Lecturing Birds on Flying

Lecturing Birds on Flying

Can Mathematical Theories Destroy the Financial Markets?

Pablo Triana

WILEY

John Wiley & Sons, Inc.

Published by John Wiley & Sons, Inc., Hoboken, New Jersey.
Published simultaneously in Canada.

For general information on our other products and services or for technical support,
please contact our Customer Care Department within the United States at
(800) 762-2974, outside the United States at (317) 572-3993 or fax (317) 572-4002.

Wiley also publishes its books in a variety of electronic formats. Some content that
appears in print may not be available in electronic books. For more information about
Wiley products, visit our web site at www.wiley.com.

Library of Congress Cataloging-in-Publication Data:

Triana, Pablo.
    Lecturing birds on flying : can mathematical theories destroy the financial
markets? / Pablo Triana.
        p. cm.
    Includes bibliographical references and index.
    ISBN 978-0-470-40675-5 (cloth)
    1. Finance.   2. Economics.   I. Title.
    HG101.T75   2009
    932–dc22

                                                        2009001895

Printed in the United States of America

10   9   8   7   6   5   4   3   2   1

To my parents, who gave me the perfect life.

Too large a proportion of mathematical economics are a mere concoction, as imprecise as the initial assumptions they rest on, which allow the author to lose sight of the complexities and interdependencies of the real world in a maze of pretentious and unhelpful symbols.

—John Maynard Keynes, 1936

Because of the success of science there is a kind of pseudo-science, social science is an example, which is not a science. They follow the forms, they gather data and so forth, but they don't get any laws, they haven't found anything, they haven't got anywhere (yet)...Maybe I am wrong, maybe they do know but I don't think so, I have the advantage of having found out how hard it is to really get to know something, how careful you have to be about checking the experiments, how easy it is to make mistakes. I know what it means to know something and therefore I see how they get their information and I can't believe that they have done the works necessary, and the checks necessary, and the care necessary. I have a great suspicion, that they don't know and that they are intimidating people. I don't know the world very well, but that's what I think.

—Richard Feynman, 1981

Beware of geeks bearing formulas.

—Warren Buffett, 2008

■ *Contents* ■

ESSENTIALS

■ It's tough to model human action ■ Finance is not as religious as physics ■ Black Swans make things harder ■ The markets are not Normal and the past is a faulty guide ■ Should we care that theorists persist? ■

■ Virginity matters ■ When describing reality was okay ■ It's the incentives, stupid ■ Many obstacles to reform ■ Heeding Fischer Black's message ■

■ Machine learning comes to finance ■ It's a computational thing ■ Models live here, too ■ Quant punting ■ Interesting enough for a movie ■

CRITIQUE

CONCLUSIONS

▨ Dangerous voluntary enslavement ▪ Let freedom ring ▨
Normality can kill you ▪ A VIXing issue ▪ Protect those
derivatives ▪

■ *Foreword* ■

I

January 2009: I am at the World Economic Forum in Davos, looking at the sorry crowd of businessmen, journalists, and bankers. There are also a few finance academics. Many practitioners look like they have just fallen off a bicycle, still confused about how to behave. All these years, they had not realized that their models underestimated the risks of high-impact rare events, allowing the buildup of huge positions that are in the process of destroying free markets, capitalism, and finance. Instead of making probabilistic assessments about Black Swans, they should have insured some kind of robustness to them. I feel sorry for the crowd, as I am certain that most of these people will not be here next year—there is effectively a mechanism called evolution, harsh to humans.

But the academics among them, equally wrong about the models (in fact, they were the ones feeding bankers with bad models), wrong about the world, wrong about the very notion of knowledge, wrong about everything, will be back next year—that I guarantee. Unless they are caught seducing graduate assistants, their jobs are safe. Nobody ever lost his tenure in social science for being wrong (the opposite may be true). There is no such thing as evolution in academic settings.

II

The biggest myth I've encountered in my life is as follows: that the road from practical know-how to theoretical knowledge is reversible—in other words, that theoretical knowledge can lead to practical applications, just as practical applications can lead to theoretical knowledge. After all, this is the reason we have schools, universities, professors, research centers, homework, exams, essays, dissertations, and the strange brand of individuals called "economists."

Yet the strange thing is that it is very hard to realize that knowledge cannot travel equally in both directions. It flows better from practice to theory—but to understand it you have nontheoretical knowledge. And people who have nontheoretical knowledge don't think of these things.

Indeed, if knowledge flowed equally in both directions, then theory without experience should be equivalent to experience without theory—which is not the case.

The myth may have all started in a Plato dialogue, *Euthyphro*, in which Socrates heckled a fellow who claimed to be pious but could not define piety. The flustered fellow, bullied by Socrates, never replied (according to Plato) that babies drink their mother's milk without being able to define what drinking milk is, or love their mother without being to explain what *love* or *mother* mean. This led to the thinking in the primacy and overblown importance of what can be called propositional knowledge—with so many side effects.

Alas, it took me a long time to disbelieve in propositional knowledge. Not only do you need to be a practitioner to realize it, but you need to ignore cultural opinions and use the raw, plain, easily obtainable, and somewhat shockingly potent evidence. And if you consider the effect for a moment, you will realize that it is more consequential than you thought.

Let me explain how the problem started screaming at me, around 1998. I was then sitting in a Chicago restaurant with a finance academic, though a true, thoughtful gentleman. He was advising one of the local exchanges on new products and wanted my opinion on the introduction of knockout options—which I had covered in some detail in my first book, *Dynamic Hedging*. He recognized that the demand for these options was great, but wondered "how traders could handle these exotics if they do not understand the Girsanov theorem." The Girsanov theorem is about a change of probability measure, something mathematically complicated that was needed to derive a closed-form formula for the options—though in the well-behaved Gaussian world. But you don't need it to understand anything about exotic options. For a minute I wondered if I was living on another planet or if the gentleman's PhD led to his strange loss of common sense—or if people without practical sense usually manage to get the energy to acquire a PhD in financial economics. Nobody worries that a child ignorant of the various theorems of thermodynamics and incapable of solving an equation of motion would be unable to ride a bicycle. Yet, why is it that we made the *Euthyphro* mistake with our understanding of quantitative products in the markets? Why should traders responding to supply and demand, little more, competing to make a buck, do the Girsanov theorem, any more than a trader of pistachios in the Souk of Damascus needs to solve general equilibrium equations to set the price of his product?

Then I realized that there has to be a problem with education—any form of formal education. I collected enough evidence that once you get a theory in your head, you can no longer understand how people can operate without it. And you look at practitioners, lecture them on how to do their business, and live under the illusion that they owe you their lives. Without your theories and your learning, they will never go anywhere.

All that can be tested. How? We can look at historical evidence. It is there, in front of our eyes, staring at us.

III

Let us take what is known as the Black-Scholes option pricing formula. Every person who had the misfortune of taking a finance class is under the illusion that the Black-Scholes-Merton formula is a gift from the three individuals who offered it to mankind and need to be rewarded for their great deed because we otherwise would not have the technology to understand these items. Without it we cannot price options. True?

Well, Espen Haug and I scratched the surface looking for the real evidence going back to the late nineteenth century. And we figured out that traders did much, much better pricing options *before* the option formulas were invented. The solid arbitrages were maintained (put-call parity, no negative butterfly, etc.). Traders, thanks to tinkering and evolutionary pressures, fumbled their way into a heuristic option pricing formula: Those who liked to short out-of-the-money options blew up in time; those who bought them survived. Traders knew what the heuristic "delta" was—about half for an at-the-money option, progressively less for an out-of-the-money option. Indeed, in our paper we interviewed veterans who confirmed that option traders in Chicago priced "off the butterfly," with "no sheets" (i.e., no pricing formula). I myself was a pit trader in Chicago in the early 1990s and saw that prominent option traders priced options without formulas.

Traders were robust to the Black Swans, these sudden events that are the scourge of option traders.

In that respect, Black-Scholes-Merton was a dangerous regression. It was made only to accommodate the financial economics establishment and portfolio theory by showing how dynamic hedging removed the price of risk—a Platonic thought experiment that was beyond the unnecessary, as it proved toxic. The exact formula they used—narrowing down the distribution to the Gaussian—had been around in its exact form since Ed Thorpe and in a different, no less realistic form since Louis Bachelier, which could accommodate any probability distribution. Various accounts of the history of financial theory ignored the point: It is not just that history is written by the winners; it is written by the losers—those losers with access to the printing press, namely finance professors. I noted while reading a book by Mark Rubinstein how he stuck the names of finance professors on products we practitioners had been trading and perfecting at least a decade earlier. History written by the losers? A prime example is how the historian managed to downplay his "portfolio insurance," a method that failed miserably in the crash of 1987.

History is truly written by losers with time on their hands and a protected academic position. In the greatest irony, the historical account of *techné* in derivatives pricing that Haug and I wrote was submitted in response to an invitation by an encyclopedia of quantitative finance. The editor of the historical section, proceeded to rewrite our story to reverse its message and glorify the *episteme* crowd.

I was a trader and risk manager for almost 20 years (before experiencing battle fatigue). There is no way my and my colleagues' accumulated knowledge of market risks can be passed on to the next generation. Business schools block the transmission of our practical know-how and empirical tricks, and the knowledge dies with us. We learn from crisis to crisis that modern financial theory has the empirical and scientific validity of astrology (without the aesthetics); yet the lessons are forgotten and ignored in what is taught to 150,000 business school students worldwide.

Note that what academics tend to call "practitioners" are often PhD-laden academics who go to practice and fall prey to the *Euthyphro* problem. This is why Pablo Triana was capable of writing this book: Like a minority of people (Espen Haug, myself), he did not go from theory to practice, but did the reverse.

IV

There is another problem with current researchers in financial economics: They are self-serving—perhaps no more, but certainly no less than other professions. Just as one of the problems with governments is that government officials have an objective function that may deviate from that of the general public, it is a myth, a great myth, that academics are there for the truth. When you hear a tobacco company talk about "health," you smirk—yet when you hear a finance professor talk about "evidence" and "risk," you don't.

Alas, academics claim to look for evidence. But they seem to *select* what evidence they need for their purpose. I have shown that value at risk (VaR) does not work, with mathematical and empirical evidence (20 million pieces of data). But the evidence was ignored. In at least one instance, it was derided. Mandelbrot was completely ignored and his work was hidden from us. Had I shown that it worked, or had other academics produced evidence that fit their point, it would have been called "evidence" and published.

Traditionally charlatans have hidden themselves behind garb, institutions, and language. Now add fancy mathematics. Robert Merton's book *Continuous Time Finance* contains 339 mentions of the word *theorem* (or equivalent). An average physics book of the same length has 25 such mentions. Yet, while economic models, it has been shown, work hardly better than random guesses or the intuition of cab drivers, physics can predict a wide range of phenomena with tenth-of-a-decimal precision.

They make you believe that their detractors are quacks by going *ad hominem* and skirting the arguments altogether. For a strange reason, I saw more solid critical thinking on the part of practitioners than academics. One common argument I've heard trying to extinguish my criticism of VaR in *The Black Swan*: "This is a popular book," implying that its arguments lack rigor. Now if all arguments lacking in rigor are popular, it does not follow that all popular arguments are lacking in rigor. You rarely find people outside academia making such a mistake.

The cost of modelization is the loss of open-mindedness, but in some areas—say, engineering—this can be tolerated owing to the low-error quality of the models and their tracking ability.

My point is that that *current* academics are bad, but that there is a tendency by nonpractitioners to idealize Platonism and fall prey to the *Euthyphro* problem—not recognize that knowledge in society aggregates through action (a point made by Hayek but that did not sink in for the economics profession). While Pablo Triana is perhaps the very first person I've met who got the point, I highly disagree with his endorsement of the sterile critiques by nonpractitioners such as Derman and others, as their conscience-clearing halfwayness causes more harm than good. I hold that anything that does not start with the basis that *techné* (know-how) is superior to *epistémé* (know what), especially in complex systems, is highly suspicious.

V

One warning before concluding. You are often told, "This is just a model; it is just an aid; you do not need to use it." I was often told that value at risk was just one piece of information among plenty—so these people providing it could cause no harm. True?

Do not put cigarettes in front of an addict—even if you give him a warning. I hold that information is not neutral. Never give a (fallible) human sterile information. He will not ignore it. These models led to an increase of risk in society, period. The providers are responsible.

VI

What should we do?

Do not waste time trying to convince academics. They will tell you, "Give me a better model or shut up," not realizing that giving someone *no* map is much, much better than giving him a wrong map. Academia does not like negative advice (what not to do).

Just put them to shame. Ignore them. Put them down. Discredit business schools. Ask for cuts in funding.

We can no longer afford to compromise.

Do what some friends have done: resign from the various associations, such as the International Association of Financial Engineers and the CFA

Institute. These institutions were promoting wrong models and will not repent naturally, no more than the tobacco industry would fight smoking in public places. You need to shame members, humiliate them. Make fun of these charlatans.

VII

I thank Pablo Triana for his wonderful lucidity, courage, and dedication in the service of the truth. This is the very first book that looks at the side effects of models, at the harm *caused* by models, and fearlessly points fingers where fingers should be pointed. I am convinced that the reader will come out of reading it much wiser, and that the publication of this book will make society a better, safer, and more risk-conscious place.

—NASSIM NICHOLAS TALEB

An Evening at NYU, Taleb's Article, and a Credit Crisis

In December 2007 I was fortunate to attend a talk by legendary hedge fund honcho Jim Simons at one of my alma maters, New York University's Stern School of Business. The founder of Renaissance Technologies (perhaps the best-performing hedge fund in the past decades, certainly one of the, if not *the*, über symbol of quantitative investing) answered several questions posed by moderator, and Nobel-prize winning econometrician, Robert Engle and by the house-packing audience on the performance of quant funds and the future for the markets.

Welcomingly, Simons offered pearly insights into his own background, the reasons that prompted a famed mathematician to abandon academia for Wall Street (his candor was remarkable: *"I wanted to make more money more than other fellow scientists,"* he shared), and how he runs his firm. He explained that the reason why Renaissance hired mostly (or only) scientists is that, not having had a financial background, it would have been difficult for him to judge the merits of a trader. But science, that he knew well, and he could tell if a mathematician or physicist was top or not. Another insightful moment came when Simons was asked to explain the notorious malaise that afflicted equity markets in August of that year.

The quant legend confirmed what many had already explained: As funds began to suffer losses on mortgage-related stuff, they had to dump liquid assets (such as blue-chip stocks) so as to gather enough liquidity with which to meet incessant margin and redemption calls.

Illuminating as all those topics of discussion were, I was most intrigued by another particular remark that Simons made following a timely inquiry by Engle. *"Why don't you publish your research, the theory behind your trading methods?"* went the question. *"Maybe not while you are active in the markets, but perhaps later on?"* After all, anyone would want to understand the quantitative philosophy behind such wildly successful quantitative trading.

Simons' reply was that there is nothing to publish. It's not physics. There is no fundamental, set-in-stone truth, no immutable laws in the markets. Financial truth changes every minute, so one would have to publish a new paper every week. In finance, the implication went, there is no eternal theorem that can help guide people through the ages. There can be no Einstein or Newton. Even the math genius raking in $1 billion a year and consistently generating 30 percent-plus returns wouldn't qualify. The terrain, unlike in the physical world, is just too untameable and lawless.

I left Stern's main auditorium quite perplexed. So the poster child of quant investing (in principle, the most sophisticated of punters out there) does not seem to believe that the markets can be theorized? That a general, overarching, all-encompassing model can capture financial behavior? And Simons, as he so eagerly clarified, walks the talk. In a hall packed with world-class professors and doctorate students (NYU is a consistent global leader in financial economics education and research), the revered mathematician loudly stated that he does not hire Finance academics. When you so obviously don't believe in the theory, what's the point of hiring the theorists?

Granted, Simons matched his matter-of-fact bluntness with graciousness towards his (by then slightly puzzled) hosts. As if to fill the void that his no-Finance-PhDs-please statement had suddenly left in the air, he promptly assuaged the audience by telling them that he was sure that they "were all going to do all right," even if not be quite able to join the Renaissance ranks. But this, I felt, came as scant consolation for all those dogma-defending finance scholars in attendance who had just heard their presumptive hero tell them that their discipline is, after all, not a science. Sorry folks, it just ain't string theory (which, by the way, Simons admitted to have never used when designing his moneymaking machines).

As I walked away from NYU and towards Manhattan's magnificently youngish Union Square, in the pleasant company of a former fellow student from the good old days, I realized that something big had just happened. Since Renaissance is particularly secretive, it is essentially unassailable for outsiders to truly understand what the heck those brainiacs are actually doing, but there is no doubt as to the general consensus held (and this would apply to equally impressive quant houses like DE Shaw or Citadel): These people are making tons of money through the use of extraordinarily complex mathematical theories, comprehension of which is way beyond the reach of mere mortals. Thanks to their armies of elite scientists, quant funds can model the markets and predict their future behavior, goes the undoubted conventional wisdom. Vanilla investors who can't mathematically map the markets stand no chance in comparison. In this day and age, conventionalist thinking would dictate, stochastic calculus and econometrics become the most essential tools for aspiring finance stars, with staid accounting and fundamental analysis consigned to the dustbin of unacceptable simplicity.

But Jim Simons, as part of an innocent university gathering, had just shattered all those notions, at least to my eyes. We can't predict. There is no theory in finance. There can't be. And none of this, of course, diminishes Renaissance's achievements one bit: I would argue that it is even more impressive to make consistent 30 percent returns when you *can't* forecast the markets.

When I got back to my apartment on 10th and 41st (conveniently very close to the glitz of New York City's Times Square), I turned on my computer and anxiously searched for a recent article that suddenly felt unavoidably urgent. The previous October, veteran trader and unrepentant iconoclast Nassim Taleb had caused quite a stir via an op-ed piece in the *Financial Times (FT)* that, in essence, deemed finance theory useless and dangerous (if you don't believe me, the title of "The Pseudo-Science Hurting Markets" seems self-explanatory). In the short space that a newspaper opinion article allows for, Taleb managed to go hard at all the sacred cows of financial economics, including a few Nobelists, and to still have some room left to ask for the irrefutable discrediting of the Nobel Prize in Economics itself. The *FT* op-ed was akin to a global debutante ball for ideas that Taleb has long espoused and talked about, and confirmed him as the leading doubter of theoretical conventionalisms.

Taken together, Taleb's take-no-prisoners critique and Simons' clarifications, delivered within a few weeks of each other, appear as earth-shatteringly impacting. Surely, many had previously voiced complaints about the unworldliness of many a financial theorem or a mathematical finance construct. But, unless I recall incorrectly, such concerns proved only mildly influential. Yes, there was a modicum of public backlash against finance academicism after the 1998 fall of mega hedge-fund LTCM (which was co-piloted, after all, by two Nobel-endowed, Taleb-irritating star professors), but no blood was shed. I don't think it would be accurate to portray those criticisms as in any way threatening to the academic status quo or to the continuous employment of quantitative professionals by Wall Street and the City of London. If anything, the weight of theory and the demand for quanty staff have only grown stronger in the past decade.

Similarly, financial economics' most illustrious device (the Black-Scholes option pricing model) survived the 1987 crash pretty much unscathed, at least when it came to its perceived condition as a supremely popular and widely used tool. Even though the Black-Scholes-inspired "portfolio insurance" strategies were a key driving force behind the largest single-day drop in equity markets, an unmistakable signal of the deeply problematic foundations of the formula, Black-Scholes was never blacklisted from business schools, textbooks, media coverage, or even trading rooms (quite the contrary, it was rewarded with the Nobel a decade later). For the past 20 years, we have basically continued trotting along, safe in the notion that Black-Scholes reigned supreme and was a wonderful discovery. Sure, its assumptions are way off base, but that has not been seen as a reason to throw it away, or doubt its position as the unchallenged standard tool.

Even the horrendous bursting of the Internet bubble in 2000, which emphatically highlighted the vastly unrealistic nature of one of finance theory's most orthodox tenets (that markets follow the Normal probability distribution and that rare events are extremely rarely present) as well as the impossibility of prediction, did not seem to make a dent into the perceived validity of quantitative finance. Models that are founded on the Normality assumption kept forming part of the core curriculum at universities, and the field of financial econometrics continued marching unopposed, even getting its own Nobel.

But this time, it seems, is different. The assault on orthodox beliefs looks strong and determined. While in the case of Simons he may have simply tried to be honest when faced with a potentially controversial question, there is no second-guessing Taleb's intentions. He is after the big guns, and wants change delivered. Orthodox theoreticians should be fearful, for two main reasons: 1) like Simons, Taleb has been around the block, having traded at the highest industry levels for 20 years; he is also quite familiar with mathematical finance and academic theories; when an educated top-level pro unstoppingly yells that the models don't work in practice and can cause harm, such arguments gain credibility and respectability; 2) Taleb is by no means an unknown; he has established himself as a widely followed, extremely successful author; he has countless devotees and detractors the world over, eager to listen to his ruminations; that is, here we have a man who can, if he wants, spread a message around like wildfire.

Other prominent figures have (in tandem or by their own accord) followed Taleb's journey into publicly displayed, warnings-filled skepticism, essentially consolidating what may be referred to as a movement. Internationally respected scientists-turned-financiers like Emanuel Derman, Ricardo Rebonato, or Paul Wilmott have in the past few years openly questioned the role of financial modeling and the value to be derived from applying quantitative methodology to the markets (though, it should be clarified, they may be accused of not going far enough, of offering critiques that are welcomed but not impacting enough; they warn against the models but concurrently teach them; they endlessly highlight the unrealism of the dogmas but do not overtly emphasize their capacity to do harm; someone has illuminatingly described some of those criticisms as *"could not make the leap from the point that ludified models were impractical to a refusal of the supremacy of a top-down theoretical background"*). To my knowledge, this is the very first time that such eminent practitioners (people who have led quant and risk management teams at top investment banks and who have become the leading trainers of future quants and risk managers) are concurrently willing to express their doubts and to let us know how things really work out there, in brave defiance of most of what we had innocently held sacred till that point.

These and other contributions have struck a new kind of blow to financial theory. As has been said earlier, the "these models are unrealistic" mantra, sufficiently heard for at least the past couple of decades, had become tired, unappealingly harmless. Almost vacuous. Neither theory nor theoreticians appear to have been bothered by it. No significant change seems to have been enacted as a result of its utterance.

The "these models are *dangerous*" mantra has been proclaimed less often, though it's an argument that is certainly not unheard of. Black–Scholes was finger pointed as a source of trouble after October 1987's "Black Monday" and again on several occasions afterwards as the model-inspired dynamic hedging practices by option traders have seriously disturbed underlying markets from time to time. Risk measuring standard tool Value at Risk (VaR) has also been portrayed as mayhem-enabling. Mark-to-model disasters associated with complex derivatives have not gone unnoticed, either. But, once more, no terminal damage seems to have been effected on the (whether perceived or real) general embrace and acceptance of theories and models. This should change, for reasons that will be described later, but the point is that up to this point it had not happened.

A new line of attack could cause real, palpable, harm to the reputation (and eventual embracing) of financial economics and mathematical finance. Simply stated, the theory may not have been as successful or popular as many had thought (some of it at least; as this book illustrates, many times the problem is precisely how intensely the theory *has* been applied out there). It is one thing to say that the models are unrealistic and dangerous. It is quite another to say that no one in the real world uses them or cares for them. What could justify the existence of things that are not only unworldly and unsafe but also not employed by those who are supposed to employ them?

Nothing illustrates this conundrum better than the Black–Scholes critique recently initiated by (here he comes again!) Nassim Taleb and Espen Haug, another former star trader with deep knowledge of the quant stuff. Haug, a bookish Norwegian who ended up working for Connecticut- and New York–based prop desks through interesting happenstances, and who dubs himself "The Collector," has painstakingly researched ancient literature on option pricing and, together with Taleb, published late in 2007 a paper where the following three shocking assertions are made:

Black-Scholes is not used, Black-Scholes was not needed, Black-Scholes was not original.

This eye-opening trilogy of critique is a force of unparalleled symbolic power. We knew that Black-Scholes (or, shall we say, Black-Scholes-Merton, BSM) was based on faulty assumptions, and that at times its application had caused turmoil. Such drawbacks have important practical ramifications: how to tweak the model to correct for the flaws, how and why it can drastically move markets, what the resultant implied volatility parameter truly stands for. The meat of Haug and Taleb's newer complaints is more a matter of semantics and terminology. Their critique is more about descriptive philosophy and the historical record than about what option traders should do or what would happen to the underlying markets. And yet, from a financial economics point of view, it is a much more devastating blow than any of the prior criticisms on BSM, arguably the crown jewel of the theoretical finance establishment and the convenient alibi that impelled the ceaseless arrival of high-tech quantitative methodology into the financial industry and the business schools.

What the inquisitive Norwegian and the author of best-selling sensation *The Black Swan* are telling us, from their position as combined 30-year veterans of the trading floor front lines, is that, frankly, we never needed BSM at all. While it may be of some mathematical beauty (it is hard to deny the innovations brought by the model when it comes to the tools, in particular the pioneer, and technically very smart, application of continuous time stochastics), it is of no practical use. Old traders (pre-1973, when BSM was released) already knew how to trade, price, and risk-manage option positions, in many cases in a very savvy way. In any case, very similar (and less constrained) models were already in existence. Most importantly, option prices may be simply the result of good old-fashioned supply-demand interactions and elementary arbitrage relationships, with no complex models involved. Lastly, even when people (as seems to have been the case) believe that they are using BSM, they are in fact not doing so. The ubiquitous presence in options markets of something called the *volatility smile* very clearly tells us that, at least since the 1987 crash, the market is not using BSM. Even if we assume that traders are actually employing a model, the latter has been manipulated so much (thus giving rise to that smile) that it can no longer be categorized as BSM. Its original spirit would have been completely fudged into oblivion. It has been made to become something else by traders looking to erase all the unworldly assumptions so as to obtain more realistic (i.e., less dogmatic) prices.

All this drives a stake through the heart of financial economics and mathematical finance. Few beliefs have been held as more sacrosanct (not only by academics and students but also by most observers and even pros and regulators) as the notions that BSM has enjoyed resoundingly successful popularity ("it's the standard model, widely used all over the globe"), that it helped launch the modern derivatives revolution ("the option business would have never taken off without the model"), and that the quant revolution that it unleashed was both welcome and necessary ("there can be no finance these days without mathematical models"). According to Haug and Taleb, this is a bunch of nonsense. It is not used and it wasn't needed. Not only conceptually flawed, but not even a first. The long-presumed king has been clothes-less for a long while, unnoticed so until very recently.

As important as the questioning of the role of models and the real relevance of theoretical inventions that the BSM critique brings to the fore is the way that academics and quants respond to it. Theoreticians have a big chance to show that they, in fact, care about the real world and its inhabitants. When confronted with the arguments of very prominent practitioners in a field that is nothing if not entirely practical, those of the nonpracticing variety should humbly listen. What would an (honest) ornithologist do if faced with a group of talking birds in the mood for sharing some insights as to how things really are up there in the blue sky? For the sake of ornithology's relevance, I surely hope that they would stay quiet and respectfully pay attention. Who knows, they may learn something of use.

Today's business schools' and mathematics departments' "ornithologists" should also jump at the opportunity offered by "birds" like Taleb, Haug, Derman, Rebonato, Wilmott, and others and try to appreciate why it is that they question the validity, applicability, soundness, rationale, and even popularity of theoretical dogma. Neither the repetition of tired exculpatory clichés nor outright neglect should be acceptable responses.

Someone who jumped to the defense of the theorists tried to offer shelter from the skeptics-launched lambasting in the following terms: *"Models . . . rely on a set of assumptions that rarely hold in the market. That does not diminish their value. Economic and financial models can be thought of as a map. If a map included every detail in the geography (trees, country roads, etc.) it would be intractable, rendering it useless. . . . The models . . . have increased our knowledge and understanding of risk immensely. Being able to put a price on risk has enabled it to be transferred more efficiently. Some investors are born with an innate sense of markets and can rely on instinct to make brilliant decisions. The vast majority of us need a little guidance; the models provide this."* I humbly believe that such widely-heard-before generalizations generate yet more, not less, skepticism. Rather than assuage concerns, they reinforce them. We are inevitably asked to just take things on faith, to unquestionably subjugate ourselves to conventionalism-appeasing dictums. In what sense exactly can constructs based on (sometimes vastly) faulty assumptions represent an enhancement, a beneficial development? Would you want to be guided by a map that asks you to assume that the mountain blocking the road is not there, or that all the other drivers will never go above 20 miles per hour, or that you should drive into the river because cars can run on water? It almost feels as if these theory-embracers envisioned the world as a place where models needed (no, *had*) to exist no matter what, and where it was our duty to find justifications (of any kind) for their presence. It almost feels as if these people had voluntarily jailed themselves inside an analytical cage and could not conceive of a situation where financial theory would not rule it all. And they want us in that jail too, us unquestioning selves.

Such clichés in defense of analyticalization appear as less than seductive. It is one thing to gratuitously state that models increase our knowledge and understanding (again, in spite of being built on admittedly shaky support?); it is quite another to actually prove it. As for putting a price on risk, another familiar bromide, why do we have to religiously assume that market players had to wait for the arrival of the nonpracticing theoreticians before financial risks could be "properly" priced? And, allow me to be bothersomely repetitious, how exactly can things built on impossibly dubious foundations help us in pricing risk more efficiently? Finally, in a supreme example of conveniently self-serving full-circleness, deep unrealism becomes not a reason to put the models down, but in fact, almost serendipitously, a reason to embrace them! After all, were the models to be perfect (i.e., actually based on real stuff), they would be totally useless! It seems hard to be convinced by the arguments of those apparently bent on defending the reliability on models at all cost and who are willing to go as far as to transform the theories' very drawbacks into forcefully blind rationales for support. Frankly, I don't think that such familiarly simplistic (yet, of course, entirely respectable) exculpatory efforts quite cut it. Time for a new approach.

Deafening silence or (as has been the case all too often) outright contempt on the part of the ivory tower would for their part only serve to aid the suspicions long held by many over dogmatists: that they are an aloof bunch interested not in searching for truth and passing on relevant knowledge, but on guild-like protecting their sheltered status. If in the process the world is put in danger through the applications of unsound analytics and students are indoctrinated wholly impractical ideas, well that's just acceptable collateral damage, right? After all, as stated earlier, theoreticians seem to have survived prior controversial moments quite unscathed. Why should they now change their working habits one bit?

And yet they should. Because, as also said before, now it is quite likely to be different. It is not just the bursting onto the scene of Taleb et al., possibly the first time that top practitioners have dared throw such a belligerent challenge at theory. The world at large may be far readier to listen these days. The recent credit crisis has served to very publicly highlight key failures in quantitative risk management, derivatives modeling, and forecasting. All the sophisticated math and the myriad of PhDs could not prevent the mess from taking hold. In fact, it could be forcefully argued that reliance on theory contributed to the mess taking place. And, certainly, this was no timid crisis. The effects have been devastating and painfully dramatic, including the annihilation of the investment banking industry and never-seen-before developments in several major asset markets.

The lessons that this watersheds-unleashing crisis presents for theoretical finance are not savory: The tools did not work and, worse, badly backfired. The mathematical risk radars did not forewarn by a long stretch; the quantitative gadgets used for pricing and rating the convoluted structures directly behind the chaos failed miserably; the regulators-sanctioned analytical methodologies for setting up capital charges proved widely inappropriate. Another poignant indictment is that the models may have been simply used as convenient alibis by risk-hungry, otherwise no-nonsense players who are quite aware of the utterly unreliable nature of the quant stuff; that is, all the glorified sophistication may have in the end been nothing more than a convenient excuse for reckless behavior, a use-and-dump enabler for self-serving rogues who couldn't care less about the equations.

None of these conclusions bodes well for theorists and their presumed relevance. If the models were useless in preventing such a big impact event (which has claimed thousands of casualties among those embracing the tools), then who needs them? Who needs mechanisms that pretend to map finance mathematically and yet don't help when help is most needed? Most critical, who needs mechanisms with the capacity to wreak destruction themselves? Secondly, if the math and the theories serve only as window-dressing for self-serving, models-mistrusting masters of the universe, then all the glorified technical brilliance would appear morphed into a demeaningly shameless sales pitch in search of a quick buck. Far from discovering the deeper truths about the markets through brilliant scientification, theorists would have been reduced to providing analytical credibility to those bent on embarking themselves and the world onto a hyperleveraged speculative orgy. People are looking for answers to the crisis. Some are also looking for guilty blood. It is undeniable that mathematical finance, either as failed preventer or enabler, has carved a prominent place for itself in the suspects lineup, along with dodgy mortgage lending practices and regulatory mishaps. Make no mistake: quantitative finance had a very large hand in what could well be the worst financial crisis in the history of mankind. It surely doesn't help theorists that it is precisely at this time that Taleb is busiest launching messages through his antidogma megaphone, or that the BSM critique has caught fire, also coincidentally.

In sum, the mood seems to be ripe for a serious rethinking of the role of analytical constructs in financial markets. This time it looks difficult for theory to escape unscratched. Neither market realities nor the strength of the attacking forces point in that direction. A wide-ranging backlash against financial economics seems to be in the cards. How the academics and the quants respond could well determine whether they will be considered worthy of attention going forward, or whether they will be forever consigned to the dustbin of irrelevance or, worse, stringently avoided as harmful to society.

Of course, there is an altogether different possible outcome. Some have called for "better models" as a suitable response to the crisis. According to this argument, we couldn't foresee or prevent the mayhem because currently used theoretical devices are not complex enough to capture reality. Only if the former were more complex, we could have avoided the worst. The solution, then, is to up the analytical ante and get busy designing even more super-charged constructs that borrow from even more super-charged mathematical and computational tools. Hire more PhDs, place even more weight on theorizing. Keep glorifying the "physics-ization" of business schools. To add a cherry on top, the pro-modeling crowd may offer, perhaps financial econometrics could be endowed with another Nobel. After all, nothing would bother that bothersomely skeptical Taleb more.

Which outcome would benefit us the most? Should theory be restrained, perhaps permanently? Should theory be given a new, stronger lease on life? Should we kill the models or build new ones? Are we safer without finance theory, or do we need a revamped theoretical edifice to feel safe? This book will attempt to help answer these questions. The main theme is the conflict between theoretical and real finance, and the potential threat that the former may pose for the latter. As we will see, there are several historical examples (not just the 2007 credit crisis) that clearly illustrate how theory-gone-wild caused real damage to market participants, and the economy (and thus society) at large. Besides specific nitpicking, it may be possible to build arguments against the application of unsound mathematical finance constructs that are of a more general scope.

On top of dealing with the harm that financial theory can inflict on the real world, we will naturally touch upon the tried-and-tested issue of whether the models are realistic (though, again, this feels slightly tired). But, crucially, we will also try to pay attention to two other, until now less discussed, remits: are the models really used? And were they needed at all?

Financial economics and quantitative finance have been generally assumed to be a prevalent and successful part of the markets for a long time (some authors even claim that theory has been "performative," that is, that its existence has in itself structurally shaped the way markets operate, so as to make the models a self-fulfilling prophecy). But theoretical and mathematical stuff may have been much less used and much less successful in real life than conventional wisdom would hold. It is also not clear whether the theoretical developments represented improvements over previously existing thinking and practices. In other words, did the models bring something new and useful? If not, why do they exist?

The BSM critique, a subject we delve into deeply, is the focal point of those two themes. It has taken more than 30 years (and the appearance of two courageous former traders) for us to realize that the Nobel-winning model may be neither popular, nor original, or necessary. When it comes to financial theory, we seem to have voluntarily enslaved ourselves to conventionalism blindness (we are quite gullible when confronted with complex mathematical symbolae enacted by holders of prestigious degrees). The BSM debate shows how important it is to nonconformistly always question everything, including the more apparently undoubted dogmas. If someone claims that a theory is widely used, innovative, and successful, we should ask for hard proof.

Interestingly, the book tries to focus on the human aspect of things. We deal with the personal incentives that both pros and theoreticians have in adopting, developing, and promoting quantitative models. Sometimes, as was said earlier, theories and tools may be used in finance because it serves the interests of certain otherwise no-nonsense practitioners. And academics and quants certainly have a very strong personal interest in convincing the world that finance is about math. Hopefully the book would allow people to see through the fog of special interests and judge theoretical developments (such as Black-Scholes or Value at Risk) entirely on their reliability merits.

The tome, then, could be accused of playing myth-debunker. Plenty of sacred cows are subjected to intense scrutiny and accused of horrible crimes. Cynicism and criticism aplenty when it comes to many theoretical contributions. But also a message of hope. Financial markets and business schools are important, valuable entities. They should be actively protected from forces that may do them harm. Unworldly theories that are stubbornly preserved and promoted would belong to that category. By providing false certainties and confidence, the models can induce pros to take far more (uninformed) risks than otherwise, potentially plunging the world into chaos. If the pain (such as in the recent past) turns out to be obscene, markets and financial institutions could become deeply disreputable, perhaps even regulated into oblivion. And the whole edifice of financial economics may be forced to crumble as folks conclude that all finance professors are unrepentant, evil, dogmatic fanatics, which clearly is not the case. Many academics and universities may unfairly suffer indiscriminately as a result.

The best way to avoid such fates is to open up the floodgates of dogma-challenging debate and discern before it is too late. Finance theory has remained both insulated and unchallenged long enough. Its (true) usefulness, relevance, hazardousness, and requisiteness need to be determinedly discussed, and action taken upon the consequent conclusions. Theory is either necessary or not. Relevant or useless. Employed or ignored. Dangerous or harmless. Short of the assembly of a "mathematical finance Council of Nicaea" that settles things once and for all, this book will hopefully be seen as a humble, worthy effort towards that lofty goal.

Penning this book has been, overall, a blessing for me. I enjoy writing very much. I believe that the topics covered here are of supreme importance, and a lot of this stuff is close to my heart. I see this tome as the final vindication of my obstinate decision more than 10 years ago to make it into derivatives, which this work deals with extensively (it is a nice feeling, managing to transform oneself from purchaser of books to author); now that I have sold derivatives, taught derivatives, consulted on derivatives, and mused on derivatives, it somehow seems like mission accomplished. Finally, I have too managed to learn a lot of valuable things from this effort.

So what prompted me to write this book? Why did I choose to muse precisely about this? Well, for one, this non-theoretician has followed with interest the quant and academic finance worlds for a while and I believe that I am in a good position to look under the right beds. I studied financial engineering at graduate school and have roamed through a trading floor. I have interacted with real finance professors (from top business schools) and with real quantitative analysts (from top investment banks). I have also been amply interested for many years in how the mathematical constructs can affect the underlying markets, having accumulated highly targeted literature and intelligence, which suddenly became richly appropriate.

Now, and as a required disclaimer, I do not particularly enjoy theoretical adventures. I can think of hundreds of better (and more productive, let alone enjoyable) things to do than to read or, worse, compose a theoretical treatise. I don't believe much in the power of theory when it comes to finance, either. And (orthodox, dogmatic) financial economists most likely would not be among my first choices for companionship on a deserted island, or at a restaurant table. Yet the writing of this book has unavoidably forced me to immerse myself for a few months in equations-laden papers and to research the activities of theoreticians and quantitative professionals. While I tried to limit the amount of technical stuff in my to-do list, in the end it was inevitable that a book like this would require from the author a larger-than-desirable number of hours in the (intellectual) company of dogmas and dogmatics.

Why did I volunteer to go through such a painful exercise? Because, again, the topic is too relevant to ignore. Even without the recent tremors, it would be utterly urgent to discuss the harm that quantitative concoctions can cause in real life; obviously, the credit crisis just made such coverage insultingly unpostponable.

The crisis simply presented too good an opportunity and made the topic irresistibly timely. The mayhem has brought to the fore the failings of mathematical finance on many, not just one, fronts. These simultaneous debacles mark this historical episode as one of the most illuminating epitomes of the havoc that unsound theories can wreak, and of how we need to be aware of and careful about the limitations of financial modeling.

Also this book, while dealing in large part with theories and theoreticians, does so in plain English, not in the mathematical language preferred by modelers. This was an added plus for me, since I believe that I have a proven (and, possibly, nonhabitual) ability to do a decent job at covering issues pertaining to advanced financial stuff in an easy-to-understand, jargon-free, perhaps even enjoyable manner. In that sense, I thought that the prospect of clearly explaining to a general-public audience (experts welcome too, of course) how financial theories can impact the markets and society was too tempting to forgo.

Another big attraction of the book were the many exciting subplots (highly relevant in themselves) that could be dealt with on top of the super-hot main central theme, including the story of the modern critique of the Black-Scholes formula; how rating agencies rated complex credit derivatives on the run-up to the crisis; how investment banks modeled those complex securities; why people may profoundly misunderstand the famous VIX volatility index; how pros may use theories to justify unfettered risk taking; what's wrong with Value at Risk; what quant funds are like and how they operate; a second-guessing of the rationale for the Nobel in Economics; why we are suckers for diploma-waving, certainty-promising, quantitative snake oil peddlers; as well as a treatment of influential historical case studies and an introduction to mysterious and intriguing characters.

One of those subplots was a particularly important motivator, namely the chance to talk about the status quo regarding business schools (which house the financial economists responsible for much of the theoretical dogmas that get dumped on the rest of us). The story of how b-schools (a universe that I have actively followed for a long time) determinedly transformed themselves from institutions dedicated to humbly describing the real world to institutions bent on scientification and the theorizing of how the world ought to be like is quite interesting in itself. I find it important to understand the personal incentives and institutional structures behind the manufacturing of the theories that have the potential to unleash mayhem on the markets.

Some readers may develop, embrace, and publicly express severe doubts as to the soundness, usefulness, and benevolence of finance theory as a result of reading this book, and in so doing might incur the wrath of some finance professor or financial mathematician, who could promptly subject the newly skeptic to insulting diatribes and blatantly rude attacks. You may feel vanquished, and excitedly begin to look for a table to hide under.

But if, alternatively, you decide to bravely confront your dogmatic confronters, here are some tips that may prove useful. First of all, everyone with a brain who lives in a nation where freedom of speech is not officially persecuted is entitled to their opinion, naturally, and to opine about the main, basic, irrefutable essentials of financial theory and the potential practical effects of ideas and tools built on such foundations. Second, there are plenty of highly respected, highly educated, highly experienced people, including leading financial mathematicians and senior academics, who would share your skepticism and who have very loudly voiced their concerns (this book is full of such testimonials). And third, if theoreticians who have never worked in the financial markets can build entire careers on the back of their (quite unshy) opining on finance themes, why can't non-theoreticians (who may boast tangible financial industry experience) opine about the opinions of theoreticians?

With luck, those tips may not be needed at all. Our newborn skeptical reader may instead encounter theory-lovers who, while not fully agreeing with him, would politely respect his skepticism. Even better, he may even encounter academics and quants who are not only willing to listen to dissenting voices (perhaps in the unpretentious hope of learning something new and useful) but may also share, to some degree, his agnosticism. And, most important, the prudence, concern, and desire to modify things that such doubtfulness would dictate. There are finance professors out there (I know, I know them) who, even if behind closed doors, openly admit to many of their colleagues' unhealthy devotion for unworldly quantitative trickeries, rather than towards what actually goes on in the real financial landscape, and who would love to endow their institutions with a sizeable dose of realism. Similarly, there are tons of quantitative professionals ready to lambast the excessive analyticalization witnessed in certain financial corners in the last decades; these pros are much more open than their academic sidekicks, maybe because their comments would be seen as much less (inconveniently) revolutionary within their own ranks.

In sum, this is a book that deals with an important topic, during a timely period, in (I hope) a fresh style, that touches upon sexy subplots, and that is bound to make some waves, create some controversies, and may act as an unavoidable excuse for a few heated-up discussions. Hopefully, it will also serve to bring (some) people on different sides of the aisle closer together in the common aims of making markets safer and academic-quantitative research more useful. After all, we should all stand to win from such realizations.

The book's structure is roughly organized around three main supersubjects. What could be deemed the "Essentials" subplot tries to introduce the playing field, presenting the unavoidable foundations and setting the background. This is the section where we analyze whether financial markets can in principle really be tamable mathematically, and where the main characters behind the churning of financial models are thoroughly presented, together with the incentives that push them into equation-blabbing.

Chapter 1, "Playing God," attempts to answer a simple question: Can the financial markets be mathematically modeled? I noncowardly put forward my own thoughts but, nondauntlessly, choose to find respected and weighty company to accompany me through the arguments. The essential message? No, the markets can't be tamed with equations. The list of obstacles is long and powerful: Maverick unlawful human action rules the markets, unexpected and unimaginable monstrous rare events shape the markets, and historical data does not appear as a trusting guide to the future of the markets. Should we care that economists and quants elect to persist theoriticizing in spite of the hurdles?

Chapter 2, "The Financial Economics Fiefdom," analyzes the sources of origin of many of the theories and mathematical dictums. Those sources are both institutional (mostly business schools) and flesh-and-bones types (the academics working inside those institutions). If we want to understand the conflicts between theory and practice and the harmful effects that theory may have, we obviously need to understand how and why those theories are developed in the first place and by whom. This chapter describes how the field of financial economics evolved from a descriptive discipline (imagine, finance professors devoting their time to explaining how the financial world actually works!) to an abstract one dedicated to technically concocting professors' own versions of how such worlds *should* work. Since the vast majority of finance academics have never been employed in the financial industry, it is admittedly awkward that their dictums may have gained so much attention (akin, perhaps, to virgins teaching at porn school). We'll try to tackle such a perplexing issue. We'll also take a look at the large personal incentives that theoreticians have to continue churning out quantitative hodgepodge. We'll humbly propose changes to academic conventionalism, mostly because business schools are important and valuable entities that should be protected (along with those valiant profs that prime relevant knowledge and instruction) from the danger of practical irrelevance, not to mention the possibility of being held responsible for terrible real-life-impacting, theory-ignited mischief.

Chapter 3, "Quant Invasion," explains how Wall Street and other financial centers became eager employers of scientists, and how scientists became eager employees of financial firms. What is it that quants really do? Why are they considered valuable? Do they also concoct theories, academic style? Can they be dangerous? We will also discuss the roles of so-called "quant funds" and examine their prominent protagonism in the market. Are quant funds an example of mathematics wreaking havoc in finance? What happened during the summer 2007 quant funds meltdown with the market turmoil that it helped unleashed?

The "Critique" subplot deals with, you guessed it, very specific criticisms of finance theory. Rather than bureaucratically list all the (notoriously familiar) technical shortcomings of the best-known models, we choose to be much more effective and hands-on (not to mention much more loyal to the objectives of this book) and devote our time to in-depth coverage of the most significant historical episodes of theory-caused, real-life market malaise, with heavy emphasis on the ongoing credit crisis, as well as to the conundrum posed by the Black-Scholes option pricing model, which may have been transformed from hero into villain by recent theory-devastating findings. Ruthlessly highlighting the blood that has been shed out there because of malfunctionings in the quantitative machines is an obvious indictment on the trustworthiness of finance theory. Even more ruthlessly elaborating on the damage very particularly caused by Black-Scholes and on the possibility that the famed construct may not be used or have been needed at all is a devastating bombardment of the theoretical temple, given the awe in which Black-Scholes (in essence, the crown jewel of financial economics) has been held by the analytical community for over three decades.

The first three chapters of this section deal with the credit crisis and how its unleashing and deleteriousness strike a mortal blow to the credibility of theoretical machinations. Here we detail why the credit crisis has made this book (timely under any other circumstances) urgently obligatory. During the mayhem, several of finance theory's creations and most sacred ideologies were distinctly rendered ineffective, misleading, and mischievous. Prior darkish episodes also served to highlight the limits of dogmatism, but it can be argued that the current damage levels warrant beyond-especial attention (after all, the investment banking industry was destroyed in the spate of a few months; entire markets became semi-extinguished; institutions had to be nationalized; the money markets froze; monetary policy became desperately unorthodox and possibly ineffective; the markets were "socialized"). Finance theory failed on several fronts at the same time, and blind devotion to it was instrumental in causing, encouraging, and not helping prevent the destruction. Again, make no mistake: Quantitative finance had a very large hand in what could well be the worst financial crisis in the history of mankind. This section introduces the main miscreants.

Chapter 4, "Copulated Nightmares," focuses on the subliminally failing mathematical models used by banks and rating agencies to dissect the creditworthiness of the exotic (toxic) structured securities at the heart of the whole debacle, in particular the so-called Gaussian Copula model. Chapter 5, "Blah VaR Blah," deals with the famous Value at Risk tool employed by everybody and sponsored by regulators, which, inevitably once more, failed to measure risks even half-accurately and, worse, decisively encouraged and sanctioned the wildly leveraged wild risk-taking that brought Wall Street (and consequently the world) down. Chapter 6, "Blue Is Not Green," concludes by denouncing the reluctance of theorists to admit their defeat even in the face of so much havoc; provides crisis-related anecdotes that show that in the markets anything, frankly, is possible; and makes a rotund call for an end to theoretical indoctrination as a way to avoid a similar future meltdown.

Chapter 7, "The Black-Scholes Conundrum," is about, well, how the Black-Scholes (Black-Scholes-Merton, BSM) option pricing model presents finance theory with a troublesome conundrum. Theorists have for a long time bragged about BSM as an invincible symbol of the prowess of mathematical finance and how it can change the world. However, at the same time, it is undoubtful that BSM presents a report card full of disappointments. The most glorified of theoretical constructs has displayed a tormentous capacity for havoc-wreaking, for example during the crash of October 1987, and is obviously not completely trusted by traders. We had known this for years, but it didn't seem to seriously challenge the perception that BSM is a successful theory. But something new, much more threatening has come up. Akin to an apparently perfect son about whom you have been relentlessly bragging in front of the neighbors and that is later found out, after many years, of having indulged in all kinds of malicious vices. Once the disturbing truth is out, should you disown your offspring, reform him, or act as if nothing had happened?

The new development is, of course, the Taleb and Haug critique that was mentioned earlier. These veteran traders and successful intellectuals have decided to let us know that BSM is in fact really not used, was not an original contribution, and was not needed in the first place. Actually, this is even more impacting than having your favorite son unveiled as a misbehaving truant. It is akin to declaring that the kid never existed at all, exposing the parents as people who had been bragging about a ghost during all these years. In this light, what had been presented as the poster child of theoretical salubriousness may become an embarrassment. That which in the past gave you honor may be transformed into a black sheep. By having pegged your own reputation and identity so closely to the object of prior admiration, your reputation inevitably suffers, too. This chapter analyzes how theorists should react to such conundrum, along with detailed explanations of how BSM can cause turbulence in the markets, the history of option pricing, and why Taleb and Haug are right when they say that BSM is, frankly, not used.

The "Conclusions" subplot attempts to draw some concluding final thoughts and underline the key, insoluble, big-picture messages that the book tries to emanate. Chapter 8, "Black Swan Deceit?" is about how pros borrow from finance theory, even if convinced of its uselessness, to achieve certain practical, personal goals. In doing so, they would be endowing the theories with copious respectability and exposure. Mathematical edifices can act as convenient alibis with which to escape blame from bad news; they can be used to enhance one's reputation as a genius and advance one's career; they can be used to help get business; they can be used to dress up simple strategies and make yourself look more advanced and intellectually exclusive; and they can be used to justify the existence of entire professions. All those interested actions by otherwise no-nonsense pros go a long way towards helping cement in the public's psyche the notion that markets are amenable to quantification, that they can be modeled, that there can be theory-driven certainty. That is, brutish players puzzlingly become unlike allies of the cloistered professors.

Chapter 9, "An Unhealthy Yearning for Precision," explains how our fear of the unknown and our desire for certainty lead us to throw ourselves into the arms of perceived "experts" who claim to have the answers, most notably finance academics. We surrender unconditionally to their dictums in our desperate search for a way out of the darkness of nonconcreteness. We trust quantitatively flavored constructs to escort us away from the gloomy reality of unmeasurable uncertainty.

And yet, in embracing quantitative finance as a bridge towards endurable order, we may be sowing the seeds of market chaos. The theory-aided search for certainty may yield untamed, out-of-control uncertainty. By looking for precise knowns through analytical machinations, we may be condemning ourselves to plunging into the deepest of unknowns.

Our self-enslavement to theoretical dictates may result in forced enslave-ment to misery and turmoil. By stubbornly focusing on measuring the unmeasurable (using less-than-ideal tools, to boot), technicians endow the financial community with a misplaced and unjustified sense of con-fidence that uncertainty has been tamed. The amount of unsound risks taken may drastically increase as a result. Rather than contribute to a bet-ter understanding of the markets and provide a reliable deciphering tool that prevents people from getting into trouble, financial economics and mathematical finance may in fact overwhelmingly contribute to make the markets a much riskier and chaos-prone proposition. The credit cri-sis, naturally, is hard proof of all this. Theoretical self-enslavement did not end well, once more.

Perhaps, with the financial system in tatters, it's an appropriate time to realize that we should fear Platonic quantitative preciseness much more than we fear earthly vagueness. We should release ourselves from the self-imposed quantitative chains and shackles and set free from harmful blind allegiance to equations-laden dogmatisms. As long as we take the brave step to remove the self-imposed blindfolds, we won't be fooled again. We need to develop an unremitting disdain for the notion that we can quantify, that we can measure, that we can understand. We need to instill in the fabric of our society an overarching sense of incredulity, a fanatical atmosphere of quantitative skepticism.

The chapter also discusses how the überprevalent notion of Normality in finance theory is particularly deleterious for the real world. To put it bluntly, the assumption of "normal" markets can deliver abnormally chaotic markets. By dreaming up a mathematically convenient tame world, financial economics can unleash raving unquietness. By assuming peaceful conditions, you get casualties-infested war. Normality, in brief, can kill us. We explain why this is so and provide real-life examples.

Finally, we highlight another essential danger associated with the preva-lence of theoretical ideology within the markets and the economy, namely the fact that we may succumb to the charms of a mathematical gadget and abide by it without actually understanding what it means. This can cause undue dislocations in the markets, as players act according to a guide that they can't read right. We can't have wildly misunderstood, influen-tial theoretical devices running loose throughout the financial landscape. The analysis focuses on perhaps the most prominent of such misread tools, the famous "volatility" index (VIX).

We conclude by remarking on what may potentially be the most troublesome side effect of the failures of finance theory and the carnage that it unleashes: a threat to the ongoing healthy existence of the (mostly value-adding) derivatives industry. As long as theory continues to display massive unworldliness and continues to be adopted into the markets, nasty episodes such as the credit crisis would recur. If derivatives, as tends to be the case, end up carrying a large share of the blame, we may witness a drastic reduction in their use as clients shy away from such conflictive tools, dealers retreat from business areas, and regulators begin to seriously meddle. All this would be disastrous. We must not allow those mathematically charged fake subduers of the unknown to deprive us of the genuine, time-tested, true unknownness-tamers.

Chapter 10, "We Need Fat Tony," calls for the radical substitution of mathematical decision making with good old-fashioned commonsense decision making. We call for the restoration to financial power of those who are completely unchained to the iron ball of qualifications and classroom-obtained erudition conventionalisms; those not the least impressed and subdued by academic diplomas and equation-solving prowess; those enslaved only to the deity of common sense and pavement-honed encyclopedism. The adoration of unworldly theories and their implementation have caused too much mayhem. We need to stop treating quantitative constructs as reliable doctrine, and start to reconsider the competitive advantage of experience-honed human common sense and intuition. Financial decision making would benefit, if only from the non-adoption of the harmful lemmas going forward. We need to hand over the keys to the risk kingdom back to freethinking, gumption-honoring, innumerate chums.

Last but not least, in the "Finale" section ("Should the Economics Nobel Be Eliminated?"), we wrap up things by being unapologetically controvertible and provocative and loudly asking whether, in light of all the wreckage that unsound financial theory can cause, the Nobel Prize in Economics (with the golden reputation that it endows on the theorists and their pontifications) should be done with. The proposed course of action? Let's not eliminate the Nobel (who am I to prohibit some Swedes from sumptuously regaling the theoreticians? These people obviously love their math, let them crown it!), but let's forcefully rename it so as to make 100 percent clear that what is being awarded is not practical at all and can be bad for your health. Libertarian as I want to be,

I also live by the motto that others' freedoms should be prevented from causing my death. Adding a big disclaimer onto the Nobel would be a reasonably beneficial step in that direction. By proceeding down that path, we would be not only welcomingly shedding light on the true meaning of the award and on the true nature of the honorees, but in the process also adding an extra layer of concrete to the fortification that keeps menacing, unworldly, quantitative dogma at bay.

■ *Mathew Gladstein's Complaisance* ■

T he investment bank Donaldson, Lufkin & Jenrette (commonly known as DLJ) has been out of existence as an independent entity for several years now, after being acquired by Credit Suisse at the turn of the century. DLJ had, of course, been a Wall Street legend for a long time, particularly famous for its leveraged finance expertise (commonly known as junk bond expertise). It is likely that not many people these days would associate DLJ with the revolution in options trading that took place almost four decades ago, much less with the revolution in theoretical finance that was gaining particular strength around the same period. And yet it is undeniable that DLJ did play a substantial role in both arenas. Leo Pomerance, DLJ's head of options, was in 1973 one of the founding fathers of the Chicago Board Options Exchange (CBOE) and its first chairman. A year earlier, Mathew Gladstein from DLJ's options department engaged Robert Merton and Myron Scholes to develop pricing and hedging tools for the firm, obviously aware of the duo's path-breaking theoretical contributions (here we are referring, naturally, to the very famous Black-Scholes-Merton formula, which was published in 1973 but had been available a few years earlier, and which was awarded the Nobel Prize in Economics in 1997).

Initially, the theoretical couple assisted DLJ to operate in the over-the-counter market and then, once equity options began to trade at the CBOE, in the exchange-traded segment, too. A source details how DLJ was anxiously waiting for the CBOE's opening day, eager to find out how reliable the option formula would prove to be in the jungle of open-outcry deal making. When the curtain was finally raised on April 26, 1973, Mathew Gladstein couldn't believe his eyes. The listed calls were being valued 30 to 40 percent above the theoretical prices calculated by the academic duo. "This model is a joke!" he panickly complained to Scholes over the phone. After a few minutes, the theoretician returned and calmly stated that the model was right, and the market was wrong. Gladstein bought it and excitedly returned to the action, decisively encouraged by the mathematical clarifications he had just received and willing to make a killing based on them.

For the past few decades, the financial world has often displayed the same willingness to believe that "the model is right, the market is wrong" as Mathew Gladstein showed on that celebratory opening day in Chicago. The same abidance by theoretical dictums, the same acquiescence towards mathematical concoctions, the same yielding to equations-laden commands. We don't know how well Gladstein did on that day, or how beneficial his firm found the assistance of the theorists (though it is tempting to assume that DLJ got value out of the relationship, given that it was prolonged). We can't be sure why the theoretical option prices were so far off from the animal-spirits-determined prices (though it is tempting to assume that the volatility estimates that go into the formula had something to do with it, or that few other players may have been using the same pricing tool in those early days). But we can be pretty sure of one thing: The enthusiastic inclination of many to, Mathew Gladstein–style, comply willingly with theoretical dictates may have caused non-negligible amounts of market trouble throughout at least the last 20 years. Several noteworthy episodes of malaise can be intransigently tracked back to the widespread use of a particular type of mathematical recipe.

That is, of course, a central theme of this book, and will be extensively dealt with in pages to follow. But let's exercise some patience and devote some time first to trying to answer a simple question: Why? Why have both financial insiders (traders, risk managers, executives) and outsiders (journalists, regulators, the public) consistently demonstrated a nontrivial willingness to treat quantifications as gospel? It is understandable that the professors would happily embrace theorization and analytical-ness as pathways towards enhanced academic prestige, perceived relevance, and a career dedicated to tinkering with adored tools. But what about the other folks? Where are their incentives? Sure, there is a subgroup of financial pros who would tend to be personally invested in adding fuel to the notion that theoretical and quantitative contributions are of the essence, but these "quants," though having experienced enhanced influence in recent times, still constitute but a tiny fraction of insiders.

What is really interesting about the acceptance of abstruse mathematical constructs into the financial game is that it has been largely sanctioned and approved by those with neither unavoidably tangible interests in nor inescapably urgent necessities for theoretical prowess. Few nonquants' professional progressions would have been supremely derailed had the industry not adopted advanced quantitative techniques; similarly, few existing products and markets would have been prevented from birth by the absence of funky technical machinations. It is commonly argued that modern financial markets owe their existence and unparalleled innovativeness at least in grand part to the adopting of theoretical dictums. I think that assertion a big exaggeration (while at the same time recognizing that on occasions quantitative models, by promising "certainties" and a sense of "security," conveniently help propel activity in some specific, otherwise size-challenged corner of the industry; such processes tend to end not well).

The market's infatuation with mathematical prodigies (symbolized by several well-known facets, including the use of Value at Risk for the past 15 years, episodes of portfolio insurance and dynamic hedging techniques applications, or the convoluted credit models employed in the past few years) is probably explained by a combination of factors. Naturally, it wouldn't be far-fetched to consider that breadwinners (traders, salespeople, asset managers) do consider, with varying degrees of intensity and sincerity, theoretical contributions useful and a source of competitive advantage. Many of these players may honestly and eagerly believe that markets are mathematically tamable and that quantitative measures can be value-adding guiding lights. This could be explained by the proliferation of scientifically trained people in financeland and by the tide of business school graduates who are ever more increasingly being taught theoretical tenets on campus.

Another possibility is that nonmathematicians may be impressed and awed by the equations, and would shy away from challenging the validity or appropriateness of the models in fear of being revealed as technically unsavvy and hopelessly backward. Such reactions may be fueled not just by the PhD acronyms inscribed on the modelers' stationery, but also by the undeniable existence of extreme success stories involving quantitative types loose in trading floors. There is no doubt that the legendary performances of the arbitrage group at Salomon Brothers during the late 1980s and early 1990s (the seeds of what later became Long Term Capital Management, naturally), or of hedge funds such as DE Shaw and Renaissance Technologies, lent a lot of credibility to the bottom-line-friendliness of quantitatively charged toiling (naughty readers may peskily note how LTCM went down amidst a system-threatening blowup and that quant funds also contributed some shaking of their own during their August 2007 meltdown). The breathtaking successes of the exotic derivatives business (kick-started in the late 1980s), which purportedly was built on the back of third-generation modeling efforts, is also an amicable presentation card for the math.

Other times quant finance is adopted because of regulatory pressures (as politicians seek to endow the financial industry with "rigor"), or because it serves some obscure interests of otherwise no-nonsense, theory-skeptic players, or because it makes for great public relations (it has been documented that the CBOE embraced the Black-Scholes formula at least in part because its ivory tower–sanctioned impressive technical fortitude gave a lot of legitimacy to the re-flourishing of the options business, which had priorly spent many decades in the shadows of finance, watched suspiciously by regulators and unfailingly dismissed as reckless gambling).

I am unaware of DLJ's exact motives for seeking the advice of two young bright men with PhDs from über-elite institutions (University of Chicago and Massachusetts Institute of Technology) and monthly paychecks from one of those über-elite institutions (MIT). It probably boiled down to curiosity about the first-ever widely publicized option pricing model in history, coupled with a lack of radical disagreement as to the model's architecture, plus maybe a sober dose of diploma-deference at a time when few (if any) doctorate-holders roamed around trading floors and when many bank executives (let alone traders) had never experienced the feeling of attending a university lecture. For the purposes of this book, the precise and uncontroversial reasons don't matter that much. What matters is that the theory was wholesomely embraced by practitioners, and thus allowed to affect the markets. DLJ presumably having been the first investment bank to guide its trading positions through Black-Scholes, its pioneering interest may have encouraged others to also seek the wisdom of the prodigal theoretical child, thereby multiplying the latter's potential real-life impact.

It is not fanatically expected that those pros who bring advanced analytics into the fold of practice would believe that the adopted models have a high chance of igniting trouble down the road. Rather, they would be assumed to be hopeful about the possible gains to be obtained by pledging allegiance to the math, whether in the shape of better prices, improved hedges, or more accurate risk measurements (the exception here would be those situations where financiers are forced by regulators to embrace a particular quantitative construct, the foundations of which they agitatedly distrust and which side effects they massively fear). Just like Mathew Gladstein was probably quite hopeful about the positive value to be derived from that innovative formula back in the early 1970s, so too with the myriad of market participants who have at one point or another borrowed from mathematical advice for the past three decades.

Thus, the dangers that finance theory may pose to the world at large would not derive from a willful desire on the part of its adopters to wreak havoc. No mad scientists plotting to deliberately cause mischief here. Quite the opposite. The real problem would derive from an exceptionally magnified belief in the capacity of the models to help and to fulfill their promise. It's those who worship the goodness of the theory who can contribute to the gravest damage. By being unaware of the potential for mishap, or extremely confident that it would not rear its ugly head, model-embracers develop an unchecked sense of indisputability, an uncontrollable urge to feel certain and safe. Thus, the model is allowed to run freely, unconstrained by undue concerns. It is in displaying such blatant act of complaisance towards the math that pros could be condemning themselves (and many others) to hubristic malaise.

It has certainly happened before. The models appeared supremely unassailable and triumphant just prior to the tremors, perfectly accepted by the academic and industry establishments. As far as most people were concerned, the theory was flawless, or at least incapable of anything but a valuable contribution. The supercomplex tools, the scientification aroma, the qualifications-inundated resumes of the theorists never failed to hypnotize many into agreeable submission. Once the math was unleashed unto the markets, the inherent imperfections of the theory were allowed to play themselves out and to massacre the confident worshippers. Sometimes it took little time for the models to unravel, such as with the 2007 credit crisis, where the dethroned quantitative constructions had made their practical debut barely a lustrum earlier. Other times it takes a while longer, with the model's potential nastiness lurking, well hidden from view, in the shadows, observing how year after year praise is heaped upon the theoretical masterpiece, calmly waiting for the right moment when, emboldened by an indefatigable faith in the mathematical groundwork, market participants would so abuse their employment of the model that the breakdown would indisputably be both inevitable and mutilating.

On October 19, 1987, Wall Street suffered its sharpest ever one-day cataclysm, with the New York Stock Exchange being forced to say farewell to almost 25 percent of its value. The main culprit: computationally charged stock-trading strategies directly inspired by the mathematical spirit of the Black-Scholes formula.

Essentials

Chapter 1

Playing God

■ It's tough to model human action ■ Finance is not as religious as physics ■ Black Swans make things harder ■ The markets are not Normal and the past is a faulty guide ■ Should we care that theorists persist? ■

E conomists (particularly those involved in financial research) are often accused of suffering from an acute case of "physics envy." If only the economic landscape could be as mathematically tractable as the physical landscape. If only terrifyingly precise theoretical predictions held in economics as well as they do in physics. If only we could also be deemed scientists.

Economics, of course, is not physics. For one very simple, yet inevitably powerful reason: In one case the laws are immutably God-made and thus permanently exact (all one has to do is go find them and, with luck, express their structure down on paper); in the other, the rules are dictated not by God, but by His creatures, us humble humans. And if there is something that we know about ourselves is that, when it comes to economic activity (which of course includes the financial markets), we tend to be reliably unreliable. Our behavior is not set in stone, preprogrammed, preordained. It is not law-abiding, but rather entirely anarchic, ever changing. While the physical terrain is characterized by its divine lawfulness, the human-determined economic domain is shaped by pagan lawlessness.

Few have explained this dichotomy better than Emanuel Derman, a former top Goldman Sachs executive and now a professor at Columbia University, and someone who as a leading "quant" has spent a big chunk of his professional life trying to determine whether the markets are mathematically tamable. Derman, who has a PhD in physics and is a globally revered expert, once offered the following beautifully stated clarifications: *"It's not that physics is better, but rather that finance is harder. In physics you are playing against God, and He doesn't change His laws very often. In finance, you are playing against God's creatures, agents who value assets based on their ephemeral opinions."*

That is, while accurate modeling and forecasting may be possible (and, naturally, desirable) in the physical world, they are likely to be impossible (and possibly entirely undesirable) in the financial world. The eventual level of asset prices will depend on the actions of millions of individual investors, constantly buying and selling. Can anybody honestly claim to be able to register such behavior with a few equations? Who knows why and when people would revert to dumping an asset, or to accumulate it? Can any type of math capture those wild spirits?

Where will the yield curve be tomorrow? That will depend on bond prices, which in turn depend on the actions of people buying and selling bonds. Where will stock prices be next week? That will depend solely on human action, too. Where will the dollar be next month? Supply and demand. Can we really aspire to predict those actions? Seems far-fetched, and Derman agrees: *"No mathematical model can capture the intricacies of human psychology. Watching people put too much faith in the power of formalism and mathematics, I saw that if you listen to the models' siren song for too long, you may end up on the rocks or in the whirlpool."*

Physicists can search for truth because in the physical world truth really exists. Once one of nature's explicitly mechanical laws is discovered by a clever scientist, it can be relied upon not to change. Ever. But there are no immutable laws when it comes to the values of financial assets. No permanent rules set at the time of genesis. No divine inevitability. In finance, there is no truth. A new reality is created every minute through the unpredictable actions of utility-seeking humans.

Let Derman deliver the final nail in the coffin: *"As a physicist, when you propose a model of Nature, you are pretending you can guess the structure created by God. Perhaps it is possible because God doesn't pretend. But as a quant, when you propose a new model of value, you are pretending you can guess the structure created by other people. As you say that to yourself, if you are honest, your heart sinks. You are just a poor pretender and you know immediately there is no chance at all that you are truly right. When you take on other people, you are pretending you can comprehend other pretenders, a much more difficult task."*

As a financial modeler you are trying to guess what other people are going to do. But their eventual actions will depend on what they think *you* are going to do. So you have to correctly guess what other people are going to guess regarding your own future actions. Plausible? Like the notion of gravitation suddenly ceasing to work.

And yet financial economists and financial mathematicians have, for at least the past 50 years (and with particular ardor for the last three decades), devoted their considerable talents and energy to theoriticizing the markets into systems of equations, statistical symbols, and Greek letters. They have embarked on a quest to formalize and axiomatize finance that is Taliban-like in its dogmatism and resoluteness. God may not have a say in the markets (a direct one, at least), but that's no reason for us to feel unattended and uncared-for. Finance theorists have shown an indefatigable resolution to step in His shoes and fill the vacuum, all too willingly enacting laws and principles that are held by those ivory towers worldwide (and throughout a non-insignificant number of nonacademic posts, including many trading floors, treasury departments, regulatory agencies, and newspapers) with the same submissiveness as that shown by churchgoing parishioners.

Call me an unrepentant atheist, but I find myself among those who seriously doubt the validity of the mathematically charged financial prophecies. I believe that humans are so unpredictable when it comes to their dealings in equities, currencies, bonds, or mortgages (by this I don't mean random, I mean unforeseeable, undetectable; stating that the markets are random, as some well-established theories do, would imply us knowing how humans behave in the marketplace) that not even a real Prophet could untangle such conundrums. It is not that the theorists are not brilliant or that the tools are wrong per se. I just don't think that financial markets can be quantitatively understood, synthesized, and predicted. Any more than one can quantitatively understand, synthesize, and predict, say, the future sexual activities of a group of diverse and unrelated strangers (in fact, this may be far easier than in the case of the markets, where new, potentially influential information constantly shows up; where the actions of some people affect the actions of the rest; and where somewhat predictable physiological necessities and personal health levels do not shape the outcome.)

As much as academics may want, as Derman puts it, to subjugate the market with axioms and theorems, the market can (and will) do anything it likes. While atoms and planets have no choice but to follow their divinely preordained paths, economic agents enjoy much greater freedom and have a tendency to stubbornly and rebelliously refuse to bow down to the authority of the mathematical sheriff. Any financial economist who attempts to scribble the market's equivalent of the Ten Commandments from the isolated confines of a university office is presupposing that the outside world will obediently oblige (at all times), thus transforming theory into reality, and theory into law. Some claim that this is indeed not wholly implausible (those who defend the *performativity* of theory, whereby the existence of a model molds reality towards compliance with the former's tenets). But, in principle, it sounds quite presumptuous to count on the unquestioned compliance of financial players, if only for the obvious reason that a large group of them may have never been aware of the theory's very existence, let alone understand it and agree with it. Apples and particles, in contrast, didn't need to wait for Newton and Einstein to publish their conjectures before they could fall from trees and move randomly inside a gas.

Emanuel Derman once wrote that *"There is an almost religious quality to the pursuit of physics that stems from its transcendent qualities. . . . It's hard not to have a sense of wonder when you see that principles, imagination, and a little mathematics (in a word, the mind) can divine the behavior of the universe. Short of genuine enlightenment, nothing but art comes closer to God."* It is only understandable that nonphysicists (like, well, financial economists) would want to reach a similar state of rapture. The same relevance and status. Just imagine being able to discover another piece of life's hidden genetic code.

However, finance theorists should humbly recognize that their field does not contain the promise of the potential discovery of immutable, transcendent, immortal truths. Finance is much less pure, much more contaminated, much more vulgar. God's creations are not only strikingly beautiful and chaste, but He also plays with a fair dice. In the universe, the rules don't change in the middle of the game, they are "stationary," thus dependable (i.e., predictable, mathematically tractable). In statistical parlance, the God-given probability distributions are not only knowable but stable. In the markets, though, things are way messier. Humans are much more treacherous. Untrustworthy. Non-dependable. They don't play fair. They change the rules constantly, without pre-warning. As such, the probability distribution is not only wildly nonstationary (what held in the past does not necessarily hold today, or will hold tomorrow) but basically unknowable. Who can model such a world?

Legendary financial econometrician Andrew Lo, a professor at MIT's Sloan School of Business with hedge fund experience, famously said that in the physical sciences three laws can explain 99 percent of behavior, while in finance, 99 laws explain at best three percent of behavior. Lo is not shy about how he feels regarding the capacities of (traditional, at least) financial theory: *"Neoclassical economics works really well in some areas. But in the markets, neoclassical economists have failed miserably."*

A big problem for finance theorists is that the markets are an area where dramatically unexpected, dramatically impacting events show a historical tendency to make themselves regularly present. That is, in finance, errors in forecasting and modeling are bound to be made very conspicuous and evident ("How could they miss *that*!"). No place to hide for under-performing economists and mathematicians. If the markets, though still unpredictable, were less subject to Nassim Taleb's famous Black Swans (monstrously unseemly, monstrously consequential occurrences) and be-haved more or less smoothly, econometricians and quants may be able to go on toiling away relatively unscrutinized and unquestioned. But, sadly for some, that is not the case here on Earth. Our financial markets are shaped by unpredictable watershed phenomena.

The 1929 Crash, the 1980s Latin American banking crisis, the 1987 Crash, the 1994 bond market meltdown, the 1997 Asian crisis, the 1998 Russian default-LTCM crisis, the 2000 Nasdaq crash, the 2001 Enron bankruptcy, the 2002 WorldCom bankruptcy, and, certainly, the 2007 credit crisis are all extremely impacting events that were not under the prediction radar (keep in mind that with the exception of the first of them, all these debacles occurred at a time when quantitative finance constructs were actively prevalent in the markets and when thousands of academics were spending their days trying to forecast events). We weren't widely warned as to their imminence, as to their inevitability (the *Wall Street Journal* of Monday, October 19, 1987, in a page-one article made the observation that *"No one is forecasting a crash like that in 1929"*; meanwhile, in the real Wall Street the market was busy that day experiencing its most dramatic one-day massacre ever.

And rightly so, since such "outliers" are bound to be mathematically untamable. It is hard to predict the future existence of something that can't really be even imagined prospectively nor is represented in the historical data. It is much harder to actually assign rock-solid probabilities to such outcomes (what's the point of models when you can't say anything about probabilities?). And what's really hard is to predict the impact of the outliers, that is, the *expectation* (probability times the associated economic result).

As the many Black Swans that have afflicted the markets show, the real tail events are the final consequences, rather than the (pretty Black Swanly in itself) occurrence that ignited the fuse. The unpredictable Russian default led to the frighteningly system-threatening LTCM meltdown; the unpredictable 2007 credit crisis led to the eye-popping sudden disappearance of the investment banking industry. Foreseeing the igniting Black Swan has proven to be insurmountably challenging; prevising the outcome result is simply not possible, as the markets can literally go to zero, countries can go broke, and banks can melt away into oblivion.

Predicting is relatively easy in Black Swans-devoid "Mediocristan," where things are boring and outcomes don't change much (the range of possible uncertain states is very limited). We know that the chance that a U.S. presidential candidate would win more than, say, 85 percent of the vote is predictably insignificant. You could rerun the campaigns over and over and such freakish outcome would never present itself. Or take sports: What is the chance that Roger Federer would lose 50 percent of his tennis matches in the next six months? Barring the Swiss champ being afflicted with some disease, zero. That is, the "Federer asset price" can't suddenly halve in value. Or consider the odds of finding a 10-foot-tall man? You could reenact the life of the universe several times and still the probability would be insignificant. In Mediocristan, it is actually possible to assign probabilities to things taking place; it is reasonable to discard the extreme as unfathomable.

In "Extremistan," where the financial markets reside, assets can halve in value (and further) in no time. The rare is not awkward, but frequent (the space of the unknown is amply ample). Outcomes are not enslaved to somewhat stringent constraints, and thus are free to explore the unexplored. In mature democracies, no single party tends to enjoy outlandish domination. In tennis, top players tend not to lose (too many games) to lesser-ranked peers. But there are no such (granted, nonscientific) rules in the markets. Nothing says that the stock market can't halve next week, or that the value of certain securities can't go to zero. This makes predicting harsh because so many alternative outcomes are possible, including many things that had never happened before. Exciting arenas full of possibilities, like the markets or book sales, are much less tamable than duller (in terms of range of outcomes) arenas like sports, height, or U.S. presidential contests.

Blogger Yaron Koren (yes, *blogger*; if anyone these days would deem such a reference nonrigorous, all I can say is, "Wake up, it's 2008!") believes that the reason we can forecast in Mediocristan but not in Extremistan comes down to the concept of conditional versus independent probabilities: *"In the Mediocristan world of sports, elections, etc., all the factors going into the final outcome are fairly independent of one another: the number of points a team scores in the first half of a game doesn't really affect the number of points they score in the second; whether a person votes for a certain candidate doesn't affect whether their neighbor will vote for that candidate. Thus, for a result to be significantly different from expectations, many things would have to go right (or wrong) independently—enough to make such a result all but impossible. On the other hand, in Extremistan, every event affects every subsequent event. If a book sells a million copies, bookstores begin displaying it prominently; the author gets invited on talk shows to plug it, etc: selling the next million becomes a much easier proposition. Similarly with the price of a stock, or the success of a website, or really most of the other interesting questions in life. . . . So there's a mathematical basis for explaining why the systems that do so well in predicting certain outcomes will fail at all the rest. And why we'll have to remain in the dark about the really important issues."*

It is obviously harder to predict in a world where conditional expectations play a key role. How to tell how one's actions will influence the actions of others? In principle, the act of me buying stock could be seen as increasing the chance of upward prices, as others follow my lead, but it could also cause prices to go down as the market may start to see the stock as overvalued and in need of a correction. It is hard to know when and if the snowball effect will take place, and in which direction. So here you would have two levels of randomness that need to be tamed: first, the original actions by a few people who kick-start a process (will a book get initially sold, will a stock get initially purchased); second, the follow-up by a thundering herd that consolidates the process into a sizeable trend. If nailing the first one could be tough in itself, deciphering the second one would be truly taxing as the range of possible future paths is expanded, in essence determined by how each individual would react to others' prior actions. That is, in Extremistan things can change much faster and in (apparently) weird directions.

And if theory is not successful at helping us prepare for the events that truly shake our world, what good is it? Perhaps less useful than trying to forecast, say, the winner of a general election by gazing at the stars. In early 2008, when the ravages of the credit crisis were inescapably abundant, Nassim Taleb put it like this: *"If the U.S. Food and Drug Administration monitored the business of financial risk management as rigorously as it monitors drugs, many of these 'scientists' would be arrested for endangering us. We replaced so much experience and common sense with 'models' that work worse than astrology, because they assume that the Black Swan does not exist."*

But, many theorists and indoctrinated outsiders would argue, surely a model, even if somewhat underperforming, is better than nothing. After all, can we afford to walk the markets analytically blind, with no quantitative guide whatsoever? Yes, Taleb says, we can and we should, because *"Trying to model something that escapes modelization is the heart of the problem. . . . Sometimes you need to say, 'No model is better than a faulty model'—like no medicine is better than the advice of an unqualified doctor, and no drug is better than any drug."* The dominance of Black Swans in the markets may make the term "finance theory" somewhat of an oxymoron. When the most important events by far (the 10 largest daily moves in the S&P 500 account for more than half the returns over the past 50 years, the 2007 credit crisis wiped out banks' gains from the previous five years, the major U.S. commercial lenders lost an amount equal to all their previous accumulated profits during the 1980s Latin American debt crisis) cannot be predicted (not just have been consistently non-prophesized, but can't by their very structural nature be presighted), can we really talk of the possibility of a theory?

Financial models suffer from two drawbacks that are particularly acute in a world, like the markets, dominated by rare events. One is that many of the sacred cows in the field assume that the Normal probability distribution reigns supreme, that is, assign negligible chances to asset prices experiencing wild swings. Another is that the present is being described and the future forecasted through heavy reliance on past historical data.

The summer of 2007 earned a notable place in history on account of the several noteworthy developments that took place under its watch. Tony Blair stepped down as Britain's Prime Minister, Apple released its iPhone, and *The Sopranos* TV show aired its last episode. That holiday period's claim to fame also rests, naturally, on events witnessed in the global financial arena, becoming yet another prominent symbol of the wild tumultuousness that can afflict the markets from time to time (we can all recall stock markets going up by 300 points one day, only to fall by 300 points the following day, only to rise by another 300 points the following, and so on). Summer 2007, and the credit crisis that it witnessed emerge, forever joined a high-profile group of dates (such as September 1998 and October 1987, among many others) that very forcefully show that in the markets the Normal probability distribution does not rule. The actual probability of the extreme is far from negligible.

It is thus with some puzzlement that many readers may receive the news that the assumption of Normality has been a staple of financial theory from its early beginnings (all the Nobels awarded to financial economics are heavily grounded on the Normal assumption; remove such tenet, and the prized theories crumble and crash). Some argue that the reason for this is that it makes mathematical modeling more convenient, as the Normal distribution is quite comfortable to work with. That is, even theorists who may know full well that the markets tend to gyrate wildly with large deviations being the norm, not the rarity, may still borrow from the Normal distribution when concocting analytical constructs. Perhaps their assumption is that other researchers will correct for the deficiency later on, or that pros will learn how to tweak the model so as to make it more attuned to the real world.

Whatever the case, it seems appropriately hard to approve of theories that assume the existence of a Platonic financial universe where the vast majority of events resemble the average and where the probability of extreme deviations is deemed to be negligible. According to the Normal distribution, events that move more than three *"standard deviations"* (the conventionally accepted measure for risk and volatility in finance, itself valid as statistical tool only under the Normality assumption) from the mean should not happen. And yet the markets are almost regularly displaying behavior that is far, far crazier. We all still remember the complaints by David Viniar, Goldman Sachs CFO, on August 2007 as the credit crisis was starting to break loose: *"We were seeing things that were 25–standard deviation moves, several days in a row."* In a Normal world such happenstance is utterly impossible. The universe isn't old enough to accommodate such small probability. Obviously, we must not live under Normality.

And that summer's travails, though particularly detectable, are not, again, by any means the only high-profile instance of the markets yelling out loud, "Don't call us Normal!" The posterior, even wilder, events in the credit, equity, and interest markets implacably bear witness, but there is also plenty of historical precedent. During the European Exchange Rate Mechanism debacle in 1992 (whereby Europe's system of officially managed currency rates collapsed), 50–standard deviation moves in interest rates were witnessed, while 1987's Black Monday was a 20–standard deviation (or 20-sigma) event. During the summer 1998 convolutions that eventually brought down giant Long Term Capital Management, 15-plus sigma deviations became the norm. Plenty of smaller (yet still sensationally non-Normal) similar gyrations have been observed in finance. So-called "one in a million years" events have been experienced, several times, by people whose age is way below one million years. Which one is wrong, the real world or the model? If you said the model, you got it right. The real probability distribution has fat (not thin) tails that grant extreme events the weighty weight that they deserve. In finance, rare events are not that rare. When it comes to wheeling and dealing in the markets, we are not Normal.

In fact, it seems to me that the assumption of Normality when it comes to the financial markets shows strong correlation with that other famously misguided imposition, namely Prohibition in 1920s America. Just like Prohibition forbade regular folks from (legally) drowning down their sorrows, Normality "forbids" investors from taking the markets beyond certain levels. Such probabilistic assumption denies individuals the capacity to cross certain lines, explore certain territories, discover certain realities. It is, thus, a very constraining assumption. A tyrannical one, you might say. Just like with any form of reactionary totalitarianism, individuals are judged to be of limited capabilities, requiring pre-set, centrally imposed, stringent regulations. They are assumed to be unable to reach beyond certain limits, forever confined to a restricted existence.

A financial theory world ruled by Normality is a world where humans (the only ones that can move a market) are prohibited from realizing their full potential, where they are caged in a dull universe of severely reduced possibilities, where freedom is only a word. Perhaps Prohibition isn't the only historical parallel with the Normality assumption after all. Do I hear . . . . . *ism*? To all those eager to break free from the Normality dictatorship, history may provide a comforting message. Prohibition and . . . . . . ism eventually did, of course, spectacularly fail. Why? Simply put, because they run dramatically counter to human nature. People (generally) want to drink. People (usually) want to be free. If one tries to set artificial limits on humans' natural desires, ambitions, and capabilities, the eventual end result is bound to be one of failure.

Real-life markets show us with astounding regularity that investors (who, despite occasional evidence to the contrary, are all too human) also want to be free. They want to spread their wings and be able to explore any possible price level, no matter how remote, no matter how inaccessible, no matter how unthinkable. They want to realize their full potential, and invariably do so. The theoretical straightjacket imposed by Normality seems as much at odds with humanity as were Prohibition and . . . . . . ism. Inhumanely unrealistic. Inhumanely unworkable. And yet all too tempting for certain freedom-denying technocrats.

Interestingly, the unavoidably obvious presence of non-Normal markets may be the direct result of a widespread belief in normal markets on the part of investors and speculators (conventional theories might have played a part in building such expectations). Bluntly stated, people's belief in the absence of rare events will eventually cause the rare event to take place. Rare events must always be unexpected, otherwise they would not occur. The assumption of Normality will make people take actions that will render the actual distribution non-Normal. The religion of thin tails will deliver the paganism of fat tails. Outliers are created by people who don't believe in outliers.

The message from a Normal distribution is that waters will be, for the most part, quite calm. No significant storms on the horizon. It is a comforting message for those considering the possibility of sailing through the marketplace. After all, most people would not dive into a market if they expect that at the end of the road there will be a crash. The possibility of a crash must be deemed negligible if a market rally is to sustain momentum. As more and more Normality-believing investors join the bandwagon, the discarding of a crash as a viable event becomes more widespread and, in effect, conventional wisdom. The more investors join a booming market, the more normal the investment looks to others. The Normality assumption becomes not just the rationale for entering into the market, but an end in itself. The market reaches a point where people are not buying any specific asset. They are buying Normality (i.e., the complete absence of nasty surprises). If they expected something else, they wouldn't have joined the party.

But with every new inflow of cash into the market, the chances of a rare event go up. The more participants in the market, the more chances that someone, somewhere would react negatively to a new development (such as corporate losses, an accounting scandal, or disappointing economic figures), would panic, and would liquidate as a result, prompting other investors to panic, liquidate, and so on all the way to a crash. In essence, when faced with the unexpected presence of the unexpected, Normality-believers will tremble and exacerbate the downfall. They never believed in outliers until they experienced one, and their reaction gives strength to the outlier, making it stronger, fattening the tails. The non-Normal distribution is thus unavoidably born, a testament to people's wildly changing trading habits. As long as people continue to not expect rare events to occur, rare events will inevitably take place.

L et's now tackle the issue of historical data. Back to Taleb for this: *"In the beginning, when I knew close to nothing about econometrics, I wondered whether the time series reflecting the activity of people now dead or retired should matter for predicting the future. Econometricians who knew a lot more than I did about these matters asked no such question; this hinted that it was in all likelihood a stupid inquiry.... I am now convinced that, perhaps, most of econometrics could be useless—much of what financial statisticians know would not be worth knowing."* Polemic stuff, no doubt. If anything, the field of "financial econometrics" seems stronger than ever, with prominent academics and academic institutions devoting lots of attention to it, and with one of its inventors actually receiving the Nobel Prize just a few years ago. And yet it seems hard to disagree with Taleb. As the famed trader-turned-philosopher says, when it comes to the financial markets econometric analysis is bound to be less than relevant.

At its core, econometrics is an attempt to forecast the future based on what happened in the past. As every former and present economics student worldwide can attest, this exercise can involve extremely complex statistical and mathematical maneuvers. It is no exaggeration to say that the proliferation of econometrics has been a decisive factor behind the outrageously excessive formalization of economic theory in the past decades.

Lately, econometrics has found its way into financial research. Past market data is used to predict future market movements, through the use of funky models with increasingly funkier names such as GARCH, EGARCH, AARCH, APARCH, FIGARCH, STARCH, TARCH, SQGARCH, and CESGARCH. But intelligently designed as these tools surely are, it is not easy to become a believer. Simple old-fashioned common sense ruthlessly dictates that past information should not be very useful in predicting the future of financial markets.

Why? Among other reasons (like the fact that you will never be able to capture all the variables that affect decision making), because, as Taleb apparently simplistically though innovatively, insightfully points out, we would be trying to predict what current financial players are going to do based on what ancient players did in the past. In the markets, prices move for one reason only: human action. If more humans decide to buy than to sell, prices will go up. If more humans decide to sell than to buy, prices will go down. Clearly, each human being has his own, independent, decision-making capabilities. The financial prices of a certain historical period would be the result of the actions taken by those individuals active in the market at that time. Those prices thus reflect the average consensual decisions of the players who happened to be around, given the relevant circumstances then present.

Econometricians would try to use those prices to forecast the prices of several periods later. The problem is that many of those individuals originally involved in setting the prices included in the time series used in the analysis would by now be either dead or no longer active in the market. Econometricians would in fact be borrowing from inactive brains, attempting to predict the decision-making process of a group of independently thinking individuals from the decision-making processes of a different group of independently thinking individuals who are no longer around. Why should Peter's particular stock pickings 20 years ago matter for predicting Paul's particular stock pickings today, particularly since Peter has been retired in the Bahamas for the last decade? It might be sensible to use data from Peter's past actions to predict *Peter's* current actions, but it definitely looks a bit suspect to use that data as a predictor for the actions of another, different, unrelated human being.

What financial econometricians are trying to do is akin to predicting the number of goals to be scored by a soccer player next season by looking at the time series of goals historically scored by his club. As any soccer fan would tell you, it would be weird to try to infer anything relevant from goals-scored data that includes players who no longer play. There are simply different people involved. Since goals (like stock, bond, or commodity prices) are all about people, it seems truly far-fetched to assume that historical time series can tell me anything about the future, no matter how complex the techniques involved. The fact that the legendary George Best managed to score 180 goals in his time at Manchester United in the 1960s tells us absolutely nothing about the scoring capabilities of today's striker Wayne Rooney.

The famous LTCM story can help us understand why borrowing from Peter to predict Paul's actions (i.e., trusting that older situations with different people present under different circumstances can provide a reliable guide as to the future) does not look like a winning proposition. LTCM took big bets in fixed-income and equity markets, making the data-backed assumption that markets return to normality. The fund had constructed money machines that would cash in big when such return predictably took place. Based on the historical evidence, such structure seemed flawless. Nothing could go wrong.

However, LTCM forgot that there was something new in the picture that distorted everything so much that it made past references useless: LTCM itself. Historical data did not reflect the existence of such a giant fund taking such giant positions in a few specific markets. It couldn't, of course, because such a giant had not existed until now. LTCM's actions had changed the game and the probability distribution because now everybody else's actions depended on LTCM's. An LTCM-less past could not be a reliable guide to an LTCM-dominated present. LTCM's boss John Meriwether put it best: *"The hurricane is not more or less likely to hit because hurricane insurance has been written. In financial markets this is not true. The more people write financial insurance, the more likely it is that disaster will happen because the people who know you have sold the insurance can make it happen."*

The data-backed return to normalcy unraveled because, once LTCM suffered a bit of trouble, the rest of the market began to trade against their portfolio, that is, began to bet against normality. As a result, things became more, not less, abnormal than ever. Courtesy of the uniquely unique presence of an entity like LTCM at that very precise point in time. New people and new circumstances can render old-timers hopelessly irrelevant.

The widespread presence of quantitative investors (or quant funds), now a ubiquitous element of the markets, may be a particularly acute case of what could be deemed the "new kids on the block" phenomenon, and of how under such situations past data becomes extra unreliable. Quant punters (in more or less intense fashion) are in the habit of employing very advanced technological and scientific tools in the quest for making money. They also tend to (a la LTCM) take a hard statistical look at the historical rearview mirror as guidance for position taking and risk measurement.

The problem with this is that, of course, never before had so many smart scientists and computer geniuses coincided in the markets, often playing exactly the same type of investment games, often armed with billions of monetary units in ammunition. So when they look at past data (notwithstanding how extremely sophisticated the lenses may be) they don't find themselves. They couldn't, because they weren't there. In the case of certain specific strategies maybe one or two early pioneers had been going at it as far as two or three decades ago, but nothing remotely close to today's reality, both in terms of the crowded number of players, the size of their wallets, and the technological prowess. Today's quant funds are employing computers and mathematical models that simply did not exist until quite recently. When the data captures neither the people nor the tools, it is impossible to confidently borrow much from such ancient wisdom.

Thus, the presence of quanty folks using cutting-edge modernish technologies to trade and with a habit to statistically analyze the past may be akin to a catch-22 situation (on occasions, at least): The historical guide is rendered faulty by the very current (and not past) existence of those folks. Take risk. A quant fund may measure the riskiness of a strategy by back-testing its past performance and building devices such as Value at Risk. But those numbers would not account for the aliveness of that fund and its contemporary siblings, clouding the picture by not reflecting the possibility, for instance, that a liquidation by one member of the quant family (for whatever reason) would trigger further sell-offs among its brainy peers, thus rendering huge losses for the strategy overall. Something like this, of course, is what happened during August 2007, when quant troubles unraveled global equity markets and, as a consequence, the returns of quant plays themselves.

In a way, all this could be labeled as "Econometrics against Econometrics"; as new complex analytical techniques are devised and applied in the markets, older strategies and strategists are rendered obsolete, and past data is irredeemably condemned to not displaying evidence of the current methodologies at play. As this process progresses, it becomes additionally hard to predict the future based on the past. If Peter and Paul engaged on simpler, fundamentals-driven analysis for picking their portfolios, the fact that they inhabit different times may be less of an issue (though still naturally a big one). It might be somewhat reasonable to draw some useful lessons given that the tools (essentially, reading the newspapers) were so similar. But not so in quantland, where the tools can be drastically renovated from one point to the next.

Besides different, dead, or retired people, using historical data suffers from another, simple problem: How far do I go back into the past, and how sure can I be that such selected past period encompasses all the possible events that can take place in the forecasted period? This is where the Black Swan issue makes a heavy presence. If on October 1, 1987, someone had used 50 years of data to try to predict the behavior of U.S. stock markets, the sample evidence would have dictated that there was no chance in hell that the market may drop 25 percent on a single day. Armed with that information you might, say, have confidently sold out-of-the-money puts on the S&P 500. If the data was right, you could make a boatload of premium money, safe in the knowledge that you would never be exercised. Three weeks later, by October 20, you would of course have been wiped out from the previous day's quite real 23 percent meltdown on Wall Street.

A Black Swan is by definition something that has never (or very rarely) happened before, making the probabilistic detection of the events that most alter our financial environment through naively looking at past data a pretty hopeless task. Black Swans (or "tail events") are prospectively incomprehensible; we only fully understand what our imagination missed after the fact. It is simply too much to ask of past data that it should consistently contain warning evidence of phenomena for which there is little or no reliable precedent.

Andrew Lo lists the following as one of his field's most important unanswered questions: *"What is the best way to measure the likelihood of rare events and manage such risks if, by definition, there are so few events in the historical record?"* Nassim Taleb's ready answer would be: "We can't." There is no way for us to conceive of a cold probability figure that can be nonastrologically assigned to a Black Swan taking place. Think about it. Someone asks you for your estimate that Wall Street would tumble by 30 percent next week or that the dollar would be worth as much as the euro by next month, what can you say? Zero chances? Not really, because the fearsome tail event lurks in the darkness of the financial world, always omnipresent, never discardable. But if not zero, then how much? How much probability would you have assigned on March 1, 2008 (share price at $80) to the event that Bear Stearns (founded in 1923, and a historical bastion of the American financial establishment) would be gone within three weeks? The fact that in its 85-year history Bear had never gone under before made for a hard prediction through the use of historical data. The Black Swan is not probabilistically discernable, and no amount of econometric complexity seems likely to change things.

A very illuminating and rabidly current example of the limited power of past data (either because it can't contain the predictably one-of-a-kind financial Black Swan or because the selected sample period is particularly deficient) are the widely publicized failings of Value at Risk (VaR) models during the credit crisis. VaR is a regulators-sanctioned, industrywide-employed risk measurement tool that aims to describe expected maximum losses (within a certain confidence interval) from a financial position or conglomerate of positions, based on historical data and statistical assumptions (mostly the prevalence of the Normal distribution). VaR models disturbingly failed to predict the monstrous subprime-related losses that have afflicted banks and others. The numbers it had been churning pre-mayhem had been way too low, way too comforting, way too unworrisome. That is, VaR (which outputs are regularly followed by senior management and disclosed in public) provided a picture of tranquility right before the world went crazy. Why?

Simple, the markets had gone through a prolonged calm phase before the summer of 2007, and thus the data (banks tend to use one to five years of historical evidence) described nothing but serenity. According to the most revered risk measure, there was nothing to lose sleep over. This placid message may have endowed financial executives with a refreshing, statistically-backed, "scientifically" reinforced sense of confidence

(VaR had worked too well for a long while). Akin to the captain of the *Titanic* accelerating the pace because recent records showed no presence of large icebergs in that part of the ocean.

Most damning for VaR, firms that ended up doing very badly out of the crisis had lower VaR figures pre-crisis than those who ended up faring relatively well (of course, many times this can be explained by widely differing balance sheet sizes; but the point remains that the largest losses, by far, corresponded to those that were reporting lowish VaR numbers). Merrill Lynch (which posted a Q4 2007 loss of almost $10 billion, its largest ever) had a much lower Q3 VaR than Goldman Sachs (which, uniquely among Wall Street peers, reported record earnings in Q4). Bear Stearns, which eventual fate does not require clarifications, disclosed a Q3 VaR (average daily VaR of some $30 million) five times lower than Goldman's. After the fact, Merrill seemed to be convinced that something had not gone quite right with the mathematical risk monitors: *"VaR, stress tests and other risk measures significantly underestimated the magnitude of actual loss from the unprecedented credit market environment,"* said Merrill's Q3 filing with the U.S. Securities and Exchange Commission. *"In the past, these AAA CDO securities had never experienced a significant loss in value."*

As the crisis progressed and intensified, VaR kept underperforming. While the theoretical expected maximum loss churned out from the model increased as market turbulence hit the roof, it wasn't even in the vicinity of a close reflection of the carnage that was about to ensue (among other reasons, because more recently incorporated data only slowly starts to modify the picture, getting lost in a vast sea of historical, non-mayhem-containing past evidence). Bear's daily VaR was still a lowly $60 million just days before the firm disappeared and $8 billion of value melted away. The number of VaR *exceptions* (the number of days when actual trading losses exceeded theoretical losses) reached outrageous levels at most financial institutions, an irreverent admission of the mechanism's utter failures as a risk radar. It's not just that VaR underperformed so savagely. The wound was so sore because the thing failed when guidance was most acutely needed. The past was inexcusably misguiding when it mattered the most.

The very disappointing performance of VaR during the crisis has fueled a debate as to how it should be modified so as to prevent similar failings going forward. Some argue that longer data samples should be used, so as to have a better chance of capturing extreme events. But others defend the opposite tactic, saying that a shorter window would act as a faster warning signal. Anyways, the problems run deeper, are more structural than the mere arbitrary selection of a certain time window. For one, VaR is calculated in terms of sigma, our familiar standard deviation parameter, which, once more, only works as measure of dispersion if we assume Normality (naturally, such probabilistic assumption works heavily in the direction of rendering unrealistically low risk numbers). Secondly, VaR may have been condemned to a hopeless task by its academic, quanty, and regulatory sponsors: the past is simply not a reliable guide to the future when there are humans around doing mischief. After all, it's not as if the 2007 crisis signified VaR's first-ever crisis of confidence.

Less than a decade ago, this glorified risk alerter went through another very painful period, again letting the financial world down. During the 1998 crisis (coming on the heels of the prior year's Asian crisis) banks experienced several acute VaR exceptions (i.e., true losses turned out to be way higher than those forecasted by the model). In one study of U.S. banks, some institutions were found to have had up to three and even five exceptions during the August–October 1998 period, when the model (at 99 percent confidence level) would predict only one exception out of every 100 working days. And not only that, the exceptions (as during the credit crisis) were quite large, more than two standard deviations beyond VaR in some cases, and more than seven sigmas in another. Under the Normal distribution, the probability of a loss just one standard deviation beyond 99 percent is virtually zero. So banks' actual P&L suffered much bigger losses, much more often than VaR had warned about. Interestingly (or, as some may have it, scarily), VaR quite possibly contributed decisively to the Russian default transforming into a pronounced tailspin for global markets, and the system-threatening LTCM collapse. Trying to predict the future based on historical data may not just be utterly impractical, but actually pretty dangerous. But that's another story that we reserve for later.

While failing to predict Black Swans is certainly a big indictment on finance theory (failing at warning when the big bad wolf is at the door), one could generously argue that, well, Black Swans are so utterly unexpected that perhaps theorists could be somehow excused (okay, may counter-punch some theory abhorrers, but then don't allow financial economists and quantitative analysts to go around saying that they can mathematically tame the markets; without Black Swans, there are no markets). But even after having been granted such generosity, theory would still present a shaky report card. It turns out that economists are also lacking when it comes to predicting the small stuff, those regular market and economic movements that, while important, are not likely to cause panic-inducing tremors. That is, it is not only that headline-grabbing crises are not being predicted, but even non-crisis-caliber, seminormal changes in key variables are consistently being widely mistargeted.

We are all familiar with how off-the-mark predictions of future GDP growth, inflation, unemployment, exchange rates, stock markets, or interest rates have traditionally been. After all, there is a whole huge market (called the government bond market) that thrives on such unreliability. Traders make bets on bonds based on their perception as to the future levels of variables such as those listed above, or on their perception as to their peers' perceptions as to those future levels, which would be affected by currently available forecasts. If such forecasts were invariably right, little money would be made in the market and activity would dry up. It is thus tempting to conclude that one of the reasons for the bond market's extraordinary liquidity is that pros have little faith in economic predictions.

Long before the appearance of the Black Swan concept (and of economists-basher-in-chief Taleb) in the scene, economic forecasting and modeling had already received plenty of negative praise. For instance, celebrity Harvard professor and author John Kenneth Galbraith once uttered that *"The only function of economic forecasting is to make astrology respectable."* Paul Ormerod, a leading UK forecaster, published in the late 1990s a polemic tome called *The Death of Economics* where he offered that *"The record of economists in understanding and forecasting the economy at the macro-level is not especially impressive. Indeed, uncharitable writers might be inclined to describe it as appalling. . . . The Japanese recession, by far the deepest since the war, was not predicted. Neither the strength of the recovery in America in the second half of 1992 nor the slowdown of the recession in Germany was foreseen by the models."* A 2001 paper commissioned by the U.S. Federal Reserve's Board of Governors opened by openly stating that *"Economists have never had much luck in forecasting asset prices in general or exchange rates in particular. . . ."* In 1994, *Wall Street Journal* economics editor Alfred Malabre's very readable book "Lost Prophets" reflected on the dreadful forecasts he had witnessed during his career: *"In late September 1969, a bare three months before a recession actually began, I conducted a survey for the Journal. The headline of my article carrying the survey results read 'Most Economists Doubt Recession Will Occur.' The consensus forecast for the year ahead was that overall economic activity would rise slightly more than 5%. . . . In fact, GNP fell in the final quarter of 1969. . . the measure continued to drop through much of 1970. . . . Most forecasters, having incorrectly signaled the start of a recession in 1968, now compounded their error by predicting recession-free growth at the very time a recession was setting in. Credentials seemed to matter little."* And so on.

In 1999, Washington, D.C.–based Heritage Foundation conducted a study on the forecasting ability of the International Monetary Fund's famous twice-yearly economic projections (presented as part of the IMF'S World Economic Outlook). Given the IMF's global clout and, crucially, its deep bench of analytically oriented PhDs (though it must be said that the Fund seems to have of late embarked on a PhDs-dismissing strategy), it could be reasonably argued that the accuracy of its forecasts can serve us well for the purpose of analyzing the general reliability of the "science" of economic predicting.

Heritage's study looked at the IMF's forecasts for 1971–1998 for both industrial and developing countries (as a libertarian über-American institution, the Foundation was trying to attest the real effectiveness of the IMF, to which the U.S. government had just allocated several billions of dollars). The findings showed that while overall forecasting performance was quite decent when it came to developed nations (it was understandably paltrier in the case of less developed ones), IMF economists had consistently missed out on key "turning points," including Latin American hyperinflation in the 1980s (inflation forecasts made mistakes in the hundreds of percentage points), industrial growth slowdown in the mid-1990s (with across-the-board overoptimistic projections in the 1–2 percent range), and Japan's economic crisis in the 1990s (persistent overestimation). In other words, some of the world's most applauded econometricians had completely missed the most decisive events.

In 2001, the RiksBank (Central Bank of Sweden) conducted its own study, testing the predicting abilities of a very large sample of forecaster-wanna-bes, including investment banks, corporates, rating agencies, and universities (all presumably employing some type of quantitative estimator). The evidence showed that, for the 1990–2001 period, crystal ballers erred annual GDP predictions (taking into account both upside and downside errors), on average, by 1.20 percent (U.S.), 1.60 percent (Japan), or 0.93 percent (Germany), and in similar inflation forecasts by 0.55 percent (U.S.), 0.48 percent (Japan), or 0.61 percent (Germany). Interestingly, the best names (in principle, those able to hire the most renowned forecasters) did not seem to perform better. Once more, turning points were not foreseen (until they had happened).

Perhaps the most illustrating analysis of how sophisticated quantitative methods fare when it comes to guessing the future is the one conducted during 1979–2000 by Spyros Makridakis and Michele Hibon (also mentioned in Taleb's *The Black Swan*), professors at the highly prestigious French business school INSEAD. They essentially conducted a forecasting competition among econometricians, focusing on business and economic time series. The goal, of course, was to see how accurate the methods proved to be. The first such test, taking place in 1979, yielded the surprising conclusion that simple methods outperformed sophisticated ones. This was not well received by the econometric intelligentsia. To respond to such criticisms, Makridakis and Hibon launched the so-called M-Competition in 1982, increasing the number of time series and of methods and, crucially, having many other experts conduct their own forecasts using their preferred instruments. The empirical results did not vary. Statistically complex tools do not perform better, in spite of their technical prowess. Such strong empirical evidence seems to have been ignored by theoretical econometricians, who have unveiled themselves to be extremely hostile to such verification exercises (they obviously don't want the world to know the results). Rather, econometricians, Makridakis and Hibon offer, have concentrated on developing yet more abstruse models without regard for the ability of those models to more accurately predict real-life data.

Faced with such an unfriendly environment, the INSEAD professors decided in 2000 to embark on a final attempt to settle the accuracy issue, through the M3-Competition which included yet more experts, yet more methods, yet more series. The shocking conclusion? Statistically complex methods do not necessarily produce more accurate forecasts. Makridakis and Hibon conclude with what may seem to many as unfettered common sense, but may be considered hostile fire inside many an ivory tower office: *"Pure theory and elaborate methods are of little practical value unless they can contribute to improve the accuracy of post-sample predictions. . . . [T]he time has come to accept this finding so that pragmatic ways can be found to*

improve predictions.... [T]hose criticizing Competitions, and empirical studies
in general, should stop doing so and instead concentrate their efforts on explaining
the anomalies between theory and practice."

In this chapter, we have provided several arguments that seem to reinforce the view that *finance theory* may be considered an oxymoronic
term. The preeminent presence of unchartable humans, the dominant
weight of unimaginable and unprecedented Black Swans, and the limited
explanatory power of historical data all indicate that financial markets are
doubtfully tamable through mathematical wizardry, no matter how complex (in fact, more complexity may result in even less reliable results).
So why do economists and quants persist? And should we care that they
do? The first question will be (tentatively) answered in the next couple
of chapters. We will tackle the second question now.

Should we care that a few hundred professors and financial engineers
choose to spend their days trying to apply mathematical models to the
practical-only discipline of finance? Many of us may deem the effort
doomed from the start and hopelessly hopeless but, really, what's it to us
if a bunch of strangers have chosen to embark down that unseemly road?
If they have been lucky enough to find university deans and trading floor
honchos willing to finance (extremely generously in some cases) such a
lifestyle, then more power to them, right?

Not only that. Perhaps quantitative finance research should actually be
encouraged (again, provided that others are the ones having to spend their
days immersed in stochastic calculus, numerical methods, and time series
analysis). Think about it. Wouldn't it be nice if the hurly-burly of the
markets could really be accurately synthesized through a few equations
and theoretical dogmas? Certainly, few potential discoveries appear as
temptingly attractive as that one. Playing God in this case would not
be entirely blasphemous: The end goal would be highly beneficial (if
you like reduced volatility and "fairer" asset prices), and the techniques
used are quite decorously intelligent. Shouldn't we actively encourage
brilliant mathematicians from Carnegie Mellon University, Goldman
Sachs, or Standard & Poor's to focus their talents on building models
that aim to unlock, and tame once and for all, the markets' DNA?
The possible upside seems obviously grand. Should we deny financial
economists the triumph in store?

Or, rather, should we protect them from themselves, and, more importantly, protect ourselves from them? It is hard to deny that thanks to the quantification of finance, market practices and research have benefited from the arrival of previously unsuspected characters (mostly from the physical sciences) who have contributed magnificently. The contributions to the finance arena of people like Emanuel Derman, Paul Wilmott, or Steven Shreve might have never happened had analytics and modeling not gained greatly enhanced relevance inside trading floors. So the theoretization of finance has produced tangible benefits, at least when it comes to the quality of human capital.

But there is a darker side. First, economists and mathematicians may be missing out on a lot by embracing abstruseness. Not only would all that time spent solving equations may be later revealed as wasted in a sea of inapplicability, but the opportunity cost from not focusing on the other stuff could be taxing. Why be involved in finance at all if you are going to turn a blind eye to the all-exciting, real-world aspect of the markets? Why hide yourself behind an imaginary, self-concocted Platonic universe, when the real version is so unmissably sexy? Renowned journalist John Cassidy once wrote that 1996's Economics Nobel winner William Vickrey apparently refused to be judged by the mathematical scheming that had earned him the prize (at age 82) in the first place, and instead insisted on being known for his ideas for solving practical problems, like subway reform and the budget deficit. Vickrey in fact dismissed his rewarded theoretical contributions as *"one of my digressions into abstract economics. . . . At best, of minor importance in terms of human welfare."* Today's financial theorists should act now and try to hedge themselves from experiencing their "Vickrey moment." Unlimited formalism might win you trophies (and gainful employment), but it may not gain you (real) relevance, possibly not even to your own eyes.

Worse, the theories may end up causing harm. In this scenario, the models would be able to claim lots of practical relevance, but of the wrong kind. This has of course happened aplenty in general economics. The applications of Karl Marx's ideas left lots to be desired in terms of human welfare. Keynesianism has been accused of several ills, including unbearable stagflation. Milton Friedman and the Chicago School may have contributed to supporting dictators in power. Reaganite "Supply Siders" created monstrous fiscal deficits. The subfield of financial markets has also been hampered by theories gone wild. While there are precise, specific instances that can be highlighted, the potential malaise may be more structurally ingrained. That is, because of the proliferation and gradual acceptance (whether real, perceived, or "faked") of financial theory, the threat that the misuse of the latter implies may be both systematic and hard to eliminate. A key theme that would make a presence throughout this book is that theories may provide a false, misplaced, inadequate sense of confidence and of quantifiable certainty, thus blinding pros to the dimension of the actual risks and encouraging (and excusing) forays into dangerous places. All this math-enabled deceit could end up very badly.

But quite possibly the most potentially harmful effect of the theories would be not so much that they provide faulty guidance based on the illusion of understanding (bad as this would be in itself, naturally), but rather that their prevalence and acceptance would do away with another possible and historically useful source of guidance, namely human intuition and wisdom. When mathematics and statistics take over as decision-making tools, the mind (with its treasure of accumulated experiences and battle scars) may be relegated to a relevance-lacking backseat role. The numbers soullessly churned out from the computer, not the softer sapience of traders and other players, become the key deciding factor. Decades of folk wisdom, passed down through generations of market warriors, may be irredeemably lost, all in the name of the scientification of that which may not be subject to being scientificized in the first place. This is important. The most profoundly insightful and informationally relevant source of financial intelligence (i.e., human experience, intuition, and oral traditions) may be entirely thrown to waste in exchange for the dominance of quantitative tools that present highly doubtful real-life credentials.

In sum, finance theory may present the world with a double threat. Not just the potential for dangerously faulty mathematically charged steering, but also the excreting of that most traditional and primordial of counselors: the experience-honed human gut feeling.

Chapter 2

The Financial Economics Fiefdom

■ *Virginity matters* ■ *When describing reality was okay* ■ *It's the incentives, stupid* ■ *Many obstacles to reform* ■ *Heeding Fischer Black's message* ■

I studied theoretical economics as an undergraduate. I went about it nonenthusiastically (though I got the highest mark in the only course that was taught American-style: you actually had to think, not just memorize abstruse theorems). In what in retrospect looks like a very wise decision, I decided not to devote the best years of my youth exclusively to microeconomics, econometrics, and topology. Instead, I mostly did other stuff during my late teens and early twenties. Like reading, almost always in the original English. Rather than spending all day locked up in a smoke-filled room trying to crack covariance matrices and general equilibrium, I read Paul Krugman and Milton Friedman's (nontechnical) tomes and religiously followed the *Economist* magazine. So one could say that in those innocence-filled years I gave up regression analysis expertise for the possibility to muse in the language of Shakespeare. Best trade I've ever made.

Distant though I was (in body and especially in soul), I still managed to develop an accurate sense of the monstrous intensity of the formalism that reigns supreme in Economics. Since undergraduate theoretical economics at top European public universities are globally famous for their orthodoxy (in fact deemed akin in complexity to the first years of a PhD at elite American institutions), I was in a good position to judge the beast from the inside.

Years later I was fortunate enough to attend (non-PhD) graduate school in the United States. This time I was way more enthusiastic about it. I got to learn about such nontheoretical things as bonds and options (the products). It was refreshing to be taught about stuff that actually exists in the real world and that flesh-and-bone individuals can in fact use. My faith in college campuses as places of (relevant) learning and thinking was frantically renewed. And yet, as I plowed deeper into my newly found discipline of financial economics, I began to notice that this academic subfield was as dominated by methodology and theoretical dogma as its mother field. This seemed truly puzzling. After all, financial economics does deal with subjects (the markets, corporate finance) that are nothing if not utterly applied. But there you had the textbooks and the journal articles describing an alternate reality, one dominated not by descriptions of the real world, but by mind-boggling equations and precepts.

In spite of my renewed passion for academic life, I felt that I had not entirely escaped the hell of economic formalism. If even finance had succumbed to the theoretical siren songs, there appeared to be little hope for descriptive, nondogmatic, actionable training in the economics arena. Paraphrasing Winston Churchill, it is likely that never have so many abstruse theorems been devised so often by so few.

Why is this so? What explains the utter predominance of theory when it comes to the studying of a field that is nothing if not practical? Law or medical schools also deal with people and their actions, yet have not suffered (by far) from the same acute case of analytization as economics departments or business schools. What factors caused financial academics to stop describing markets and to begin to tell markets (from the isolated confines of an ivory tower-sheltered office) that they should behave according to the enslaving dictates of certain mathematical precepts? If we want to understand how finance theory affects the real world, we must understand what kind of people and institutional structures have contributed (and are contributing) to the design of many of those theories.

Financial economists mostly work inside the business schools that house the finance departments of a given university. Thus, it helps in our quest to understand the forces behind the mathematical constructs that can shape the markets if we get a good idea as to the B-school status quo. This will allow us to comprehend the characters and incentives behind the churning of financial theorems.

This is important. After all, without the theoreticians (and the academic institutions that pay them for their analytical production), there would be that much less theory to worry about. And, as we will see, the current foundational structure of B-schools (the one that has reigned supreme for the last 50 years) goes a long way towards explaining why finance theory is both so prevalent and so, well, theoretical. As long as B-schools retain the same status quo, potentially dangerous unworldly models will keep being developed unfetteringly.

In the last few years a barrage of criticism has befallen the formerly glorified B-school establishment. While the sources of criticism are varied, one particular issue is emphatically highlighted, namely the fact that B-school faculty simply do not, in general, possess any significant real-life business experience. B-schools are filled with finance professors who have never closed a deal or traded a bond, marketing professors who have never marketed anything, management professors who have never managed anyone, and strategy professors who have never designed or implemented any business strategy. Akin to cooking schools having as teachers people who have never fried an egg. Or golf clubs having as instructors those who have never hit a swing. Or, yes, having virgins teaching at porn schools.

If we find it risible that a hypothetical sex school would allow a virgin to lecture students, why should we be, in principle, less outraged by the fact that business students are being taught by people who have never worked in a business? It gets worse: Just like the virgin prof from porn school would be telling students who have (presumably) already had plenty of sex in their lives how to interact in the sack, in B-school we find that students who have had significant real-life work experience (in many cases, positions of responsibility in highly regarded firms and even in their own entrepreneurial activities) are getting lectured on how the business world works by people with zero practical experience.

Someone might reply that real-life experience on the part of professors is not as relevant in the case of a B-school as would be in the case of, say, a porn school. Sex (like cooking or playing golf) is a purely practical activity where you simply cannot teach anyone anything of value unless you yourself have done it before. Like academics Warren Bennis and James O'Toole mentioned in their inspirational anti-academicism declaration, you cannot be a piano teacher if you have never played the instrument. Same with teaching the art of sexual positions or how to make crème brûlée. However, does the same dictum really apply to business academics? Should we not care much that B-school faculty don't have practical experience since business academics can be taught even by inexperienced people, straight from the textbook?

The answers to both questions are, of course, yes and no. Business is nothing if not a practical, nontheoretical discipline where the difference between having done it and not having done it can be the difference between real knowledge and make-believe. Borrowing from player-turned-prof Peter Hahn, *"You would probably be scared to death if your surgeon told you she had learnt all her surgery from a book, or only read about your required surgery in a journal."* The textbook (most likely authored by a business virgin) cannot replace hands-on, sleeves-rolled, real-world business experience. In fact, if the textbook were enough, why would I need to pay $150,000 for an education that I could acquire at the public library for $10 in late fees?

Not requiring business professors to have relevant practical experience sends the message that it's okay to be isolated from the real world and that, furthermore, any knowledge regarding the real business world is not required to succeed as a B-school academic. Just publish more of those multiple regression econometric papers explaining the relationship between the amount of snow on Mt. Kilimanjaro and the correlation between the Dow Jones and the New Zealand bond market.

This last point is perhaps the gravest. To be perfectly honest, while it would be great if all B-school profs carried at least a decent amount of real-life experience, the truth is that some people just don't like to work in a professional, nonacademic environment, or perhaps never had the chance. In a letter to the editor of the *Financial Times*, I stated that *"The real world simply does not offer many of the perks offered by business schools, endowments that some people may find extremely valuable, worth even severe monetary sacrifice. A flexibly scheduled life devoted to (hopefully practically relevant) writing, teaching, and thinking, surrounded by bright young things from all over the world, and inhabiting a comfy and resource-filled university campus does not sound entirely unappealing. For those who can achieve it, that is."*

One must not immediately assume that business academics are academics because they couldn't be doers. Some people who could *do* may choose to ponder instead, on account of the many attractions that campus life holds.

However, and this is the key idea, their interests would extend from the purely theoretical to the practical, and as such they would follow real-world events very closely and constantly network with leading practitioners. What they publish and what they teach would have immediate practical value for both seasoned and wanna-be practitioners. This type of people would obviously still be wonderful additions to the faculty roster of any business school, in spite of their lack of hands-on actual work experience. Anyone would want to attend the lectures and read the intellectual production of such scholars, even if they haven't quite been around the block. These are the kind of professors who (together with other perks, such as the energetic environment and the window of opportunities on offer) would make attending B-school a very appealing proposition.

Unfortunately, such a person would likely be an exception at most B-schools these days. There is even the danger that he might be penalized because of his interest in practitioners and their world. The other day I was watching a re-run of the movie *Patch Adams*, where an idealistic young doctor, wonderfully portrayed by Robin Williams, is relentlessly subjected to attacks and harassment by the medical school's dean, mainly for the unforgivable sin of spending lots of time at the hospital interacting with patients. Apparently, the dean believed that more hours immersed in theoretical books instead of dealing with real patients and nurses is what a true doctor needs. In the end, Patch is purportedly dismissed from the school, only to be rehabilitated by a panel later. Applying the movie's message to the state of B-schools, we might ask ourselves: How many professors want to be like Patch Adams, always priming practice and customer attention over theory? Do B-school deans show the same prejudice in favor of theory and taste for the repression of alternative views as the one in the movie? Do professors have Patch-like willingness and courage to confront a system they may deem too narrow-minded?

For anyone who has followed business academics in general and financial economics in particular for the last few decades, it may seem surprising to hear that those fields had not always been overtly mathematical and theoretical. In fact, the analyticalization that appears today as obviously inevitable only began to take root some 50 years ago. Things were quite different prior to that phenomenon—much less quantitative, much more narrative. Much less theoretical, much more descriptive. Or, to borrow from orthodox academicism-speak, much less "rigorous," much more "unscientific." Most of the articles in the *Journal of Finance* (the field's leading academic publication, founded in 1946) *"had to do with Federal Reserve policy, the impact of money on prices and business activity, taxation, and issues related to corporate finance, insurance, and accounting. . . . In issues up to 1959 . . . no more than five articles could be classified as theoretical rather than descriptive. The rest contain plenty of numbers but no mathematics."* The year 1959 may in fact be seen as the high-water mark for the nontheoretical, descriptive (down to earth?) period of business finance in particular and business academics in general. Soon afterwards, little would be left of the so-called institutionalist approach, having been flagrantly railroaded by the new economics–like ways.

As two B-school staff members put it a few years ago: *"During the past several decades, many B-schools have quietly adopted an inappropriate, and ultimately self-defeating, model of academic excellence. Instead of measuring themselves . . . by how well their faculties understand important drivers of business performance, they measure themselves almost solely by the rigor of their scientific research. . . . Some of the research is excellent, but because so little is grounded in actual business practices, the focus of graduate business education has become . . . less and less relevant to practitioners. This scientific model is predicated on the faulty assumption that business is an academic discipline like chemistry or geology. In fact, business is a profession, akin to medicine and the law."*

Thus was born the modern system that allows and encourages the churning of mathematically charged finance theories from ivory tower confines. But why, exactly? What initial forces contributed to the challenge to and eventual demise of the old descriptive, nonscientific order? And how were things like before the technical apparatchiks took over?

A crucial watershed-like turning point, and the purported kick-start to the unfettered theoretization of business academics, were the famous 1959 Gordon-Howell and Pierson reports, sponsored, respectively, by the Ford and Carnegie foundations (which, apparently, believed that the professionalization of management education could aid in the war on communism; also, *"the high prestige of the natural sciences after WWII encouraged the widespread belief in the 1940s and 1950s that 'science' could be applied to managerial and business problems and that scientific research into these problems should be supported."*). They blasted business schools for having narrow trade-focused curricula, for employing poorly trained faculty and attracting academically inferior students, and for implementing simplistic teaching and research methodologies.

The two reports constituted an academic bombshell, rudely jolting business schools into a drastic strategic U-turn. The key message from those two wealthy foundations was that B-schools needed to be endowed with "academic respectability," akin to that enjoyed by the social and physical sciences. Grant money was offered towards that end. No wonder that the focus of business academics switched in absolute favor of so-called rigorous research (it is interesting to note that the institutions that were singled out as commendable examples were those that had already embraced quantitative and scientific methodologies, thus already boasting a "serious" curriculum). After all, when they are calling you a simplistic hick and they offer you a lot of dough to become more like an economist or a mathematician, what can you do if not oblige?

Between 1957 and 1965, the Ford Foundation made grants totaling $46.3 million as part of its effort to strengthen business education in the United States. The Foundation terminated its funding because it believed that its main goals had been amply achieved, and (conveniently reformed) B-schools could now be left to their own devices. Among the goals that the Foundation deemed mission-fully-accomplished were the following: shifting the emphasis from vocational undergraduate programs to professional graduate programs, strengthening curricula through the incorporation of social science concepts and rigorous quantitative methods, and raising the scholarly levels of business faculty members to full equality with their counterparts in other disciplines.

While B-schools have certainly flourished since (and perhaps primarily because of) those generosity-filled days, some see in the foundations-directed revolutionary actions the sowing of the seed of today's discontent. The case can certainly be made that today's abject abstractionism would not roam so freely inside B-schools had the lavishly financed push for scientification not taken place five decades ago. Interestingly, the Ford Foundation itself admitted that things may have gotten out of hand, by noting that *"One of the few criticisms of the program is that its doctoral studies and research activities may have become too theoretical and esoteric."*

So the key question becomes: Were things really that bad prior to the scientification-seeking intervention of the charitably giving foundations? Is the exaggerated esotericism an acceptable price to pay in exchange for getting rid of an unacceptably primitive structure? Did Ford and Carnegie deliver us from evil? Those who supported the abrupt transition towards the scientific method certainly thought so. Critics of the trade-focused approach *"questioned the proliferation of narrow, excessively specialized courses and the heavy emphasis on detailed descriptions of current practice and rigid rules of business management"*, and *"decried what was termed as excessive vocationalism."* Even those who voice loud complaints about the theoretical status quo are quick to remind us of the limitations of the ancient predecessor: *"For the first half of the twentieth century B-schools were more akin to trade schools; most professors were good ole boys dispensing war stories, cracker-barrel wisdom, and the occasional practical pointer. We remember when the production class at MIT School of Industrial Management was taught by the manager of a nearby General Motors assembly plant. That was a useful, but hardly comprehensive and professional education. . . . Going back to the trade school paradigm would be a disaster."*

And yet it is tempting to argue that the old ways had some things going for them. In the 1950s a typical finance course would cover matters such as *"institutional arrangements, legal structures, and long-term financing and investment projects,"* which, frankly, sounds conveniently useful. I, for one, wouldn't mind one bit if my production class was being taught by a guy who is actually a, well, production manager. Just like I wouldn't mind if my options class was being taught by a guy or gal who was actually getting his or her hands dirty as an options trader, cracker-barrel wisdom or not. And I can attest that I wouldn't be alone in having such preferences.

I have taught at top international B-schools, in packed lecture-halls populated by bright young things from all over the world. My derivatives courses are 100 percent practical, 0 percent theoretical/ analytical/mathematical. I borrow heavily from my own investment banking experience and exclusively from real-world developments. Students leave the classroom understanding how people actually use derivatives (both simple and über-complex) out there. The rigor part is placed entirely on the side of applied rigorousness. Students become extremely rigorous at understanding what a swap is and why a corporation may want to use one, or why knock-out options exist, or why credit derivatives can help reduce the risk of receivables default. And the funny thing is that students seem to love this approach. They don't mind learning nontheoretical stuff one bit. It may amaze you to know that I haven't found them averse to acquiring knowledge that can be put immediately to good use in the real business world. I have never had anyone complain about the lack of equations on the board. Or walk away from the class disgusted by such a torrent of unfettered "vocationalism" (how dare he teach us things that can be hands-on applied in the trade?). So perhaps, unbeknownst to them, today's students are paying homage to those ancient, now forgotten scholars who primed description over imposed dogmatism.

Scholars like Arthur Stone Dewing, finance professor at Harvard Business School in the early decades of the past century. Dewing, a popular teacher who apparently never shaved his beard (he was on occasions confused with a Maharaja) and who resigned from Harvard in 1933 after being accused of unlawful gold-hoarding (though the gold withdrawal later turned out to have been intended as a hedge for one of the many utilities that he owned throughout New England), authored what was considered the primal finance textbook of the pre-theorems period. *The Financial Policy of Corporations* first appeared in 1919 and was subsequently enlarged all the way to 1,500 pages. What was the holy bible of pre-scientification finance all about? What did such symbol of backward primitiveness ponder? What kind of topics did stochastic calculus–illiterate Neanderthalist professors deal with?

Well, Dewin's era-defining magnum opus *"presented corporations as institutional and legal entities"* (imagine that!), *"discussed the ways in which corporations raise money by issuing securities"* (who needs to know that?), *"discussed the overall valuations of public utilities and of corporations, the basic techniques of accountancy, the causes and forms of business expansion"* (the simplicityness of it all!), *"contained many historical asides"* (yeah, yeah, but where is the math!) *"and some allusions to psychology"* (you mean, it made actual humans actually relevant?). In other words, the main finance textbook in the years before the Ford and Carnegie foundations saw a need to endow B-schools with science-backed respectability, was an unfettered example of descriptive pureness, with no fancy analytics beyond elementary arithmetic. The effrontery, Professor Dewin!

In essence, through the scientification process initiated in the late 1950s, B-schools traded descriptions about institutions and actual business practices (perhaps not as intellectually enchanting as rocket science, but undeniably useful and harmless) for quantitative models of human behavior. In doing so, they were heavily influenced by the freshly mathematicized economics sibling. Since the beginning of the twentieth century the latter had been progressively becoming more theoretical (less narrative), culminating in the neoclassical movement that became tyrannically dominant after WWII, centered around the key gospels of rational optimizing economic agents and an idealized general equilibrium world (if you have studied Arrow, Debreu, you know what I am talking about).

A crucially important gift from these new theoretical economists to their even newer finance abstraction soul mates originated in the mind of that most famous of social scientists, Milton Friedman, who, in what has been termed the central statement of modern economics, stated that theories should not be judged based on the realism of their assumptions, and that the presence of wildly unrealistic assumptions is no reason to discard a model as useless. Such arguments, coming from such an eminent figure, gave, in practice, carte blanche to the new breed of quantitatively oriented business academics. Friedman's essay became a very convenient alibi to wave in the face of opposition from more traditional, descriptive, untheoretical scholars. A great marketing, self-justifying tool, if you like. No wonder, then, that one of the most prominent early financial theorists, Merton Miller, bluntly stated that *"Around here we just sort of take for granted Friedman's viewpoint."* While some financial economists cared somewhat more than others about the actual verisimilitude of the assumptions, the eventual unrealism of the latter did not score points against the models in the new brave world of scientific finance.

In sum, B-schools discarded tangibly accurate knowledge and information while embracing what may be deemed as analytical make-believe. Business academics were thus given free rein to play God and to do away with the inconveniently nontechnical task of having to describe the actions of God's subjects.

Interestingly, such swapping did not go along without a fight. Today's absolute mathematical dominance of B-school academics may blind us to the fact that not so long ago one could find fierce resistance to the spreading of such analyticalness. It could be argued that a civil war of sorts broke out within B-schools, with those trying to preserve descriptiveness on one camp and those trying to culminate the scientification revolution on the other. That there was resistance to the new scientific approach in the specific case of finance is evident, for instance, in the following testimony: *"In finance, one can almost sense the shifts by leafing through the volumes. The early years were filled with descriptive articles, with a heavy institutional flavor.... Slowly, the mathematical and model-building revolution was revealed.... And feelings (pro and con) ran high.... It was the battle between the 'new' versus 'old' finance. Some complained about the lack of relevance in the newer approaches, others confessed that they could no longer understand what was in the journals. Younger members wanted more 'rigour.'"*

A member of the old guard once said that *"Some of these bright young men spent so much time studying mathematics and theory that they learned too little about finance. Once in a while one of my quantitative colleagues comes to me with a question about some instrument and institution that reveals abysmal ignorance."* And perhaps the most notable critic of the path that financial economics took, once the old business finance field had been vanquished and obliterated, summarized his views in the following manner: *"The new finance men have lost virtually all contact with terra firma. On the whole, they seem to be more interested in demonstrating their mathematical powers than in solving genuine problems; often they seem to be playing mathematical games."*

Most interesting, the objections to the new financial economics did not involve an all-encompassing objection to quantitative methods. MIT's David Durand, a leading academic in his time, pointed out as part of his critique that quanty stuff was not in fact new to finance, with actuaries having used statistical modeling for years. The key difference, however, was that while the actuaries were using the tools to solve workaday problems (even if possibly dull and unexciting) which solution clearly required some math, the new financial economists seemed to care much less about the application and almost exclusively about the tools. In other words, the new quantitative finance profs were much less effective than the preexisting ones, who at least kept *"one foot on the ground."*

Divisions even broke out among those who had supported the scientification push. Most illustrating were the disagreements within the hallowed walls of Carnegie Tech's Graduate School of Industrial Administration (now Carnegie Mellon's Tepper School of Business, a world leader in management, financial economics, and quantitative finance education). Carnegie Tech had been at the forefront of the theoretization efforts, a prime destination for grant money. In principle, its most senior bigwigs appeared to fully agree on a science-based operation, but not entirely on the precise type of science. Future Nobel and father of artificial intelligence Herbert Simon held the *behavioral* parapet, embracing observation-based empiricism and avoiding dogma-based economic theory. He ruthlessly ridiculed the financial economists' assumptions about human action and habit of building up theories based on irremediably unobservable variables (such as expected return). The economics camp responded by developing the early stages of rational expectations theory (über-dogmatism taken to its limits) and the Miller-Modigliani capital structure irrelevance theorem (heavily grounded on traditional economic thought's tenet that the real-world invalidity of a theory's assumptions is nothing to be concerned about and certainly not a reason to doubt the soundness of the mathematical construct). Judging by the subsequent popularity within academic circles of the latter pieces of work (and thus their acceptance as conventional wisdom outside the ivory tower, including the granting of two Nobels), it seems safe to conclude that the guys focused on observable behavior lost and the ones focused on (mostly) unworldly hypotheses won.

We have seen how the new scientific paradigm made initial inroads inside B-schools through generous grant support from those interested in more rigorous, professional management education. But what made it stick? Why did theory eventually rule supreme, all the way to today? Why did neoclassical financial economics consolidate into dictatorial dominance? Perhaps it all came down to ego and comfort. Listen, listen to what some profs have to say about the shameless embracing of the scientific model by their colleagues: *"Although few B-school faculty would admit it, professors like it that way. This model gives scientific respectability to the research they enjoy doing and eliminates the vocational stigma that B-school professors once bore. In short, the model advances the careers and satisfies the egos of the professoriat. And, frankly, it makes things easier. Though scientific research techniques may require considerable skill in statistics or experimental design, they call for little insight into complex social and human factors and minimal time in the field discovering the actual problems facing managers."*

That is, the mathematical flood allowed formerly disreputable (to the eyes of other academics, that is) business faculty to now become scientists in the innocent eyes of the world. The new status and ways of doing things in turn attracted new young PhD students eager to establish themselves, too, as business scientists and to spend all day solving equations, and so on until all remnants of the old order disappeared into oblivion. Once finance theorists and other residents of the B-school began to win Nobel prizes, all respectability issues became logically assuaged and washed away, at least within the campus (and for the most part also outside). The scientific method became an unassailable ideology, almost a religion, with not much chance for dissent to rear its head.

Theoreticians knew that they had a very good thing going and were not about to let anyone take it from them. Since the slightest crack in the dogmatic glass house could expose the deep unworldliness of some of the lemmas and force demands for a heavy dose of mathless realism, the equation-lovers tightly closed ranks and ruthlessly defended the analytical parapet from enemy intrusions. No way they were going to let anyone deprive them of their beloved scientific status just on account of minion technicalities, such as practical relevance. The unquestionable supremacy of the theoretical approach was implacably imposed within the B-school ivory tower walls, and strenuous efforts to spread such unquestioning outside of the walls were conducted.

As regards comfort, yes, while it may sound somewhat counterintuitive, doing advanced theory may be far easier than developing truly valuable practical insights about real-world business developments (not to mention actually implementing stuff in the real business arena). Once you have mastered the analytical toolbox through your PhD training, churning out research output may be simply the result of repeatedly applying well-worn techniques, in many cases to deal with some minute detail from some other well-worn theoretical construct. The amount of true innovativeness may be limited. Much more creativity is required from those who can come up with applicable actionable breakthroughs and hard industry knowledge.

The mathematics are specially comfortable because they allow you to build your own alternative world. Getting to understand, let alone comprehend, the real financial world can be a lengthy, complicated, maybe even utterly hopeless affair. It is just too darn chaotic out there, and anyone interested in gaining some insight would definitely have to mingle with a lot of doers, which would take a substantial effort. Much easier if you can concoct your own reality from the safe comfort of your university office, and with the help of methodologies that are actually held in very high esteem by your peers and bosses. While it may be hard to differentiate yourself from others when trying to analyze the real financial arena (after all, there's only one such reality), the mathematics allow you to come up with your uniquely unique contribution, a chance to claim one-of-a-kindness and see your name in ivory-tower lights.

In this sense, it is tempting to argue that many of the best-known scions of financial economics (which are all grounded on severely Platonic hypotheses; Milton Friedman would have been proud) gained their stardom precisely as a result of their obscenely obvious intrinsic departures from real life. Perhaps Merton Miller, Aldo Modigliani, Harry Markowitz, William Sharpe, Fischer Black, Myron Scholes, or Robert Engle were not the first to conceive the ideas that made them all famous (I am not talking plagiarism here), but were rather the first to dare espouse them in print, with their names indelibly tied to the dictums. Others may have shied away from such boldness precisely because of the unacceptably insurmountable level of abstractionism that such ideas entailed. They may have considered the whole thing notoriously ridiculous and, fearing public ridicule, may have thrown the drafts to the nearest wastebasket.

Miller et al., in sharp contrast, and unabashedly under the inebriating influence of the new theoretical age, may have shown no such remorse whatsoever, more than happy to associate themselves with those theories. That is, when Platonicism becomes the rule of the land, those more willing and less hesitant to embrace radical abstractionism get promoted, as those with even the slightest modicum of interest in at least appearing to cater to the real world (and who might otherwise be superior scholars) take themselves out of the game, leaving gaping openings for people who are not so picky. He who publishes gets noticed, naturally, and gets to be exposed to outsiders as flag-carrier for academic advancement. Promotion and notoriety may thus be determined by the degree of abstractionism one is willing to embrace, not by innate capabilities. Great news for those who believe only in equations.

Related to this, there could be a third major reason why academics lovingly embraced scientification. With theories, you too can feel like a player. A puppet master, moving markets with your dictums. If you are just describing what others (the *real* players) are doing, you are mastering no puppets or moving no markets. Describing is just too humble, too undignified; it limits your potential for glory so much more. But what if you could come up with a theory (say, something that says that no one can beat the market or that an option can be priced through a dynamically replicated portfolio) and, with the help of the academic establishment and outsiders' qualifications blindness, consolidate it as conventional wisdom? Have Wall Street listen? Perhaps even obey?

Now, that would be power. You, too, would be a player. A bit like Soros or Buffett. Or even better, because you would appear as much more thoughtful and intellectual than those street-smart rogues.

Hedge fund manager John Seo (who holds a PhD in biophysics from Harvard) once analyzed financial academicism in the following terms: *"These academics couldn't understand the fact that they couldn't beat the markets. So they just said it was efficient. And, 'Oh, by the way, here's a ton of math you don't understand.'"*

It is slightly tempting, borrowing from Seo, to think that, had certain notable finance theorists gotten a job as hedge fund traders or derivatives salesmen rather than a university post, scientific market theory would have never taken flight. After all, when you are making it in the real game, there is no need to concoct an alternative, imaginary, virtual-reality game that allows one to conjecture that he, too, is playing.

Almost half a century since the publication of the Gordon-Howell and Pierson reports, the process that they helped initiate looks back at its founding fathers from a position of glowing triumphalism. Theory rules the B-school ivory tower with an iron fist. Sure, many prominent members of the team have in recent years furiously attacked its dominant strategy, but no earth-shattering changes seem to have been effected on the status quo. In a widely distributed article titled "Where is the B in B-Schools?" the former dean of MIT Sloan School of Business, Richard Schmalensee, stated that *"Management school faculty often focus on academic fields such as game theory or econometrics, not on management practice, and their work may have little to do with real business problems.... Unfortunately, under the current academic reward system, what matters most is having an impact among peers, mainly by getting specialized research published in influential journals. The system isn't designed to evaluate or reward someone who invests significant time in the field learning about industry X and working on its problems.... [T]he academic system's current methods for hiring and rewarding professors don't necessarily attract or encourage the kind of practitioner-oriented faculty we need to make business-school research and MBA education much more attuned to meeting today's and tomorrow's management challenges.... [B]usiness schools' research agendas must become primarily driven by real-life management problems. But in order for this change to happen, problem-driven research must become recognized and honored as a great way to advance, not jeopardize, an academic career."*

What Schmalensee is trying to say is that B-schools have been kidnapped by people who mostly don't know or care much about business, and they must be rescued from such a freakish state (it is slightly ironic that for all the chest-thumping machismo typically displayed by MBAs, they may have allowed their B-schools to be completely dominated by technical people who haven't seen much action).

Jeffrey Garten, former dean of Yale School of Management, is also not shy about telling us what he truly thinks: *"The current model of business school education needs to change dramatically. I think there should be different criteria for hiring and retaining faculty.... What business schools need to do is add some criteria for promotion. One of them should be some real-world experience, in the same way that a doctor teaching at a medical school would have had to see patients."*

But you need soldiers to lead a revolution, and those would-be George Washingtons will find it hard to enlist recruits among more junior faculty members. For one simple reason: the rewards from strictly abiding by the rules are too tasty, and the penalties from not doing so too taxing. It all comes down to something called *tenure*, perhaps the biggest incentive for toeing the official line ever invented by humankind (bar perhaps the long whip). In essence, this tenure thing guarantees that the theoretical order goes internally unchallenged and thus trots along ever-lasting. Because under the scientific model, the number one criterion for being granted tenure (a wonderful gift, as will be explained shortly) is the production of peer-reviewed theoretical research. And because focusing instead on nontheoretical, applied, actionable, descriptive, institutional stuff would probably be the surest way *not* to be given the keys into tenure paradise. But don't just trust me on this, listen to actual veterans of the game: *"A management professor who publishes rigorously executed studies in highly quantitative journals is considered a star, while an academic whose articles appear in the accessible pages of a professional review, which is much more likely to influence business practices, risks being denied tenure. We know of no scholar with a good publishing record who has been denied tenure or promotion for being a poor teacher or for being unable to teach effectively in executive education programs. But we do know of a professor of finance who was denied promotion when his department decided that he was not a serious scholar. The damning evidence against him included seven articles in Harvard Business Review and the highest teaching ratings in his department. The stated ends of business education may remain the same: to educate practitioners and to create knowledge.*

But the means make that end impossible to achieve because rewards are directed elsewhere."

When the obscurantists take over, those who try to shine some light on practical affairs and who have the ability to communicate insightful notions may get mercilessly railroaded. Those Torquemada-like equations-only academics who engage in hunting the witches who can do other things, such as expressing useful ideas to the general public or teaching students in an engaging way, are probably only too aware of the fact that the best way to guarantee that the area where you can excel (abstruse analytics) remains the only possible path towards success is to relentlessly discredit and persecute those who can excel in other areas. Needless to say, everybody else would lose from such arrangement: no real knowledge may be created, students may be badly indoctrinated in nonapplicable stuff, and professionals may not be able to draw anything of much use. And the overall reputation of B-schools could one day abruptly sink, naturally.

So what exactly is tenure and why are so many business academics willing to sell their soul to the analytical devil in exchange for it? One could see tenure as the equivalent of passing the European top public servant exams: a reason to bring the family together in celebration because bright little Johnny (or Antonio, or Anuj, or Chen) had finally, after long years of solitary confinement that made many of his cousins wonder if he was still alive, achieved permanent, relatively well-paid, relatively prestigious, relatively stress-free employment. Somewhat akin to a bureaucrat figure, but on a higher level (easier for your mom to brag about to her friends). While academic tenure is not by definition permanent, it is in practice for-life. It is not unheard of for tenured profs to be revoked of tenure, but the percentage tends to be minimal and you would have to do something quite weird in order to be discharged (like encourage students to blow up a university facility or plagiarize the works of others and lie about your ethnic background).

B-school professors can make good money, particularly if they are finance professors. A newly minted PhD in financial economics from a good institution that gets recruited by a, say, top-50 school will make around $150,000 in the first year, plus interesting benefits (including the opportunity to reside and work in the midst of beautifully green campuses). That in itself sounds to many people like a very good reason to try to perpetuate the situation. But it can get better with time.

More senior profs not only get salary raises but are also included in highly remunerated executive education programs. On the back of their academic reputations they may get juicy book contracts and consulting arrangements. Perhaps even a board seat or two. All in all, a senior finance professor at a good U.S. (or UK) school can put together an annual package in the very high six figures. But you need to have been tenured first before you can become a senior prof. Thus the very tempting nature of tenure. You can't get fired and you can make a pretty good living down the road, certainly a much better one than European civil servants. Thus, the very strong incentive to do what it takes to achieve it.

And what does achieve tenure? Tons of theoretical research. Interestingly, tenure is defended by academics as a way to protect freedom of thought and speech, but judging from the totalitarian dominance of tenure-determining analyticalness inside B-schools, it could be argued that the complete opposite effect has been achieved here; dissent and individualityness don't seem to earn lots of brownie points, while conformity and submission appear highly rewarded.

A recent case quite clearly highlights the completely dominating preponderance that the tenure process affords to the scientific research establishment. How the total supremacy of theoretical contributions is guaranteed and protected by such rewards system. How all other types of ("softer") contributions are mercilessly steamrolled, rendered hopelessly incapable of earning benefits to the contributors. How tenure impedes progress to those with the ability to shine glowingly at other, nontheoretical endeavors (such as, sin of sins, teaching or student services). How tenure ruthlessly dictates that all that eventually matters when it comes to holding on to a highly paid, eternal, ivory-tower job is to please the theoretical apparatchiks. In sum, such a case is a great example of how tenure could reasonably be seen as a tool that protects the analytical status quo. The kind of status quo, of course, which has for decades dumped unhealthily (and, potentially, dangerously) unworldly finance theorems on the rest of us (tenure as it stands today drastically encourages such dumping and guarantees that it will go on).

In January of 2008 it was announced that the Olin Business School at Washington University in St. Louis, Missouri, had decided to terminate the contract of assistant professor of accounting Tzachi Zach. He was denied tenure and let go (he was happy to quickly find suitable employment at the very prestigious accounting department of Ohio State's Fisher School of Business, where he will also be able to enjoy first-class college football and basketball games). Olin students immediately and forcefully came out to oppose the decision. The school's student newspaper became flooded with angry commentary and praise-filled platitudes honoring Zach. Alumni went the distance and created a Facebook group titled "Olin School of Business needs to rethink its priorities," encouraging other complainers to complain to the chancellor.

Why all this activism and disappointment? Simply put, Zach was a widely loved teacher. And he was loved most by the people who (should) matter most, his students. *"I thought he was the best teacher I had at Wash. U. by far, not even close,"* sophomore Ryan Grandin said. *"Professor Zach has had a significant impact on some students and is the reason why some kids are accounting majors."* Zach Freedman, a junior accounting major, who met Zach as a prospective student at Olin's spotlight weekend, said that *"I think Olin is trying to get their name out there and trying to enhance their image among students, and Tzachi Zach is one of the biggest draws for people."*

"I absolutely think the University made a mistake, and we're letting one of our most respected and coveted teachers go," said Yoni Dina, a sophomore accounting major and a teaching assistant for Zach. Former student Kristin Haggerty wrote that Zach was more than just an admired prof: *"Admired is the understatement of the year. How many students at this University can say they have a professor who has truly touched their lives?... a professor whose teaching has influenced not only their career paths but their personal goals and behaviors while also establishing a life-long connection with students. Professor Zach is a professor who truly inspires his students to reach their potential. And he does that while teaching the driest of dry subjects: accounting. I know I am not the only CPA who owes her career path to Professor Zach, and though I graduated two years ago and have not been his official student in five years, my loyalty to him is as strong as ever."*

Current student Alex Neumann, in a piece dubbed "Stop Forcing Out the Best Professors," declared that *"Zach is a shining example of the lecturers that Wash. U. students want. We want professors who are engaging, witty, intelligent and articulate."* In 2007, Zach was awarded the Reid Teaching Award.

So why exactly was Zach denied tenure, and thus afforded dismissal? Because of an apparent lack of theoretical research prowess. Mahendra

Gupta, Olin's dean and the person who eventually signed Zach's death certificate, said that *"Zach is a very good researcher. However, he has not been able to produce, which is unfortunate."* While the value assigned to each component of a professor's job (teaching, research and service to the school) remains confidential, students worried that in Zach's case, the university placed undue emphasis on research and ignored his teaching abilities. A former dean of the school, who admitted that Zach is a dedicated teacher widely admired by his students, brushed asides those concerns by flatly stating that students just *"don't understand the role that research plays in teaching and the importance of scholarship in their education. They're going to have trouble understanding that, unless they understand the importance of ideas in their undergraduate education."* The implication, of course, is that the truly important ideas and knowledge come from abstract equations-laden theoretical research (real-world developments and professionals be damned!). And if you don't get that, then you are just not getting it. Pretty convenient argument, if you are part of the guild that is.

Alumna Kristin Haggerty, for one, found such a way of reasoning insulting: *"Students do not mindlessly attend Zach's class and consider him to be a favorite professor solely because his jokes are funny or even because he is always willing to help his students with academic or personal challenges. Professor Zach is a one-of-a-kind professor because he does these things while giving his students a first-class education. Any current or former student of his, and other accounting faculty members, can attest to the challenging level and appropriate coverage of his classes.... [A] lack of published research is most certainly not indicative of a lack of technical knowledge.... Dean Gupta even stated that the issue with Professor Zach was not his research abilities (and therefore not his level of expertise) but rather his lack of published articles.... Is it really more important for the people who actually read* Accounting Today *to suppose that the students of the Olin Business School are getting a great education than for the students themselves to know they are getting a great education?"*

The Zach case (and the more than probable existence of many similar other cases) illuminatingly highlights how the B-school establishment operates. A superstar teacher is effortlessly expendable because he didn't play by the rules dictated by those favoring theory above all else. No doubt as to what truly matters under the scientific method. Saul Kopelowitz, a senior and former teaching assistant for Zach, thinks Olin's decision sends a clear message to the students: *"The administration is blatantly saying that the students' input is inferior to consideration of faculty research. They're saying the research mission is their priority over educating students."* Good point, Saul, but I believe that students are not the primary intended recipient of such message. Rather, the message is directed primarily at other academics: If you want a job for life, you better get on with the theoretical program. Zach's story shows how the incentivizing powers of tenure guarantee that B-schools will continue to produce theorems. The Ford and Carnegie foundations couldn't be prouder. The beast they helped create displays unremitting resilience, including the Saturn-like capacity to devour its most promising sons.

In yet another note of support, another Olin student asked administrators to *"Prove to us that teaching quality and outside-of-class interaction with students matter in some significant way in your review process,"* and lamented that *"Ultimately, Olin and its students will lose the most in the decision to let Zach go.... [S]tudents will lose a phenomenal teacher, a great mentor, and a one-of-a-kind friend,"* concluding with a teary-eyed good-bye: *"Professor Zach, thank you for touching our lives. We wish you all the best."*

After having been exposed to the above diatribes, some readers may find themselves puzzled. Finance departments typically are the most important and prominent segment of any B-school. Finance professors (along with many of their academic peers) tend to not have relevant real-world experience and to err on the side of analytical abstraction. They are heavily incentivized and encouraged by their superiors to go in that direction. And yet it is undeniable that B-schools have overwhelmingly enjoyed relentless global success in recent decades. How can this be? Why do B-schools succeed, on the face of such (in general, there are always exceptions) unworldly structure? This is a nontrivial point. As long as B-schools are perceived as successful, there will be no real challenge to the status quo, thus no stopping the production of realism-challenged finance theories that carry the ivory tower seal of respectability and that, mostly for that reason, can have a harmful effect on the real financial and economic landscapes. We need to understand the factors, besides obvious internal forces, such as the tenure system analyzed earlier, that allow dogmatic financial economists to trot unchallenged and that oil the machines that churn out an unstoppable amount of theoretical output.

There are two main reasons why B-schools don't see the need to yield to demands for change: 1) in many cases, the negative aspects of inexperienced professors and theoretical dominance are conveniently ignored by both students and recruiters, thus effectively becoming harmless; 2) the positive aspects presented by (good) schools continue to be attractive enough to compensate for the disappointments.

B-school professors, in general, lack applied professional experience and conduct only theoretical research. "So what?" many students and administrators may reply. "We are not going to press for change to the status quo." Truly, these two groups have very few incentives to internally promote a revolution towards practical relevance. Once admission has been granted, a student (enrolled, say, in an MBA) has not much to gain from loudly proclaiming that the education he is receiving is less than useful for the real world. Why diminish the value of his investment? Why voluntarily hamper his job-seeking prospects? It may be smarter to keep the anger to oneself. And certainly few program directors and deans would (at least prior to undertaking some reforms) publicly admit to the theoretical dominance prevailing inside their institutions.

For their part, those in charge of hiring MBAs have also traditionally had a certain interest in not questioning the academic status quo excessively. B-schools (again, the good ones) offer a very convenient way to access a reliable pool of ambitious and (usually) talented youngish things, highly valued assets for, among others, investment banks, consulting firms, and private equity houses. Why question something that seems to have worked so well?

And, at the end of the day, the promise of juicy job offers from such elite players (together with the possibility of meeting people from all over the globe, enjoying an idyllic resource-filled campus, and, on occasion, learning new useful stuff) continues to draw students to B-school. The true paradox is that Goldman Sachs and McKinsey, by incessantly hiring MBAs, make it possible for the financial economics virgins to continue to afford with impunity their cozy, isolated, theoretical life far away from reality.

People are typically prompted to borrow in excess of $150,000 and decide to confine themselves into a B-school for a couple of years for three major reasons: the first one is the possibility of getting a highly paid prestigious job after graduation; the second is the chance of obtaining a highly paid prestigious job after graduation; and the third is the opportunity of gaining a highly paid prestigious job after graduation. So as long as students believe that an MBA will open the doors to great career opportunities, B-schools have no incentive whatsoever to change the way they operate and how they organize themselves. Why make drastic and potentially painful changes when your customers keep coming back year after year? Sure, there are occasional applications droughts, but the market always returns to normal levels.

In essence, B-school professors' lack of practical experience and knowledge goes internally (and externally, at least by those who matter most) unchallenged because none of the parties that could push hard for a change have any real incentive to do so. B-school administrators are not going to publicly admit that such malaise exists if the buyers of the product (the employers of MBAs) seem content with what B-schools churn out year after year. Making a fuss and starting a comprehensive internal process of change might send the message to the outside world that perhaps what's going on inside B-schools was not of very much quality after all. You don't tell recruiters that you have been fooling them for years, sending graduates their way who have not received relevant training. As for students, well they have even less of an incentive to press for change as long as they are getting job offers. Ever heard of the MBA student interviewing for a $200,000-a year job who boasted what a total waste of time their purely theoretical B-school education had been? Me neither. And as for recruiters, B-schools have acted as reliable fishing ponds for a long time, and the fact that the education received may be overtly unpractical has never been too much of a deal-breaker. One only has to take a look at graduate training programs inside investment banks to realize that (in general) MBAs are not assumed to have learned a lot while at school.

Of course, by self-interestingly not pressing for reform, both students and recruiters lose out. Isn't it obvious that a student's Wall Street prospects would be much better served by gaining exposure to what's really going on out there than to what certain nonexperienced theoreticians think should be going on out there? The more they know about the products and the markets (as opposed to the abstruse math), the greater their chances of landing a really good job and of making an immediate impact. Similarly, recruiters could save a lot of money and time on redundant training programs and would get staff that can truly hit the ground running (let alone avoiding the risk that too much theoretical indoctrination may direct those new recruits towards actions that prove deleterious to the institution).

In sum, change-abhorring finance academics should probably rest easy. Those who could most effectively threaten their prized status quo are unlikely to do much about it. Such reluctance in turn denies any effectiveness to the efforts of more determined outsiders. Renowned pros have in the past used the pages of periodicals like the *Financial Times* to make a resounding case against conventional financial economics. The familiar argument is that finance theory is so unrealistic that it shouldn't be taken seriously by those living and operating in the real world. By expressing those views, those pros are quite likely not just trying to expose the unworldly tenets but also their adherents. However, and while those articles must have surely won tons of new converts for the skepticism cause, it is highly doubtful that they succeeded at personally annoying the economists. Even for those who do read the *Financial Times* and who are open to considering the views of nontenured individuals, those words likely didn't generate an inch of pain. Some indignation perhaps, but nothing tangibly harmful. No financial economist will lose his job or see his academic reputation massively damaged as a result of the unveilings. The articles (the equivalent of publicly catching the economists with their hands in the cookie jar of irrelevant theorizing) may not even cause a significant reduction in the number of students registering for the theorists' (dogma-filled) courses.

The Achilles' heel of those critics of financial orthodoxy lies in the fact that as loud and as frequently as they shout their message, they can't get to their enemies. The theorists' main line of defense is precisely the unworldliness that the pros so desperately highlight. Orthodox financial economics has been so successful at sheltering itself from the real world that its health cannot be altered whatsoever by anything emanating from that real world. The triumph of dogmatism has reached such levels that finance academics are not overwhelmingly expected, let alone required, to pay heed to market realities. When teaching and publishing material that is relevant in the real world is not a requirement (could very well be an impediment) to building a successful academic career, no amount of noise emanating from (nonrecruiting) practitioners can have any real effect on the status quo of the theorists. And savvy theorists, of course, are only too aware of all this.

To most finance theorists and financial mathematicians, Fischer Black is a hero. A guiding light. A referential icon. A pioneer at whose altar one should bow. He is credited with having decisively contributed to firing up the quantitative finance revolution that has allowed so many academics over the years to make a profitable career out of the applications of heavy-duty mathematical, statistical, and computational methods to financial issues. And yet in adoring the father of modern option pricing theory, analyticalists may be worshipping the wrong kind of idol.

For Black was not just an avowed skeptic when it came to the excessive mathematization of finance in the first place, but was actually quite openly critical of the financial economics academic establishment. A passionate searcher of financial and economic truth, he spent a decade at MIT and the University of Chicago but readily left for Wall Street when Goldman Sachs came knocking. His most noticeable quality, according to his Goldman colleague Emanuel Derman, was *"his stubborn and meticulous devotion to clarity and simplicity. . . . Because he liked clarity, and perhaps because his training was not in economics, he avoided excessive formalization. His papers were the antithesis of the unnecessarily rigorous lemma-filled research papers of financial economics journals."*

That directness dictated that his approach to research *"seemed to consist of unafraid hard thinking, intuition, and no great reliance on advanced mathematics. . . . He was tenacious in trying to attain insight before resorting to math."* In modeling, *"he liked to describe the financial world with variables that represented observable phenomena rather than hidden statistical or econometric factors. . . . Fischer preferred reality to elegance."*

Derman recalls how in a short essay circulated informally inside Goldman, Black struck at the foundation of financial economics: *"Certain economic quantities are so hard to estimate,"* wrote Black, *"that I call them 'unobservables.' . . . "One such unobservable,"* he pointed out, *"is expected return. . . . So much of finance from Markowitz on, deals with this quantity unquestioningly. Yet, wrote Fischer, our estimates of expected return are so poor that they are almost laughable."* Perhaps an even bigger blow to the theoretical intelligentsia came when Black stated that *"In the end, a theory is accepted not because it is confirmed by conventional empirical tests but because researchers persuade one another that the theory is correct and relevant."*

But certainly the most impressive contrarian moment came in October 1994, when on being awarded the prestigious Financial Engineer of the Year award, he flatly stated that he much preferred applied research to pure research, and that professors should be hired, promoted, and paid for their teaching, and not their research (which should be voluntary, not mandatory). He likened the university system to the bureaucracy-ruled, inflexibly uniform Soviet empire, adding that

"The basic problem with research in business and economics is not that it's too theoretical, or too mathematical, or too divorced from the real world (though all of these are indeed serious problems). The basic problem is that we have too much research, and the wrong kinds."

It is extraordinary to realize how much of what Fischer Black said sounds exactly like the arguments put forward by today's take-no-prisoners critics of finance orthodoxy, such as Nassim Taleb. Think those messages would be generally well received in today's B-school environment? Neither do I. Almost serendipitously, the presumed paragon of theoretical purity becomes the standard-bearer of beliefs that are as anathematic to orthodox academics as kryptonite would be to Superman.

And yet it would be immensely helpful if finance departments picked up the glove and heeded Black's message, more than a decade after his untimely death. And if finance profs won't do it, their superiors should. B-schools are important institutions. They provide a key link between talent (or just flesh)-seeking employers and ambitious young things. They provide unique transformational opportunities to those willing to make a mark in new fields. They provide second chances to valuable individuals who missed their first boat (if you didn't get into Harvard University, you can always try to get into Harvard Business School later). In doing so, they can play a decisive role in enhancing the globe's human capital.

They should be made to matter, and they should be actively protected from those forces (like excessive formalization or physics envy) that threaten to make them practically irrelevant. Borrowing from Fischer Black's ideas would be a giant step in the right direction. And it's not like he lacks academic credentials. Far from being a crazed outsider, Black earned a PhD from Harvard, taught at two of the world's superelite schools, and would obviously have won a Nobel had it not been for his untimely death from cancer. In other words, Black's contrarian views wouldn't lack the respectability seal. There would be few excuses then not to act on his guidance.

Brave deans and heads of finance departments intent on endowing their domains with worldly relevance could do worse than borrow from Fischer Black's playbook. In doing so, they would achieve a glorious triad of valuable objectives. First, even though we mentioned earlier that the unquestionable success of B-schools (as measured by steadily strong demand, career-enhancement possibilities, global clout, and enthusiastically expansionary activities) reduces the urgency and incentives for reforms, administrators should not show unfettered complacency. Certainly not in the face of so much recent external negative publicity (attacking business academicism seems fair game of late). When notoriously notorious imprints like *Harvard Business Review* or *BusinessWeek* publish thundering critiques of the current B-school model, the outside world at large notices and begins to wonder. For administrators not to react would smell of arrogance or indifference. The potential outcome of inaction could well be a prolonged period of decadence, potentially resulting in a progressive abandonment of the MBA market by corporate recruiters. Once such abandonment has reached a critical point (i.e., once Goldman Sachs does not hire B-school students any longer), then the institutions themselves might be in jeopardy. Even mogul Donald Trump is sensing a market need for applied, rather than theoretical, business training and has launched his own online university, offering courses in strategy, marketing, and real estate; one can only imagine B-school deans' cold sweats at night at the possibility of having to go head-to-head with the star of *The Apprentice*. Better act soon and free B-schools from the analytical straitjacket, thus preventing the gravest threat to their continuing success.

Second, by unabashedly embracing practical relevance over darkening dogmatism, business professors would be not just best serving their students' interests but also appropriately honoring their role as teachers. Financial economists must understand that they have chosen to become academics in disciplines that are applied by nature and that they are not the ones effecting the applications. Other people out there are making the real decisions that shape the financial world. Unless professors want to switch fields and become physicists, they must understand that they have chosen to associate themselves with a discipline that is only practical, only human-driven, unscientific. And if they want to teach and not do, then they should humbly learn what it is that practitioners are doing, synthesize it, and pass it along to students in a comprehensive, informative, and entertaining way. Only then would their (sacred) roles as instructors and mentors be truly abided by. Only then would their many talents be put to their best academic use.

Finally, academic honchos would have a chance to perform a welcomed public service. To act as statesmen of sorts, defending the public good. To become gatekeepers of the relevance shrine, ruthlessly filtering out anything dangerously unworldly. It is clear that any resistance to theories with the potential for wreaking havoc upon the markets and the economy at large should include those institutions that have so far provided ready shelter for the theoreticians. Once a theory is churned out and unleashed into the world, with the ivory tower pedigree laced around it, it is much harder to avoid the possibly fatal consequences. Those outsiders blinded by officialdom and qualifications are seldom easily convinced of the flaws of dictums fathered by prestigious PhD-holders from prestigious universities who count on the public support and endorsement of hundreds of other prestigious PhD-holders from prestigious universities ("If those Harvard endowed chaired professors say that's right, then it must surely be right, right?"). Once the theory is out and about, in essence an ingrained part of the established financial economics universe, it becomes quite hard to fight it effectively. Too many people have simply chosen to voluntarily enslave themselves to the official line.

No, for any resistance to harmful theoretization to be effective, it must start at the roots. Deans should confront the threat head-on, helping protect the world from the danger of wildly unrealistic mathematical machines that can turn against their users. In this sense, a particularly sensible step might be the abolition of the PhD in Finance as it is conceived today, to be replaced with a degree which contents would be supervised by practitioners (can you imagine a PhD in cooking where cooks don't have a say?). Or tenure could be abolished, or at least vastly reformed. No less a figure than Steven Levitt (yes, the tenure-endowed *Freakonomics* guy) has proposed just such measure. All this would guarantee that future finance profs embrace an entirely practical approach and devote all their efforts to adding real value to both students and no-nonsense pros, rather than to pleasing fellow academics through yet more abstract mathematical gimmicks that have the potential to unleash mayhem onto the real world.

I am not going to judge for the reader whether the evolution from business finance to financial economics was a blessing or a curse, or something in between. I won't pass verdict for everybody else on whether B-schools have chosen the wrong path or not (though, as this chapter shows, I do naturally have my personal opinions on the issue). And the message of this book is certainly not that finance theory is an outrightly bad thing. I am sure that many people consider the evolution towards financial economics a gloriously valuable one, and marvel at the mathematics in awe. Finance theory might have even delivered tons of positives to the world (one very prominent author presents the theorists as *"innovators and tinkerers who showed us how it ought to be.... [T]hey help investors deal with uncertainty, they provide benchmarks for determining whether expectations are realistic or fanciful and whether risks make sense or are foolish, they have reformulated such familiar concepts as risk, return, diversification, insurance, and debt.... [O]ur heroes may not be household names among the investing public but the spirit that ignited their revolution now touches virtually every decision that investors make.... [T]he theorists... can also help us to make our system even better"*).

The simple truth is that the quantification of finance has meant many things to many different people and has had several different effects. For example, an impact on the underlying financial markets, and one that can be (and has on many occasions been) quite negative. That potentially dangerous outcome is the main thrust of this book, not an all-encompassing bad-mouthing of theoretical endeavors. Of course, if an unwordly theoretical device can wreak havoc in the markets, then we should look at it with deep suspicion and take preventive actions to remedy the situation. But this should not imply that all academics should stop playing with the theoretical toys that they love so much. If they want to spend their days on such labors and if they find employers ready to pay them well for such efforts, who am I to pass judgment? I am most certainly saying that bad, harmful finance theory should be confronted, but I am not saying that finance theory should be outlawed. I am most certainly saying that the scientification process kick-started 50 years ago resulted in and encouraged the production of bad, harmful theory, but I am not saying that all the ramifications from such process were negative. I am most certainly saying that I personally don't believe that the markets are amenable to mathematization, but I am not saying that those who think otherwise should be instantly impaled.

Rather more humbly, what I can do is recollect the basic themes, and let readers decide for themselves. Here are the indisputable facts. Business finance was thoroughly grounded on describing real-life practices and institutions. It taught you stuff about the real business world. It didn't use too much fancy math. Financial economics brought the rigor of advanced mathematics and economics-style lemmas. It thoroughly grounded itself on having people with no practical experience theoreticize about what the financial world should be like. And its whole modus operandi was based on the idea that whether a model's assumptions are wildly unrealistic should not affect the model's reputation and, crucially, should not count as an argument to refute the model's embracing and acceptance. Ancient business finance seems conveniently harmless. Modern finance theory can have (and has had) unpleasant effects on the financial and economic landscapes. In other words, if you are a fan of scientific models and don't mind too much about possible detrimental spillovers, you may conclude that the arrival of financial economics was a wonderful thing. On the other hand, if you are more into harmless bread-and-butter institutional and descriptive stuff, you may rue the day when scientification took over.

Rocker Bryan Adams famously sang his praises to the summer of '69. Perhaps it wouldn't be surprising to find that many of today's worried observers of the academic financial theory scene yearn for a return to the good old dogmatism-deprived, description-dominated best days of the summer of '59.

■ *Chapter 3* ■

Quant Invasion

■ Machine learning comes to finance ■ It's a computational thing ■ Models live here, too ■ Quant punting ■ Interesting enough for a movie ■

I first learned of the quantification of finance in the mid-1990s. I was then living in Washington, D.C., trying to get a job at a multilateral organization (the World Bank and similar). Thanks to my undergraduate "education" in theoretical economics, I had no idea that things called options or swaps existed. My frequent trips to Dupont Circle and K Street bookstores consistently took me to the international economics and political science shelves. Completely ignorant of derivatives, I saw no reason to go looking for tomes on structured products or stochastic calculus.

All this changed around 1996, for two main reasons. First, I was fortunate enough to attend lectures at American University (AU) that happened to deal with important real-life issues (and not just econometrics or topology, as had been the case during my bachelors years) like, well, derivatives and risk management. I learned about the products and the very exciting cases of Orange County or Procter & Gamble. I became hooked. But so far, no heavy-duty quant stuff. So far, derivatives were simply another type of financial product and the derivatives industry just another line of business (though particularly sexy), not the apparent subfields of scientific endeavors. During the initial virginity-losing phase of my indoctrination, derivatives were about finance, not about math. Funny how things sometimes come full circle if given enough time.

Secondly, one day I was walking down the hall at AU's Economics department and I stumbled upon a poster announcing the Math Finance program at Columbia University. It boasted of the place's strengths in stochastics, numerics, and financial applications. My interest was certainly piqued. I went and took a look at the web site. The program seemed exclusively targeted at math geniuses. For an inexplicable reason, I found it extremely enchanting that money could be made in the markets through the use of supersophisticated quantitative methodologies. That combination of braininess and profitability, wrapped up in a cloud of mystery and exclusivity, proved irresistibly tempting. On my following trip to the bookstores I decided to venture into the unknown and visited the finance and mathematics sections. Thus began a lengthy tradition (somewhat diminished in intensity as of late) to spend thousands of dollars on (at best half-read) derivatives-related books.

During the 1996–1997 period (in which I managed to get that multilateral organization job, much to my later regret) I got to discover all the other new graduate programs in quant finance. Preponderantly impressive among them was Carnegie Mellon University's, which also happened to have been the pioneer in the field. In those earlier days there was a rumor that you needed a PhD in Physics or Computer Science just to be considered for admission. The curriculum certainly felt threatening. Carnegie Mellon's Robotics Institute seemed to play a role, and there was a course intimidatingly called "Machine Learning for Finance." To me, the whole thing felt like NASA-meets-Wall-Street. Carnegie Mellon (and the bunch of other schools pioneering similar programs) appeared as counselor of a new breed of financial professional, with a set of skills and intellectual prowess never seen before.

These elite corps of "financial astronauts" seemed destined for unlimited glory and riches. I began to develop an incontrovertible urge to join their ranks (this was both a very naïve and very strange infatuation, as I have never been specially skillful or interested in advanced math or computer programming). I mean, who wouldn't want to be an astronaut *and* a millionaire in one convenient package? In those youthful days, no other career prospect looked more unavoidably cool and modern than the derivatives industry, turbocharged (or so it seemed) by Einstein-caliber rocket scientists.

How did we get to that point? What explains the proliferation of quantitative pros in the markets? How did stochastic calculus and Wall Street ever get to be in the same paragraph? What is it that the trading floor astronauts (aka "quants") really do? And, are they as capable of potential mathematically driven mischief as academics?

There is an old Spanish tale about the bullfighter who was introduced to a philosopher. "So, what do you do?" asked the über symbol of manliness. "I think," replied the philosopher. Perplexed, the bullfighter could not fail to admire (even if perhaps not entirely respect) the other guy's savviness. "Man, you can never go unemployed!" came the summation.

This story popped in my mind not long ago as I was reading an interview with a top quantitative finance personality where he was walking the familiar line of "It is important to understand the models so as to know where they fail." It just hit me that in using that well-trodden alibi, financial modelers display self-serving survival skills that would have earned the admiration of our feisty bullfighter. Say you build a wrongful model. Big deal? Failure? Out of a job? Not at all, for you see, people need to understand why your model is wrong, and who better to explain it than you? Even if the theories are flatly wrong, we need to learn them so as to know why they are wrong. In fact, this twisted logic may encourage the buildup of bad, not good, models. The more badness, the more need for explanations. Employment for life, just like with the Spanish philosopher!

Of course, there is a caveat here: Someone, somewhere on some trading floor may become as perplexed as our bull-executing hero was and wonder why one would need to employ a bad model in the first place, notwithstanding the ready presence of dozens of modelers willing to help us fully understand why the model is rotten to the core.

The unquestionable truth is that investment banks, hedge funds, and other financial players hire a considerable amount of quantitative analysts (though quants are still but a small minority of the financial professional spectrum). In spite of the apparent limitations to mathematical taming of the markets described in prior chapters, some of the most shrewd and penny-conscious people on the planet make the decision, year in and year out for at least the past two decades, to hire legions of PhD-endowed physicists, statisticians, mathematicians, and computer scientists. The best quant finance graduate programs consistently place their students at the world's leading institutions. In other words, no one can deny that banks and funds are in the habit of recruiting those who may be best termed "modelers."

So what is it? Are the models wrong but no one inside the trading floor has decided to do much about it, or perhaps has fully bought into the "you need me to understand why the model I built fails" line, and so these modern-day math philosophers are perplexingly allowed to continue enjoying eternal employment? Or, alternatively, are the models gloriously right and thus the quants are more than deservedly kept around? Both possibilities may contain some truth to them, but perhaps there is a third option. Perhaps there is another factor that explains the undeniably extended presence of quants in the financial scene. Perhaps whether models are wrong or right is not the crux of the issue.

Perhaps the key reason why quants are hired and invited to stay in spite of the purportedly limited power of math in the markets is that not much hard-core modeling goes on anyway. For, you see, one dirty little secret of the quant world is that, while some creative mathematical envisioning certainly takes place, the main duty of modelers seems not to be pure modeling. Rather, they tend to spend most of their time on technology-related issues, coding away at their desktops and building the software, interfaces, and databases that allow traders and other breadwinners to efficiently run their businesses. In that sense, it is not surprising that the quant explosion witnessed on Wall Street or in the city of London coincided with the advent of the computer revolution.

Satyajit Das, a derivatives player in the early days and a subsequent well-regarded author of derivatives books, explains this phenomenon in less-than-technical language: *"Traders didn't quite know what quants could do. Upon arriving in academia [Myron] Scholes and [Robert] Merton found that their computing skills made them useful to older researchers. In trading rooms, it was similar. Quants provided essential computer literacy. . . . It hasn't changed a lot in modern dealing rooms. . . . Gradually, quants became a fixture. . . . A key to this was the almost total dependence on computers in trading. Quants held the key to maintaining the technological infrastructure that supported trading—they became indispensable."*

Quants began to arrive in earnest in the early 1980s. On top of the availability of computers (IBM first introduced the PC in 1981), two other significant factors determined the need for people with the capacity and willingness to spend long hours performing technical work. On the one hand, markets became much more volatile and unpredictable in the second half of the 1970s, following the death of the Bretton Woods system of fixed exchange rates, the oil shocks, and the end of Keynesian-style official control over interest rates. Such freshly-unleashed mayhem made risk management a much bigger priority, enhancing the demand for derivatives products, both traditional and ever more complex. It has traditionally been assumed that you need quantitative know-how to design and manage such creatures. On the other hand, suddenly a lot of people with high-level technical skills became available. In the late 1970s (at least in the United States) physicists and other members of the scientific crowd began to experience difficulties trying to find academic employment. With too many PhDs having been churned out in prior years coupling with a sharp reduction in research funding, those who got their physics spurs in the post–Vietnam War period struggled mightily to make room for themselves. The best that could be hoped for was a lowly-paid nomadic existence, haplessly trotting from one short-term university contract to another. Many chose to betray their (pure) scientific aspirations and decided to answer the call of Mammon.

Initially, technical people were hired to conduct research. These passengers of the quant Mayflower got into finance way before the nerd flood permanently altered the cultural landscape on Wall Street and the City. A very prominent member of the original crew was Martin Leibowitz, a math PhD who helped build a legendary fixed-income research department at Salomon Brothers in the early 1970s. Some of the future most powerful members of hedge fund giant LTCM honed their skills initially as quant researchers under Leibowitz's tutelage. Stanley Diller at Goldman Sachs was also a notable pioneer, founding and running Goldman's quantitative research (and later mathematical and computational modeling) efforts from 1976 to 1985.

Originally treated as awkward exotic pets never to be displayed in public (especially to clients), quants are now part of the mainstream. Not only is their existence fully acknowledged, they have almost become a de rigueur asset for financial institutions, an indispensable sign of modernity, forwardness, and, dare I say, even coolness. Quants have become extremely assertive of late, perhaps payback for those early days spent in humiliating seclusion. Quants are now a big source of revenue, for instance, for book publishers, conference organizers, and universities.

Headhunters avidly fight for them. So-called quant fund managers are among the richest people in the planet. In what may be the sweetest victory, the world at large now seems to accept (even if slightly naively) that advanced scientific training is key for a successful career in finance. While I wouldn't exactly term it "revenge of the nerds," it certainly must feel good for quants to witness such an enhancement in public reputation.

To be perfectly honest, some of the original quants did get the royal treatment by their employers early on, being touted as star senior hires rather than lowly techy support staff. Case in point is of course Fischer Black, who joined Goldman Sachs in 1984. Black was poached from the academic world as a direct request of none other than Robert Rubin, then Goldman's head of Equities and naturally its future co-chairman (not to mention other modest future roles as U.S. Treasury Secretary and Citigroup chairman). Far from confining Black to an isolated basement to crunch numbers and code computer software, he was taken on board so that he could calmly think big thoughts that may help some of the firm's business areas perform better through the improvement of certain existing practices or by embarking on completely new ventures. That is, Black was a quant whose number one mandate was to act as the in-house, big-picture, intellectual guru who could help traders and salespersons make more money through the value added by the deep thoughts of a demonstrably deep thinker. In other words, Goldman very much wanted Black to be influential where it really counted. Not just a technician with a PhD in Mathematics, but someone who could actually alter the firm's strategy. In mobspeak, a special consiglieri to the dons and their executioners, not the bean counter balancing the books. After a brief and successful trial period, Black was actually made a don himself (he won a coveted Goldman partnership in 1986). Clearly, this was no hidden exotic pet.

Naturally, Black also devoted a considerable part of his time and energy to managing hands-on, get-dirty analytical projects. During his time at Goldman he participated in the development of some of the most notorious sons of mathematical finance, such as the Black-Derman-Toy and Black-Litterman models. He was (on occasion, at least) not above the nitty-gritty of designing computational programs, including interfaces that would help traders operate more comfortably. He helped build some of the most impressive quant teams on the Street and imbued them with the same pragmatism and taste for applicability that characterized his career and intellectual production.

This was a very important contribution from Goldman's point of view, at a time when its senior management was bent on "building up the quant side of its operation but still unsure what kind of a quant operation would fit with the Goldman culture." Given Black's ingrained skepticism towards pure theoretical/academic contributions (as highlighted in the prior chapter), Goldman was guaranteed that its future quants would be mentored in a nondogmatic, no-nonsense, analytically unpretentious way. In a way, then, that would prime practical relevance over quantitative wizardry. Not a bad thing for an institution committed to doing business in the real world.

Emanuel Derman has been amply quoted in this book so far. This is not gratuitous name-dropping. Derman is a highly useful source not just because he was (is) a very successful quantitative finance pro, or because he is a globally recognized brand, or because he worked at leading Wall Street firms, or because he happens to say insightful things in brilliantly expressed plain English. On top of all those conveniences, Derman was also one of the early pioneers who witnessed the revolution from a front-row seat. While perhaps not quite a crew member of the quantitative Mayflower, he was certainly among the first waves of pilgrims to celebrate quant Thanksgiving on Wall Street *("They had maybe 10 or 20 people there. I was early, but I wasn't the first.")*. He is thus an irreplaceable window into the evolution of the quant landscape.

Derman reminds us how things differ between the trading floor and the university office. Upon arriving at manly Goldman Sachs in 1985, he was asked to refine an existing options model and, still very much the traditional scientist, Derman proceeded in studious fashion, trying to learn as much as possible on the topic. But to his surprise, his bosses, by now impatient with his lack of deliverable progress, explained that erring on the side of fast-delivery simplicity is more valued around trading floors than erring on the side of delivery-delaying analytical perfection. *"You know,"* Derman was explanatorily told, *"in this job you really need to know only four things: addition, subtraction, multiplication, and division, and most of the time you can get by without division!"* The South African–born scientist soon learned (and eagerly embraced to this day) the key notion that, unlike in isolated dogma–ruled academia, in the real world actionable simplicity is always preferable to undue abstractionism. Another illuminating corollary of the story is that, while Derman did improve the model, the part of his efforts that traders found most welcome was the new user-friendly interface that allowed more business to be handled at once.

Derman also comes in handy when trying to understand the differences between academic theoreticians and the quantitative pros actually employed by financial firms. While both sets of species would belong to the modelers family, and thus to that group which can potentially wreak havoc through a latently potent belief in the power of mathematical descriptions of markets, they can be quite dissimilar. For one, the PhDs would be in different disciplines. Financial economists, of course, carry PhDs in Finance (though a few also boast science PhDs; I recall reading some years back about a hot, freshly minted Stanford University Finance PhD of Chinese extraction and being acutely impressed by two of the article's claims: one, the sought-after academic star was being unseemly compared to Keanu Reeves, and two, the lucky guy had previously earned a PhD in Physics from Cornell). Quants mostly have PhDs in a hard science instead of finance, presumably because employers are much more seduced by PhDs in a *real* science.

I guess the market is voting with its paychecks, when it comes to the issue of whether finance theory has tons of valuable contributions to make to no-nonsense pros. Faced with the need for technical staff, banks and hedge funds appear to much prefer the scientists and engineers used to getting their hands dirty solving practical problems than the economists used to daydreaming about a Platonic world. Even when it comes to nerdy types, financiers know how to pick up the doers (of course, this is a generalization; as with all generalizations it may be both exaggerated and unfair; there are well-known cases of financial economists who end up involved in the industry, but they look like a minority compared with the physicists or the mathematicians).

Besides what's printed on a diploma, quants appear distinctly distinct from academic theoreticians in another key respect. Quants are much more willing to admit to the limitations of modeling than finance professors. Whether such humbleness is born out of innocence-depriving trading floor happenstances (or, conversely, permitted to flourish by the removal of dogmatic academic vigilance) or just something that scientists are naturally endowed with, there seems to be no denying the fact that (many) quants have been much more known for their capacity and willingness to share with us that math can be an inconvenient companion in the markets. Those who receive a monthly check from financial institutions tend to view models as modest tools for thinking, not as arrogant calculators of incontrovertible numbers. Derman has always presented himself as particularly honest, but he is not by any means the only quant subject to admit to his emperor's clothes-less state. *"Watching quants pursue sacred laws for the profane production of profit, I sometimes find myself thinking disturbingly of worshippers at a black mass. . . . How can traders put faith in this stuff?. . . Isn't this endeavor the misguided consequence of some sort of physics envy, an inappropriate attempt to model messy human systems with the wrong paradigm?. . . Is quantitative finance a science at all? And finally, are quants scientists or cranks?"* So said the quants' quant.

You wouldn't be likely to hear the same self-criticizing ruminations emanating from a finance academic's mouth (or pen, or laptop). And really small would be the chances of the financial ivory tower regaling us with the following utterances: *"The mathematics of economics is so much more formal than the mathematics of physics, much of it reads like Euclid or set theory, replete with axioms, theorems, and lemmas. You would think that all this formality would produce precision. And yet, compared with physics, economics has so little explanatory power. Everything looks suspect: questions abound."* In their desperate attempts to attain the same status as physicists, financial economists may have become hopelessly, incomprehensibly dogmatic, even to physicists.

Another big dissimilarity between trading floor mathematics-lovers and their academic siblings is the differing degrees in which doctrinal rigorousness reigns supreme. Both quants and academic theorists use advanced complex tools, but while for the latter the math-enabled lemmas are the absolute last word (an end in themselves), for the former they are simply the start of the conversation and may eventually be entirely discarded and dustbinned. Quants may produce elegant papers that purport to answer some key question pertaining to some relevant issue afflicting their employer. But that does not mean that the model may be eventually used, at least as it was originally conceived. The initial level of complexity may be substantially watered down so as to make it compliant to the tastes of end users, aka traders and salespersons. That is, the mathematical games of quants are subjected to the veto of those whose number one goal is the making of monetary profits, as immediately as feasible. Needless to say, no such veto exists within ivory towers' walls. While the quants' models must pass the no-nonsense money-seeking test, theorists are free to abstract away as much as they want. In other words, while abstraction gets rewarded in academia, it is kept under check in the real world (that's not to say, of course, that banks and hedge funds do not employ unworldly theories, only that it is harder for analytical sobriety to rule unquestioned).

In the real world, many times übercomplex products are not priced directly from a mathematical model, even if one exists, but rather from the quoted market prices of much simpler instruments, with models being used simply as linkage mechanisms between the known and the unknown. Such a practical, engineering-type approach is a testament to the fact that quantitative doctrinarism must take a backseat to pragmatic functionality when real cash is at stake. Emanuel Derman once said that *"It's common to imagine that physicists on Wall Street spend their time predicting the future. They rarely do. Most of us work in quantitative haute couture, using models to create custom-tailored risk profiles from off-the-shelf products."* I vividly recall explaining to a fellow trading floor colleague the mathematical subtleties (based on academic papers, now long forgotten by me) involving the pricing of digital and barrier options (two types of exotic derivatives), only to be cut off by his pragmatism-dominated assertion that he couldn't care less about those equations, given that those kind of options can be replicated (and thus valued) through a combination of plain-vanilla contracts. Perhaps the number one difference between academic finance and real finance is that you absolutely must incorporate abstruse analytics in the former case, while that is certainly not a requirement at all in the latter. That is, profs are much more pedantic, and quite likely utterly unnecessarily so.

Finally, a crucial divergence between quants and finance profs concerns computer programming, both its use and its dominance. To put it bluntly, you can't be a quant if you can't code (C++ much preferred). To put it blunter, you would be hard-pressed to find a finance academic who can code (particularly in C++). Take a quick look at graduate programs in quantitative finance and those in financial economics; what's the number one unsameness? The ridiculously ubiquitous presence of computer programming courses in the former, and their conspicuously abrasive absence in the latter. This discrepancy goes to the heart of what quants are and professors are not, namely implementers. Quants are useless unless they can implement (i.e., code away) the models and the software infrastructure that contains them. Traders are not likely to do it, and salespersons surely won't do it (that would leave the CEO . . . not likely either), so that's why you hire PhDs in physics or computer science.

In fact, as anticipated earlier, most of what most quants seem to do is not pure mathematical modeling, but the building of administrative and procedural computational applications (databases, systems, interfaces, back office IT stuff, deal validation). Some time ago, Derman explained that *"At Goldman Sachs, despite the models we build, the papers we write and the clients we visit, only four or five of our group of 30 people in quantitative strategies in equity derivatives are directly involved in modeling: that is, in isolating financial variables, studying their dynamical relationships, formulating them as differential equations or statistical affinities, solving them and, finally, writing the programs that implement the solution."* Renowned London-based quant headhunter Dominic Connor says that 60 percent of quant work is computer programming. Former quant Mark Joshi concurs: *"[A]ll forms of quants spend more than half of their time programming"*; he also adds that there is a trend towards more routine tasks and less research. Some specific types of quants, known as "quant developers," spend *all* their time programming. This creates tensions within the quant family, with developers eyeing with jealousy how their "desk quants" brethren chattily interact with traders, actually do some math, and, worse, participate in a tastier bonus pool (apparently some would-be quant developers are baited in by banks with the later-unfulfilled promise of having a desk presence and thus partially escaping the coding grind). In any case, as Connor offers, quants in general have to code away so much that all could be seen as developers, really.

As a master of the universe, I may not need theoretical daydreamers, but I surely need software designers. In that sense, one could see the finance theorists versus quants dichotomy as somewhat akin to soccer journalists versus soccer coaches. Neither of the two plays the game, but one of them gets to actively help the players by creating a (hopefully) valuable working structure. The other watches from afar, at best describing what players do (and perhaps offering some useful actionable advice and insights based on those observations), mostly theorizing about what they should do.

So it turns out that quants and finance academics are entirely different breeds of theorists, of modelers. While quants may be much more, well, quantitatively versed (after all, we are talking about actual mathematicians and computer scientists), they may be much more constrained as to how profoundly to use all that firepower. They face the veto of traders and salespeople, so the success of an idea will be determined entirely by its practical usability and, crucially, its capacity to solve real-life problems (combined with the capacity of the quant to explain it in plain English). Such stringent requirements can be of the in-your-face variety, as many quants literally sit next to traders' desks. Just like a pupil facing a cold-calling session by his teacher, it can be prohibitive for quants to do anything with their time but focus exclusively on solving practical problems for their testosterone-filled colleagues. If those problems happen to not require too much in the way of analytical creativity, well that's just too bad. Professors, of course, don't face the constant vigilance of the practicality police (in fact, such enforcement officers may be banned from the premises) and are thus free to engage on grand thoughts or on issues that may serve the purpose of demonstrating technical prowess but which might hold negligible relevance.

This primal dichotomy of roles presents us with a challenge when trying to decide which type of modelers could do more harm. On the one hand, secluded, uninhibited, uncensored profs have a much better launching pad for whatever theoretical concoction they may come up with. Not much of a realism filter here. In that sense, the models made in the ivory tower could be seen as having the potential for being more unworldly, less reliable, extra dangerously illusory.

But there is another side to that coin: The quants have a much more direct influence on actual doers. A trader may have never read the *Journal of Finance* or *Econometrica* (let alone acted on what they publish), but he is definitely accessing the quants' models through his computer, on a daily basis. What quants put together (whether in the end more or less mathematically complex) has the power to move (and create) markets. Right away. The conclusion must be that while quants may churn out less dogmatism and more pragmatism than academics, the penalty for faulty assumptions can be both much more greatly and rapidly taxing on the markets. In the end, while we admire the humble matter-of-factiness and resourcefulness of quants (to which academics should become welcomingly addicted), our concerns for the welfare of the world may dictate that we worry disproportionately about the possible flaws in their high-tech amalgamations. We may have a softer spot for quants, but we might nonetheless be forced to scrutinize them stringently.

What is the main difference between the role of models in academia and the role of models in trading floors? Academics take models much more seriously. And, equally important, they are truthful in their Gnosticism: not only do they tirelessly proclaim the gospels, they in fact passionately believe in the theoretical God and its infallibility. Pros (including many quants), on the other hand, tend to take models much more lightly, almost unrespectfully so. While not exactly atheists (quants, particularly), they don't bow to the Theoretical God with nearly the same ardor as the cultish professors. Of course, banks and hedge funds do employ models, sometimes blindly so. But it seems also true that on occasions the perceived embracement of mathematical toys by financial players may be an act of convenient self-serving, either as means to look more sophisticated to the outside world, excuses to take more risk, or as alibis to justify possible bad news (much more on this in Chapter 6). The models used inside financial institutions should be a concern for the rest of us, given the very immediate impact that they can have. But don't always take at face value pros' self-proclaimed faithfulness in the analytical commandments. No one, on the other hand, could ever accuse ivory tower residents of fake zealotry.

Inside trading floors, models are much more likely to be treated as experimental toys than as evangelical doctrine. The goal is not to win a Nobel Prize or to earn the awe of the academic community (at least not primarily), but to allow traders and salespersons to be able to start a conversation with the market and with clients about what the value of a financial product should be, roughly. A model can be used for something as simple as a communicating tool, say quoting the price of an option in terms of volatility. It should help pros go from the easily understandable (prices of vanilla products, standard market variables) to the hardly comprehensible (prices of exotic products, nonstandard variables), in a convenient manner. But perhaps that should be it. Not much else should be asked of models by those who use them in the real world. Listen to Derman: *"I think a model works (serves its purpose) if it's a useful way of thinking about things. . . . What will happen to my position if interest rates go up, if volatility goes up or if dividend yields go up? I honestly think that's about as good as you can do—having a rational way of exploring what might happen to you in a world in which you've articulated the variables that can affect value."*

Quants devise utensils with which moneymakers can experiment and play out the consequences of different scenarios. Whether the model is acted on or not is up to the moneymaker. Sometimes the model serves as guidance for action, other times it is entirely discarded. Of course, students in a finance class are not allowed the same latitude (imagine a financial economics PhD candidate telling his professors that he has made up his mind and he would rather go on through the program without studying any of the models on offer). This points to another key issue: In the markets, bad models may have a much shorter shelf live than in academia. In the real world there is, as derivatives guru Stan Jonas once put it, a very straightforward and powerful criteria of refutation: when traders lose money the model is either completely changed or entirely refuted. In any case, the end result is that the original model is no longer in play (even if we think that it is; Black–Scholes is a very good example of this, as we will see later in the book). In academia, ac-cepted theories die much harder (if at all). Just like John McClane-Bruce Willis stubbornly survives year after year, attack after attack, movie sequel after movie sequel, the sacred cows of financial economics have never been internally refuted, in spite of well-known deficiencies. Rather, they continue playing prominent roles in the curriculum and receive Nobel backing.

What this means is that while bad quant models may do lots of harm due to their proximity to the action, the harmfulness may be short-lived, as the refutation criteria dictates that the culprit would be exterminated (perhaps to be replaced with something worse, but one has to assume that the market learns its lessons). Bad academic models, on the other hand, always live to fight another day. Thus, whatever negative effects they may cause would not be prohibited from reemerging later on, as veteran players (fully aware of the theory-enabled mishaps) are replaced by fresh recruits, who may be ignorant as to the recent past and thus naively receptive to the theoretical dictums, in practice opening the doors for new, similar debacles. As long as the theories are not refuted they naturally retain a good chance of entering and reentering the hallowed grounds of conventional wisdom. In this sense, academic models, while farther from the action, could be seen as the ones posing a more perennial influence on the real world.

Can we imagine a world without models, either academic or quant? Or, to put it slightly differently, which type of financial models would have a greater shot at longevity, even immortality? Touching upon some of what has been said already, it looks as if academic modeling may be able to boast a more secure future. It seems implausible (right now, at least) that the scientific revolution launched through the generous monetary support of the Ford and Carnegie foundations in the United States in the 1950s will suffer from a drastic turnaround anytime soon. It isn't exactly likely that financial economists will suddenly decide (or be forced to decide) that all that math and econometrics should be discarded and replaced with a softer institutionalist-descriptive approach. It is a safe (though not totally unassailably so) bet that theory will continue to reign supreme inside finance departments at B-schools. The unmistakable truth is that few finance profs dream at night cuddled to the tunes of a John Lennon–inspired ballad that would go something like this: "Imagine there's no models / It's easy if you try / No GARCH below us / Above us only real-life / Imagine all the academics / Living for the market / You may say I'm a dreamer / And I'm sadly the only one / I hope someday someone will join me / And we won't do any more math."

But what about banks? Are models equally safe here, within such brutish environment? So far, the models have been allowed to stay, even under the stringent condition that unsuccessful ones be (purportedly) promptly radically reformed or reduced to ashes. But, surely, nothing guarantees that this should be the normal state of affairs going forward. Is it really impossible that one day the bigwigs may decide to stop the mathematical dance and ban all quantitative modeling (though not the quants, they would still be urgently needed for computational stuff) from the premises? Or that some interested third party may force them to stop all that dancing? Stan Jonas was possibly quite prescient here, answering his own query as to whether banks should invest in modeling: *"If we take a look at the models that we always create and the ways derivative securities are produced, it seems as though we have bright analytical people creating models on one side, and then we have what are postured as rather naive (unscientific) people buying these products on the other side. Ironically (and in some moral sense, thankfully), over the long haul, it always seems that those naive people make a lot more money than the people who sell the product. As a financial institution's shareholder I would feel that there's something wrong with how we devote our resources when somebody who simply reads a newspaper and makes a bet based on what he thinks Alan Greenspan is going to do makes more money on a risk-adjusted basis than a team of former Russian physicists, who are trying to figure out what the correlation is and will be between, say, two-month LIBOR and 10-year LIBOR for the next 10 years. Perhaps it is a waste of resources and the risk capital at hand. If I were an investor, a shareholder in the bank, I just wouldn't want my money spent doing that."*

This raises a key and, to my knowledge, entirely innovative issue. Should bank shareholders and hedge funds investors become more concerned about the use of models by their investments? They just may have to become more inquisitive and start asking conveniently inconvenient questions: Why exactly do you use models? What if you had no models? What are the gains from models? What are the risks? Why do we need models? Can you give us hard cold examples of situations when a model was helpful and beneficial? Should we pay you to model? All this interrogation would of course become ever more pertinent following the all-too-recent credit crisis, where mathematical concoctions played a non-irrelevant role. I know of at least one set of shareholders (those who invested in a certain investment bank which stock went from $100 to $2 in a few weeks, as a result of savage losses from complex positions whose valuation decisively depended on modeling assumptions) who would have loved to have been prospectively more aware of how sensitive the return on their hard-earned dollars was to the use and performance of mysterious quantitative models.

Perhaps we will soon see financial institutions creating the position of Chief Modeling Officer (wait, that would read as CMO, which may not be the smartest of acronyms given the recent travails associated with collateralized mortgage obligations; let's settle for CQO, or Chief Quant Officer) to deal with such concerns. Of course, this would be in sharp contrast to the academic arena, where stakeholders (students, deans, school administrators) are not likely to subject their modelers to the same scrutiny. The end result would be a much less inquisitive university corporate governance regime, subject to much less accountability than their quant cousins. In other words, the perfect environment for theory to eternally blossom unquestioned.

I met Neil Chriss (for all of 10 minutes) in September 1999. I of course had known about him for a while, mostly through his very well written *Black-Scholes and Beyond* book, and was fully aware of Chriss' standing within the quant community. Even without the other accomplishments and accolades, his then current position, the number one reason why I got to share the same space as him for those brief moments almost a decade ago, by itself spoke volumes of his financial engineering reputation. As director of the math finance program at New York University's ultra prestigious Courant Institute of Mathematics, Chriss held the keys to attendance to any of the lectures on offer by the program (consistently among the global elite in its field). Though I was a student at NYU's business school, I was doing a specialized degree focusing on derivatives and financial mathematics and thus was very interested in attending a class at Courant (which, for those not in the know, sits just in front of the B-school). My own program's extraordinary flexibility allowed me to do so, but I obviously also needed special permission from Courant. In asking for such granting, I was crossing the short divide between both schools in the least popular direction, as by far many more math students seemed to want to roam around the B-school than vice versa.

I knocked on Neil Chriss's office door and got in. I don't remember much, but the place was dark and small, definitely unassuming. I think that we had a brief chat about how hard it was for his students to cross-register with the B-school (particularly famous, of course, for its finance department), which may have caused me to worry that he would decide to reciprocate the treatment. What truly matters is that he eventually granted me permission to enroll in the "Banking and Finance" course, taught by a former Salomon Brothers arbitrage head and a former Chase derivatives head. I must (should) have thought how privileged I was to be in the company of such prominent pros and academics.

These days, almost 10 years since I robbed 10 minutes out of him, Neil Chriss is one of the most relevant quant fund managers out there. After a few years spent honing his skills inside the quantitative asset management arms of a couple of bulge-bracket investment banks (he also spent some time as a desk quant in the mid-1990s, helping Emanuel Derman build innovative option pricing models at Goldman Sachs), and after a successful entrepreneurial experience in the form of an electronic derivatives brokerage, Chriss joined notorious U.S. hedge fund SAC

Capital in 2003, with the mandate to build a quant trading business. He did quite well, and four years later the University of Chicago math PhD set out on his own, founding Hutchin Hill Capital, a New York–based quant hedge fund that received unapologetically determined financial backing from Renaissance Technologies, likely the world's biggest and most successful quant shop.

So what exactly is it that Neil Chriss and his quant trader peers do? What explains the tremendous success of (many) quant funds? What makes a fund quant as opposed to, say, traditional? And are quant fund managers "quants" or do they constitute an entirely different type of breed?

Very simply stated, a fund may be deemed quant if it largely allows computers and mathematical/statistical instructions, rather than humans, to select its investments and to dictate which positions should be taken. Expressed in rather more formal terms, *"An investment process is fundamental (or traditional) if it is performed by a human asset manager using information and judgment, and it is quantitative if the value-added decisions are primarily based on quantitative outputs generated by computer-driven models following fixed rules."* Hybrid approaches seem to be quite prevalent, as many traditional managers routinely use some computer-based, statistically-aided tools, adding some computational flavor to their beloved judgmental strategies. Obviously, the computer must be told what to do and how to go about being an e-portfolio manager, and herein would enter the technical expertise of those working inside quant funds, the scientific PhDs endowed with the task of creating the right software. What is less clear is whether behind such computational designs would lie convolutedly complex predictive models of security prices (kind of trading floor–made finance theory) or rather more straightforwardly basic instructions. That is, you don't seem to absolutely need to act that quant in order to run a quant fund.

The first step to a model-driven investment strategy seems to be selection of inputs (data, rules). Then you build the forecasting engine, which provides, well, forecasts of future prices and risk. Then both the inputs and the forecasting engine are fed to the portfolio construction engine. Do managers interfere with this automated process? It depends on your degree of quant fanaticism. According to some, the model should never be overridden. Others allow for a small amount of interference, just to make sure that the numbers make sense and that trading orders do not outlandishly contradict influential last-minute market developments. In the words of a manager at a firm that combines purist quant strategies with so-called fundamental overlay, *"We read annual and quarterly reports and the footnotes plus looking at, for example, increases in daily sales, invoices. I expect that we will continue to use a fundamental overlay; it provides a commonsense check. You cannot ignore real-world situations."* Another mixer gives an example of the value of a hybrid approach: *"We don't use fundamental overrides in our quant funds, but if we want to make a big move, a fundamental view can be of help; for instance, if a model suggests to buy shares in a German bank when the fundamental analyst knows that German banks are heavily invested in subprime."*

The in-fashion move into hybrid portfolio management seems to be characterized mostly by traditional outfits incorporating quanty ways (through so-called "quant screens" that place constraints on choices), attracted by success stories from the computational side of the fence. Pure quant houses, on the other hand, may partly embrace fundamentalism as a way to differentiate themselves from competitors in their space. For both camps, embracing the other would appear as an attractive way to obtain diversified alpha. According to someone known for a scientific approach to moneymaking, *"Presently, only a small percentage of our business is run by fundamental managers. Going forward, we would like to grow this significantly. It's a great diversifier. But there will be accountability. Fundamental analysis will keep their own portfolios, but quantitative methods will be used for screening, performance attribution, and risk control."* As a general rule, though, a quant process worth its salt should keep judgmental oversight (or overlay) at a minimum. After all, the whole idea is to keep those pesky emotions out of the game.

What are the rationales for investing in a quanty way, whatever the actual degree of computational intensity chosen? Why does money chase after quant punting? A survey of market participants and assorted experts found that there are five top motivators: tighter risk control, more stable returns, better overall performance, diversification benefits, and founders' profile/in-house culture. Certain specific advantages of quant versus traditional investing are cited, including the ability to back-test strategies, the capacity to offer an ample menu of distinct products, and having an edge when it comes to complex applications.

Have quant funds truly delivered outstanding performances? Evidence is apparently scant. Model-based investing is a relative novice. There are perhaps 10 years of active records, compared to many decades for traditional punting. It is usually argued that quant funds returns are perhaps not overwhelmingly spectacular, but they sure are stable; as one expert put it, *"Because quant funds are broadly diversified, returns are watered down. Quants do not hit the ball out of the park, but they deliver stable performance."* Stable, if perhaps not stellar, performance can be a pretty good presentation card. And of course we do know that the best of the quant bunch do perform stably spectacularly. New York–based Renaissance Technologies, for instance, has produced consistent annual returns over 30 percent for the past 20 years. Its 1982 founder, Jim Simons, a former university math professor, makes hundreds of millions of dollars (much of which he donates to charitable causes, such as autism research or mathematical education). Also New York–based DE Shaw (founded in 1988 by, naturally, computer scientist David Shaw, a former academic who did quant trading in the mid-1980s at Morgan Stanley's famed statistical arbitrage group) has also done pretty nicely; during its first 10 years of existence the fund was reported to be delivering average annual returns of close to 20 percent, and while it did go through a rough patch during and immediately after the Russian crisis of 1998, it seemed to have recovered well from those mishaps; today, DE Shaw manages about $30 billion of assets (similar to RenTec, mid-2008 data) and has diversified into venture capital and value investing. Chicago-based Citadel ($20 billion under management as of mid-2008, founded in 1990), another behemoth fund known for its quantitative approach, has also typically been (notwithstanding more recent setbacks) a symbol of outstanding success with a record of plus-25 percent annual returns; Citadel's founder, Harvard grad Kenneth Griffin, paid in 1999 $60 million for a Cezanne.

According to sources, 2007 was not a good year for quant investing, in general underperforming more traditional activities (of course, we had that pesky "quant fund crisis" during the month of August; more on that later). This was in sharp contrast to the extremely quant-friendly 2005 and 2006 exercises. Most quants seem to favor value investing and suitably performed well during the 2001–2005 value market. By 2006, the stock market went back to growth, and quant funds got hurt as a result. What this implies, naturally, is that quant performance is not isolated from cyclical patterns.

Another key factor behind disappointing quant results in more recent times is a homogenization of strategies, models, and data among managers. As more people go quant, returns suffer from such copycatting. It used to be harder to become a player in the quant arena, with inputs being much more proprietary and secretive. As those hurdles got removed and performances famously shot up, plenty of wanna-bes joined the dance. In a way, then, quant investing may have suffered (temporarily, at least) as a direct result of its success. This could bode ill for the future of quant funds, their impact on the markets, and their public reputation. When you have lots of money being managed by lots of people who behave mechanically (or semimechanically) and who follow the same models with the same factors, big trouble may ensue as soon as things go slightly sour. If you need to unwind your position, there may be no takers at all. This can lead to a liquidity stampede and massively destabilizing sell-offs, which is just what happened during the summer of 2007's equities meltdown.

Even if returns can sometimes disappoint, the mathematicians and computer scientists are said to be better risk controllers anyway. Quant funds have been found to offer a pretty attractive risk-return trade-off (i.e., a superior risk-adjusted performance). One study found that in the case of U.S. large cap stocks for the period 2002–2004, quant funds bested fundamental managers with half the risk. Quants, as a group, were found to be better at risk management. Others concur, indicating that risk control is one of the biggest plusses of quant asset management, in contrast to traditional alternatives that may many times be unaware of potentially insalubrious exposure concentrations. So if, as an investor, you decide to go quant (and don't mind putting up with fees that can be substantially more taxing than in the boring, staid, traditional cases), you not only know that the moneymaking track record seems to be decent, but also that the potential for nasty surprises may be, in principle, more limited.

How far should one go in quantland? Is full automation the best approach, or perhaps a hybrid that combines human judgmentalism with quantitative inputs? Should models serve human decision makers, acting as technical support? Or should humans slavishly bow to the mechanical genius and serve as hands-off caretakers who humbly ensure that the machine is allowed to operate undisturbed? One initial source of advantage for the computer is the undisputable fact that machines can put in many more hours than flesh-and-bones types, and their efficiency is not abducted by tiredness or the distraction of personal issues. And in the end, not having to put up with unavoidably human factors may be the best reason to go full-auto.

Perhaps the key to quant funds is not so much the presence of abrasively high-tech models and techniques, but instead what they avoid by going the computational way. When a machine does the picking, human emotion is obviously erased from the picture. This could well be the primordial intended consequence, after all. You go quant not entirely because you have unlimited faith in the predictive and theoretical powers of your PhDs, but because you want to eliminate some of the presumed nasty aspects associated with more traditional portfolio selection. This characteristic of quant funds may be an important reason behind their appeal to investors, which had expanded substantially in recent years (for instance, at Vanguard Group, which launched its first quant group in 1985, the amount of money managed quantitatively went from $4 billion in 2002 to $20 billion at the end of 2005). The computer could be given instructions against accumulating heavy exposures to given names or industries, guaranteeing a disciplined approach to risk taking that no gut-endowed human could offer. The possibility of irrational exuberance on the part of traders would thus be subdued, an attribute that many investors may find highly valuable. It is harder for a computer to be seduced by fads or suddenly consumed by paranoid fear (it is, though, critical to highlight the paradox that a discipline that was designed to avoid traditional herd behavior ended up creating its own brand of herd behavior, a key reason for the disaster that struck quant funds in the summer of 2007).

Crucially, a particularly positive (to quant-friendly folks) attribute of computationally driven asset management rests with another key limitation that it helps avoid, namely the limited capacity of humans to absorb the seemingly unlimited amounts of financial information that bombards us ceaselessly. Computers obviously don't suffer from such handicap. Even when recognizing that human behavior cannot be entirely captured by models, the modern need to quickly analyze and process huge amounts of information is offered as a powerful argument (perhaps even *the* argument) in favor of quant investing.

Thus, it should not be surprising to find that many quant funds unapologetically emphasize their humanless predisposition when marketing themselves to investors. They certainly portray it as their main comparative advantage. *"There is a clear advantage of a quant approach over a fundamental approach. The former is less susceptible to behavioural biases, and these biases are increasingly recognized as important to results. Quant processes are, of course, susceptible to biases because quant models are programmed by humans. If a modeler examines propositions that have worked well in the past and sets them up in the future, it might turn out that they worked out in the past purely by chance. But quant processes are more systematic,"* stated one defender of the faith. *"A quant approach takes out the weaknesses of humans. It is objective and has a standard, repeatable way of looking at things. One stock is looked at in the same way as another. The quant process strips out the subjectivity. The manager does not fall in love with a stock or a CFO,"* added another fan (note, though, that such pitch may be less than spectacularly appealing to those yearning to devote their money to more glamorous, "story" stocks punts).

Just like with the case of plain-vanilla quants, quant fund managers have long ceased to be seen as weird additions to the financial animal kingdom and have, too, managed to transform themselves into protagonists, in this case in a particularly acute way. Some of those of a more traditional bent may still choose to deride quant traders as nerdy types with zero insights or knowledge about (let alone interest in) the economic and business worlds. Investors used to devouring balance sheets and newspaper articles, and to cultivating personal relationships with captains of industry, may profoundly dislike the arrival onto their scene of a misfit band of scientists who appear to be interested only in the data that markets generate, not in the people and organizations behind such hurly-burly. How can anyone make trading decisions without reading the *Wall Street Journal* and watching CNBC?

But the truth is that traditional players are the ones who may now look like the odd man out. Quant funds are not just much more irre-sistibly mysterious or house a far larger concentration of IQ. The best of them have also delivered sky-high returns (consistently for many, many years), enabling their managers to enjoy 9- and 10-figure paychecks. It is probably true that for those with the right attributes (which in-evitably tend to include a science PhD from an elite institution and a track record of top-notch research and technical production), joining a place like Renaissance, DE Shaw, or Citadel would outshine any other possible alternative within the financial industry. That is, quant funds have achieved the feat of counting themselves among the most profitable and sought-after money-chasing entities on the planet. If Derman's peers are happy claiming that they are no longer exotic pets that get consigned to the I-bank basement, Jim Simons, David Shaw, and (in spite of a bad 2008 that saw key Citadel funds lose half their value) Ken Griffin can be much louder and proudly say that they have confined a lot of their nonscientific competitors to the cellar of inferior performance and that they look upon the financial landscape not as peculiar specimens that excite some curiosity but as entrenchedly dominating forces.

We seem to have spent a considerable amount of time discussing quant funds without explaining the possible impact of their mathematical and computational games on the markets and thus on the rest of us. It's nice to present a picture of what quant funds do and who runs them (an important part of our initial effort to present those who toil in finance-land with the help of analytical tools), but if we want to abide by the central motto of this book we should at least try to analyze whether quant punters can influence, even hamper, markets. Luckily, the credit crisis presented us with a wonderful opportunity to do just that.

Naturally, an indelibly perennial characteristic of the crisis has been tumultuous tumultuousness in the world's stock markets. In a series of seemingly unending disturbing volatile moves, we have seen equities in the past two years experience behavior that would have priorly been deemed impossibly rare. On an almost daily basis, stocks have climbed 5 percent only to immediately dive another 5 percent. Long gone are the times when a 1 percent daily variation (up or down) would be described as a shocking development; in fact, the markets have very seldom varied by *less* than 1 percent during the troubles. Several countries have experienced historical equity happenstances throughout this period (including the largest-ever one-day points drop on Wall Street, or the largest one-day percentage rise ever for Spain's stock exchange). Such a continuous roller coaster was first witnessed during summer 2007, with those memorable episodes when the Dow Jones went up and down 200 to 300 points in breathtaking succession.

The conventional wisdom tells us that behind such pioneering shoot-the-chute lay the activities of quant hedge funds. After all, it's not for nothing that the turbulence was nicknamed "the quant crisis." Briefly put, a lot of quant punters (some of them quite sizeable) were forced to take drastic actions in the stock markets, catching innocent bystanders off guard and indirectly inflicting heavy setbacks on third-party investors.

Why exactly did this take place? What prompted the PhDs to act so rashly so suddenly?

Let's lazily borrow once more from conventional taglines. The generally agreed-on story would go something like this: Many multistrategy funds that used quant equity ammunition were also invested in complex structured credit stuff; as the latter's market value began to steer south with particular ardor (due to the unleashing in force of the subprime crisis, with considerable mortgage defaults and rating downgrades that caused a bloodbath among those eager to bet that none of those contingencies would take place), the funds faced sharp margin call increases. In other words, they needed to raise cash, fast; given the (drastically enhanced) illiquidity of the complex credit market, punters were left with no option but to sell only that which could be readily sold, namely equities; this unexpected and unscripted dumping in turn affected the entire myriad of equity quant funds (for reasons that will be detailed shortly), which, too, were forced to sell equities in order to deleverage and cut risks; the quant stampede may then have inspired surprised nonquants to also join the dumping party (or to engage in what may have looked like irresistible special-of-the-day bargain buying) in response to the unexplained volatility jump.

Excitingly interesting as the theme surely is, we won't delve deep into the actual strategies pursued by the quants or the nitty-gritty of the affair. Rather, we will focus on an issue that is of much more direct concern for our main purposes. What is it specifically about those using quantitative trading tools that can pose a menace for the stability of the markets, and did that commonality show up during August 2007? Was August 2007 just an accident, a freak coincidence, or the very public materialization of an innate danger presented by quant traders? Can quant funds, by their own intrinsic nature, be harmful to our health, and did August 2007 show just how much?

Simply stated, and as anticipated earlier in the chapter, quant punters can be dangerous because they can be wildly successful. The riches to be reaped by going quant can be so tantalizing that soon jealousy and envy run amok, with many wanting to become the next Simons, Shaw, or Griffin. And, and this is the key, copycatting can be easier in the land of the brainiac than in more gentile grounds. When "quantcentration" has reached a certain critical point, you have a lot of people backed up by a lot of money essentially owning the same positions. This is similar to very dry grass on a very hot summer day in California. The slightest disagreeable development can trigger a wildfire of uncontrollable dimensions.

Of course, trade concentration is an issue for any type of strategy, quant or not. But quant trading may lend itself to be particularly exposed to such risk. The real caveat, again, is that overcrowding may be more feasible in quant territory, on account of the intrinsic nature of the quant approach. To put it bluntly, it may be far easier to copy each other's moves (in exquisite detail) when computational programs, math, and theory give the orders. After all, quant people mechanically abide by their models, so if you want to be like them and know what approach they are using and replicate it, you are pretty much guaranteeing that you will both behave similarly, all the time. A hunch ("buy Google") is more difficult to be faithfully imitated by a precise group of people. In contrast, a theory-model is easily shared by like-minded people who studied in the same universities and under the same professors (or were even the professors themselves), and by those who are aware of which models those other guys are using; hunches are much more intrinsically individualistic, much less replicable, much less knowable, much less disseminateable; the hunch is never mistaken for a certainty (even if you fanatically believe in the hunch you know, deep inside, that it's only a hunch), the theory-model can very much be assumed to be an inviolable certainty, thus easily shared by analytics-adhering folks. Precise mathematical concoctions are much more amenable to exact replication and copying than human emotions. That is why a bloated quant universe may pose a destabilizing threat to market stability, because what happens when all those who have been flatteringly imitating each other have to dispose of their portfolios at the same time?

The indisputable evidence is that quant investing had exploded in size in the years just preceding the August 2007 meltdown. One source estimates that during 2000–2005, quantitative-based equity funds grew at double the rate of all other alternatives. Another indicated that between 1998 and 2007 the number of quant funds increased by a number of six (from some 130 to around 800). Again, good performances had been the norm prior to the crisis. Many of the new entrants apparently were not hard-core believers, but rather opportunistic multistrategy players attracted by the potential profits of computer-guided punting and the greater access to information and intelligence regarding how to put on quant strategies. Crucially, the new kids on the nerd block contributed to a general enhancement in leverage, as the increased crowding out of trades required bigger plays to make the same buck (it is important to point out that leverage had anyway been immodest on account of very low official interest rates and low volatility, reducing both the cost and risk of overleverage). And yes, a lot of the quant equity players, both old and new, used the same moneymaking tactics.

So by the start of the summer of 2007, there were hundreds of well-financed, über-leveraged quant shops holding identical positions. Any disturbance to the markets could ignite serious chaos and inflict pain. And painful were the effects for the quant family, including the most notable names. During the first 10 days of August, Renaissance Technologies' institutional equities fund lost 8.7 percent, Highbridge Capital Management (owned by JPMorgan) suffered an 18 percent decline in its Highbridge Statistical Opportunities Fund, DE Shaw's Composite fund was down about 15 percent. It is important to note that many (though certainly not all) quant players recovered swiftly from the setback, with RenTec and DE Shaw, among others, even managing to turn a net profit for August. But notwithstanding such prompt comebacks, the crisis very illustratively showed that machines left to their own trading devices can be dangerously destabilizing and that quant funds are not infallible in spite of the brain power and can create severe turmoil through their affinity to the crowded trade phenomenon. In fact, August 2007 may have been the first public demonstration of such perils, a revelation, in the words of an insider: *"It was the first time that it became obvious that this quant equity strategy was a crowded, run-for-the-exit type trade. Until it actually happened, no one knew that the cross-ownership was so huge."*

Paradoxically, as a result of the crisis, quant funds may be forced to disclose what they do more openly, lest they witness a drought of investors' money. Of course, such disclosure may make future crises likelier, as the troublesome copycat process becomes even more feasible and convenient. This concern was fully expressed by a quant manager: *"One lesson from the events of July–August 2007 is that we will be more circumspect when describing what we are doing. Disclosing what one is doing can lead to others replicating the process and thus a reduction of profit opportunities."* For those of us wishing for a mayhem-less financial architecture, the idea of a more secretive quant world sounds appropriately appealing.

Highly interesting, and placing emphasis on a key topic of this book which will be inexhaustibly expanded on in future pages, Value at

Risk failed its users and likely contributed to the turmoil in a non-negligible manner. The scientifically backed, Nobel-endowed, regulatory-sanctioned market risk guidance was heavily misguiding: As the period prior to the crisis had been characterized by stability, the VaR numbers (which borrow massively from the past) were "forecasting" placidity throughout. Those same minion "risk" figures possibly encouraged excessive complacency and contributed to the leverage buildup (it has been estimated that equity quant funds had at least doubled their leverage between August 2005 and August 2007, on the back of a very low VaR that granted permission). Once the chaos ensued, VaR made things worse. Brokers drastically and brusquely increased their margin requirements, not trusting VaR's dictates (a reference for funding purposes) on the face of extremely enhanced market volatility, resulting in the hurried demand for more capital and forcing further liquidations by awed hedge funds.

That is, even the mathematicians and the theoreticians can fall prey to the deleterious influence that quantitative finance constructs can inflict when let loose in the markets. Misguided and flawed theories can be so ruthlessly damaging as to refuse to spare even those who unapologetically defend the utter superiority of the algorithms over human wild spirits.

We have seen that a lot of what quants (the classical ones, not the punting types) do would feel a bit more bureaucratic than what we previously had in mind. Rather than dreaming up new breakthrough theories and designing awe-striking models built upon mind-boggling mathematics, quantitative folks seem to spend most of their time providing technical support to traders and salespeople, whether via database design, software improvements, or value-at-risk calculations. This reality, needless to say, does not in any way diminish the value that quantitative folks bring to their employers, or the reputational strength of such contributions. In fact, I would argue that having the capacity to successfully involve oneself in the nitty-gritty of things and to act as efficient engineers rather than idle daydreamers should be seen as a big *plus*, not as something to feel mathematically ashamed of. If the job market demands that you behave less like a research purist and much more like a look-under-the-hood guy or gal, and if you have the capacity and spirit to oblige, then you should be commended for your exemplary predisposition towards practicality. If pure thought and grand reflection is your cup of tea, perhaps the ivory tower would be a more welcoming space.

The testimonials regarding the actual professional activities of quants seem to agree with what I personally experienced in the trading floor. Quants and risk managers were essentially another (wonderfully useful) resource at the disposal of deal makers. This could be taxing on quants. Many deal makers did not understand how the spreadsheet-based models worked, even after 10 prior explanations, and were constantly pressing the quants for tutoring. Similarly, a risk manager could be asked to calculate the at-risk amounts of a potential trade several times during the same day, for several days in a row, as the structure suffered the inevitable modifications along the way and as markets moved. I always felt that quant folks were overexploited and somewhat abused. They had to always be ready to service the deal makers in what were mostly repetitive and creativity-devoid tasks.

And this is probably a key reason why PhDs tend to fill quant and risk management roles. Sure, you need technical skills to perform such jobs. But you also need to be personally comfortable doing those jobs. If what you want is action, meeting clients, and the thrill of the kill, then you can't be a quant or a risk manager. Two weeks into the job you would be bored to tears and quit. Banks clearly can't have such people as quants or risk managers because, well, they would quickly run out of quants and risk managers.

But things are probably way different with PhDs. Plainly speaking, a quant or risk manager position at a bank would be considered a winner for those whose alternative occupation may be grading undergraduate exams inside the confines of a silent university hall, making meager wages. Offer such people the chance to become part of a heavily populated trading floor and make six figures, and they would probably not think twice. They would be eternally grateful, love you forever, and work enthusiastically, even if most of what they do consists of building databases, finding glitches in the software, and making hundreds of daily at-risk calculations.

If you want quants and risk managers, you need people who are happy being quants and risk managers, and for whom being quants and risk managers would be among their very best possible career paths. PhDs fit this pattern better than most. Yes, their technical skills obviously come in handy. But that is not enough. You also need the right personality.

You need people who are not too action-driven, who are not too en-trepreneurial, who are not too anxious, who are not too adventurous, who are not too practical, who are not too restless, who are not too allergic to repetitive tasks, and who, perhaps, are not too money-hungry. Science PhDs are possibly endowed with all those attributes, and that is probably a big reason why science PhDs became (and remained) quants and risk managers.

Of course, even if their roles and personalities are perhaps not as sexy as what we had assumed them to be, quants definitely play an important role in modern finance and their core contributions are a very welcome addition to the firepower of financial institutions. It wouldn't be unreasonable to say that the world needs quants. But, necessary as they are, are quants as unexciting as I seem to portray them in above paragraphs? Are they indispensable but boring? In other words, are quants needed but not rip-roaring? No, I don't think that's an obvious conclusion. Quants can be as interesting, if not more, as testosterone-filled, wild-eyed traders. Behind all the computer coding may lie a beguilingly alluring story dying to be told. Perhaps even worthy of its own on-screen immortalization.

Take Emanuel Derman, for example. The "dean of quants" certainly symbolizes a nontedious, nonordinary, non-run-of-the-mill life. Brows-ing through Derman's memoirs for the umpteenth time (these days I no longer read books, I randomly browse through them searching for eye-catching passages), I couldn't help thinking that someone, somewhere, someday should make a movie out of this great tome.

Have I gone insane? A movie about a quant's life? Do I want to irremediably jeopardize the possibility of a future Hollywood career for myself? Am I really that bad picking cinematic projects?

Call me crazy, but I think that people would want to see a Derman-inspired flick. I know, I know: You are probably imagining the long line of science PhDs eagerly waiting to see their idol immortalized on the screen. But I don't mean just brainy types when I talk about the potential popularity of the movie. I very much mean the general public.

What prompts me to believe in *Derman: The Movie*? Well, his book (his life) touches upon several experiences that I think can be quite appealing. The lonely young foreign student that lands in crime-infested New York. The PhD seeker at a legendary physics department. The aspiring academic doing the postdoc rounds. The Wall Street success story at the most famous of institutions. The revolutionary quantification of finance.

But even more than these individual biographical bits, the main selling point for the movie would be the presence of a major essential theme, one that inspires and that would be bound to attract attention from folks. When traveling through Derman's life, it is impossible not to detect a sense of betrayed innocence, a nostalgic yearning for lost love, an indefatigable yet hopeless attempt to satisfy a relentless passion. Derman is a man who loves deeply and who fights very hard to have that love reciprocated, only to be disappointed by unfavorable circumstances. Derman's love interest is, of course, physics. We see him as a young idealist bent on doing physics all day for the rest of his life. This is a quest for him, an absolute must, life-defining. And he wants to do physics for the purest of reasons: He wants to find truth. In order to achieve that romantic goal he is willing to make the toughest of sacrifices and to incur untold pain. He continues to fight and hope under strain, refusing to give up the dream.

For the reader, it is impossible not to root for the hero. We want Derman to succeed; we desperately wish that by the end of the chapter some university has finally offered him the coveted full-time position. When disappointment comes knocking again one final time, we sink with Derman. Innocence is lost, the dream is gone. The search for universal truth would have to be postponed.

But if we shed some tears at the sight of our hero departing from his beloved physics path, we glowingly smile when he eventually finds happiness, fulfillment, and untold recognition on Wall Street. We feel elated that life has vindicated him. We find his triumph an act of justice. We bow at the altar of the humbleness and modesty that Derman continues to show even after having reached the pinnacle at that most illustrious of institutions, Goldman Sachs. And we surrender to his never-ending intellectual curiosity.

I think that regular people would also side with our hero at movie theatres. I think they, too, would be moved by the story of this man who came to New York guided by a passion for scientific truth, who became a marveled inhabitant of a genius den at Columbia, and who struggled relentlessly in the quest for a life of science. I think people would sink, too, when the hero has to finally confront the inevitable reality that he will not be able to pursue his dream further. It would break their hearts to see Derman leave physics, just like it broke our readers' hearts. And, just like it happened to us bookworms, it would energize and inspire them to see his victory later in life. Patrons would leave the theater with an open smile (fitting for a movie about the man who first modeled the volatility smile).

In sum, I would recommend the Hollywood honchos to do this movie for several reasons. One is that it contains lots of interesting subplots. The youthful pursuit of scientific accomplishment at a genius-filled top university could be appealingly presented (did you like *Proof*?). The hardships associated with finding an academic job could also be made attention-grabbing. The use of esoteric quantitative techniques to make money and manage risks on Wall Street is definitely a winning theme. And Derman has certainly met his share of intriguing eye-catching characters (all of whom should be portrayed in the film).

But again, the biggest selling point would be the portrayal of an idealistic, likeable man who sacrificed so much for the pure love of science, who had to brusquely and tragically abandon his life-defining quest, but who eventually found extraordinary worldly success without betraying his basic traits and his never-ending passion for intellectual achievement.

Wouldn't it be nice if the final scene were that of Derman satisfactorily returning (as financial engineering professor) to his beloved Columbia after so many years, to the place where he dreamed of endless days of physics, the place where innocence still ruled supreme?

Critique

■ *Chapter 4* ■

Copulated Nightmares

■ *Abrupt reform, if not so much prison* ■ *Modeling death*
■ *The 2005 pre-warning* ■ *Rating us into hell*
■ *A disapproving grin* ■

Around mid-July 2008 (with the then one-year-old global credit crisis still fuming on all cylinders, having recently forced U.S. authorities to bail out stricken mortgage giants Fannie Mae and Freddie Mac) the following, rather unshy, ruminations appeared on Nassim Taleb's idiosyncratic web site:

> Having a risk number is not trivial. It does lead you to do foolish
> things, even if you knew that the measure was wrong. If I can
> show that, many people [who offered quantitative risk measures in
> finance] will have to be held accountable—and I can show that!
> One of Fannie Mae director's, a quack and proponent of "Modern
> Finance" charlatanism, kept promoting "scientific" risk
> measurement methodologies that do not measure risks adequately,
> but lead people to TAKE MORE RISK foolishly thinking they
> know something. [This is the reason I singled out Fannie Mae in
> *The Black Swan* as a firm sitting on dynamite and the International
> Association of Financial Engineers as a society of snake oil vendors
> harmful to society]. After > 1 trillion in losses I can safely say that
> my statement that the banking system has been taking more risks
> than they thought SHOULD HAVE BEEN TAKEN MORE

SERIOUSLY. So I hold that giving someone a bad risk measure
was just as CRIMINAL as giving someone the wrong medicine.
For a long time nobody sanctioned doctors who poisoned their
patients. Why don't we take on the proponents of quantitative risk
management, put them in jail so they stop harming us?

It is clear that widespread reliance on quantitative methodologies and
constructs was, at least in a large enabling role, behind the mayhem that
originated in the summer of 2007, first in an obscure corner of the U.S.
residential mortgage market and then spread-out like a virus throughout the world's credit and financial markets. It is also clear that previously conventionally accepted (or at least widely sanctioned) quantitative
techniques and the "ideologies" supporting them became unappealingly
discredited amidst the chaos.

What should we do about it? We could, as Taleb proposed, imprison
all those directly responsible for this "quantitative 9/11," perhaps make
some room for them in Guantanamo Bay, next to Osama Bin Laden's
henchmen. After all, if we are to fully endorse the arguments of Taleb
and similar critics, finance theorists and financial mathematicians have
committed criminal acts that are not exactly outside the realm of Taliban-
size dimensions.

But such course of action may be impractical, and not just because of
human rights or legal process concerns. Short of donning quant types
with orange jumpsuits and sending them out to the Caribbean, we
could, rather less aggressively and a tad more efficiently, voice the need
for unavoidable reform. If the credit crisis (in the words of George Soros,
curiously a strong opponent of Guantanamo, the gravest since the 1929
Crash) shows something, it is that the role of quantitative tools in finance
must be entirely rethought, reconsidered, and reevaluated.

In this sense, a sensible initial step would be to ask ourselves a very
simple question: Why does finance need quantitative tools? Why does
finance need theorems? Granted, finance, by its very nature, has always
depended and will always depend on a certain amount of math and
lemma-like truisms. But these are of a very soft nature. Because there
are numbers involved, you need to be able to do some arithmetic (you
know, if you buy 1,000 shares and each share is worth $25, you will
need $25,000) or at least be able to employ a machine capable of doing
the arithmetic for you. And because there are products with predefined

payout formulas, it is possible to infer unquestionable relationships (if bond prices go up, yields go down; or when the price of the underlying asset goes up, the price of a regular call option goes up). But do we need extra math and lemmas beyond these simple bedrocks? And, more pointedly, do we need such extras to be as incredibly complex as they have become through the years?

The quantification of finance was a process most likely not dictated by a real, existing, indisputable need on the part of math-challenged ancient pros (if we exclude, naturally, the computer revolution, which unleashed the need for people who could produce software and design interfaces and databases; but here we are focusing on the modeling-forecasting-theorizing aspects of quant finance, not on the more habitual technical plumbing activities of those deemed quants), but rather was a need artificially (and forcibly) imposed on insiders by a mass of outsiders, with the aid of a smallish fifth column of insiders who (either out of pure belief in the value-adding capabilities of the tools or as means to enhance their own internal relevance) eagerly engaged in active pulling.

What I mean by all this is that finance is, in itself, not a fiendishly complex activity, even after products and markets have become incredibly more sophisticated. You really don't need much beyond the basic elements highlighted earlier (provided, again, that you can count on technical computational support). You don't absolutely need advanced mathematical theorems in order to run a modern-day financial institution. Scientific prowess is *not* a requirement in order to be successful as a hedge fund, an asset manager, or an investment bank. Nothing in the markets or the products dictates that you must have mastered econometrics or numerical methods prior to being allowed and able to play. Even 20 years deep into the derivatives revolution, elementary arithmetic and solid practical market knowledge remain the only true requirements. Until someone designs a financial market where payouts are determined by the solution to a stochastic differential equation or a multivariate regression model, things will remain so.

This is not to supinely argue that advanced quantitative methods can't be of help, simply to underline that, whatever their potential benefits, they are not irrefutably needed. The same markets and the same products would have emerged without the development and presence of the fields of mathematical finance and financial economics (but surely not without the advent of the computer, at least at the same level of activity).

There was no extreme, unavoidable urgency on the part of players to be equipped with funky forecasting and valuation tools. If they are available and they can help, great for the traders, punters, and deal makers. But if they are not, no irreparable harm would be inflicted, no innovation would be prevented, no solution would be lost. If consenting adults want to make a market in whatever asset or to take an existing asset market to the next level, they can and would do that without waiting for mathematical authorization. The history of derivatives (perhaps the most sophisticated financial arena) shows us that professionals are more than willing and capable of creating new stuff long before the technical paper has been published.

Much more urgency would be urged, in contrast, by those endowed with the skills to design and implement the tools, and who desire to join the financial industry or to multiply their relative relevance within it. You are likelier to praise the contributions of financial econometrics and to peddle its solutions as God-sent if you are a financial econometrician. You are likelier to argue for the utter necessity of modeling if you are a modeler. And, throughout history (though less markedly today than yesterday), modelers and theoreticians have been overwhelmingly outsiders.

What motivates quanty outsiders (academics, scientists) to want to colonize the financial planet? Well, the rewards are potentially very tasty and the sales pitch has a more than decent chance of working. By rewards I don't just mean monetary ones. Quantitative finance can be a very exciting intellectual adventure, full of challenging potential discoveries. Who wouldn't want to try his hand at unlocking the mysteries of the market through fancy ultrasmart mathematical manipulations? Who wouldn't want to be the first to obtain a (purportedly fair) price for a new hot product? The markets are also tailor-made for those with a disproportionate taste for research and analytics in one very important sense, namely the availability of tons of reliable data to play with. Finally, there is also fame and power. Finance promises more of both to those scientists unsure of their Nobel prospects.

Having a chance at achieving all those rewards (i.e., having a chance of being hired by a financial institution) is appealingly not impossible. These days, and continuing with a process that was kick-started some 30 years ago, investment banks and hedge funds hire a substantial number of quantitatively trained individuals. If you are a nerdy type who wishes to go into finance and have the patience to do a numerate PhD or the money to enroll in one of the increasingly prevalent specialist Master's programs, it is indeed quite possible to achieve your dream. In spite of the nonabsolute necessity for mathematical wizardry exposed earlier, there is little doubt as to the habit of financial institutions to let mathematical wizards in. And while (as has been detailed earlier in the book) most of these brainiacs spend most of their time doing no mathematical modeling or undecipherable forecasting, instead becoming highly skilled technical assistants who provide the computational support essential for any financial organization, it is likely that such reality would not prevent finance from appearing insurmountably superior to other alternative occupations in the eyes of many scientists.

The ubiquitously numerous presence of quanty types around trading floors (many times reported by mass media) may give the impression that fourth-generation analytical tools (those, again, beyond computer power) are indispensable if you want to make a buck in the markets. All these quantitative people certainly have a strong vested interest in having the world believe that finance does need advanced quantitative tools (though we must highlight the admirable honesty displayed by many top quants when they loudly voice their skepticism as to our ability to mathematically tame the markets). Sometimes, no-nonsense nonquant pros contribute to that story line, for self-serving reasons of their own. These impressions are mainly illusions, but they also rightly convey the message that certain mathematical and statistical constructs have indeed become mainstream elements of the financial industry, a revolutionary development that sharply differentiates modern market practice from its historical predecessors.

While, it must be again emphasized, impressions are not quite reality in this case (the undeniable presence of scientists does not imply that finance is a science, and not just because those former scientists don't really perform much science in their new financial environment), there is no doubt that the quantitative and theoretical invasion unremittingly launched in the late 1970s and early 1980s has established very solid beachhead in financeland. Mathematical models are (partly at least) routinely embraced, statistical measures are (rather more profoundly) followed, econometric guidelines are (not exorbitantly frequently) sought. Existing markets, products, and practices may have emerged in a math-deprived environment anyway, but that does not negate the fact that advanced math has, for the past few decades, been used. Possibly not as intensely and religiously as conventionally believed, but used nonetheless.

The financial markets of May 2007 were faithful adherents to that three-decades-old legacy. The financial order prevalent just as the horrendous credit crisis began to rear its ugly head was one where theoretical models and quantitatively charged dictums enjoyed a privileged existence. Far from being widely shunned, many of them were adoringly abided by and wholeheartedly accepted as backbones of the system. A few skeptical outsiders had been crying wolf for a while, but those who matter (the practitioners, the rating agencies, the regulators) had overwhelmingly decided not to entirely ban the math from the premises. The financial *Titanic* that hit the iceberg in the summer of 2007 and then began a painfully lengthy descent into total darkness was, in modern fashion, inescapably inhabited by quantitative machinations. As we shall see, such machinations not only failed to forewarn of the iceberg in advance, or may have actually directed the ship towards it. They helped *create* the iceberg themselves.

There is reason to believe that May 2007 could represent the high-water mark for the application of quantitative tools in finance. A backlash against theoretical devices seems to be in the works. Simply stated, the crisis has highlighted too many failings at the same time. Models did not work, guiding measures failed horribly, sacred assumptions broke down. The math did not forewarn, afforded excess complacency and misguided confidence, and justified lethal business practices. Above all, the mayhem has helped confirm what many had always known or at least suspected: Markets are not quantitatively tamable, and efforts in that direction can destroy us.

It is difficult to see how something that is not really necessary for the evolution of finance, whose success is quite improbable, and which can contribute to generating untold pain, could continue to play a prominent role in the markets. It is one thing for academics and maybe a few insiders to spend their time thinking big mathematical finance thoughts (not much downside, maybe some significant upside if someone does come up with valuable insights), but quite another to allow such ideas to unfilteredly affect practice. Perhaps it is time to turn back the clock 30 years and return to a world in which theoretical "certainties" were not an ingrained part of the financial industry.

When asked about the reasons behind the credit crisis, pundits, analysts, politicians, and other assorted outsiders would be overwhelmingly expected to cite the myriad of oft-cited usual suspects: horrendously lax mortgage lending policies, unsustainable housing bubbles, securitization run amok, asleep-at-the-wheel regulatory practices, untold investor greed, retold bankers' greed, and so on. But few (if any) would be expected to show rebellious originality and point towards the direction of something called *Gaussian Copulas*. Before you let your imagination run wild with visions of Germanic sexual activities, it may be prudent to clarify that a Gaussian Copula is a mathematical model, broadly used to probabilistically quantify and predict the interdependence of different individual variables. Such constructs, originally the obscure preserve of statisticians, made their way into finance some 10 years ago, becoming endorsed with particular ardor in the credit derivatives arena, both by quants and academics. The valuation and rating of many of the complex structures that unraveled during the crisis drew from the dictates of Gaussian Copula models, which, naturally, suddenly appeared as less than perfect. Simply put, what the models had been theoretically crowning as highly valuable and highly trustworthy became downgraded by real life to the status of worthless and unreliable.

Quantitative models should be added to the list of guilty parties when discussing the crisis, perhaps displayed prominently atop the rankings, just a few notches below NINJA loans. Without the model-based confident assessments of traders, quants, and rating agencies, the vast securitization of less-than-salubrious credit and its spreading throughout the far corners of the financial universe might not have taken place. Or it might have been that much less carefree and trigger-happy. Those mathematically sanctioned AAA ratings made everyone feel safe and secure, decisively aiding business. Pricing tools that purported to be able to summarize überly complex trades into one neat number and that ruled out the possibility of such number being zero (or, more to the point, of not being at all) convinced bank executives and trading floor honchos that restraint would be a wasteful course of action. Without the misplaced certainty afforded by elegantly sophisticated analytics, the mayhem may have been no more significant than a mild hiccup.

A Copula (in a statistical sense) is a way to obtain multivariate, or joint, probability distributions that, technicians affirm, is particularly simple and convenient. Once we know the marginal (i.e., individual) probability distributions of each of the concerned variables together with the correlation structure (how closely the variables move in tandem; this idea obviously implies nonindependence), the copula function can be used to marry those univariate marginals to their full multivariate distribution. Roughly, we would be trying to model the likelihood of various different events taking place jointly, with those events depending in some way on each other. That is, you are not simply interested in the chances of X and Y taking place together; you want to know how often X and Y take place together once you know that X can cause Y, or vice versa.

An obvious financial application of this wizardry is the modeling of dependence between defaults, which, naturally, happens to be at the heart of those modern multiname credit derivatives structures which, certainly, happen to be at the heart of the 2007 crisis. Why would default probabilities of many single bonds or loans be assumed to be interdependent? Or, to put it technically, why would copulas be needed to model products where the default probabilities of many different assets matter? Wouldn't the single, marginal distributions be enough on their own? The answer is no. Or at least, the theoreticians, quants, traders, and rating agencies said that the answer is no. And they appear to have a point. The alternative assumption of independent credit risks may seem unrealistic.

As the pioneer of the application of copula methodology to credit derivatives put it, *"The default rate for a group of credits tends to be higher in a recession and lower when the economy is booming. This implies that each credit is subject to the same macroeconomic environment, and that there exists some form of positive dependence among the credits."* If one or more companies default on their obligations, this could trigger further defaults as the original devastation breeds further destruction through several plausible channels (tighter credit, disruption of supplies, loss of customers, enhanced general economic malaise). Needless to say, such interconnectedness would be deeply enhanced if the companies belonged to the same industry sector.

Creepily paradoxically for the mathematics behind tools that caused so much financial obliteration, the original modeling efforts were inspired by work done on the correlation of (human) death rates. There is a concept in actuarial science known as the "broken heart": People tend to die faster after the death of a beloved spouse. Cracking such co-dependence can be quite useful to life insurers. Believing that *"Default is like the death of a company, so we should model this the same way we model human life,"* quant David Li borrowed from his death-modeling academic friends, who first gave him the idea of using the technology of copulas. When he published his path-breaking paper in 1999, Li and his One-Factor Gaussian Copula (the "one-factor" refers to the fact that the performance of each individual asset is linked to a common additional factor, typically economic variables; the "Gaussian" part implies that the model's architecture is influenced heavily by the Normal probability distribution) concoction contributed to opening up the floodgates of the complex credit derivatives explosion, by providing a simplicity-embracing way to calculate joint default probabilities and default correlations for a bunch of fixed-income securities pooled together.

This model became the standard ever since. It borrows from the market's assessment of the default probability for each loan or bond, runs those individualistic projections (together with correlation estimates, which are assumed to be stable in time and structurally flat) through the copula function, and out comes the theoretical probability mapping the joint default behavior of all the assets (i.e., how likely are assets to default if others default, or to remain solvent if others do so). This number has direct implications for the value and returns of derivatives based on the contingency that a credit event would affect more than one security. If the churned out likelihood is low (a small theoretical chance that all credits survive or default), the model would be saying that the risk of joint default should perhaps not be excessively rewarded or valued inordinately high. Alternatively, if the output is substantial, tasty potential returns should possibly be offered to those eager to face the risk. Similarly, a high default correlation would narrow the gap between the yield presented to those willing to invest in the riskiest part of the pool and the one destined for more conservative tastes (since both parties would seem to have a similarly high likelihood of suffering pain).

It is generally held that an investment in the riskiest slice (or *tranche*) is long default correlation, since it has little to lose from a joint deterioration in creditworthiness but lots to gain from a joint improvement in nondefaultness, while the safest slice is short correlation, since it has little to gain from a joint improvement and lots to lose from a joint deterioration. Take those famous collateralized debt obligations (CDOs), the instruments arguably behind the true mayhem that led to the crisis and that were assessed by punters and rating agencies through Gaussian Copula lenses; they are comprised of many different fixed-income securities (loans, bonds, mortgages) or derivatives based on those securities, and investors can choose which risk tranche to invest in, with the riskiest slice (called "equity" in the jargon) being hit first by any default-related losses in the portfolio, and the safest slice ("super senior") being hit last. Default correlation would determine the performance of each investment. Equity investors want high correlation because their only chance of survival lies with an extreme scenario (no or negligible, joint defaults; that is, very low losses). Senior punters, on the other hand, want low correlation because their existence is only threatened by extreme scenarios (lots of joint defaults, very high losses).

It becomes now clearer why the correlation number is of such high importance in the brave new world of credit derivatives: it determines the returns to be earned and the market value of the product (and, crucially, the rating, as will be seen later). Modeling default correlation right can bring large benefits, just like modeling it wrong can unleash untold disaster. The Gaussian Copula model calculates the spread (or return) that each tranche should offer based on the individual spreads of the underlying assets and, of course, assumptions about correlations. However, and this is key, the correlation number that typically goes into the model is so-called "asset correlation," not actual default correlation. The latter is simply too complex to estimate, since there is very little data available (defaults, after all, happen not that often). On the other hand, data about asset price correlation is quite abundant (think equity prices), so pros concentrate on it as a proxy for default correlation, hoping that they somehow have something to do with each other. In fact, one of the attractive things that the Gaussian Copula model offers is the possibility to infer (theoretical) default correlations, given default probabilities and asset correlations.

Naturally, if actual market default correlation turns out to be way different from the one implied by the model (based on the initial asset correlation estimate), then the theoretical outputs would have underperformed significantly. Given that Gaussian Copula assumes a stable and flat correlation input, undue volatility in the underlying credit markets could easily do the trick (by being erected on Gaussian foundations, the model endows a low chance to extreme, or tail, events taking place; correlations would be expressed with Normal distributions, thus guaranteeing an output that assigns little chance to all hell breaking loose). This is what happened, for instance, in May 2005, during the conveniently termed "Correlation Crisis," a loud forewarning that, maybe, theoretical finance devices are not always safe from disagreeable real-life developments.

One of the outputs from the model is the so-called *Delta ratio*, which indicates how one could, theoretically, hedge a credit tranche play. Just like in the case of currency or stock options, this ratio attempts to measure the exposure of the value of the position to small changes in the underlying reference variable, based on a mathematical model that links them both. If you believe in the formula, then you can put your trust in delta as a hedging guide. It has been amply known for a while that delta is a deleteriously deficient aiding kit when it comes to the markets where it was first tested (forex, stocks, interest rates, commodities); delta hedging simply does not work there, for several reasons. It turns out that analytically charged hedging has also been shown to be lacking in the credit arena. And just like the real-life failures of delta in more conventional waters prompted a backlash against its mathematical begetter (naturally, the Black-Scholes option pricing model), the failures of delta in the credit universe unleashed a no-holds-barred criticism campaign against the Gaussian Copula concoction.

Encouraged by the perceived, scientifically sanctioned, confidence offered by the copulated delta (whether because they truly trusted the math or because they thought that it could be used as a convenient alibi for their punting of choice), many traders had by early May 2005 entered into a particular type of play known as "equity vs mezz." The idea was to capture profits that were, in principle, perfectly hedgeable and thus riskless. Since the returns offered by a long position in the equity tranche of a CDO are tastier than those offered by a similar position in a mezzanine tranche (more senior up in the pool's capital structure; several losses in the underlying portfolio need to take place before this slice endures pain), one could do worse than buy the equity (i.e., sell protection on that tranche, collecting the corresponding yield) and sell the mezzanine as a protection (buy protection on that tranche, paying the corresponding yield). But how much protection to buy exactly? How can I be sure that I am neither underhedging nor overhedging?

I'd love to do the promising equity-mezz thing, but it just looks too complicated to get the whole thing right! Luckily for the profits-revering punter in you, mathematical finance comes to the rescue. David Li's baby (together with posterior, better-bred siblings) tells you exactly how to do it.

Let's see how this might work through an example. The table below gives quoted parameters for the equity and junior mezz tranches of the five-year iTraxx (European) basket index on May 4, 2005, just one day before the crisis:

	Up-front	Spread	Delta
iTraxx 0–3%	29%	500	17
iTraxx 3–6%	0%	168	6

That is, the equity slice (suffering the first 3 percent of losses) offered an up-front payment of 29 percent of the invested notional together with an annual payment of 500 basis points (5 percent). The mezzanine slice (suffering the subsequent set of portfolio losses, up to 6 percent) did not commit to any up-front disbursement, and just an annual outflow of 168 basis points. In other words, the equity-mezz trade would yield, net, a 29 percent up-front inflow plus a positive annual inflow (dependent on how much of each slice is traded). The play would of course be exposed to the risk that the equity tranche would suffer from defaults in the underlying pool (forcing the investor to incur severe monetary loss) while the mezzanine tranche doesn't.

Given a certain investment amount in the equity tranche, how much mezzanine notional should be committed so that the overall net position is a hedged one, mark-to-market? That is, what should be the size of the mezz play that guarantees, in theory, that the value of the play does not suffer from mark-to-market gyrations? Whatever the ratio of the two deltas (the equity's and the mezz's) says. This ratio can be interpreted as the sensibility of the value of the equity tranche to a small movement in the index, divided by the sensibility of the value of the mezzanine tranche to a small movement in the index, assuming everything else (including correlation) is constant.

Imagine that in the above example the equity play is selected to be $10 million. The deltas ratio is $17/6 = 2.833$, indicating how much more sensitive to a widening of the index the equity slice is with respect to the mezz slice (this would seem to make sense, as the slightest enhancement in uncreditworthiness in the portfolio could wipe out the riskiest tranche). Thus, if we want a delta-neutral play (one that does not have exposure to index movements, theoretically), we should build a short mezz position of $28.33 million. The net position would promise the following cashflows: $2.9 million up front plus $24,000 in annual carry ($10 million × 5% − $28.33 million × 1.68%). At zero market risk, according to widely accepted scientific methodologies. No wonder that many hedge funds (which, let's not forget, get 20 percent of performance) would find such windfalls irresistibly enticing. The mathematically conceived delta was shouting from the rooftops of quantification, "Hurry, invest in the equity tranche and revel in the yummy returns, safe in the knowledge that if the value of your play goes down you will not suffer abruptly!" Appealingly appealing.

There are, obviously, two main problems with all this. First, again, the 17 and 6 numbers may be as worthless as a bond issued by Tsarist Russia, as untrustworthy as an Enron balance sheet. They only make sense in the mathematical world dreamed up by the quants and academics behind the credit models. The mathematical delta tells us (rather arrogantly) by how much the value of the position will change as the index moves, but of course in real life the value of the position can do whatever it wants (whatever those behind the demand and supply of the asset collectively decide). Second, the delta ratio hedge assumes that both tranches would respond in the same direction to a change in the index: If spreads widen, both the equity and the mezzanine would be worth less (both would also widen), only that with differing intensities. Thus, a short mezz position (which, in principle, would gain value as the index widens) can be a hedge for a long equity position (which, in principle, would lose value as the index widens). Using the deltas, you can safely sell equity protection by buying mezz protection, and collect a nice windfall as long as the assumptions come true.

On May 5, 2005, this beautiful fantasy was brusquely shattered by that most inconvenient of party poopers, real life. Following the market turmoil that was ignited that day, both legs of the trade went against the trade maker. As credit spreads shot up, the equity tranche widened and the mezz tranche tightened. That is, the riskiest part cheapened while the more conservative slice gained in value. The deltas were rendered useless (not just in magnitude, but also when it came to the arithmetic signs), precisely at the most stressful time when shelter was most unavoidably urgently needed. Huge mark-to-market losses were inflicted. There were reports of wounded hedge funds considering abandoning altogether the now demonstrably hazardous, complex credit space. Many punters apparently grew angry at the models.

What triggered the massacre? What helped bring mathematical sacredness down to earth? What helped expose the unreliability and perilousness of the models? The downgrade, on May 5, by Standard & Poor's of carmakers General Motors and Ford to junk debt status, which inspired a sharp rise in idiosyncratic risk and a widening of credit index spreads. While those spreads eventually returned to precrisis levels, the effects on the correlation market (the market for tranches) proved more structural, with relative tranche valuations adapting to the new reality much more resiliently. Why did Ford and GM have such a large impact? For starters, they are pretty big borrowers and many credit structures contained their names as references. They had also been in trouble for a while, keeping the market nervous and on a constant state of alert. On May 4, such sleep-depriving concerns appeared welcomingly assuaged after über-investor Kirk Kerkorian announced a large investment in GM. Hope reigned supreme among pros. So when S&P dropped the junk bomb the very next day, the short-lived dream was shattered so violently that the whole thing unraveled badly. And it did so in unexpected ways, affecting the values of different CDO tranches in such fashion as to render the mathematical guidance dangerously unhelpful.

Why was it deemed a "correlation crisis"? Because, as we know, the values of the tranches vary, in principle, with the correlation parameter. To say that a long equity position went down is similar to saying that correlation went down in that space; to say that a long mezz position went down is similar to stating that correlation went up in that space. It's simply just another way to word things. Just like option traders in other markets talk about "implied volatility" when they mean price, so in the credit sphere "implied correlation" becomes the term of choice when analyzing changes in value. Just like with the more familiar role of implied volatility in the case of Black-Scholes, it is possible to obtain an implied correlation parameter from traded tranche spreads through the Copula model. (Unfortunately, the commonality extends to the famous "smile"; as in the volatility arena, there seem to be more than one implied correlation quoted by the market, with each tranche level quoting its own different correlation level in direct violation of the Gaussian Copula fine print, an indication that credit traders, like their currency or stocks counterparts, don't seem to entirely trust the purported standard pricing model, and feel that valuation adjustments must be made through manipulating the correlation parameter; or it could simply mean that credit traders are not using the model after all, with values being the result of simple supply-demand interaction and implied correlation being not the purported indication of consensual correlation estimates, but rather an illusion churned out backwards from a formula that is not employed; just like option traders may not be inputting any volatility estimate in any formula when trading, credit traders may not be inputting any correlation estimate in any model; both implied volatility and implied correlation many not mean anything in themselves, certainly not market estimates of volatility and correlation, but they may still be used as communication tools, essentially signaling changes in asset values, either up or down.)

During the crisis, implied correlation on the iTraxx equity fell (its value went down, with up-front reaching 50 percent) from above 20 percent to below 15 percent, just as the index blew out above 55 basis points. Implied correlation on the mezzanine slice also went down as spreads (mostly) tightened. Take the Dow Jones CDX North American investment-grade index: According to the models, as the overall index widened by around 3 basis points in the two days following May 5, the mezzanine tranche should have widened by around 20bp; but, to the surprise and dismay of most traders, it instead tightened by 16bp to 212bp. The so-called correlation curve, which can be thought of as indicative of relative price across the different tranches, became much steeper, as can be seen in the following table. There was a "breakdown in correlation": The decline in equity implied correlation was accompanied by a decline in mezz implied correlation, and delta hedging failed (note that the equity-mezz play was long-long correlation). As long equity plays became despicably unworthy, short mezz plays turned irresistibly wretched. All in a wildly unpredictable fashion.

	May 4	**May 5**	**May 6**	**May 17**	**May 26**
iTraxx 3%	0.23	0.22	0.21	0.16	0.18
iTraxx 6%	0.33	0.32	0.31	0.30	0.29

What exactly caused such theory-negating market movements? Dealers (i.e., investment banks) had apparently placed (i.e., sold) lots of CDO mezzanine tranches into the market in the years prior to the crisis (as much as $132 billion by some accounts, mostly to real money accounts like insurance and pension funds that were attracted to selling mezz protection by the safety-return trade-off on offer), and had decided to warehouse (i.e., not distribute away) the risks. Following the Ford and GM downgrades and the spread blowup in the U.S. auto sector, the increase in credit dispersion (the tendency of credit to move in an uncorrelated fashion) shifted risk away from mezz to equity, with the latter appearing urgently riskier and suffering the consequent market value bloodbath as everyone rushed to buy equity protection. As mezz spreads began to tighten (as mezz tranches began to rally, probably reflecting some kind of *safe haven* effect), those mezz protection-buying dealers needed to hedge their mark-to-market exposures, which in many instances meant going out and selling mezz protection themselves. This sudden accumulation of long mezz trades resulted in a sharp tightening (rather than widening, as delta would suggest) of mezz spreads, just as index spreads were widening like there's no tomorrow.

Naturally, all that activity coincided with, or possibly encouraged, the forced unwinding of equity-mezz punts put on by hedge funds and others, drastically snowballing things in a testament to how trades based on the promise of quantitative certainties can yield pesky turbulence when the math proves wrong. The following table reflects such tranche behavior, highlighting how once the waters had receded (after May 17, the toughest crisis day), a fundamental structural shift had taken place, with equity levels (quoted as up-front payment) remaining above their precrisis numbers (i.e., lower valuations had been solidly established) and mezz levels (quoted as spread) remaining well below their precrisis figures (i.e., higher valuations); this is the truly remarkable aspect of the affair, the equity-mezz dislocation or correlation breakdown that caused delta hedging to fail and so much pain to ensue. We can also see how index reference spreads widened and then reverted to their old selves.

	May 4	May 5	May 6	May 17	May 26
Eur 0–3%	29%	30%	31%	49%	34%
Eur 3–6%	168	158	165	170	122
Eur 6–9%	49	41	41	49	41
Eur 9–12%	25	23	23	34	24.5
Eur 12–22%	16	14	15	24	15
Ref (Eur)	44	43	45	57	44
U.S. 0–3%	44%	46%	47%	62%	51%
U.S. 3–7%	235	229	211	275	185
U.S. 7–10%	55.25	54	47.5	54	51
U.S. 10–15%	28	28	24	30	22
U.S. 15–30%	10.5	11	9	18.5	12.5
Ref (U.S.)	59	60	60	78	60

These developments were very bad news for the Gaussian Copula (and the general reputation of theoretical finance) for several reasons: The model assumes constant and flat correlation, inconsistent with the presence of the smile and the fact that different tranches experienced exaggeratedly dissimilar implied correlations numbers during the crisis; markets are not Gaussianily normal; delta hedging did not work. (Some observers have tried to excuse this by saying that the strange changes in the relative values of the tranches was due to strange behavior in correlations, and that delta captures spread risk alone, not correlation risk, so we shouldn't be too hard on poor mathematical delta; but just like Black-Scholes assumes constant volatility, the Gaussian Copula assumes that correlation does not move, so delta should be the only risk that theoretically matters; also, the correlation alibi may be structurally flawed anyway because the market may not have changed its correlation estimates or used a model at all, with implied correlation simply being a model-transmitted reflection that values changed, and with such variations being entirely explained by index spread swings and the animal spirits behind them, yielding results directly in contradiction with the mathematical delta.)

Did traders collectively decide that correlations had changed and thus their model-inhabiting parameters should be modified accordingly? Maybe. Following this argument (which assumes that traders do wholeheartedly use models when valuing tranches), the dislocations experienced during May 2005 were the result of modified views regarding the probability of joint defaults among the assets in the pool. Tranches' value changes would be fully explained by hastily revised correlation forecasts. Under this scenario, delta should be blamed for not taking correlation swings into account; and the model for assuming that correlation is constant and that the equity's delta and the mezz's delta would move in the same direction following a spread widening.

But there is another possibility. Perhaps traders did not use models that much after all (when pricing CDO tranches, that is; those embarked in the equity play did abide by model-dependent delta), so no updated correlation view was mathematically expressed. Implied correlation simply went up (or down) because tranche values went up (or down), for whatever reasons. Market values changed first, then implied correlation was calculated backwards from the model. In this sense, implied correlation would be wrongly used to explain tranche behavior, which may have had a less-mathematical genesis (staid supply-demand interaction), and could be conveniently employed as alibi for the predominance of models (just like the concept of implied volatility is used in other option markets as "evidence" that traders are using Black-Scholes and inputting a volatility forecast into it). Under this scenario, the models wouldn't just be wrong; they wouldn't *be*. Quite likely not the preferable conclusion for modelers. The *"traders decided to abruptly change their correlation estimates into the model and values thus varied"* tagline would sound better to quants and academics than the alternative *"flesh-and-bones rogues just came to the collective conclusion that tranche A was worth less and that tranche B was worth more; there was no model involved and correlation had nothing to do with it really"* matter-of-factness.

It is one thing for the models to become (just temporarily perhaps) disreputable, and another for the world to hear that technical constructs previously considered unassailably popular are in truth not that much employed by pros in real life. While math propagandists could live with the former argument (hey, it may even be spun into a chance to build an entire new line of better models), they surely can't stand the latter.

One of the most shocking aspects of the credit crisis is that many of the losses that dealers reported were derived from their holdings of senior and super senior CDO tranches, the ones that are assumed to be iron-cladly sheltered from turmoil (and thus the ones that return most modestly relative to its tranche siblings, but still more generously than most other comparably-rated securities). For instance, UBS reported in Q4 2007 losses of almost $8 billion derived from super senior tranches of subprime CDOs. The Swiss bank explained that the deterioration in the U.S. residential mortgage market was more sudden and severe than any such event in recent market history, and that increasing homeowner delinquencies fueled the expectations of future write-downs, thus sinking the market value of structured credit assets. UBS also lost $800 million through their exposure to super senior Alt-A CDOs (less risky mortgages than subprime, though still reasonably suspect). In Q1 2008, UBS lost another $5 billion from its super senior subprime CDOs and $430 million from its super senior Alt-A CDOs. Q2 2008 yielded respective downfalls of $750 million and $42 million, respectively (by that time UBS's total exposures to the U.S. mortgage market had been reduced very substantially, through asset sales and write-downs). What about, say, Merrill Lynch? It recorded losses on its super senior subprime CDOs of almost $15 billion in 2007, $1.7 billion in Q1 2008, and $3.5 billion in Q2 2008. Other investment banks had similar stories regarding the insultingly unsenior-like behavior of what had been assumed to be senior.

This sad, unlikely reality has unavoidably highlighted the dangers associated with tail events, in particular when the mathematical tool that has guided many through the credit market jungle is one built on the assumption that rare events (defined, in this case, as the contingency that a lot of names within the pool would either default or begin to be perceived as serious candidates for default) do not happen with outlandish regularity.

The rating agencies that awarded AAA wrapping to those senior tranches also used Gaussian Copula-type methodology when coming up with their (back then) revered letter soups. As a gadget that yields joint default probabilities and correlations that assign very little chance to a lot of bad credit news taking place concurrently, the model facilitated things quite a bit. If you want to make sure that three straight As are churned out from the mathematical sausage machine, you could do much worse than mixing your ingredients with the Copula shaker. The analytical rating framework of the three major agencies was similar in the years preceding the crisis. Fitch, Moody's, and Standard & Poor's all applied the seminal Merton 1974 structural model and derived correlated default values with the Gaussian Copula model. The differences between the agencies' methodologies lay in the way each derived the core input parameters of individual asset default probability, individual asset recovery rate, and asset correlation.

Merton's model borrows heavily from the Black-Scholes-Merton option pricing theory (published a year earlier) to derive the probability of default for a given company, defined as the probability of zero equity (i.e., the probability of the value of the assets being smaller than the debt). This model, which contains certain limitations, has been extended by mathematicians to fit the brave new world of structured credit. Such framework is the one used by the agencies to arrive at default probabilities. Once those are arrived at, the Copula machine is used to derive the (multivariate Normal) joint distribution. Then Monte Carlo simulation yields a multitude of possible default scenarios which form the basis for the ratings of the tranches. The joint default distribution that results from the Gaussian Copula approach, as we know, has a lognormal shape. The probability of both few defaults and many defaults is low. In other words, those tranches at the top of the capital structure (those that only suffer when a lot of defaults take place) would be assumed to be pretty much risk-free, and thus gloriously worthy of that most sacred of adornments, the AAA crown.

And let's be crystal clear: The real factors behind the unprecedented mayhem that has had unprecedented consequences were the vast mortgage-related CDO positions that investment banks accumulated in their balance sheets. We would have survived pretty unscathed if the only piece of bad news had been the default per se of a few subprime borrowers in the United States. Without the uncontained transformation of those loans into convoluted securities, the pain would have been so much more acceptable. It was the devastation caused by the unmitigated tumble in that CDO market from early 2007 that caused the monstrous trading floor losses that unleashed the hell of billions-sized quarterly write-downs, the initial freezing of the interbank lending market, and the initial financials-driven stock markets roller coaster, which in turn contributed decisively to the all-encompassing spreading of fear and the disintegration of confidence in the world's credit and equity markets that ultimately sank Wall Street's most venerable institutions, engulfed stocks in an unending volatility nightmare, and restricted lending across the board, which in turned forced governments to intervene and to socialize the economy in ways that would have made Lenin proud. Without the

CDOs, Hank Paulson's bald head would not have been a familiar fixture on TV sets around the globe.

Without the reassuringly reassuring three straight As, that devilish side of the CDO business would never have taken flight. (Ratings played a key role in the very birth of the overall CDO segment; the legitimacy provided by the rating agencies was a decisive boost in the early days of an industry that in less than 10 years reached a size in excess of $2 trillion.) Not only are many investors, like money market funds, prevented from investing in anything less than super senior, but banks had a very strong incentive to hold very highly rated, and yet amicably yielding, assets given the friendly regulatory treatment (in terms of capital charges under Basel II). In other words, without the compliance of the rating agencies the poster child of the credit crisis would have been a poor, unemployed, rural American family saying good-bye to the six-bedroom mansion of which it had been the unseemly inhabitant for the prior two years thanks to a NINJA loan offered by the local thrift, not the disappearance of Bear Stearns or a hastily approved $7 billion bail-out package. The AAA-ing of subprime CDOs guaranteed that the malaise would compete with 1929's for historical supremacy. And mathematical finance, in the shape of its proud Gaussian Copula creation, helped a lot in that respect (at least one notable source suggests that the default probabilities and correlation assumptions under the Copula approach were more relaxed than under prior rating methodologies, leading to more relaxed creditworthiness verdicts).

The latest crisis to have afflicted the financial universe has, of course, been indistinctly labeled a "credit crisis," a "subprime crisis," and an "investment banking crisis." Such denominations would naturally not be off the mark. And yet, as much as any of those things, the crisis has also been foremost a "ratings crisis." In fact, without the latter, the other members of the crisis family may not have grown up to be so big. It is quite likely that never before have credit ratings proved to be so disastrously wrong. On so many occasions during the past two years, and so successively so, securities soberly deemed AAA were rendered to be very close to worthless. As a leading expert put it, the rating agencies dramatically failed not once, but twice: First, they assigned overoptimistic ratings to so-called Residential Mortgage Backed Securities (RMBS), the original securitizations of the residential loans (mainly subprime, given their recent predominance and the extra yield that such higher-risk assets promised; as we all know, a big motivation for the drive into structured credit products was a desperate search for enhanced returns during a prolonged era of low official interest rates) originating mostly from the U.S.; second, they again assigned overoptimistic ratings to the CDOs of those RMBS, or CDOs of ABS (as in Asset-Backed Securities), in effect securitizations of securitizations, or re-securitizations. Ninety percent of the CDOs that were downgraded by the agencies in 2007 were CDOs of ABS. The performance has been so miserly that few players and observers may believe in ratings anymore (this is reflected, for instance, by behavior in the credit default swaps and bond markets with yield and spread levels totally at odds with what ratings purport to indicate). That is, the ratings-enabled crisis may have claimed the agencies themselves as victims. Another (quite high-profile) casualty of the misplaced faith in quantitative finance.

Let's delve a bit deeper into the disappointing performance of the agencies. For instance, in a report released in 2005 and 2006, Moody's showed that the performance of BBB-rated CDO tranches had not performed better than BB-rated ones. For humble nonconnoisseurs such charge may seem harmlessly innocuous, but in fact it is a big deal. Triple B is the last line of defense of the so-called "investment grade" world; anything less aristocratic (i.e., BB and lower) would belong to the much less dignified, much more plebeian, much less illustrious "speculative grade" world (really just a better-sounding substitute for the more descriptively accurate "junk"). Not being able to discriminate between, say, AAA and AA would be much milder in comparison. You have to be extra careful when you discriminate between BBB and BB, because the implications are particularly serious. When you say "BBB" you better mean it and you better make sure that the tools that allowed you to be so open-mouthed are notoriously sound, because a lot is on the line. You can hurt a lot of people if BBB and BB turn out to be the same thing. On the one hand, many investors are not allowed to invest in anything below investment grade, but if the BBB stuff ends up behaving like the BB stuff, the perceived agencies-provided security blanket would have been a complete farce. The investment may not have been categorized as junk, but it did behave as such. Secondly, capital charges can be determined by credit ratings and they can be especially taxing for those securities placed in junk territory; if the BB stuff turns out to act like the BBB stuff then plenty of people may rightly feel cheated and overcharged.

In early 2007, the market suddenly and brusquely reached the conclusion that the ratings could no longer be trusted. The disagreements were exaggeratedly accentuated in the crucially relevant BBB tranches (with similarly-rated tranches showing differences in pricing of almost 1,000 basis points), but could also be detected in other segments. Such until-then-unprecedented discrepancies voiced an unassailable message: CDO ratings are very, very wrong.

If the bad news on the CDO front (which would lead directly to the unleashing of hell that has come to be known as the credit crisis) began in earnest in the Spring of 2007, the underlying problem began to rear its ugly head a couple of years before, in the decidedly less sophisticated U.S. subprime lending arena. Significant increases in delinquency rates over there started to take place around mid-2005, and by the end of 2006 the numbers looked worryingly somber, with 14 percent and 10 percent of subprime adjustable rate loans and fixed rate loans, respectively, deserving the delinquent label. Interestingly, a major factor behind that sudden outburst in naughty behavior may have been the subprime CDO business itself. At the time, the demand for BBB mortgage-backed bonds by CDO arrangers (hungry to satisfy their yield-hungry customers) was insatiable, and this raw need may have translated into a sharp decline in lending standards in the already notoriously loose subprime universe, even including the possibility that sound borrowers may have been misled into taking riskier mortgages. Of course, we know that a lot of those CDO of ABS tranches were kept by the investment banks on their balance sheets, not distributed away to other investors, but here the rationale for furiously dabbling on subprime junk was equally solid.

As was mentioned earlier, it is likely that those BBB high-yield bonds that became the collateral pool for the CDOs (the illiquid assets that make up the structured vehicle; in the case of subprime CDOs, the ABS bonds typically rated between BB and AA, being BBB on average) were never "investment grade" to begin with. Some may wonder, what's the big deal about that? I mean, I can understand why there would be a vested interest in having the actual tranches receive BBB and better, but couldn't the agencies have just given out those favorable ratings anyway, without having to also be overly generous with the underlying asset-backed securities? Why the need for such double wrongness?

There is a key reason why it was important that the ABS ratings were good (and not only that it's clearly easier to deem a tranche AAA if you haven't previously labeled the underlying assets as junk): The CDO structurers finance the purchase of the underlying assets (the subprime loans and so on) by issuing bonds; it is tantamount that those bonds yield as little as possible (i.e., that the costs of financing the CDO are as unassuming as possible). A time-tested way to get lower yields is to obtain very high credit ratings, and it is certainly easier to be endowed with generous ratings if your assets are high quality. In other words, by being generous when rating the ABS, the agencies guaranteed that the CDO arrangers could get cheap funding and that business could proceed. (So-called CDO trusts made large net-present-value profits by buying high-yield assets financed with low-yield debt; and according to the rating agencies, at no substantial risk. Of course the agencies had it wrong both times: Neither the ABSs nor the CDOs were so trustworthy. Some have said that the monetary incentives for being generous were far too tasty for the agencies, given the fees to be earned from successfully arranged CDOs; for instance, Moody's made more than 40 percent of its revenues from structured credit rating). That is, the agencies failed three, not two, times: when rating the original ABSs, when rating the subsequent CDO tranches, and when rating the bonds issued by the structuring and packaging CDO trusts (and the famous *structured investment vehicles*, or SIVs).

The rating agencies began to react to the voracious deterioration in the subprime mortgage market during the summer of 2006, issuing several warnings. Moody's was apparently the first to jump the gun and in November downgraded subprime loans that had been issued on that very same year. In February 2007, Standard & Poor's unprecedentedly placed on watch transactions closed just the prior year. By Q3 2007, S&P reported that 66 percent of CDOs of ABSs had been downgraded (44 percent downgraded from AAA to junk, including default, sometimes in a matter of a few days). During the second week of July 2007 alone, S&P downgraded more than $7 billion of mortgage-backed securities sold in 2005 and 2006, with Moody's soon reciprocating by slashing ratings on close to $20 billion in 2006-originated securities (many of them deemed AAA at origination), blaming it all on the poor performance of such loans. Not to be left out, Fitch also participated in the subprime downgrade fest.

The carnage continued as 2007 progressed. In October, S&P down-graded residential ABSs totaling $22 billion, and during November and

December Moody's axed another $50 billion of shaky debt, while plac-
ing more than an additional $100 billion under review. In all, between
Moody's, S&P, and Fitch the notional amount of CDOs of ABSs downgraded in 2007 approximated $250 billion. Hundreds of billions more
were announced for 2008. And, again, on many occasions the haircut
was not just a simple trim, subjecting AAA tranches to the indignity of
junk denomination in the blink of an eye. Up to this crisis, AAA was
supposed to have stood for solid stability (think U.S. Treasuries and the
World Bank). Not anymore.

Clearly, something was amiss in ratings-land. Such changes in opinion
(forced by unavoidably visible market developments) were simply too
brusquely brusque. Obviously, the methodology was revealed to have
been obstinately flawed. Both joint defaults and recovery dependencies
were sensationally inappropriately modeled, and that is why previously
considered unassailable super senior subprime tranches were wiped
out almost as soon as much-riskier equity tranches suffered that fate.
In vintage Gaussian Copula fashion, default correlation revealed itself
as having been severely underestimated. As in so many other similar
happenstances in the financial past, by not considering the possibility
of the Black Swan, theory led to a bloodbath. Also in historical fashion,
looking at the rearview mirror did not help much. When calculating
individual default probabilities, recovery values, and asset correlations,
agencies borrowed from past evidence. But yesterday is not a good guide
to tomorrow in the markets, particularly to tomorrow's very likely and
very uniquely idiosyncratic rare event. Let's thank the crisis for forcefully
providing yet another reminder of that basic fact.

So, what was it? Did the agencies know that what they were churning out was crap but went on nonetheless blinded by the golden calf of
stupendous CDO fees? Or did the agencies honestly believe that their
methods were sound and were caught completely off guard by unforeseen developments? In either case, reliance on quantitative finance was
the convenient enabler. By relying on complex analytical trickeries, the
agencies achieved two things: One, they provided scientifically sounding
essential support for the growth of the low-quality-mortgages-backed
CDO business; two, they provided scientifically sounding legitimacy for
the out-of-control speculating on those CDOs that ultimately led the
world into untold chaos. Whether the mathematics were truly abided by
or simply employed as an effectively deceitful smoke screen is not the

main issue for the purposes of our discussion (though it would be particularly sinister, naturally, if everybody involved had been theory-agnostic
all along and the math had been borrowed and selected simply as conduit
to obtain the desired results and to hypnotize investors, regulators, and
assorted outsiders; in this light, the Copula approach would have been
chosen not on account of its engineering beauty and a sincere belief
in its wonders, but precisely because its proclivity to rule out extreme
events would be a nice way to assure that tranches backed by very toxic
stuff could receive high enough ratings and the subprime game could be
played out in earnest). The inescapable main point is that overt reliance
on flawed advanced technicalities obstinately facilitated reckless and misinformed punting, and the financial industry and the overall economy
paid dearly as a result.

A key lesson from the CDO ratings debacle is that we shouldn't allow
critically influential institutions (like, well, rating agencies) to outsource
their decision making to quantitative wizardry. Particularly, of course,
when the magic dust can be obscenely improper or easily made so
(in a particularly poignant case, S&P for a while rated CDOs under
the assumption of zero interindustry correlation, that is no dependence
whatsoever between credit names in different sectors; obviously, such
assumption outrightly diminishes the perceived risks of well-diversified
asset pools, going a long way towards the obtainment of very favourable
ratings; facing heavy criticisms for such an unseemly assumption, including accusations of falling prey to "ratings shopping" by CDO arrangers
and trying to win business from the competition by guaranteeing a most
friendly result, S&P had no option but to change its correlation assumption from 0 to 5 percent in late 2005, instantly instigating the placing
on watch of several tranches priorly rated by that same agency, on many
cases carrying the AAA denomination).

So reliance on quantitative models (whether honest or deceitful)
caused the worst credit ratings disaster ever, which collateral damage included the destruction of Wall Street and the almost sinking of the world's
economy. Our blind devotion to theoretical concoctions (especially if
sponsored by rigorous-looking individuals with PhDs from prestigious
universities) helped. If we didn't succumb so easily to the siren songs of
mathematical sobriety, the ratings horror may have not happened, and
the CDO nightmare might have not occurred. Rating agencies could
happily trot along surrounded by a sea of equations because we take

it as an article of faith that more math is better than less math, that more "rigor" is better than less rigor. They knew that few would doubt the unassailable wisdom of going super quant. Only an impudent rogue could question the appropriateness of such high-tech sophisticatedness.

Now that the superquant stuff has been exposed as a hoax, and our blindness as exceedingly self-wounding, what? What can we do? The CDO of ABS business is busy taking care of its own reform, essentially shrinking itself into oblivion. But what about the rating agencies? Well, regulators should look into shaking that world up more than a notch. As for us, let's propose something bold: Stop basing such important decisions on impossibly hopeless analytical machinations! Some, in typical quant-lobby style, would protest, "we can't stop using math, what's the alternative, there's no alternative." No, there is. It's called experience-honed common sense and intuition. The math had its chance, and couldn't have gone any wronger. The bar has been set exponentially low by the models and the statistical games. I'm sure that good old human judgment is up to the task of raising it up again from such immense depths (we can't be *that* bad). If anything, by departing from quantland we would at the very least prevent convoluted constructs from being used as intimidating alibis to justify stamping a "AAA" on a bundle of poisonous, mayhem-prone, NINJA loans.

The unavoidable conclusion is that the Gaussian Copula model (the mathematical driving force behind, certainly, the credit ratings and possibly the market values assigned to the complex structures most directly responsible for the crisis; and, surely, delta-hedging strategies like the ones that malfunctioned in the 2005 meltdown) has proven to have unsavory effects. The apparatus is simply wrong and it has contributed to too much wrongness. Another loud defeat for quantitative finance in the real world.

In this light, we shouldn't perhaps be judged too harshly for proposing that the model be hidden (under lock and key) in the drawer of practical irrelevance. At least one internationally renowned expert would concur, *"The most common argument that we have heard from people who disagree with us [that is, die-hard Gaussian Copula defenders] is that i) everybody uses it, and ii) it is very easy to use. As a matter of principle we endorse the view that those two arguments, in no particular order, are probably the worst possible justifications ever*

offered for anything; clear evidence that there is something rotten in Denmark!
To sum up: the one-factor Gaussian Copula method is a flawed technique
to model something (default correlation) that does not exist—two very good
reasons to move on and leave all this correlation/copula nonsense behind. Future
efforts should be focused on estimating default probabilities better. Period. End
of Story."

Interestingly, fanatical Gaussian Copulists would counterattack by
pointing out that, hey, pros certainly know that the model is founda-
tionally not exactly right, but can correct for such shortcomings through
the very useful built-in self-correcting mechanism that it is magnificently
endowed with. This in itself, the apologists would argue, would be reason
enough to continue tagging along in Copula company. If the less-than-
right model can be easily righted, should we really disrespectfully label
it as the wrong approach?

Of course, the market does seem to know that the Gaussian Copula
probabilistic approach is not entirely accurate. The correlation smile tells
us so: Even if we assume that the model is widely used as a valuation tool,
pros would be tweaking it so that it delivers more acceptable outputs (e.g.,
ones that take rare events into account). The correlation parameter is
manipulated in order to compensate for the non-Normality of rebellious
real life. While the model assumes constant and flat basket correlation,
implied correlation for the different tranches quotes ununiformly, with a
grin-like shape developing as seniority is enhanced, a clear testament that
traders believe that less risky slices deserve a spread bump (i.e., should be
worth less) as the possibility that a large number of assets get in trouble
is deemed more weighty by the market than by the model. Interestingly,
the credit smile grins on both sides, with equity implied correlation also
getting a bump, which, as we know, in this case symbolizes a gain, not
a loss, in value (see Figure 4.1). In sum, those who matter appear to
be confident that basket default correlation can be very high, with both
extreme outcomes (vastly numerous or starvingly limited instances of bad
surprises) likely to be shockingly prevalent. Needless to say, the credit
crisis showed the wisdom of such revisionist views.

But the point remains that the model is wrong. Even if it can be easily
manipulated into "rightfulness," such convenience should not count as a
respectability-granting compliment. It should, rather, be seen as the conduit through which unrepentant criticism towards the model is ruthlessly
transmitted. Many (including, at one point, the author of this book) have

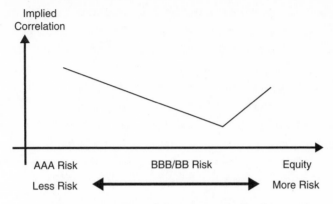

Figure 4.1 Typical Correlation Smile Curve

seen in the volatility smile a glorious vindication for the Black-Scholes formula, a symbol of its victory, the reason why the model is embraced and popular. The mathematical device may be imperfect, but it contains the seeds of its own correction, a built-in self-fixing mechanism that allows traders to heal the theory from its inescapable structural flaws. According to this view, the smile would be friendly smiling at the model. This, I now think, is a wrongful interpretation. Quite to the contrary, the smile would be frowning at the model. A symbol of failure, not success. A symbol of rejection, not embracement. If people truly loved the model, there would be no reason for corrective manipulative measures. And, by the way, through such manipulation, traders are essentially making sure that the model used would no longer be the original, whether Black-Scholes or Gaussian Copula. When something that was originally engineered to have a flat correlation structure is transformed into something churning out a smiling structure, the new thing would be so different from the original that it should no longer bear the same name. Even when traders are using a tranche pricing model originally called Gaussian Copula, it no longer is the Gaussian Copula model.

Even quants are now coming out of the closet, irresistibly impulsed by the impossible-to-ignore neglect of the model's soul by market forces. A new breed of credit models is being unshyly put forward, in a development probably fueled by the combination of a practical desire to correct a malfunctioning machine and a personal ambition to replace David Li as the analytical godfather in this area. Even before the crisis hit, some dealers had been pondering a move away from Gaussian Copula models to those that consider a heightened possibility of tail events. *"Some credit models have not done terribly well recently,"* said Martin Baxter, a leading London-based quant. *"Under the Gaussian distribution, extreme events are slightly rarer than they are in practice."* He offered this as justification for his bank switching from Gaussianland to other models that assign more weight to rare events.

Other modelers are going a step further and, rather than contenting themselves with making a few probabilistic modifications to established structures, are peddling a whole new set of constructs that would claim to be able to capture all and any factors affecting defaults. Likely fed up with mathematical monuments erected on the shaky foundations of a handful of assumptions, and that get torn apart in the arena of public opinion when the inevitable breakdown of one or all of the assumptions takes place, these ambitious theorists don't want to leave anything to chance and seem to pretend to insulate credit models from any possible further attacks. By introducing a so-called "frailty factor" into the inevitably deemed "frailty model," the hope is to be able to capture any unobservable variable that might have an impact on outcomes. In other words, this new modeling technique tries to isolate itself from the habitual critique that the math does not reflect reality by, almost literally, accounting for anything that could affect defaults or credit spreads. The credit carnage witnessed since the summer of 2007 certainly emphasizes the importance of trying to capture the myriad of factors that contribute to making extreme tail events such a harmful reality.

If you can't observe those unobservable factors that drive credit events, how can you model them? Do you just make them up? Not really. You characterize the frailty factor borrowing from (unexplained) historical default clustering. By doing so, you hope that your model is capable of predicting default correlations much more accurately than humbler one-factor, or two- or three-factor, models. In a way, you are trying to insulate your number-crunching from the unexpected surprises that typically descend on credit markets and that can't be captured by simple models which outputs depend on factors that are not just limited in number, but possibly entirely irrelevant as indicators of future happenstances. Frailty models are more analytically sophisticated, but at the same time their existence is a testament to the tiringly habitual failings of analytics. A forceful recognition by quanty folks that models are, after all, quite imperfect.

An example of a frailty (and its importance) comes handily from the credit crisis: the horrendously lax ways in which subprime loan documentation and borrower credit quality were recorded and assessed. Clearly, it seems too much to ask of a modeler (particularly those theorizing from the secluded confines of an isolated, dim-lighted university office) that he should have the ability and God-like vision to ascertain the shady lending practices taking place in back alleys throughout the four corners of the United States (and yet, of course, such events are the ones that matter the most, so what good are models that stand no chance at capturing that which really, or even solely, matters? but let's leave this point for now). But the new frailty-encompassing mathematical kids on the block attempt to precisely capture such inscrutably uncapturable phenomena. They borrow heavily from the past, something that may deliver less than stellar results.

Alistair McLeod, associate director in portfolio management at Barclays Capital in London, put it like this when asked about the applicability of frailty models: *"You're making a brave assumption that the patterns of default you've observed in the past are likely to repeat in the future. One should be very cautious about doing so."* Such charge is, certainly, applicable to many of the sacred cows of finance theory. Frailty models, though, lend themselves particularly well to such well-trodden complaint. Simply put, those unobservable, unidentifiable, undetectable factors are, well, unobservable, unidentifiable, undetectable. There is certainly no guarantee that the unobservable event that mattered yesterday will matter (or even repeat itself) tomorrow. Lax subprime lending was the key factor in the latest crisis, but how can we be sure that it will be a deciding variable going forward? Should the very idiosyncratic odd variables behind the 2007 credit crisis be important for measuring tomorrow's expected default correlation?

Andy Payne, managing director in the portfolio management group at Barclays Capital, emphasized this point by noting that sources of credit turmoil have varied heavily through the past few decades, *"With hindsight, if we look at the peaks, where clustered defaults happen, the drivers of those defaults were very different. In 1991, it was recession and a collapse in property prices. If we look at the early part of this decade, it was accounting fraud."* Such drawbacks throw cold water onto the ability of frailty methodologies to predict the next waves of (predictably idiosyncratically idiosyncratic in themselves) clustered defaults and tail losses. How can one forecast the future behavior of factors that are, as of yet, mysteriously unknown? *"As a practical matter, introducing frailty factors makes default-rate forecasting more difficult since one needs to forecast the future path of unobserved latent variables. Frailty modelling can be important in quantifying the uncertainty surrounding model output, but it may be of limited use in actually generating model forecasts,"* asserts Albert Metz, a senior credit officer at Moody's.

Possibly the best-known (though not the pioneering) work on frailty models has been that of top credit theorist Darrell Duffie. In his revolution-inciting "Frailty Correlated Default" paper, co-authored with three Wall Street quants, the Stanford University mathematical finance guru opens up the debate in clarifyingly direct terms: *"The probability of extreme default losses on portfolios of U.S. corporate debt is much greater than would be estimated under the standard assumption that default correlation arises only from exposure to observable risk factors. . . . [C]onventionally based estimates are downward biased. . . . This paper provides a more realistic assessment of the risk of large default losses than had been available with prior methodologies."* As we have seen earlier, conventional credit models derive conditional default probabilities for a pool of assets based on the individual probabilities, a correlation estimate, and one or a few more extra factors (typically, the economy's performance). This, Duffie and his friends assert, is not enough and produces substandard results. The underlying borrowers may be exposed to common risk factors, the effects of which are not captured by the individual distributions or asset correlation levels, resulting in a poor estimation of the actual portfolio loss distribution. Since it is not possible to ex-ante identify all relevant observable variables, *"Our approach is to directly allow for unobserved risk factors whose time-series behavior and whose posterior conditional distribution can both be estimated from the available data by maximum-likelihood techniques,"* proclaim the theorists.

The main idea is to assume that default probabilities depend on several observable factors (so-called *distance to default*, a volatility-adjusted measure of leverage; trailing one-year firm-specific stock returns; three-month U.S. Treasury Bill rates; and trailing S&P 500 returns) and on two unobservable factors (one firm-specific, and another of macroeconomic dimensions—the real frailty variable, which is the main focus). They use 25 years and the data of almost 3,000 firms. Using the data on observed variables, an econometric exercise estimates the sensitivity of portfolio loss to each of the selected factors (both observed and unobserved). Through these machinations, it is possible to obtain the theoretical impact of each variable. The results show that all factors carry importance.

Once this econometric intelligence is gathered, the distribution of the frailty process is calculated (the frailty variable is allowed to dynamically change over time as credit realities change). Back-testing the accuracy of the joint default probabilities with and without including the common frailty effect, the study finds that the latter underperform when it comes to detecting portfolio losses. For instance, for the period January 1998 to December 2002 (which witnessed 195 real defaults), the no-common-frailty-thanks models assigned zero chance to the event of more than 200 defaults taking place; in contrast, the I-love-common-frailties approach would have predicted around 215 and 265 at the 95 and 99 percent confidence levels.

Let the brainiac authors themselves sum it all up: *"This paper finds significant evidence among U.S. corporates of a common unobserved source of default risk that increases default correlation and extreme portfolio loss risk above and beyond that implied by observable common and correlated macroeconomic and firm-specific sources of default risk. We offer a new model on corporate default intensities in the presence of a time-varying latent frailty factor. . . . Applying this model to data we find that corporate default rates vary over time well beyond levels that can be explained by a model that only includes observables. . . . A test for data between 1980 and 2003 shows that a model without frailty significantly underestimates the probability of extreme positive as well negative events in portfolios of credit risk, while a model with frailty gives a more accurate assessment."*

Notwithstanding the brilliance of the work, we shouldn't be too shocked by the conclusions. We knew that Gaussian Copula type of approaches underestimate the likelihood of extreme credit scenarios, thus the presence of the smile as a timely reminder. We fanatically suspected that a bunch of observable factors could not account for the whole explanation as to default occurrences, so it makes only sense that a statistical analysis that includes parameters deemed "everything else" would certify the importance of such unobservables. But once those beliefs have been confirmed through enchanting analytical prowess, what next? It is not enough to say that defaults are explained by a bunch of mysterious stuff. It seems hard to rely on a model which number one message is that modeling may be utterly hopeless and that offers as unique solution an all-encompassing, take-on-faith wastebasket into which anything not captured by what's observable gets to be dumped. As was indicated before, frailty models could be useful when assessing standard model error (by the size of the waste), but perhaps not as valuable as forecasting tools. That is, as models.

In any case, we need to be ready to extract practical conclusions in case frailty constructions do eventually reign supreme inside trading floors. There are two obvious potential consequences to this, one tentatively good and the other demonstrably bad. On the one hand, since frailty models generate more conservative loss estimates (i.e., those pesky impacting tail events are, presumably, more effectively captured), their embracing by dealers should result in higher VaR figures, with the consequential increase in capital charges. Similarly, structures previously endowed with AAA ratings (on account of their perceived modest clustered defaults risk) may lose such shiny endowment if we applied frailty methodology. This theoretically charged dose of enhanced conservatism could prove quite helpful. Had the market embraced frailtiness fever a few years back, senior CDO tranches may have been designed with prudent overcollateralization, or had their ratings and prices drop, putting a break on the bubbly buildup of positions. Or equity tranches may have become more expensive (i.e., less tasty for protection sellers, as the bump up in theoretical correlation yields the investment less risky), maybe discouraging the avalanche into the equity-mezz trades that ended up causing so much trouble. In general, the model could have forced a retrenchment in excessive risk-taking, put a brake on speculation-gone-wild, dampened transactional delirium, in so doing limiting the odds and impact of a massive credit-driven crisis. That would be a welcome contribution from frailty concoctions.

But there is a darker side, too. Frailty models could result in sloppy risk management, as people might feel unduly overconfident in the assumption that all possible risk factors have been taken into account, so there's nothing to worry about. Traders and their supervisors may become careless and stop paying close attention to possible sources of bad news. A major point of this book is that it is when they create a false sense of scientifically backed security that models can be summarily dangerous. This is true of the Gaussian Copula approach, and therefore irredeemably truer in the case of models that purport to correct past quantitative failings by making the pretentious claim of being able to estimate all that we can't see. The potential for hubristic trouble could be exactingly calamitous.

■ *Chapter 5* ■

Blah VaR Blah

■ Insalubrious charlatanism ■ Tracking a true culprit ■ Credit truths ■ A long rap sheet of evidence ■ The police are in on it ■

I magine that you are thinking about buying a new car. Eager for tempting alternatives, you walk into a dealership, where a smiling salesperson instantly grabs your arm and offers his unlimited assistance. You emphasize that, while design and gasoline consumption are important factors, you most care about safety. The salesperson replies "No worries!" He has the perfect risk-management vehicle in store, if only you would please follow him. Confronted with a view of the car, you can't but confess to yourself that the design is certainly slick, and, from the manual, the engineering appears to be technically sophisticated. You are almost sold, just a tiny unresolved detail. "What about the air bags?" you press. "Do they work?" The salesperson loses none of his confidence: "Of course they do, all the time. Except, that is, under extreme circumstances. If you suffer an accident, they won't work. But hey, what's the chance of that happening, eh?"

Many readers would probably concur if someone proposed to endow such imaginary car salesperson with the "charlatan" adjective. After hearing that you would be protected except when most needed, you would turn off your ears to the incessant charlatanism. The salesperson may continue to make the pitch unabated, but you would have ceased to listen. No extra attention should be wasted on someone capable of peddling such fraud.

The financial landscape has been dominated in the past 15 years or so by a device that promises to act as an air bag at all times bar exceptional times. In this case, however, the sales pitch has not been outrightly rejected. Far from it. While some influential figures have indeed accused its peddlers of charlatanism, this has not prevented a large number of customers from succumbing and buying the car, apparently believing the safety measures to be more than satisfactory and worthy of embracement. Value at Risk (VaR) may only provide a picture (doubtably reliable in itself) of "all the time" financial risks, leaving aside extreme scenarios, but it is hard to deny its popularity. Banks, hedge funds, public entities, corporates, asset managers, and regulators all over the world follow this risk guide rigorously, and base many of their most important decisions on its dictates. Protest all you will about charlatan salesmanship, but the VaR air bag has been a hit ever since it appeared in the market. Far too many people have simply bought into it.

All this may change post the credit crisis. The wreckage has been so fatal that the many VaR flaws that have been exposed along the destructive path cannot be ignored or conveniently swept under the carpet of convenient conventionalism. VaR possibly is facing the gravest challenge to its continuing relevance, and that's saying quite a lot, given the less-than-perfect historical record of the artifact (particularly, naturally, during times of stress). As hedge fund manager David Einhorn says, *"Risk management is the air bag that must always work, but only in the multi-sigma event where you have an accident."* In other words, the complete opposite of what VaR promises and delivers. For a long while prior to the summer of 2007, the financial highway offered placid routes and not many accidents were recorded. VaR worked under such conditions. Then, suddenly, the road became much less accommodating, and drivers who had previously been able to freely speed ahead were now suffering mortal accidents, exceedingly often. VaR miserably failed under those conditions. The much-needed air bag refused to inflate.

What is VaR? It's a model-based number that purports to indicate likely maximum future losses for a portfolio of financial assets based on past historical data and certain probabilistic assumptions about how the markets work. VaR assumes a world ruled by normality, where rare events are extremely improbable. It believes that the past is a good guide as to the future. Borrowing from standard finance theory, it depends on two variables (standard deviations and correlations) that only make existential sense under normality. It paints a picture of how dispersed (*volatile*) financial markets have been during a prespecified prior period, and then translates that estimate into expected results going forward, using a very large degree of confidence but not quite yet 100 percent. That is, VaR does not capture the more unlikely setbacks.

The problem with this is not just that the effects of rare events may be devastating, but that the normal world of VaR assumes an unrealistically low chance that those happenstances will happen. In other words, the VaR number (generally purported to be a reliable guide to the market risks faced by a financial institution) excludes the potentially most troublesome scenarios and assigns an unseemly high probability to the (selected) past repeating itself.

No wonder, then, that VaR models failed during the crisis. Markets spectacularly revealed themselves to be non-normal, and the historical sample periods used in the calculation (which range from a few months to several years, depending on the institution) did not contain some of the things that uniquely took place beginning in the second half of 2007. Both volatility and correlation behaved in insultingly different ways from the recent past. The risk forecast proved spectacularly lacking. The official guiding light misguided aplenty. Neither the likelihood nor the speed or the severity of the downfall were predicted.

But before we delve deep into the actual details of how VaR did not succeed during the crisis, let's anticipate a central theme of this book: VaR not only fails at measuring, preventing, or predicting humongous risks, it can actually help create them. By leaving aside the extremes and operating from a philosophical platform that vastly underestimates the (real) probability of rare events, VaR can yield numbers that are so low that complacency is unmitigatingly bred and risk taking runs amok. Trades can be shown to be almost negligibly risky at the 95 or 99 percent (or even 99.9 percent) confidence level, thus affording the perfect stamp of approval. Not only would the trade be executed, little capital would be set against it, creating in effect a largely leveraged position for the institution. In other words, the mathematics of VaR would have encouraged the firm to enter into situations where bad news (even slightly so) can cause a lot of damage and manufacture enormous losses, certainly way above those indicated by the glorified risk radar. These types of positions are the stuff market crises are made of: A negative development in some obscure corner of the financial world gets translated into a wide-reaching massacre through huge, highly levered gambles. Once the mayhem takes place, VaR limits are naturally breached, rendering its prior outputs utterly useless. That is, VaR will show a stubborn tendency to be misguiding as long as VaR is.

David Einhorn is one of those who believe that VaR was a major force behind the credit crisis. *"'Now we understand why investment banks held enormous portfolios of super-senior triple A-rated whatever. These securities had very small returns. However, the risk models said they had trivial VaR, because the possibility of credit loss was calculated to be beyond the VaR threshold. This meant that holding them required only a trivial amount of capital, and a small return over a trivial amount of capital can generate an almost infinite revenue-to-equity ratio. VaR-driven risk management encouraged accepting a lot of bets that amounted to accepting the risk that heads wouldn't come up seven times in a row,'* states this unrepentant VaR critic. *Unfortunately,"* as Einhorn notes, *"In the current crisis it has turned out that the unlucky outcome was far more likely than the backtested models predicted. What is worse, the various supposedly remote risks that required trivial capital are highly correlated; you don't just lose on one bad bet in this environment, you lose on many of them for the same reason. This is why in recent periods the investment banks had quarterly write-downs that were many times the firmwide modeled VaR."*

Interestingly, regulators may have decisively facilitated trouble here. For the past decade or so, VaR has been embraced by the regulatory community as not only the widely accepted risk radar, but also, crucially, as the widely accepted (and required) method for determining capital charges (i.e., how much cash and other liquid assets financial institutions should commit to their trading book).

More recent developments made things more poignant. Take the United States' Securities and Exchange Commission (SEC). In what some have salaciously deemed the "Bear Stearns Future Insolvency Act," the SEC established in 2004 a rule that allowed large broker-dealers to use their own risk management practices for capital requirements purposes, recognizing outright that charges were destined to be lower under the new approach. VaR was predictably sanctioned as the main method of calculation, but the ruling went beyond that. Illiquid securities ("no ready market securities" in the jargon), which previously would have been subjected to 100 percent deduction for capital purposes, were now afforded the same VaR treatment as more conservative and conventional alternatives: If the mathematically driven number happens to be low, the required capital charge will be low. In other words, engaging in unapologetically risky activities instantly became much more cheap and convenient. In this sense, perhaps we shouldn't be surprised by the fact that financial institutions have gorged on less-than-perfectly-liquid, übercomplex stuff. The VaR-transmitted regulatory encouragement was probably too tempting to resist. The end result may have been a highly levered, undercapitalized financial industry; or, in slightly different wording, a ticking time bomb.

In fact, it could be argued that its role as capital charge setter made VaR the true decisive factor behind the credit crisis. Such assertions would be expected to sound shockingly unconventional to many. To most people out there, the crisis that sank the financial markets and the world economy was undeniably caused by Alberto Ramirez, Maria Avila, and Brad Morrice. Blaming the trio (and their many resemblers throughout the land) is comforting because it fits well with a simple and conventional explanation: The oft-called *subprime crisis* was triggered by those participating in the subprime mortgage business. No doubt, the take would inevitably go, it was subprime mortgages and those individuals who took them, sold them, and lent them. They did it. They condemned us to misery and chaos.

In November 2006, Alberto Ramirez stopped making payments on his California home's $720,000 mortgage. The non-English-speaking strawberry picker (who was making around $15,000 a year by the time he obtained the loan and purchased the home), finally gave up after several months of excruciatingly struggling to meet the monthly $5,378 bill. It is likely that he didn't invite Maria Avila to his Christmas Eve dinner party the following month. The real estate agent had arranged for the original transaction. Instead of a party invitation, Alberto and Rosa Ramirez sent a letter of demand to Maria's agency, claiming the brokers breached their fiduciary duties by selling him a home he couldn't afford. But perhaps Avila was unfairly targeted. After all, she didn't provide the financing without which no $720,000 four-bedroom, two-bathroom property would have ever been owned by someone earning $300 a week and without a predisposition towards down payments of any kind. That side of the deal fell into the lap of New Century Financial, which happily obliged. As it was, anyways, expected to. Propelled by the vision of his founder and long-standing CEO Brad Morrice, the lender couldn't find a low-income, assets-challenged borrower that it didn't like.

The majority of those awed by the destruction and havoc that have been unleashed onto the markets would readily accuse Ramirez, Avila, and Morrice for the carnage. How on earth could the first agree to a contract that he had no hope whatsoever of ever honoring? How on earth could the second peddle such an obviously unaffordable house to such an obviously inadequate customer? How on earth could the third finance such an insolvency-promising adventure? By acting so recklessly irresponsibly, this unsavory trifecta (borrower-broker-lender), the familiar tagline dictates, sealed our fate. That naughty threesome!

Of course, this is not quite exactly how things unfolded. Defaults on junk mortgages can be blamed for lots of wreckage but they were not, per se, responsible for the worst financial collapse since the 1929 crash.

As slightly more informed observers know full well, the credit crisis owes its strength (and glowing place in history) to the monstrous losses accumulated by investment banks, hedge funds, and other institutions on wildly large, wildly leveraged punts on the value of the type of loans that Brad Morrice gave to Alberto Ramirez through Maria Avila. Not the loans themselves, but übercomplex speculative bets on their performance (actual or perceived).

But we can go one further. If the setbacks from those impossibly toxic punts that sank Wall Street did sink the world, what made such punting possible in the first place? No, I don't mean bankers' greed. That one's too easy and obvious (though certainly not untrue). We can dig much deeper in search of the holy grail of truly causational forces. Why did the banks gorge so portentously on mortgage-related stuff? For three main reasons. One, because thanks to those lax lending policies, high-yielding loans to Ramirez and his peers became amply available, and because thanks to enhanced financial engineering expertise the loans could be transformed into easily accessible investments. Two, because the rating agencies acted (as we saw in Chapter 4, with the decisive aid of the Gaussian Copula alibi) overly generously when ruling on the creditworthiness of those investments. Three, because glorified risk radars (i.e., VaR) allowed one to proclaim that the plays were unassailably secure and to have to post but very little capital up front in order to play the game.

Let's now shoot for the moon, perhaps inexcusably snoopy. Of all those guilty parties, which one was, frankly, the worst offender? In other words, which was unremittingly essential for the nasty chain of events to unfold as it did? Which truly did the trick? Well, the loans and the complex engineering were exceedingly required. Without subprime CDOs you can't have subprime CDO-related losses. The AAA-ing fest was key too, for it decisively aided the creation of CDOs and it actively abetted banks' investments in them. But even if you have the know-how to design the product and the rating alibi, you need to be able to afford the investment in order for the investment to become an asset that you own. Just because a Ferrari exists and the automobile inspectors attest to its superior quality that doesn't mean that you can just own it. You have to pay for it first.

And how exactly does a bank "afford" an investment in a trading instrument like a CDO? By having to incur as modest capital charges as possible. Kind of like being able to buy that Ferrari by just depositing a tiny amount of collateral. Obviously, if the charge was, say, 100 percent, playing the CDO game would be expensive indeed. Plus take into account that CDOs are not the only attraction in town. As a bank or a fund, you naturally would also want to take other trading rides, which in turn require their own capital charges and make their own demands on the overall capital pot. Luckily for those unrepentant gamblers, the tool that has for the past years been sacrosanctly endowed (by regulators and bankers alike) with the power to set capital requirements inside trading floors tends to do a very good job at churning out extremely low numbers.

Why does VaR produce underestimated figures? For two main reasons. On the one hand, because as we explained earlier it heavily borrows from past data, and if, during the selected sample, volatility was tame (as was certainly the case in the run-up to summer 2007) and the presence of extreme events was limited or nonexistent, then the amount of capital required will be one in accordance with such apparently placid environment (i.e., a pretty lenient number). Even if the past did contain tumultuousness, who is to say that such agitation would be a good predictor of future, yet-to-be-seen, perhaps doubly (or more) agitated developments? Financial markets are dominated by extreme events for which there can be little historical precedent, so chances are that when such freakishness presents itself, capital levies calculated by looking at the past would be rendered exceedingly inadequate.

Secondly, the probabilistic foundations on which VaR rests don't assign large odds to the extreme materializing out there. VaR's calculation assumes a Normal distribution, inappropriate to the realities of a world where abnormal events take place often. Also, the tool's churned figures can be substantially depressed through the intervention of the so-called correlation factor, which says that your overall risks could be assumed to be less than meet the eye because some of your positions offset other exposures within your portfolio. But the correlation guidance is in itself drawn from past behavior, which naturally does not have to hold in perpetuity. We are mighty tired of witnessing how asset families that are theoretically believed to be uncorrelated or negatively correlated (and thus constitute an offsetting match) irremediably turn out to move cordially in tandem, particularly when it comes to all sinking together during a meltdown. The correlation alibi that can aid in producing humbler capital requirements looks pretty suspect, too.

By indicating the need for just minion charges, VaR dictated that banks could take huge CDO positions cheaply. No wonder that the balance sheets of Bear Stearns, Lehman Brothers, Merrill Lynch, and the like became inundated with subprime-related assets, in amounts larger than the firms' entire equity bases. But of course, leverage works both ways. As soon as things turn even slightly sour, things can get very sour. If the value of your investments declines, even not astoundingly, the decline in net income can be nightmarish when compared to your capital resourcefulness. Big losses on top of a minion equity base don't make for good returns.

In sum, the hugely sizable, hugely geared bets on subprime-related assets designed through cutting-edge financial engineering and the generosity of Standard and Poor's and Moody's, and which are the real reason why the United States may have transformed itself into a socialist nation, were ultimately made possible by an industry-standard, regulators-endorsed, risk-management concoction with a habit for downplaying upcoming market turbulence and for recommending timid capital requirements. The concoction, not Alberto Ramirez, was the true culprit.

What exactly happened VaR-wise during the dawn of the crisis? Well, the third quarter of 2007 (the first quarter to fully incorporate the troubles) witnessed a superlative amount of investment bank VaR exceptions. Trading losses wildly exceeded the loss limits predicted by the model. While VaR always allows for a few breaches (2 or 3 a year in the case of a 99 percent confidence level; about 12 a year in the case of 95 percent confidence levels), the third quarter of 2007 presented a heavily concentrated cluster of exceptions. Some banks that report 99 percent VaR admitted to exceptions figures above 10 or even 15. And this in spite of the fact that VaR itself was naturally going up as the turbulence was enhanced and, crucially, that banks may have been conservatively reporting too high a VaR in the period preceding the crisis as a way to avoid bothersome regulatory nit-picking (under Basel capital rules, penalties can be imposed if the number of exceptions is eye-catchingly abundant).

In all, Lehman Brothers revealed 3 exceptions at 95 percent; Goldman Sachs 5, also at 95 percent (with only one in the first half of 2007); Morgan Stanley 6 at 95 percent; Bear Stearns 10 at 95 percent (also with only one before the crisis); Credit Suisse 7 at 99 percent (just 2 in the year's first half); and UBS 16 at 99 percent (its first exceptions since the 1998 Russian-LTCM crisis). That is, daily losses during a short three-month window exceeded theoretical losses much more often than theoretically assumed. This shouldn't come as a big surprise. The dependence on historical data and normalness was glowingly revealed as the insurmountable flaw that it is. Not only had the recent past been relatively mild (riding the good side of the cycle), but the records did not contain much activity, if at all, in many of the markets and products that had become redundantly habitual in more recent days (such as complex credit derivatives and mortgage-related trades). Also, correlations between different asset families broke down, as different classes moved together in ways that the model did not capture; what was supposed to be a diversifying factor turned out to be a risk enhancer (past theoretical correlations proved, once more, not to be a reliable estimator for future co-movements). UBS itself made it abundantly obvious: *"Since VAR is derived from historical market data, it is not expected to predict the losses seen in unusual stressed conditions of this type."* The car buyer himself is accepting as de facto that the air bag won't work if there is an accident. Again, what type of driver would buy into a risk-management device that admittedly only works under nonstressed situations? And why should he expect the rest of us to believe that he has risks under control?

The problem with VaR is not just that historical episodes from time to time destroy its reputation. The poor thing never had a chance, on account of the mathematical structure with which it was endowed. VaR is calculated by multiplying the sigma (standard deviation, or *volatility*) of the given financial positions, times the size of the positions, by a number representing a certain degree of statistical confidence. For instance, in the case of a 95 percent confidence interval you would multiply sigma by the number 1.65. If you want 99 percent confidence, you multiply sigma by 2.33. Thus, according to the Normal probability distribution that rules in VaR-land, the probability of any deviation beyond three sigmas is basically zero. In fact, VaR would likely ignore such freakishness as they would not fall under the interval (the probability in any given day of a 3-sigma event is less than 0.15 percent, or about once every 750 trading days; this is roughly equivalent to a 99.9 percent confidence, or 3.2-sigma event, which allows for one off-radar major loss every four years). That is, the theoretical maximum loss derived from VaR is mathematically constrained to be no larger than around 3 times sigma times the size of the position. The VaR radar will not, by definition, register a figure higher than that.

Unfortunately, in the real financial world, 3-sigma and more events take place quite often, certainly more than once every three years and definitely more than once every 125 years (the probability of 4-sigma events, 99.995 percent confidence, according to the Normal curve) or every 14,000 years (5-sigmas, 99.999 percent). In August 2007, the markets witnessed 25-sigma events, several days in a row. According to the Normal distribution, that is impossible, and thus hopelessly unforeseeable by its VaR offspring. Real in real life, utterly unreal in theoretical life. If the probability of a 5-sigma event is equivalent to a single occurrence since the last Ice Age, the chances of a (single) 25-sigma event are way smaller than once since Big Bang (12 to 14 billion years ago). So no need to dwell too much on the theoretical odds for a series of consecutive such happenstances. Someone has compared them to winning a high-stakes lottery more than 50 times in a row. Since VaR limits are destined to be breached as havoc inevitably strikes the markets, VaR paradoxically becomes a tool that becomes less relevant just as it claims to be offering increased accuracy. Going from a 95 percent interval to a 99 percent, or even 99.9 percent, won't do much in terms of preventing breaches (remember that anything beyond 3-sigma, a pretty habitual sight in financial land, will shatter VaR), but it would reduce the scope for error, as now the number of exceptions required to deem the tool a failure are much reduced and thus more probable. Thus, enhanced "certainty" is sadly transformed into enhanced unreliability.

Of course, no coverage of the latest VaR disaster would be even in the vicinity of complete without detailed analysis of the Bear Stearns and Lehman Brothers stories. After all, both of them did go down as a result of the crisis. We are not talking here about some bothersomely larger-than-usual setback, we are talking about the disappearing of two of the most venerable and traditional financial powerhouses in the world. How did VaR fare? Did it even slightly so, prewarn of the potential for total destruction? Did it provide some clues as to the danger of unfettered oblivion? Did the most revered and accepted risk-measurement tool manage to capture, even modestly so, the possibility that Wall Street legends would sink in a matter of weeks?

As part of its very last 10-Q filing with the Securities and Exchange Commission, covering the quarterly period ending on February 29, 2008, Bear Stearns publicly divulged its VaR for the final time. For starters, we should invariably point out that the bank itself, like so many of its (former) peers, was more than willing to admit to the shortcomings of the measure. As Bear sincerely stated, *"VaR has inherent limitations, including reliance on historical data, which may not accurately predict future market risk, and the quantitative risk information generated is limited by the parameters established in creating the model. There can be no assurance that actual losses occurring on any one day arising from changes in market conditions will not exceed the VaR amounts. . . . VaR is not likely to accurately predict exposures in markets that exhibit sudden fundamental changes or shifts. . . . Furthermore, VaR calculated for a one-day horizon does not fully capture the market risk of positions that cannot be liquidated in a one-day period."* But that long list of defects didn't matter much in the end because, as the befallen giant added, *"However, the Company believes VaR models are an established methodology for the quantification of risk in the financial services industry despite these limitations."* In other words, don't finger-point at me, everybody's doing it! When I sink, we all sink together! There's safety in numbers (pun intended) when it comes to risk assessment, too.

On February 29, 2008, just days before the institution finally sank in mid-March (in a process that saw the stock price go in one week from a listed price of $70 to a worth of $2, a destruction in value of

$8 billion; the bank was at one point in 2007 valued at $19 billion), Bear Stearns was reporting an aggregate VaR (one that takes advantage of the diversification benefits of a portfolio of different asset families) of $62 million. The number for May 31, 2007, the crisis predawn, was a paltry $28 million; the one for August 31, already heavily in the midst of the tragedy, barely higher at $35 million. The average VaR (one-day, 95 percent confidence) for the quarter ending February 29 had been $60 million (high of $72 million); that for the quarter ending November 30, 2007 just $45 million (high of $69 million). There were eight VaR exceptions during that period (as opposed to just one during the same period 12 months earlier). The firm attributed this to substantial losses in the mortgage-related and leveraged finance areas. Similar alibis were previously employed to justify the 10 VaR exceptions registered during the quarter ending August 31, 2007 (as opposed to zero for the same period one year before).

It is true that Bear's VaR (predictably) went up as the crisis unfolded. By way of comparison, its typical VaR in calmer days had been inferior to $30 million ($28 million on both February 28, 2007, and November 30, 2006). So VaR did predict more danger as danger became ubiquitous. But it was nonetheless breached much more often than theoretically expected (about three times over). More importantly, it didn't seem to anticipate the sudden escalation of troubles (May's VaR was equally low as that reigning at the beginning of the year). And a $62 million VaR possibly does not qualify as a good indicator of expected sadness when just a few days later the company (and thus its trading portfolio) is deemed to be pretty much worthless (precisely because of a tumultuous deterioration of its trading portfolio, the kind of risk that VaR is supposed to measure). From a theoretical −$62 million (one day) to a real −$8,000 million (the difference between Bear Stearns' approximate market value at the beginning of May and the $250 million that JPMorgan agreed to pay for the whole thing on May 15th). Pretty impressive.

Of course, VaR deals with market risk, and Bear (though rather on the side; the firm was mostly a fixed-income trading house) did other things besides market activity, so comparing expected market losses to the entire fall in value of an investment bank could, as a matter of principle, be seen as somewhat inappropriate. After all, Bear could have fallen because of some odd, market-neutral happenstance, like the destruction of New York by alien UFOs, and VaR could thus be wholly excused.

However, given that we know perfectly well that the fall of Bear was entirely predicated on the meltdown into oblivion of its market positions due to prolonged adverse mortgage-related market movements (all those messy write-downs, all those inconvenient internal hedge fund disasters), it is indeed entirely reasonable to compare the $62 million figure to the $8,000 million one. The portfolio that was VaR's to watch and monitor was fully responsible for the nine-zeros deprivation.

And, of course, an inaccurately dwarfy VaR did harm not just because it hopelessly underestimated the approaching malaise but because, as we have comprehensively analyzed, it most likely contributed to the buildup of positions that contained the seeds for future irreproachable malaise. By late summer 2007, Bear's balance sheet showed around $13 billion in equity supporting around $400 billion of assets, which included at least some $40 billion in "no ready market" stuff. These (VaR-supported) leverage and illiquidity excesses sank Bear, as counterparties and creditors said enough is enough and ran on the bank (though at least one influential observer believes that the bank was not undercapitalized under prevailing regulatory guidance and that a crisis in market confidence is what truly brought it down, with VaR being unfairly fingered).

What about Lehman Brothers, the other mythical investment bank to also disappear as a result of the crisis? How did VaR do? Well, it remained lowish throughout, with average VaR below $100 million during Q2 2007 and Q3 2007, and (depending on the calculation method) Q4 2007, Q1 2008, and Q2 2008. Just like in the case of Bear Stearns, Lehman engaged in wild leverage throughout, aided and abetted by such permissive VaR numbers. On May 31, 2007, the firm boasted $600 billion in assets (with half of those being financial instruments) on top of $20 billion of equity. By February 29, 2008, the proportion had shifted to $785/$25 billion, yielding a similarly abusive ratio. Less than four months before the firm's final demise, Lehman's $640 billion in assets ($270 billion of the financial variety) could still only count on the meager support of a $26 billion capital base.

VaR breaches were modest except for, crucially, the quarter ending May 31, 2008, which witnessed nine VaR exceptions, three times above the predicted amount. What's more, these violations referred to *weighted* VaR, which was substantially higher ($123 million quarterly average versus $84 million average for the nonweighted calculation) given that it assigned greater influence to more recent (more turbulent) events. That is, in the months closer to Lehman's September 15 bankruptcy, the risk radar was malfunctioning badly. While the bank suffered a monstrous, fate-sealing, loss during Q2 2008 (almost $3 billion, in contrast to a $500 million gain in the prior quarter and a $1.2 billion windfall in Q2 2007), VaR numbers were lower than those registered in the six months prior. Just as risk seemed (mathematically, theoretically speaking) friendlier, nastiness ensued.

And, since we are on the subject, what about the VaR of those other financial behemoths who just came short of gliding into unfettered oblivion as a result of market troubles? I mean, it's not an absolute requirement that you failed completely for us to analyze the performance of your VaR during the crisis. Institutions that almost fell would serve, too. Take Swiss (former?) giant UBS. It was the European firm to come closer to Bear- or Lehman-style fate. We saw earlier how its VaR deplorably underperformed in Q3 2007, the first reported results to include the reverberations of the tumultuousness. Unfortunately for VaR fanatics, that was just warm-up. Q4 was almost as naughtily misbehaving, with a grand total of 13 exceptions, even though the bank had implemented tweakings into its VaR calculation that generally made it higher. That is, those single quarterly gaps alone rendered UBS's annual VaR showing despicably inaccurate (at 99 percent confidence, you can't have more than two or three exceptions a year for the tool to be rendered on-the-mark). In all, UBS's 2007 exercise was not one for the museum of VaR golden achievements: the bank recorded about 30 exceptions. Yes, that's right—10 times above theoretical predictions. And the gaps between actual trading losses and VaR forecasts weren't modest, either, with more than 10 episodes representing a negative mismatch in excess of CHF150 million.

The bloodbath continued in 2008, with Q1 exceptions still proudly in two-digit territory, at 11 (with several gaps beyond CHF300 million). UBS has an alibi here, though: In late 2007 it decided to exclude toxic illiquid credit derivatives stuff (CDOs, subprime) from VaR, noting that the glorified risk radar is *"neither an adequate measure of the risks in such illiquid positions nor an appropriate risk control tool. These risks are therefore now excluded from VaR limits. The regulatory treatment has also changed, from trading book to banking book. These positions were previously the dominant contributors to interest rate VaR."* Largely as a result of such change, VaR went down significantly (to about 50 percent of the prior period's VaR), and thus became much easier to breach. In this light, Q1 2008 exceptions (by themselves, five times above the theoretically allowed level for the entire year) could be mercifully half-excused, though of course one wonders about VaR's report card as a viable risk indicator when it can't reflect those market exposures that matter by far the most. In Q2 2008, the number of exceptions too equaled the number of players in a soccer team (though the gaps in revenue losses proved rather smallish). Were UBS to manage to keep up this rhythm through the end of the year, 2008 may yet best 2007 as *annus horribilis* for VaR.

Let's continue this walk down VaR memory lane with, naturally, Merrill Lynch. Just like UBS, it didn't quite sink (it was bought, cheaply, by Bank of America before that could happen) but it certainly competed head-to-the-head with the Swiss for the headlines when it came to big-game mortgage-related write-downs. As of mid-August 2008, a month before Merrill ceased being Merrill, the still-single Wall Street firm had accumulated $52 billion in credit-related markdowns, second only to Citigroup's $55 billion, with UBS coming in close third at $44 billion. Merrill doesn't seem to have reported the number of VaR exceptions during the tremors, but it did still provide some useful information. First, it should be noted that Merrill's VaR was unsurprisingly mild precrisis ($50 million average daily 95 percent VaR during 2006) on the heels of a prolonged quiet historical period. Just like in the case of Bear Stearns and Lehman (and others), such calmness would have resulted in less-than-impressive capital charges and exorbitantly optimistic complacency. By December 31, 2007, Merrill had $31 billion of equity supporting more than $1 trillion in assets (some $60 billion mortgage-related). In 2004, the same amount of equity had to support half the assets. Short-term borrowings ($316 billion) and long-term borrowings ($260 billion) were twice the corresponding 2004 amounts. It is beyond doubt that Merrill, on the back of generous VaR levels, managed to become notoriously leveraged in the years leading up to the nastiness.

As soon as the restlessness started, Merrill's VaR predictably went up to above $75 million average levels for Q2 and Q3 2007. (These numbers, like those of other banks, were much lower than otherwise because of the so-called diversification benefit of owning assets that are, in principle, "uncorrelated," VaR rewards theoretical uncorrelatedness, but what if markets turn out to be not so unchained after all and consensually move in the same direction?) Clearly, those timid VaR figures of old did not forewarn spectacularly, with the tarnished Wall Street legend posting trading-originating losses of more than $2 billion in Q3 2007 (compared to gains of $3 billion 12 months earlier). Merrill was quick to point out at risk management failures: *"VaR and other risk measures significantly underestimated the magnitude of actual loss from the unprecedented credit market environment during the third quarter of 2007, in particular the extreme dislocation that affected U.S. subprime residential mortgage-related and Asset-Backed-Securities CDO positions. In the past, these AAA ABS CDO securities had never experienced a significant loss of value."*

After posting a devastating $9.8 billion loss in Q4 2007, its biggest ever, Merrill decided to revisit its handling of the risk-management function. The massacre experienced by the entity that year (which saw a net downfall of $8.5 billion) is a poignant reminder of the insultingly misguided limitations of VaR, as Merrill was one of the investment banks with the consistently lower (if not the lowest) VaR numbers. Goldman Sachs, with a VaR double Merrill's, performed much better during the credit tempest, going as far as posting record earnings in some quarters. The institution with the (much) inferior theoretical risk turned out to be a much more severe victim.

In spite of its relatively minor VaR, Merrill made attempts to trim it further. It tried hard to reduce its size by reducing positions, only to see VaR actually creep up due to the enhanced market volatility created by those very liquidations (more on this later). Much more consequential, it decided to follow UBS and boldly exclude all the exotic mortgage-related structures from VaR's calculation. The excuse sounded equally Swiss, *"Given the market experiences of U.S. sub-prime residential ABS CDO and residual securities, the modeling of these positions using traditional VaR measures is of limited interpretative value due to the known limitations of VaR and the illiquidity of the positions themselves. Therefore, for 2007 the scope of the portfolio covered by the trading VaR has been changed to exclude the U.S. subprime residential ABS CDO and residual securities positions."* In other words, since there is no reliable market value for the tanking toxic waste and liquidity is but a distant illusion, I'd rather not take the chance with that volatility time bomb, which could drive my VaR to the moon on very short notice. Predictably, once you remove your number one source of risk, the risk measure drops like a fly. The year-end 2007 subprime-less VaR was reported at barely $65 million, yielding an identical figure for daily average throughout the annum. Had the toxic stuff been kept in place, the respective VaR would have been a decisively more abrasive $157 million and $83 million.

Merrill's VaR continued on its southbound quest in the first half of 2008, with daily averages of $65 million and $57 million in Q1 and Q2 2008, respectively. The bank incurred losses of $6.6 billion during that period (once more, mostly trading-related). VaR may have been lowered but that doesn't mean that the source of risk is no longer. The toxic mortgage stuff is still there, lurking in the dark, waiting to be downgraded yet again. By choosing to separate VaR from the most illiquid positions, Merrill guaranteed that the measure would be an even less reliable loss forecaster and an even less trustworthy reflection of the firm's exposures. Of course, VaR had it coming on account of its flawed foundations.

As a final note to this section of the book, allow me to muse sparingly about the VaR record of two other not-unimportant financial institutions who count themselves among the comparatively least castigated by the credit agitations. Credit Suisse experienced 10 exceptions during the first half of 2008, at 99 percent confidence interval, five times more gaps between actual losses and theoretical losses than predicted for the entire year. Average daily VaR was CHF193 million and CHF194 million during Q2 and Q1 (as with all other banks, precrisis VaR was lowish, at CHF100 million). Credit Suisse lost almost CHF1 billion during those 6 months ($2 billion setback in Q1), compared to a $6 billion gain 12 months earlier. Morgan Stanley, for its part, saw its VaR perform rather better, with just three exceptions during H1 2008. At 95 percent confidence, that's well on track to abide by the Normal distribution for the full year. Average VaR during Q1 was just above $100 million and just above $110 million during Q2 (just below $100 million during Q4 2007). Morgan Stanley made $2.5 billion in H1 2008 ($4.6 billion in H1 2007). It seems fitting that those making, not losing, money would witness a more modest number of VaR breaches. What is striking is that for those in the red, VaR proved such an underperforming radar.

As we see, different financial heavyweights experienced different VaR behavior during the beginnings and maturation of the crisis. This non-identical state of affairs is to be entirely expected given the differing asset portfolios and the differing calculation methodologies (VaR is not entirely comparable between firms, rather best seen as an indicator of a trend within each particular institution). Two key messages can be communalized though: Firstly, VaR abstrusely underperformed; the number of exceptions was simply too large. Rules are rules, after all: If the tool says x exceptions at most, and real life delivers $3x$ or even $10x$, then the tool is unappealingly broken. Those VaR-loving radical defenders of concrete metrics should be expected to notice when a very precise numerical rule, imposed by the quantitative machinations that they so favor, does spectacularly not hold. The disarray was stringently not forecasted (if VaR is a few dozen million dollars and you lose billions, something is amiss). In sum, the credit crisis is but the latest evidence that what is deemed intolerably inconceivable by VaR can and does happen in real life. The accidents that VaR is not equipped to deal with do take place, monstrously so. The differences between the prediction and the fact are so unassailably immense that the whole thing would be laughable if only the pain and suffering inflicted on market players and the economy had not been so harsh.

One particularly big drawback that was unavoidably highlighted by the crisis was anticipated earlier, namely the very distorted picture of illiquid exotic risks that VaR can provide. Obviously, the 2007 crisis was caused primarily by illiquid exotic products. VaR couldn't cope, not just because past data may not have been abundantly endowed with prior activity in such markets, but notably because of the large swings in valuation that those products can experience when the hurly-burly ensues (a big reason why some fed-up banks decided to stop including these illiquid positions in their VaR). Exotic stuff (like CDO tranches) can spend long spells under "fuzzy" valuation regimes, being marked-to-model or to a market that may not be fully revealing its cards, or even marked-to-make-believe. Such state of affairs may be harmless under placid circumstances, but could prove disastrous under more stressful conditions, as the market could experience large all-at-once revaluations once the "truth" about such illiquid assets emerges. Simply stated, when it comes to less-than-standard financial fare, the past (even if very immediate) could be an even less creditable source of guidance than usual. And VaR, it follows, an even less reliable figure than usual.

The second key message regarding VaR disclosures during crunch time is that banks showed a passionate tendency throughout to publicly denounce the validity and usefulness of VaR. Without going as far as yelling "Ignore that worthless piece of charlatanism!" the truth is that regulatory filings are adorned with more VaR disclaimers than a Christmas tree has ornaments. That is, VaR reporters are obviously not entirely sold on VaR, and they go to great pains to let you know of that unsinkable fact. In prior paragraphs we have introduced some of those complaints. Let's now add an additional set of representative pronunciations, those of matter-of-factly Merrill Lynch (we have already analyzed how the firm gave VaR a mouthful on account of its inability to properly accommodate the most toxic stuff): *"The calculation of VaR requires numerous assumptions and thus VaR should not be viewed as a precise measure of risk. Rather, it should be evaluated in the context of known limitations. These limitations include but are not limited to the following: VaR measures do not convey the magnitude of extreme events; historical data that forms the basis of VaR may fail to predict current and future market volatility; and VaR does not fully reflect the effects of market illiquidity (the inability to sell or hedge a position over a relatively long period)."* So shared Merrill, toeing a line familiarly familiar to its peers.

And yet, notwithstanding the public lynching by those who invented the gadget and vouched for it in the first place, as long as VaR is prominently displayed in those regulatory filings and annual reports, VaR will matter. Shareholders and investors (who should not be summarily thought of as probability experts) will believe that it does mean something and that it does have something valuable to say about a bank's risks. So will analysts and journalists. And don't get me started on policy makers. If you display VaR profusely under the ever-important, ever-followed "Market Risk" heading in your printable communications with the world, people will endow it with relevance and meaning, and their opinion of you will vary according to the VaR of the moment. Do you really want your share price, maybe even your job, to be affected by what others think about your salubriousness based on a measure that you know to be impossibly wrecked? Perhaps you should bravely walk the talk and take measures so that the flawed measure does not have to be disclaimed about ever again.

The failures of VaR during the credit crisis (which strength was built up on the back of VaR-sanctioned leverage and complacency) are doubly troubling for two simple reasons: one, VaR had caused tangible troubles before; two, the merits and solidity of the theory had been subjected to ample intellectual debate. That is, at the start of the twenty-first century it wasn't exactly impossible to find evidence (both hard and soft, both practical and ideological) that pointed a heavy finger in the direction of VaR's potential for misfiring and for unleashing hell. There was, therefore, plenty of warning. We deal with the applied side of the evidence in bits and pieces throughout this book, but suffice it to say that it wouldn't be incredibly adventurous to proclaim that VaR oiled the conduits via which uncontrollable market chaos consolidated itself and brought down mega hedge fund LTCM (and almost the entire system) in August–September 1998.

And many believe that VaR was also behind the prior year's almost-as-devastating Asian crisis; listen to derivatives maven Stan Jonas: *"What will be the consequences? I think we will see what we all saw in the Asian marketplace before last July. Not only was every VAR system incorrect ex-post, but they were totally inappropriate. In fact . . . much like portfolio insurance in 1987, the prevalence and apparent statistical comfort that VAR gave people probably increased the size and the risk of the exposure that banks were willing to take ex-ante. It would be interesting to see an academic exercise. . . . [S]ystematically what were the consequences of having so many participants using, effectively, the same "stop loss" programs?. . . Of course, it's ironic that JPMorgan, as the progenitor of VAR, had to take such a large haircut recently against its positions in the Asian marketplace. . . . What happened? Where was that vaunted 24-hour system so widely advertised and even sold to others?"* As for the early philosophical debate (that included Stan Jonas' above ruminations), which indelibly and presciently highlighted the potential for trouble and ineffectiveness, let's concentrate on that now.

Interestingly enough, the most influential conversations about VaR took place at the very beginning, just as VaR was being gloriously crowned as the de facto risk measure by regulators worldwide. The exchange between Nassim Taleb (then a quantitative trader who had just published his applied option hedging opus) and Philippe Jorion (then as now an academic, who had recently published his VaR opus) in 1996 remains a lessons-filled classic. Being interviewed by a then top–notch e-derivatives magazine, Taleb came on swinging: *"VAR has made us replace about 2,500 years of market experience with a co-variance matrix that is still in its infancy. We made a tabula rasa of years of market lore that was picked up from trader to trader and crammed everything into a co-variance matrix. Why? So a management consultant or an unemployed electrical engineer can understand financial market risks. To me, VAR is charlatanism because it tries to estimate something that is not scientifically possible to estimate. It gives people misleading precision that could lead to the buildup of positions. It lulls people to sleep. All that because there are financial stakes involved. To know the VAR you need the probabilities of events. To get the probabilities right you need to forecast volatility and correlations. I spent close to a decade and a half trying to guess volatility, the volatility of volatility, and correlations, and I sometimes shiver at the mere remembrance of my past miscalculations. Wounds from correlation matrices are still sore."*

Fine, but what about the claim that VaR is nonetheless an improvement over the mathless past? Rubbish, offered Taleb: *"That's completely wrong. It's not better than what you had because you are relying on something with false confidence and running larger positions than you would have otherwise. You're worse off relying on misleading information than on not having any information at all. If you give a pilot an altimeter that is sometimes defective he will crash the plane. Give him nothing and he will look out the window. Technology is only safe if it is flawless. A lot of people reduce their anxiety when they see numbers.... Before VAR, we looked at positions and understood them using what I call a nonparametric method. After VAR, all we see is numbers, numbers that depend on strong assumptions. I'd much rather see the details of the position itself rather than some numbers that are supposed to reflect its risks."*

Taleb was also among the first to draw serious attention towards the destabilizing powers of VaR, and what can happen when a lot of players choose to follow mechanical trading rules (such as having to liquidate positions if VaR limits get breached) and when a lot of other players are fully aware of such choices. *"VAR players are all dynamic hedgers and need to revise their portfolios at different levels. As such they can make very uncorrelated markets become very correlated.... VAR is a school for sitting ducks. Find me a dynamic hedger who is a reluctant liquidator and I will front-run him to near-bankruptcy."* In other words, if the financial industry were to (as it did do) widely adopt VaR, there would be a danger that everyone would have to liquidate stuff at the same time, taking different markets down concurrently. Savvy punters could take advantage of such theory-imposed actions and try to front-run the VaR-worshippers by kick-starting the kind of turbulence that may force them to fire-sale, in a lucrative snowballing process that leads to overall chaos. By voluntarily enslaving themselves to mathematical mechanics that are public knowledge, VaR-embracers (members of the dynamic hedging family) set the stage for meltdowns.

The perils presented by VaR-inspired liquidations are compounded by the fact that many times punters own very similar portfolios. Certain trades simply become fashionable, certain asset classes just turn voguish. So when something bad happens somewhere, a lot of people would hurt at the same time, would see their VaR numbers go up at the same time, and would have to dump stuff at the same time.

"My first premise is that after a given period of time, everybody has pretty similar trades. After 10 successful years, everybody is doing the Thai baht carry trade. Why? Because even though you think it might be a risky trade, all your friends are getting rich doing it, and after a while it becomes difficult to resist the pull. . . . Plus, the statistics show that it's a risk-free trade. After eight years, it's an immutable fact—Thailand doesn't devalue. So you begin to look like a person who is not scientific. . . . What results then is that people have portfolios that are diversified in virtually the identical fashion. . . . And then you have some shock to the system. Under a VAR approach, everybody tries to shrink the size of their aggregate portfolio. Because under a VAR system, when bad things happen, the way to make sure you don't lose any more than a certain amount of money is to shrink all of your portfolio. . . . Explicitly, what we see is that Brazilian Brady Bonds begin being sold as a hedge against things that happened in Korea, because the same people owned both Brady Bonds and Korean bonds. . . . All of a sudden, Brady bonds begin moving down. That triggers other sales, so you end up having contagion effects," explained a well-known expert, who highlighted the flakiness in the theory's assumption of eternally unlimited liquidity: *"Then you can see that if everybody has a similar portfolio, everybody can't shrink their portfolio at once, because, in this world, the major fallacy of diversification is that somebody else has to be outside of the ostensibly diversified system to hold the risk. And those value buyers, whoever they may be, are traditionally slow to come into play. So, for a long period, it's the famous Keynesian analogy. When you go to the football stadium and you can't see because somebody's standing in front of you, you get up and you can see the game. But if everybody gets up, nobody can see the game. And this is exactly what happens when you have a VAR system where people have similar portfolios and they all try to shrink their portfolios at the same time."*

That is, VaR-dictated risk reductions will only work if others want to buy whatever you are trying to dump. But that means that you need a lot of people out there who are not abiding by VaR. Thus, the sinister contradiction that VaR becomes less successful the more people embrace it.

In sum, what Taleb and other critics back in those pre–school days were eager to emphasize is that VaR is a purported risk-management tool that won't forewarn right when it actually matters, that VaR can actually generate new risks, and that false confidence in a flawed methodology can only make things worse.

By far the most commonly employed argument in favor of VaR is that risk quantification, while admittedly full of shortcomings, is better than nothing at all. Listen to the pope of VaR, Philippe Jorion: *"The essence of civilization is measurement, and value-at-risk measures things in a way most people can understand. . . . Value-at-risk won't tell you the worst case; that's what stress testing is for. It is better to quantify and look for ways to improve predictions than do nothing at all."* Leaving aside for the moment the possible contributions of VaR to our having evolved as more civilized than chimpanzees, Jorion's clarifying words offered a wide-open window into the minds of theory-defenders. In their universe, the alternative to mathematization is nothingness. Beyond math lies the most lugubrious emptiness, the most desolated vagueness. To them, if you don't do theory, then you are doing nothing. It's math or bust in their world.

That, needless to say, is a bit limited. Believe it or not, there is more to financial markets and financial risk management than theories and convoluted correlation matrices. There is this weird thing called human intuition, common sense, judgment, and experience which, who would have guessed, had been busily at work for centuries by the time the nerds Platonized risk-taming 20 years ago. Jorion's statements are an insult to the thousands of real-life financial professionals who have effectively dealt with risk through the ages. He is denigrating and deriding their hands-on experience as a wasteland of nothingness. The drama here is not only that the cloistered professor is insufferably belittling the no-nonsense warriors who have toiled (and shaped) the markets, but that nonquantitative risk management never sank the entirety of Wall Street, while the mathematical stuff so heavily promoted by Jorion and his peers has had a hand in precisely that.

And in any case, again, it is highly doubtful that we can measure financial risk, anyway. The credit crisis (and all the apocalyptical predecessors that have taken place in the space of time since finance was quantified) provides the brutishly hard evidence, but Taleb explained it rather more elegantly 10 years ago: *"Frank Knight of the University of Chicago defined two forms of random events. One of them he called measurable risk, the other he called nonmeasurable uncertainty. I think that it's a grave mistake to try to mix the two. Measurable risk is when you have a handle on the randomness. If I throw a pair of dice, for example, I can pretty much measure my risk because I know that I have one-sixth probability of having a three pop up. Nonmeasurable uncertainty is when I'm throwing the dice without knowing what's on them. In the real world, most social events are nonmeasurable because nobody hard-coded the rules of the game."* If you don't know the probabilities and the possible outcomes, you can't measure uncertainty, as simple as that. The disappearance of Wall Street in 2008 was not just an event which probability was utterly unquantifiable, the event itself could not even be considered.

Nassim, please continue: *"It all comes back to one problem. If the distributions were stationary and you had a recurring event that happens every five years or so, the world would be a better place. Because then we would, in 20 or 30 years, detect these problems and build defenses against them. The problem is that the distributions are not stationary. What is alarming is not the fact that we have a standard error. The problem is that we don't quite know what the standard error is. When I use a thermometer, I may be aware that there is one or two degrees of error in my measurement of the temperature. But here, I don't know much about the instrument, particularly when it comes to rare events. Finally, we should not confuse risk with variance. Most people believe that risk is variance. Risk is not variance, except for a symmetric normal distribution. Risk is what can really hurt you. What can hurt you is a large move down, and these are entirely uncharted waters for us."*

Most damning for the scientification-seeking financial economists, Taleb argues that VaR shows that *"Being scientific does not necessarily mean being quantitative. Medicine is very scientific, in the sense that it has the rigor in its search for the truth, but it is not yet quantitative. . . . Look at a time series—say of Mexico. Someone who's purely quantitative, just from looking at the data, might infer that there is no volatility and that Mexican currency presents no risks to investors. But take someone who has read the newspaper, who's rigorous in his thinking, and who took the time to get familiar with the dynamics of foreign exchange markets and central bank reserves. He would know that something that takes place in Korea could spread to Mexico. Such an approach is scientific—that is, rigorous in searching for the truth and understanding the risks—but is not the least bit quantitative. . . . One of the mistakes I made was using the VAR, without much intuition about the data, and losing money. Then I got wiser and learned the existence of the trap. I start by trying to understand what was going on in the world, and I'm wiser by using statistical methods as a mere appendage to my reasoning. Value-at-risk should be nothing but a small footnote in the way we view the risks. Not the dominating tool."*

So the choice is not, as Jorion misleadingly presents it, between math and nihility, but between inexcusably flawed and dangerous math and experience-honed common sense. Now, that has another ring to it, hasn't it?

VaR proponents should not be allowed to continue to get away with the simplisticly vacuous (and deceiving) "it's better to quantify than to do nothing" slogan. The point of risk management should not be to quantify for the sake of quantification, but to be effective in protecting risk-takers. Soundness, not mathematical prowess, should be the yardstick in the real world. A measure that hopelessly fails can't be better than a lot of things.

Philippe Jorion said that had VaR been in place, the famous derivatives disasters of the early 1990s could have been prevented. In particular, when referring to the spectacular collapse of Orange County in California, Jorion stated that *"There was no regulation that required the portfolio manager, Bob Citron, to report the risk of the $7.5 billion investment pool. As a result, Citron was able to make a big bet on interest rates that came to a head in December 1994, when the county declared bankruptcy and the portfolio was liquidated at a loss of $1.64 billion. Had a VAR requirement been imposed on Citron, he would have been forced to tell investors in the pool: Listen, I am implementing a strategy that has brought you great returns so far. However, I have to tell you that the risk of the portfolio is such that, over the coming year, we could lose at least $1.1 billion in one case out of 20. The advantage of such a statement is that this quantitative measure is reported in units that anybody can understand—dollars. Whether the portfolio is leveraged or filled with derivatives, its market risk can be conveyed to a nontechnical audience effectively."*

There is only one minor caveat with all this, of course. The "at least $1.1 billion loss in one case out of 20" assertion is simply not true. That was *not* the risk of the portfolio. It was a theoretical estimate that assumed the future to be exactly like the selected past sample period and the markets to be Normal. Since none of those two tenets holds in the financial jungle, the reported figure would be an utter falsehood. Is that how investors would be best served? By telling them Texas-size fabrications? By portraying as risk something that can't have any hope of representing risk?

Another helpful rumination by the VaR godfather is the admission (a little too late, perhaps) that the glorified risk tool may, after all, be ruthlessly unable of coping with risk. For what is risk if not worst-case scenarios? Average, hopelessly timid, boringly laid-back events are not risk. Never have been, never will be. Risk is what can harm me, what can dismember me, what can erase me. Saying that a risk measure can't cope with the harmful stuff is like saying that an air bag can't function if you hit a wall. Such a puzzling sales pitch gets compounded by the fact that what Jorion deems worst-case tends to be almost average in the real world, and yet utterly undetectable by VaR. It's not as if the "worst-case" scenarios not covered by the revered bell curve referred solely to a 50 percent drop in the Dow Jones or the disappearance of the euro. VaR leaves out scenarios that happen almost on a daily basis (how many 300-point moves have we witnessed on Wall Street in the past 18 months alone, basically on a continuous stream?).

So the worst-case disclaimer-excuse-alibi is not just utterly self-deprecating in itself (no risk tool worth its salt can admit to failing when it matters the most), but it actually shouldn't be entitled to donning that label because in the non-Platonic real world what Platonists categorize as excruciatingly rare is in fact exorbitantly common. VaR does not just leave out the one-million-year hurricane or the asteroid hitting the Earth; it leaves out tons of harmful events that take place exceedingly often. Alibiing VaR by using the worst-case line is not just implying that your air bag will not work out if you are in trouble, but that the only possible kind of trouble is you hitting a giant pink elephant who's skateboarding down the highway.

So stop using that tired "Var is not for worst-case scenarios" justification as if that which is not covered were an impossibly distant possibility that no risk radar could ever be asked to cover. A lot of what VaR doesn't cover is far from distant, and it only seems extreme to VaR peddlers because their calculations do not belong in the real world. VaR allows you to excuse the highly probable by incorrectly labeling it highly improbable. Theoreticians have a great thing going on here, as any breach of VaR can be apologized for as the result of the rarest of rare events, and which tool could be reasonably demanded to capture such oddities?

And not just theoreticians. Pros could too take comfort in the probabilistic con afforded by VaR. Once more, let Taleb explain: "*Nor am I swayed by the usual argument that the VAR's widespread use by financial institutions should give it a measure of scientific credibility. . . . I believe that the*

VAR is the alibi bankers will give shareholders (and the bailing-out taxpayer) to show documented due diligence, and will express that their blow-up came from truly unforeseeable circumstances and events with low probability—not from taking large risks they did not understand. . . . I maintain that the due-diligence VAR tool encourages untrained people to take misdirected risk with shareholders', and ultimately the taxpayers', money." More than a decade later, and in the midst of the credit tragedy, such pearls could not appear any more prescient.

Allow me to conclude this section by revisiting Philippe Jorion's linkage between measurement and advanced civilization and how VaR should be defended as a continuation of such a formidable tradition. When protecting the VaR flag during an encounter of experts, Jorion borrowed from a literary work called *The Measure of Reality*, which apparently contained irrefutably enlightened and confirmatory inspiration for VaR-faithful around the globe. *"Some 900 years ago,"* stated Jorion, *"Europe was populated by dull people in a barbaric state of civilization. Europe was much less advanced than the Arab world, for instance. Then 400 years afterward, Europe embarked on a wave of imperialism that seems to have no precedent in history. The book asks, How did this happen? The thesis of the book is that this change happened as Europe started to measure the material world. What happened was a change in the mentality that induced people to start measuring space and time. It was the beginning of clocks, measuring space, measuring the material world and the environment. That led to huge technological progress in Europe and explains why Westerners seems to have been able to conquer all other civilizations they met. In a way, value-at-risk is along the same lines."*

This is presumably Jorion's argument/defense: If we want Western civilization (with its freedoms, its prosperity, its scientific prowess, its melting pot) to remain in place, we must support VaR. The best tool to defend Western values from those bent on destroying them is VaR. Want to fight Islamic fanaticism? Forget armed conflict, stop searching for Bin Laden throughout dimly lighted caves. Convert the Middle East to VaR, that'll stop the conflict. Honor the legacy of Newton, Darwin, Churchill, Bill Gates, and so many others who did so much to establish, protect, and expand civilization, and spread the gospel of VaR throughout the land. Who cares if the risk clock perennially malfunctions and causes harm? What's that compared to preserving and expanding a 400-year-old way of life? Let that covariance matrix civilize the uncivilized.

One would tend to assume that a widely shared reaction to all the disappointments and disastrous performance during the crisis (which came on the heels of historical disappointments and disastrous performances, let alone plenty of publicly available warnings) would be to shy away from VaR-embracement and to discard the safety mechanism that won't protect during turmoil (that in fact discards the very possibility of turmoil). But while these would surely be hard times to enhance the ranks of devoted VaR groupies, voiced reactions by those in the game seem to lean not towards the annihilation of VaR, but rather towards its reform. The goal seems to be to try to preserve the preponderance of the tool through a few technical twitches, not to humbly admit that a failed (and, once more, inevitably so) guide should not be kept around. By going that route, those non-annihilators contribute to increasing the risk of unfettered and misguided risk-taking and of the subsequent market catastrophes.

The technical amendments recently suggested for VaR range from the use of a larger data sample (go further back in history so that you can capture a larger myriad of events that may possibly result in a more reliable mirror on future events), to the use of a shorter data sample (go less far back in history so that recent events are "read" faster by the model), to the disproportionate weighting of more recent data (so that what happened yesterday counts more than what happened last year), to the more regular updating of the data sets (shift from monthly or quarterly to weekly or even daily as a way to capture sudden changes in market environment). But this is like our fictional car dealer trying to make up for the nonfunctioning of the air bag during accidents by offering an upgrade in its texture and manufacturing material. Those technical niceties won't help a bit as long as the damn thing continues to refuse to inflate as we crash against the concrete wall. The main issue simply would continue to be avoided and stubbornly left in place, unaltered, ever dangerous.

The problem with VaR is not that the historical data is too short or too long, but that it is entirely based on historical data. This makes it a hopeless task, and not just because the past is not a wonderfully accurate reference. Readers should keep firmly in mind that one would obtain an *entirely different* VaR figure depending on the historical data sample chosen. And that such choice is entirely arbitrary (i.e., there is no set-in-stone golden rule; it's up to you and your intrinsically intrinsic self). Basel II

constrains personal selection to a minimum of one-year observation period, but beyond that it's your call (by the way, what's so great about one
year of data?). And whether you go for a two-year or five-year window
will make a big difference to your VaR number, with direct implications
on your risk-taking and your capital charges, and on how exposed you
are deemed to be by others. For example, Morgan Stanley's 95 percent
trading VaR as of May 31, 2008, was $99 million if using a four-year
database but $127 million if using simply a one-year sample; discrepan-
cies were even worse for the 99 percent case, $165 million versus $257
million. This is not simply to highlight the technical difficulties involved
with the calculation process, but to emphasize how utterly unreliable,
almost childishly so, the tool is. If something as inevitably inexact and
as insultingly arbitrary as the mere selection of a data sample can impact
final results so much, can we honestly trust VaR as a rock-solid measure of
anything?

Worse, the data is interpolated into the future, employing deeply unrealistic probabilistic assumptions. The unreliability aspect captured in
the old adage that "Past performance does not guarantee future performance" is compounded by imagining a fantasy, make-believe future.
The financial markets are non–Normal creatures dominated by extreme
events. Many times, these Black Swans are debutantes, never having been
seen in public before they struck out. Therefore, it is impossible for past
data (even if one million years old) to be able to reflect such extremes,
leaving VaR totally unprepared when the rarity does take place.

In sum, the reaction to the VaR meltdown during the credit crisis
has the feel of charlatanism protecting charlatanism. Via this process,
the reputation of VaR and its defenders sinks further. The world does
not need risk managers who, when confronted with the unavoidably
horrendous failure of their tools, choose not to arrange a passenger escape
in the lifeboats of common sense and let the big bad ship of hampering,
misplaced mathematical certainty sink, but rather tie themselves (and the
rest of us) to the mast while explaining that the many leakages through
which the water is inexorably coming in can be fixed by painting the
sails red.

Of course, risk managers and their employers may have their hands
tied and may not be entirely free to act as they wish in this matter. VaR

being the regulatory requirement that it is (VaR just has to be calculated and reported), banks may have no choice but to abide. Ever since the Basel Capital Accord was revised in 1996 so that banks would have to measure and apply charges with respect to their market risks as well as their credit risks, VaR has become the mathematical reference that determines capital charges. And, naturally, VaR is religiously reported as part of quarterly regulatory filings and annual reports, a must-show piece of information. International regulators have tended to provide lots of leeway to financial institutions as to how exactly they should calculate VaR, but the main idea remains intact: Whatever this statistically derived single number says, goes. In a summer 2008 revision to this so-called Basel II regime, detailed amendments to the requirements concerning the technical aspects surrounding the actual calculation of VaR were presented, but, again, the key theme was left unaltered: Each bank must meet a capital requirement expressed as VaR (the previous day's or the average of the last 60 days, whichever is higher) times a multiplication factor (of no less than three; more if the model turns out to be a bad predictor of actual risks).

That is, regulatory pressures dictate that you may want a low VaR (so as to reduce the amount of committed capital) but not *too* low (so it's not breached so often that capital charges get mandatorily enhanced anyway). Such Goldilocks-style incentives can lead to actions by banks that generate market turbulence and that, depressingly ironically, can turn out to be completely ineffectual. Bankers eager to reduce their VaR levels, for example, after markets have become slightly more volatile and risk limits have been or are about to be breached, may reduce the size of their positions. But such actions, if concurrently shared by several other financial institutions, could trigger extra volatility in the markets, rendering the positions that have been kept riskier and thus pushing VaR up. No net VaR reduction may be achieved at all. As one astute commentator proposed, this would be akin to "running only to stand still." In fact, the new volatility may breed so much additional volatility that VaR may end up actually being pushed up by the attempts to push it down. The net result: more capital charges, much more risk. People have long been aware of the dangers posed by VaR-dictated asset liquidations that can take markets on an unstoppable downhill march, potentially leading to a massive crisis. What we are saying here is that the origin of all those liquidations may well be a strategy to *reduce* VaR. Talk about nasty side effects. VaR is a tool that can lead to much more risk precisely as a direct result of trying to trim risk.

And something like that apparently took place in the fall of 2007, following the exciting events of the prior summer. In an attempt to lower their VaR, several entities unloaded a portion of their most daring assets (mortgage-related), but the dumping was on such a scale that VaR rose, rather than fell. Fire sales that should have halved VaR (under constant volatility levels) failed miserably in the face of the VaR-caused price swings. For instance, Merrill Lynch complained in its Q3 2007 reported results that its late-September VaR was higher than its late-June VaR even though positions were reduced substantially between both dates, with the culprit being of course the offsetting effects inflicted by the increase in market volatility during that three-month window. The purported risk-managing gadget can become a deleterious risk enhancer. Those who designed and adopted VaR forgot that the presence of VaR itself changes the rules of the game and drastically affects the outcome. VaR can make VaR irrelevant. In their rush to embrace the sophistication of mathematically backed risk management (perhaps as a convenient substitute for raw cluelessness), regulators forgot about such fine print.

Highly interestingly, one of the changes that the Basel Committee wants introduced dramatically highlights a key failure of VaR, and one that as we know may have proven particularly misleading during the credit crisis, namely the treatment of illiquid securities. Given the short holding periods reflected by VaR (which puts a premium on ease of liquidation), sometimes it may not be possible to include risk measurements for complex positions for which little or no market liquidity may exist at any particular time; naturally, this exclusion would translate into lower capital charges, compounding the natural tendency of VaR (because of its absurdly unrealistic statistical foundations) to deliver hamperingly size-challenged charges. The "Incremental Risk Charge" amendment (to be tentatively introduced in 2010, and to deal with factors such default risk, credit migration, and liquidity risk) would run alongside VaR, with the inescapable goal of clamping down on banks' leverage levels by making them put up more cash to play. In other words, it took a VaR-aided Poseidon-like market sinkage for regulators to finally revisit the VaR-ruled risk framework that has been causing trouble for the past 12 years. But VaR (for now, at least) survives the crisis pretty much regulatorily unscathed, with officials scrambling to perfect its engine, as detailed above, but certainly not contemplating its execution (it's almost shocking how little the "quantitative standards" section of the Committee's market risk documents has varied throughout the years). And, of course, the new incremental charge will have to be calculated through a model. In fact, the first thing that catches one's eye when inspecting Basel II's plans for its latest market risk innovation is that dreaded breach-prone figure, the 99.9 percent confidence interval.

Quantitative professionals definitely have a vested interest in the unquestioned acceptance of math-driven risk management, and bank honchos may also (for a variety of reasons) enjoy the notion of being able to present to the world their exposures wrapped up in an easy-to-understand single-number format, but at the end of the day regulatory orders make it all happen. In fact, as repeatedly stated earlier, pros may be perfectly aware as to the limitations of VaR (as yet another exemplary quote, Credit Suisse's chief risk officer stated last February that *"VaR is a tool for normal markets and it is not designed for stress situations. It would have been difficult for VaR models to have captured all the recent market events, especially as we were emerging from a period of relatively benign volatility"*), but even if they wanted to stop paying attention to it they now can't. VaR has been allowed to become too central a figure of the financial universe. The risk radar that the industry invented more than a decade ago (JPMorgan first introduced VaR to the world) may have become a regulations-aided Frankenstein.

Regulators thus appear as relentless defenders of misplaced certainty, derived from flawed technicalities. And as we know, such defense can render destabilizing crises likelier. A low VaR (typical during calmer, prolonged prosperous market periods) can give carte blanche to excessive risk taking by diminishing the requirements for pledged capital. The consequent high VaR (typical during a turbulent, troubled period) can in turn cause undue precaution, as risk taking is limited by the much higher capital requirements. VaR blindly assumes that if the recent past has been calm, then the present and the future can be considered placidly safe, a good environment to be a tad more daring; on the other hand, if recent history has been turbulent, VaR would assume a dangerous panorama, a good time to be conservative and reduce your risk appetites. But the opposite could well be truer. Relatively durable calm periods in the markets may indicate danger ahead, not placidity, as the trouble-free reality signals the unopposed buildup of a bubble, fed by uninterrupted bouts of good news and good performances that breed complacency, encourage excess, and seductively invite new entrants into the game. Not the time to be demanding *low* capital charges from players. Conversely, hurricane days may indicate that the worst is about to be over and that a more tranquil equilibrium awaits around the corner. Perhaps not the best moment to demand *high* capital changes that help stall the much-needed recovery. VaR can effectively be adding fuel to excessive excess and putting brakes on salutary risk taking because of its obsessive credence in the future being a reflection of the past.

That is, not only can VaR help cause (or encourage) malaise, it could have, as openly indicated by a group of leading experts, a dangerous overall procyclical effect, destabilizing the economy at large by adding fuel to both boom and bust. The bubble is assisted, the posterior recovery is handicapped. This is regulatory-driven economic destabilization, the consequence of having an irremediably malfunctioning mechanism given the power to set bank capital charges.

So let's blame quantitative finance fanatics and their sponsors for endorsing tools that failed to provide any meaningful guidance as to the storm of risk brought about by the credit crisis, and that may have in fact contributed decisively to the unleashing of the torment. But let's not forget that the main culprit may lie elsewhere, in the shape of inappropriate math-sanctioning, unrealistic analytics-endorsing, fantastical precision-loving public servants. Yes, the salespeople are peddling air bags that fail during stress, but they are under pressure from the police to do so.

Chapter 6

Blue Is Not Green

■ *Lehman did die* ■ *Anything is possible* ■ *Buffett versus
the Black Swan* ■ *Stubbornly holding the theoretical fort*
■ *An end to indoctrination* ■

For those of you lucky enough to be in New York City, if you trot from Central Park to Times Square you will inevitably come face to face with what used to be Lehman Brothers' headquarters (with the nice candy store by the side, and the glittering billboards just a few meters southwards). Pre–credit crisis, the lights on the building used to be shiny green, reflecting the color of Lehman's logo. Now they are blue, reflecting Barclays Capital's logo. One of the very first things that the Brits did upon taking over was to proudly (and rather conqueringly) install the new flag. Literally overnight, the building turned from green to blue.

Such picturesque modification allows us to play a little guessing game. What's the difference between a regular (sane) person and a finance theoretician? Simple: The regular fellow, when asked about the color of the building's light, will matter-of-factly answer "blue." The theoretician, on the other hand, will answer "green."

What do you mean *green*? Yes, green. For you see, according to standard finance theory Lehman is still alive and kicking, healthy as ever, gloriously present. Thus, the building's logo would still be Lehman's logo. Green. For the theorist, Lehman is alive because the credit crisis did not happen. How could it, when the accepted models and risk

measures deny it any chance of ever happening? Such a dark, ebony-
ish, inky, Black Swan is simply not possible in Normality-abiding, rare
event–denying theoryland. The two most influential mathematical constructs during the period leading up to the crisis (Gaussian Copula and
VaR) tenaciously refuse to conceive of a world where a rare event of
those proportions could even be hypothesized as a distant possibility.
The quantitative philosophy behind the Nobel prizes showered on financial economists would testify in court as to the utter unattainability
of such outcomes. If you abide by the orthodox tenets, the investment
banking industry is still with us, the Dow Jones never fell by 777 points
in a single day, and AIG doesn't owe the U.S. government a cent.

The crisis did not happen. Lehman is alive. The logo is green. We may
be able to understand why the theoreticians choose to hallucinate and
rabidly Platonize (they make a living out of it, they may actually believe
in their models), but why have we regular folks followed them so often
for so long? Not just followed them, avidly defended them (remember
how lonely Nassim Taleb was at the beginning of his anti–quantitative
establishment crusade?).

And that is a key lesson from the crisis. Self-serving theoreticians will
always see green where there is blue. Left to our own devices, we will
see blue, but we will see green when accompanied by the theorists.
When we walk alone, blue is blue. When we walk with the theorists, blue is green. Such utterly insane, blatantly ridiculous, scandalously
degrading hypnosis is the price we pay (or used to pay) for our unconditional self-enslavement to the dictates of a group of people who,
equations in hand, pontificate about markets without having ever toiled
in them.

As the still-unfolding mayhem proves beyond any reasonable doubt,
our unnegotiable conformity with theoretical dictums has caused us unlimited pain. On par with lax mortgage lending practices, failing structured finance vehicles, and unsound regulation, quantitative finance is to
blame for the crisis. Simply put, the models and the risk guides used to
value and rate credit structures, and to measure future turbulence and set
capital charges, encouraged untold complacency and insalubrious leverage. Without the scientifically sanctioned, out-of-control, madly levered
punting, the chaos would not have unfolded as drastically as it had. By
putting faith in the complex math, we killed ourselves. Confusing blue
with green is dangerous. We shouldn't fall for it again.

As much as certain theoreticians may dislike the notion, blue is not green. The crisis did happen, dragging down with it the reputation of many a theoretical gospel. We could (as we have done, and will continue to do, in this book) nit-pick and finger-point several specific instances where particular quantitative applications horrendously failed. But let's try here to underline the more big-picture themes, more for-the-ages lessons that undefatigably emerge from all the rubble. Two interconnected conclusions bother us particularly harshly on account of their insistent obviousness: We can't predict, and anything is possible.

Don't give us mathematical recipes for how the world will operate or, worse, how we should operate. You couldn't forecast even one of the innumerable mega-Black Swans that have taken place in successive/ consecutive motion, each of which, in itself, has earned a place in the history books. Forget about your inconsolable incapacity to describe tomorrow's stock prices or next week's foreign exchange rates. You couldn't get what truly matters right. Not even close to being close. How many financial economists had forewarned on December 31, 2007, that in barely six months the investment banking industry would be gone? When you can't even detect that which most impactingly impacts our lives, why should we consider you and your tools worthy of our admiration and allegiance?

Second, don't pretend that you can measure and that you know the probability distribution. Particularly if the distribution of your choosing is one where a huge range of possibilities is off-handedly discarded as impossibly far-fetched, where the realm of the possible is reduced to a limitingly limited range of outcomes. We don't know the distribution, we don't know the range of outcomes, and we don't know the ramifications. If 2-sigma is the best that you can do, you are obviously hopelessly out of touch, out of sync. The real world left you behind a long time ago. The crisis has amplifyingly shown that you can't prepackage future events and their impact in a nice little box, adoringly adorned with standard deviations and correlations. Reality is much more ferociously untamable. The randomness is not just wild; it's savagely uncageable, abominably undomesticated. No equations can subjugate it, control it, or decipher it. Where anything can happen, there are no mathematically imposed bounds. You could never build a model that could accommodate all the possible impossibly impossible future happenstances, let alone assign them a (trustable) chance of occurring.

Fittingly, coincidentally with the credit turmoil, we witnessed two specific, noteworthy, and widely reported episodes that demonstrably highlight what can happen under an untamable environment that grants permission to exist to any kind of occurrence. That is, what can happen under an anti-theory (yet very much real, naturally) environment. One of them is a direct by-product of the mayhem and serves to pass verdict on the merits of a particularly famous and particularly predominant trading strategy that thrives on (succumbs under) Normality (non-Normality). The other is less directly related to the crisis (though it does deal with a high-profile financial institution, and the depth of the malaise was indeed magnified by the crisis-enabled market depression), and it would have happened nonetheless. But it seems like a good tongue-in-cheek way to bring home the point that we do inhabit an utterly unpredictable, impossibly uncontrollable, certainly uncertain terrain.

Veteran speculator and indomitable iconoclast Victor Niederhoffer counts himself as one of the victims of the credit crisis, in spite of not being a renowned CDO punter or a gobbler of subprime financing. As widely reported by the media, his flagship funds went down after the summer 2007 turmoil, causing a near total wipeout in value. This is the second time that the former squash champion blows up. The first disaster took place 10 years ago, when investments in Thailand turned sour and positions taken in the U.S. stock market as a way to cover for that setback turned sourer still. Many are wondering whether the PhD-holding, clarinet-playing maverick will be allowed a third chance in the markets.

Niederhoffer's travails provide us with a good excuse to revisit a trading strategy that very clearly highlights the perils of betting against the markets behaving abnormally. That is, of betting against the rare event. Of betting against the philosophical backbone of orthodox financial theory (VaR, Gaussian Copula, the Nobels, all abhor Black Swans). We are talking about option selling, a punt endowed with a distinctly "heaven-and-hell" nature. Niederhoffer has always been a well-known option seller, and at least a sizable chunk of his troubles can be explained by option selling gone bad. He is not the first, and won't be the last, player to be wiped out through such conduit. Bluntly stated, selling options has historically been too tempting for many to resist. Such temptation can blind investors as to the (very substantial) potential damages that may await in the future.

Why is option selling such a tempting proposition? Because it allows you to generate a constant stream of cash (the premium of the sold options) for what could be a very long time, thus helping you produce very tasty returns as the strategy does not require an initial capital commitment on your part. And the strike of the options could be set in such a way that the probability that things would turn nasty is (in principle) highly diminished. For instance, a time-honored tradition (embraced by Niederhoffer, among many others) is to sell deep out-of-the-money puts. While the premium money collected would be inferior (as the underlying asset needs to go down a lot for the owner of the option to receive a payout), only a market crash could wipe you out. As long as the market behaves "normally," you can continue happily pocketing premium cash and looking very good to your backers. Niederhoffer was indeed very successful for a while, and was actually at one point declared the best hedge fund manager in the world. Another famous player that went the options selling route as a way to enhance returns was mega-fund LTCM, which was so active in that arena that it was dubbed the "Central Bank of Volatility" (as selling options is akin to selling volatility).

But as soon as you sell your soul to the devil of easy put premium money, you expose yourself to Mephistopheles one day coming back to demand compliance with his side of the bargain. If the underlying markets tumble and/or if volatility goes wild, chances are that you won't live to tell. You will be left nakedly facing very large real payouts to your counterparts or very large mark-to-market losses which would ignite impossible-to-meet margin and collateral calls. In any case, you will be wiped out. Take LTCM. When long-dated implied volatility on European equity indices, steady for months, jumped up significantly in the fall of 1997 as a result of Asian crisis—originated stock markets turmoil, LTCM decided that the time was right to sell options to the market. With historical volatility in European markets traditionally lowish, LTCM thought it had a clear winner. It was selling volatility at historically very expensive levels, with a data-backed expectation that turbulence would soon return to its normal, much lower levels. If you sell options and implied volatility nosedives, you get nice mark-to-market profits. Of course, were volatility to *rise*, not fall, LTCM would be in big trouble.

LTCM bet big on the future being like the (rather placid) past. After Russia devalued and defaulted in mid–August 1998, the financial world went insane, and implied long-dated volatility on equity indices climbed above the levels at which LTCM had sold options. Suddenly, the fund was being hit with insurmountably huge margin calls from its counterparts. As implied volatility kept being pushed upwards, LTCM simply run out of money to keep playing the game. In all, LTCM's equity index volatility trades lost $1.314 billion.

Niederhoffer blew up through option selling first during the 1997 Asian crisis–inspired malaise. Like LTCM, he was short equity put options, this time with an exposure to U.S. markets. When the S&P 500 experienced a one-day drop of 7 percent in late October, Niederhoffer's short put positions killed him, in a single day. While LTCM had to be rescued (and thoroughly disassembled into nonexistence) by a consortium of banks, Niederhoffer was forced to auction his precious personal belongings to cover his losses. Such are the unpleasant fates that can await the options-selling Fausts.

The decision to sell options thus needs to be based on sound probabilistic assumptions. If you expect chaos and mayhem, obviously you would be less willing to generate returns through premium money. If you expect placid times, your willingness would go up. What option buyers (like Nassim Taleb) would tell you is that option selling is doomed to fail because the rare event will always unavoidably materialize, sooner and stronger than anticipated by conventional wisdom.

For instance, during August 2007 the VIX volatility index (a measure of equity option costliness traded in Chicago) reached historically peaky levels, something that would have been deemed as improbable by many in the face of very low VIX recordings for the prior few years. As a result of such extraordinary turbulence (a measure of the stock market ramifications of the subprime mortgage crisis), those short equity options got hurt, badly. Mark-to-market losses prompted sudden margin calls, a typical tool to assuage counterparty credit concerns. Victor Niederhoffer was among those being demanded more cash in order to stay in the game. Niederhoffer was reportedly asked to double the amount of capital supporting his S&P 500 options positions, but found it difficult to raise the necessary cash. As a result, he was ordered by his brokers (i.e., creditors) to liquidate his portfolio, thus crystalizing big losses. Had he been able to ride it out, things could have turned out okay. The stock market soon rallied and volatility almost halved.

Just like with LTCM, Niederhoffer lost big because he did not have enough capital to survive a short-lived, dramatically impacting mega-rare event to which his option selling trades had fully exposed him. And also like LTCM, the Brooklyn-born risk-taker blamed everything on unanticipated market movements no one could be prepared for (the "perfect storm" argument). A big lesson from Niederhoffer's second bust-up in a decade is that the best preparation would have been not exposing yourself negatively to the rare event in the first place. Because, as we have been reminded so forcefully of late, there is nothing rare about rare events when it comes to financial markets.

Interestingly, none other than Warren Buffett may be (a big *may*) next in line to join the club of wounded option-sellers. In Q1 2008, Berkshire Hathaway saw profits tumble by 64 percent on the back of almost $2 billion of unrealized losses tied to short options positions, a direct result of the crisis-igniting market chaos reigning around that time. Warren Buffet has also sold equity puts (together with, less sizably, short high-yield credit positions). In return for tasty up-front money, he is willing to bet that mainstream stock markets will not nosedive and/or become crazy. The plays have longish maturities (2009 to 2013 in the case of credit, 2019 to 2027 in the case of equities). Berkshire claims to have cashed in to the tune of $3.2 billion (credit plays) and $4.5 billion (equity plays) in received option premium. What's Buffett's rationale? Well, he must believe that high-yield defaults will be limited, that U.S. and foreign stock markets will perform with dignity (these puts were struck at-the-money, so any downward move puts Buffet intrinsically in the red), and he must have plenty of confidence in his ability to invest the premium proceeds.

It is undeniable that Buffett has shown extreme bravery and self-belief. He has chosen to defy the Black Swan that has sunk so many protection sellers throughout history. And he seems certain of his capacity to put the cash raised to very good use. We can almost hear him screaming, "Bring it on! I will make so much money out of those $7 billion that I don't care what happens to my short option positions." The sage's bets look both sizeable and daring. Take the put options on equity indices. As of March 31, 2008, the notional value of the sold puts was a non-negligible $40 billion, representing a mark-to-market liability of over $6 billion.

Berkshire will be fine as long as the Black Swan does not rear its threatening head, sending stock markets into a sharply slumping whirlwind that inflicts large real monetary losses and/or earnings volatility and mark-to-market malaise. Buffett has chosen to leveragely expose his firm to abyss-seeking, wildly turbulent stock markets making an appearance during the next 10 to 20 years.

Would you have made such a bet? Is it implausible, indeed impossible, for the S&P and foreign siblings to experience sharp shoot-the-chute behavior at certain points in the next two decades, including horrendous declines at several specific intervals? Buffett's valiant play has a lot going for it, including substantial up-front capital, Berkshire's long-proven capacity for generating outsized returns, equities' presumed healthy long-term performance, friendly collateral agreements, and the possibility that inflation may reduce the pain of future liabilities. But if financial history (including the most recent kind) teaches a stubborn lesson it is that no matter how advantageous your situation prospectively appears, the apparently rare is not to ever be discarded.

On October 3, 2003, magician Roy Horn was mauled by a white tiger during his famous act at the MGM Mirage in Las Vegas. As a consequence, the "Siegfried and Roy" show had to be indefinitely canceled. Losses for the casino became enormous. Siegfried and Roy was considered the most successful display in the history of Vegas, directly generating annual revenues in excess of $50 million, and much more indirectly (through the sales of food and beverages, hotel rooms, and gambling activities). And to top it all, the Mirage's brand got seriously hampered, given the substantial symbolic value of Siegfried and Roy as publicity tools.

Roy Horn's case, perhaps paradoxically, helps us analyze the fraudulent trading episode famously experienced by French bank Société Générale (SocGen) in early 2008, victim of nonauthorized transactions that ended up yielding a massive loss of 5 billion euros. The main lesson in both cases is that the most impacting and devastating risk can be hidden in the least suspected and monitored places.

MGM Mirage had spent hundreds of millions of dollars in high-tech surveillance systems and mathematical models in order to prevent large setbacks on the gambling floor. The casino seemed to be fully prepared to control that type of exposure, considered the most urgent (and most conventional). However, the events that caused the most consternation lay outside of the models. Besides the tiger attack, a disgruntled contractor tried to blow the place apart with dynamite, and an employee forgot to fill out certain fiscal requirements, resulting in a monstrous fine. At the end of the day, the monetary value of those improbable events represented a much heavier toll than what the more orthodox and monitored risks would have ever caused. Off-model risks can be much more devastating. The most dangerous exposures may not even be under the risk radar. The exposure that can truly kill you can originate in the most unsuspected location. Anything, truly, is possible.

SocGen fell victim to the rare event, and the impact has been as destructively nasty as in the Mirage episode. The financial institution's tiger is called Jérôme Kerviel and, while this time the show will go on, the tamer has again bled massively. The €5 billion loss (materialized when trying to liquidate a longish bet amid tanking, credit crisis–infected stock markets) places SocGen as indisputable leader in the pantheon of rogue traders' victims, way above the hitherto dominators, Sumitomo Corp. and Barings Bank.

Top-rated banks such as SocGen invest large amounts of resources in managing their market, credit, operational, and legal exposures. Hundreds of pros use the latest technologies to model and measure those risks, attempting to create fast-response alarm systems that impose limits and send warning signals if these are breached, in which case positions must be cut until acceptable levels are reached again. That is, those types of risks are amply monitored, and while it could be argued that the methods employed present deficiencies, there is no doubt that senior management is fully conscious of the possible origin of the potential bad news.

When it comes to rogue traders, the surprise factor is much bigger. It is quite likely that neither Daniel Bouton (SocGen's then chairman) nor the vast majority of SocGen's executives had ever heard of Kerviel prior to the scandal. "Kerviel risk" was not under the radar, not at the same level as currency risk, or subprime loans risk, or interest rate risk. In fact, Kerviel particularly exemplifies the improbable rare event.

As opposed to Nick Leeson, the rogue trader who sank Barings in 1995, Kerviel had a very junior rank, made little money, operated in familiar markets through low-profile strategies, and worked from central headquarters in Paris. In sharp contrast, Leeson was Barings' star trader, wielded enormous influence within the bank, was revered by the most senior bigwigs, made huge bonuses, operated in exotic markets, worked from faraway Singapore, and was in charge of the back office (he policed himself and approved his own trades).

That is, while "Leeson risk" could have been considered obvious pre-crisis (and it is clear that Barings incurred tremendous control mishaps), "Kerviel risk" was much less obvious. Even though it is true that his previous middle office experience allowed Kerviel to commit his fraud, it is undoubtable that his profile was very low, undetectably so. Surely, he wasn't under Bouton's (or any of his lieutenants') immediate radar. It didn't seem probable that someone like that would have the potential of causing such destruction. The negatively highly impacting rare event in the shape of Jérôme Kerviel appeared as impossibly unlikely. As utterly improbable (and yet so real) as a tiger becoming a casino's number one risk factor. Or, dare we say, as the investment banking industry disappearing from the face of the earth in but a few months.

We have seen how the credit crisis has been less than generously amicable in its verdict on quantitative finance: All that math-driven theory can fail us and hurt us. It really is an untamable world full of possibilities out there, not a ridiculously limited one where things can be quantitatively forecasted and tidily measured. And the tools that some use in that futile pursuit can go Mr. Hyde and breed tenebrous nastiness. It may thus not be entirely illusory to hope that as a result of the record-setting malaise (all those befell investment banks, all those bust-up insurance companies, all that historical stock market volatility, all those mortgage lender nation-alizations, all those disappearing hedge funds, all those bailout billions), many erstwhile defenders of the quant faith would become converted to the rather softish, equations-lacking, commonsense protestantism. If not voluntarily converted, then at least forcefully so. It is obvious that we need to fight quantitative indoctrination when it comes to the finan-cial arena. The crisis has taught us that. It's time to say enough and to release the stop sign. Watershed times require watershed measures. We must make a concerted effort to prevent the theoretical finance madrassas from graduating disciples willing and able to mathematize us into trouble.

And yet, it seems that a lot of folks continue to eagerly wrap themselves around the dogmatic flag. Zero wishes to be known as "hitherto theory devotees" here. These resilient defenders of the faith act not just as if the lessons from the crisis should be ignored or deemed non-watershedy, but actually go as far as arguing that a passionate renewal of the mathematical vows is the response that's truly needed. Even when your spouse of so many years has been unveiled as a harmful impostor (and everyone around you reminds you of that fact), some quantitative lovebirds propose a reconfirmation of the relationship, demanding only a slight makeover from their objects of desire. No divorce plans here. If such forgiving and forgetful enamoring gets its way, we may be in for a destructive heartbreak down the line.

Take renowned financial engineering guru Robert Jarrow. According to the Cornell University professor, models had nothing to do with the crisis. Quite the contrary, states the math maven, modeling would have delivered us from the mayhem. *"Better and more thoughtful modeling would have alleviated, and perhaps even made impossible to happen, the subprime crisis,"* says Jarrow, who believes that far from demanding a cutback in the quanty stuff, the meltdown demands an enhanced quant presence in finance. Not one to mince words, Jarrow unshyly proclaims that *"The subprime crisis is a cry, a manifestation of the need for better models."* As you can notice, not a word of self-criticism from this most established member of the theoretical establishment. Not a hint that perhaps, maybe, the crisis shows that the mere attempt to introduce advanced science into the markets can deliver a bit of sourness and disappointment. Not a modest display of humbled modesty with the timely recognition that this might be a good occasion to sit down and thoughtfully analyze whether quantitative finance is not all wine and roses after all.

Now, in total fairness, we shouldn't judge Jarrow and same-minded fellow academics too harshly. In their shoes, we may follow an identical path. They simply have too much invested in the notion that no models is not an acceptable option. If current models go wrong, that's fine. You never admit to their failing being an overall indictment on the quantification religion, while fastly suggesting the need for better, improved, fine-tuned machinations, which you gladly volunteer to produce in short notice. Anything but admitting, even with the slightest of winks, that perhaps finance is not about advanced science. When you have built an entire career based on the peddle that finance is science ("applied math," according to Jarrow), we shouldn't be extremely surprised if you turn down our offer to show some humbleness in the face of theory-lambasting chaos.

Of course, dogma-defending theoreticians know perfectly well that the world has endowed them with the most glorious of gifts, the perfect antidote against any theory-threatening developments: a perpetual re-munerated call option. The most efficient method to encourage people like Jarrow to engage in theoretical research. There is tons of upside and no downside. If you do well you get paid very well and may even get a Nobel. Crucially, the theory doesn't have to work in the real world or bring benefits to the industry; it simply has to look fabulous equations-wise. If the models fail in real life and even wreak havoc, no suffering accrues to you. There's no downside. You won't lose your job or the re-spect of your peers (and vast numbers of diploma-hypnotized outsiders). You might even still have a chance at the Nobel (Black-Scholes won after Black Monday and with 10 years of the volatility smile smiling out there). There may be, actually, and as anticipated, tremendous upside in the shape of new opportunities for "better" research.

The credit crisis shows that many theoreticians are not about to let go of that call option just because the world is in flames and finance theory may have had a lot to do with it, let alone having demonstrated (once more) monstrous shortcomings. Now we know, for sure, that the quan-tification priests will never accede to renouncing their lemmas-idolatry (those willing to show some self-doubt after the credit carnage, please speak louder, we can't hear you) and will never cease to attempt to convert the rest of us, no matter how grandiosely sinister, how ruthlessly devas-tating, how unequivocally destabilizing the side effects of their theology may be.

The venerable Sloan School of Business at the venerable Massachusetts Institute of Technology has recently launched a new educational pro-gram, its very own Masters in Finance. For those less than exaggeratedly interested in the graduate education landscape and who may doubt the relevance of such news, let me assure you that Sloan's initiative is nothing short of revolutionary. It is the first time that a truly top U.S. business school has decided to offer a fully fledged specialized finance degree, in a pioneering move that may soon be imitated by some of MIT's privileged peers (the likes of Harvard or Stanford).

In doing so, Sloan joins a bandwagon that had steadily become globally crowdier. The past few years have witnessed an unmistakable explosion in the number of finance university programs worldwide, housed by both notorious institutions (Oxford, Cambridge, Princeton) and by a myriad of less mythical schools. Such development comes on the heels of a prior, even more pronounced, burst in the number of graduate degrees in quantitative finance, financial engineering, and computational finance, subdisciplines that concern themselves with the heavy-duty mathematical, statistical, and software-design skills typically employed by the brainiac quants found inside investment banks and hedge funds.

In sum, it wouldn't be far-fetched to say that the international financial education field is experiencing its own bubble, glowingly exemplified by MIT's jump into the market. Paradoxically, of course, this bubble is reaching peaky dimensions precisely when the bubble that had afflicted the real financial world for so long is being pricked at a horrifyingly accelerating rate. Will all those newly minted finance graduates be welcomed by such a lackluster job and earnings environment? Could the pricking of the real financial bubble hasten the prickle of the educational bubble?

I, for one, hope that is not the case. As a very strong defender of the rationale for (real-world-grounded, practically oriented, that is) specialized finance programs (I kind of forecasted MIT's move a while back), I would hate, in principle, to see such valiant efforts hampered because a bunch of irresponsible players decided to bet the house (pun very much intended) on the possibility that people with no income, no jobs, and no assets would not default on their unseemly mortgage loans.

But such initial declaration of love does not imply that these new finance degrees are mistake-free. In particular, the contents of many of them are perilously close to being irrelevant in today's shaky environment and, worse, may contribute to helping restore and perpetuate notions and practices that have clearly been key driving forces behind the latest malaise and turmoil. To put it bluntly, many of these programs indoctrinate students into the sacredness and hallowedness of techniques and tools that have consistently shown (in this crisis as well as before) their unrepentant capacity to wreak havoc in the markets.

There is no doubt that a big casualty of the credit nightmare that began in the summer of 2007 has been the validity of theoretical and quantitative methods in finance. The complex mathematical models used to value and rate complex credit derivatives structures proved spectacularly lacking. Value at Risk was revealed clothes-less by much-bigger-than-indicated losses. Advanced econometric forecasting tools did not provide any warning. The central tenets of Nobel-sanctioned financial economics (markets behave normally, rare events don't happen, liquidity is not an issue, standard deviation is a reliable measure of risk) were savagely dev-astated by a tidal wave of hard-knocking reality. Quant funds suffered huge setbacks (though it is not entirely clear the extent to which such computer-aided punters care for finance theory at all).

And yet, the flavor of many of the new finance programs is indelibly theoretical and quanty. Most of them concentrate excessively on technical tools and theorems rather than actual products, markets, and institutions. Rather than being treated as supportive tools that may or may not be used by a minority of specialists in the real world, subjects like econometrics, microeconomics, and stochastic calculus are often accorded royal treat-ment, prominently placed as integral and undoubted parts of the core curriculum. The undiluted message from these schools is that finance *is* econometrics, microeconomics, and stochastic calculus. When learning GARCH models and Ito's lemma (which are, at best, utilized by but a tiny fraction of professionals) becomes more important than understand-ing capital markets or derivatives accounting, you know that quantitative indoctrination has run amok. As we have just been (once more) re-minded, blind, sectlike belief in the dictates of mathematical finance and financial economics can provoke quite unsavory outcomes.

Unfortunately, MIT appears to have chosen to tag along the quanty lines. Given the institution's impressive status, the clear and present danger is that such endorsement may be seen by many as an irrefutably positive indictment on the merits of the theorems. It may be difficult for some to conclude that the equations were behind the crisis when concurrently with the bloodbath one of the world's most elite educational outposts is busy surrounding its pioneering decision to launch a finance degree with unmistakably intense quantitative cred.

Listen to how the Sloan School advertises its new dish: *"Modern finance is a high-tech industry, requiring increasingly sophisticated quantitative tools to assess and manage risks and returns. The development of modern finance came in part from breakthroughs in research, including the Black-Scholes-Merton deriva-tives pricing model, the Cox-Ingersoll-Ross model of the term structure of interest rates and the Modigliani-Miller theorems on corporate financing and valuation.*

Much of this research was pioneered by MIT faculty, and in some cases these pathbreaking ideas appeared in the Sloan curriculum well in advance of their widespread adoption by industry professionals. " This is theoretical convention-alism run amok. Out-of-control mathematical establishment–honoring. Unmitigated equation-blindness. Dangerous propaganda. Unfettered in-doctrination. Finance is high-tech. Finance requires (I guess "needs" is no longer enough for the financial economics priests) sophisticated quantitative tools. Finance owes its modern existence to research break-throughs. Finance pros use the tools widespreadly. Of course! I believe you! Please, tell me when the collection basket is passed at the theoretical church, I just became irredeemably converted and want to make a large donation!

By fervently promoting such naive (almost childish), tired, empty slo-gans, Sloan is, surprisingly for such a cutting-edge and forward-looking place, living in the past. Such utterances look 20 or 30 years old. They definitely don't belong in the age of the iPod and Google (or history-making credit crises that deprive us of the investment banking industry). Is it really appropriate to peddle a finance degree that will debut in 2009 by mentioning Miller-Modigliani, a 1950s theory that says that it doesn't matter if a firm is leveraged or not? Or by referring to Black–Scholes, a 1970s concoction that, more than any other scion of financial economics, has proven spectacularly wrong and harmful?

It is not so much that theory has moved on (though in some ways it has; interestingly, one of the most revolutionary, anticlassical economics contributions comes from Andrew Lo, a leading finance prof at Sloan), but mostly that the real world has so evidently moved on. Decades ago you may have been forgiven for enthusiastically embracing the new, complexly beautiful enactments. They seemed full of promise, and they promised so much. But not these days. Only someone outstandingly blind to real-life developments would want to equate finance to sci-entific discoveries. Only someone extraordinarily neglectful of the real world would elect to promote a finance education program through the quantitative sales pitch. When you go that route after Black Monday, LTCM, the Nasdaq boom-and-bust, dynamic hedging's failures, VaR during the Asian Crisis, VaR during the Russian Crisis, VaR during the Credit Crisis, VaR during the Quant Funds Crisis, Gaussian Copula, the 2005 correlation crisis, the rating agencies disaster, and the volatility smile, you are presenting yourself as an irreverent indoctrinator bent on disseminating a creed that has long been largely discredited. You might as well seclude yourself and your indoctrinees in an isolated, cloistered convent and vow eternal withdrawal from the outer world.

At a time when the mathematical finance edifice is crumbling harshly and when the obsession with assigning precise, concrete figures to unknown parameters such as expected loss or default correlation has proven sensationally erroneous, is it the right approach to loudly promote those failed tenets from the far-reaching academic confines? Masters in Finance graduates are being touted as an elite corps of financial wizards, the chosen ones who will lead the finance industry into the future. Given the troubles that an unfettered faith in quantitative "certainties" can provoke, we would all be that much safer if those individuals joined the financial world free of any illusions as to the true value of theoretical and mathematical gimmicks.

Varied have been the measures demanded by pundits and politicians as a result of the credit crisis. Tougher regulation, revised benchmark lending rates, less exoticism, and a deep revision of the rating agencies business have all been loudly petitioned as prerequisites to avoid a repetition of the mayhem. Equally important as all those important steps would be a transformation inside the university campus. When it comes to the classrooms and the impressionable future players that inhabit them, finance needs to go back to being about finance.

Chapter 7

The Black-Scholes Conundrum

■ *Once upon a time at MIT* ■ *Frowning, not smiling*
■ *How Black was that Monday* ■ *A devastating KO*
■ *The Taleb & Haug critique* ■

S ometime in the spring of 2007, I attended an all-star derivatives seminar organized by the Stern School of Business at New
York University. The keynote speaker was Myron Scholes, a
practitioner-academic most famous for having co-authored the most
famous financial formula ever. He wasn't there to talk about his formula,
but rather about his new life as sophisticated asset manager. However,
the formula did, perhaps disappointingly to him, inevitably come up at
one point during the talks.

One very prominent former quant (and currently very prominent
academic) took to the podium with the intention of complimenting
the option pricing model that Mr. Scholes and Fischer Black (with
the help of Robert Merton) had put together almost 40 years earlier.
His compliment consisted of endowing the formula with the nametag
"sophisticated vulgarity." Trust me when I tell you that that was meant as
a compliment. I was there and could look the speaker in the eyes, distill
his intentions through his tone of voice. Besides, I knew the man and his
beliefs, and was aware of the illuminating fact that he had worked in the
past with Black and had consistently had nothing but perennial accolades
towards his persona.

Unfortunately, Myron Scholes did not get the joke. Sitting right next to our man, and being observed by some of the world's top finance professors and quants, Scholes wasted no time in expressing his outright displeasure with the terminology selected by his praiser. Instead of allowing his mind to dig deeper into the actual meaning of the term that had just been showered on his precious mathematical construction, he seemed incapable of not being irredeemably turned off by the "vulgarity" stuff. Believing that he had just been insulted and demeaningly deemed vulgar, the Nobel Prize winner appeared unable to accept the (extraordinarily gentlemanly and outlandishly public) apologetic clarifications from his reluctantly-turned-nemesis complimenter, who a few minutes after having finished his speech raised his voice again to explicate that he didn't intend to insult the formula one bit. Quite the opposite, actually.

This narrative serves us to gain clarifying understanding about two key themes: one, the value that the Black-Scholes-Merton (BSM) model can provide (when actually used by traders); two, the saintliness with which BSM has been unconditionally surrounded by the theoretical establishment since it first came on stage, with anything resembling harsh criticism being mercilessly corralled and lambasted. Both issues are critically important to this book, as they go to the heart of the debate regarding the validity of finance theory. BSM has traditionally been portrayed as the crowning achievement of financial economics, an unassailable symbol of triumph for the equation-fetishizing crowd; thus, excessive criticism upon the model has always been seen as akin to pit-bully attacking theoretical achievements overall. Note in this respect that BSM has been amply found to be somewhat faulty by many academics and quants, but such reactions have led not to a point-of-no-return demonization, but to the mathematical fine-tuning of a mathematical structure that has been otherwise respectfully kept in place. That is, there have been numerous calls for the modification of the formula, but not for its extermination.

Scholes's "critic" would belong to that school of complainers who have worked hard at correcting the model's technical malfunctions but who haven't gone so far as to qualify it as useless or even irrelevant. By "sophisticated vulgarity," the quant-academic who incurred Scholes's wrath actually meant that BSM is a shining example of the best that mathematical finance has to offer. The best models, the homology-throwing quant-academic stated, are those that use "vulgar" variables but in a sophisticated setting. By *vulgar*, he meant variables that are actually used by people in the markets and that are thus readily observable. Variables that are the result of the dirty, sweaty, degenerate actions of market players could be sensibly termed as unrefined, plebeian, or, yes, vulgar. Once you combine such unwashedness with ultra-complex theoretical/mathematical platforms, you obtain something that can be trusted, something that's usable—sophisticated vulgarity.

BSM would appear to be the most obvious poster child of such glorious combination. No one can doubt the sophistication of the concoction. In its fully fledged version, it incorporates decisively unplebeian things like Geometric Brownian Motion, partial differential equations, stochastic calculus, and probability theory. At the same time, BSM glowingly allows for unfettered vulgarity in the sense that it fully employs (in fact, generates) boorish market jargon through something called implied volatility, a variable that is supposed to express the market's consensual view of future asset returns turbulence and that is obtained directly from BSM (as we will see repeatedly in this chapter, traders as assumed to include such view into the model's volatility parameter). Such implied figure can then be used to value all types of options, from vanilla to exotic, safe in the knowledge that one is using market-parented intelligence. Thus, vulgarity would get spread out, mixing itself with ever more sophisticated platforms. The vulgar part would actually allow the sophisticated part to play a role, by endowing it with street cred. Scholes had it twicely wrong: The criticism was in fact a powerful exercise in flattering, and the vulgarity that it helps create and transmit is the most valuable aspect of his Nobel-caliber baby.

To be perfectly honest, I left the NYU seminar a bit upset at Scholes's reaction towards our open-minded, creatively waxing, quant-academic friend. It wasn't just a matter of less-than-perfect fairness, or the fact that the discussion became impossibly awkward once the podium infighting was unleashed. What I most disliked was that the co-father of modern option pricing theory (aka the co-father of modern finance theory) was not recognizing the aid and assistance that he was receiving and misinterpreting. No, I am not talking here again about the failure to comprehend that calling his model vulgar was akin to calling it wonderful. I am talking about something much more important, much more decisive: Scholes had chosen to lambast someone who was voluntarily contributing to sheltering his fame-granting formula from its gravest menace, the unveiling of which would certainly provide a real reason to truly get upset.

In making his misunderstood flattering, the quant-academic was assuming all along that BSM is used in the markets. The sophisticatedly vulgar tool was indisputably thought of as being widely popular among traders, an indelible inhabitant of trading floors and exchange pits around the globe. Scholes should have instantly gotten off his chair and run to the podium to hug the quant-academic for sending such life jacket his way. For you see, it is not entirely clear that (as we had come to religiously believe for more than three decades) BSM is in fact employed by pros.

Since the appearance a couple of years ago of earth-shaking research by two former senior traders with quantitative knowledge, we can no longer safely assume that the sophisticated vulgarity should be deemed BSM or, even more Bastille-stormingly, that the sophisticated vulgarity is used at all. Perhaps option traders do not use mathematical devices as often as conventionally enshrined. It could all be the result of plain, staid, untheoretical supply and demand. In other words, the whole thing would be one big vulgarity, with absolutely no role for sophistication. This would obviously be a much bigger indictment of BSM and financial economics than the mild effrontery of harmless name-calling. By taking for granted that BSM is used in real life, the quant-academic was throwing an olive branch, not a gauntlet, to the best-known exemplar of theoretical finance. Given the unprecedentedly powerful latter-day existence-denying criticisms of the model, theoreticians would be well advised to show gratitude, not derision, towards those still in the habit of toeing the traditionalist line and portraying BSM as an employed success.

The story of how BSM came to be has been overwhelmingly told in dozens of books and articles, so allow me to try to summarize such untamable amalgamation of information. In January 1965, Fischer Black (a recently minted PhD in Mathematics from Harvard) joined Boston-based consultancy Arthur D Little (ADL), to help businesses improve their computer use. Soon he began to develop a strong interest in financial matters, upon meeting his ADL colleague Jack Treynor. Treynor is the least-known of the two co-inventors of the Capital Asset Pricing Model (CAPM), an indisputable bedrock of modern finance theory. Black soon became irremediably enamored with CAPM, a love affair that was to last throughout his fruitful and varied life. Without such steamy encounter, it is possible that Black would have never become involved in option pricing.

Fired up by Treynor's mentorship, Black caught financial economics fever. He began to mingle with leading academics, and in mid-1967 initiated his lifelong tradition of penning working papers dealing with financial risk, corporate investments, and assorted finance-related stuff. These initial ruminations were dominated by CAPM in an almost obsessive fashion. A CAPM world is a world where equilibrium reigns supreme and markets are efficient. This ideal appealed so much to Black that he decided to devote his existence to making it come true. The future father of modern option theory staunchly believed that the future belonged to CAPM. It is thus not surprising that back in those early days Black would reach the conclusion that CAPM could be applied to solving just about any financial problem, including, yes, option pricing.

That particular quest received an extra push when Black enlisted a partner-in-crime. Shortly after arriving at the Massachusetts Institute of Technology's Sloan School of Business in September 1968, rooky finance professor Myron Scholes telephoned Black at next-door ADL and met him for lunch. Having heard about Black's finance work through a fellow PhD student at the University of Chicago (soon-to-be star academic Michael Jensen), Scholes thought that here was someone that he could collaborate with, a devoted fan of the new finance theories with an unrestrained interest in applying them to real-life problems. So eager was Black to embark on the theoretical crusade that he quit his ADL job in early 1969 and set up a consultancy deemed Associates in Finance, with Scholes as reliable contributor. His first assignment consisted in proposing a CAPM-compliant investment strategy to Wells Fargo Bank, which was not eventually adopted. Not to be discouraged, Black and Scholes continued to toil together along similar lines. Soon, they found an extra reason to pick each other's brains.

It is not entirely clear why Fischer Black began to be interested in options, but it may all have boiled down to his mission to apply CAPM to all kinds of assets beyond the model's original focus on stocks. Whatever the initial inspiration, by June 1969 he had distilled the challenge of valuing a stock warrant to a partial differential equation (a complex, difficult-to-solve, mathematical expression). He was unfortunately unable to solve it by himself, so he put the whole thing aside. Nonetheless, he was convinced of his work's breakthroughness, for one crucial reason: The stock's expected return was nowhere to be seen in the equation. That is, he seemed to have found a formula for warrant (option) pricing that did not require one to have to forecast the future stock path, a decisively subjective and inaccuracy-prone task. Previous efforts suffered precisely from that problem, as we will see in a second.

It was thus with more than a passing interest that Black reacted to Scholes' disclosure of his own work on warrant pricing a few months later, apparently inspired after supervising a thesis from one of his students. They both tackled the problem from the same philosophical angle: CAPM-compliance. Scholes was familiar with arbitrage-enforced pricing and tried to apply the notion to the warrant affair by building a portfolio made up of the warrant and stock; by going long the warrant (which goes up in value if the stock price goes up) and short the stock, he reasoned that you could build a market-neutral position, or, in CAPM-speak, a *zero-beta* position, uncorrelated with the overall market and thus, according to CAPM, one that should earn a risk-free rate of return. But at that point, he didn't know how to construct such portfolio. Like Black, his solo efforts were roadblocked.

Black was familiar with the modeling of the relationship of variables that depend on each other, thanks to work that he had done with, certainly, Jack Treynor. He had used such tricks (including the famous Taylor-series expansion) to get to his differential equation. Black and Scholes understood that the partial (mathematical) derivative of the warrant price with regards to the stock price was the key to building the zero-beta portfolio: that derivative (or "delta") tells you how much you have to trade of the stock in order to keep the portfolio's value insulated from market movements. The end result of this reasoning led again to Black's equation. Scholes' arbitrage arguments thus provided confirmation that Black had been on to something. They were now certain that they were in a zero-beta scenario and, thus, according to CAPM, a risk-free one. The portfolio's expected return should be equal to the riskless rate. But they still could not solve the equation.

What did they do? They went back a few years and borrowed from one of the previous attempts at theoretical option pricing, armed with their belief that this was now a zero-beta universe. In 1961, Case Sprenkle, a PhD student at Yale University, had come up with a warrant formula based on the mathematical model for stock price movements overwhelmingly embraced by modern financial economics (i.e., his methodology was status quo–compliant). The formula asked of the user to make guesses as to the stock's expected future return and the investor's risk preferences. Seen eight years afterwards from Black's and Scholes's zero-beta world, the latter was assigned by the duo a value of zero (equivalent to a risk-neutral individual) and the former was assigned the risk-free rate. And, voila, the legendary Black-Scholes formula was born. Since the formula satisfied the differential equation, it was valid not just for zero-beta stocks but for all kinds.

It should be blindingly obvious that Black-Scholes was a theory whose validity depended on the validity of another theory. Black-Scholes was presented as the right approach entirely because it came with the CAPM stamp of approval. The sleight-of-hand that allowed them to shout "It's risk-neutrality!" and thus to avoid the pesky task of having to make a call on the stock's expected return and on personal preferences (a big reason why previous theories had not been applicable) was CAPM-sanctioned. Without CAPM, no riskless rate. Without CAPM, no glorious transition from neglected, shadowy Sprenkle to future Nobelist Black-Scholes. It should be clear that this was a theory justified entirely by another theory. Talk about Platonicity.

When Robert Merton took a look at Black's and Scholes's analysis in the autumn of 1970, he instantly appreciated the potential of the contribution. Ever since joining MIT as an Economics PhD student in early 1967, Merton (a brilliant mathematician with a longtime interest in financial affairs) had been working under the wings of Paul Samuelson, a towering figure in the field who had developed an interest in warrant pricing. Merton took to this wholeheartedly, and did considerable research on the topic (Black's own initial interest in the problem may have been inspired by Merton's and Samuelson's intellectual production). His attention was certainly piqued when his MIT colleague Scholes disclosed his work with Black.

Merton's enthusiasm did not owe to the CAPM stuff. He didn't care much for CAPM, faithfully following his mentor Samuelson's thinking. He deemed Black's and Scholes's approach "intuitive" rather than "rigorous" (but note that by employing CAPM as an alibi, their method, notwithstanding its intuitive feel, was crowned fully permissible by the theoretical intelligentsia). He didn't like the fact that you had to take the formula on CAPM-faith, but he saw potential elsewhere. He loved the no-arbitrage part, the idea that you could find a price that is enforce-able and independent of pesky, human-dependent unobservables.

Merton agreed that risk-neutrality was at the end of the road, but he conceived of a superior (to him) way to get there different from CAPM-cultism. The key to him was the warrant-stock position, which can be made riskless through delta trading. If you could maintain the position continuously during the life of the warrant, readjusting the delta as the market moves, you could erase all risk from the transaction. By dynami-cally rebalancing the delta nonstop, one could build a combination made up of stock and cash (to finance your stock activities) that is at all times equal in value to the warrant. Thus, a portfolio made up of the war-rant and the stock-cash combination would be a riskless proposition. It should earn the risk-free rate since they both match each other perfectly. Otherwise, there would be arbitrage opportunities, an impossibility in an efficient universe. A dealer selling a warrant could hedge his liability by manufacturing the replicating portfolio, safe in the (theoretical) knowl-edge that they will always mirror each other all the way to maturity, allowing him to run a riskless business. The cost of the portfolio thus becomes the premium to charge for the warrant (or else arbitrageurs would make sure that any discrepancy is ruthlessly ironed out until the match is perfect once more).

Merton could handle such continuous replication exercise because he was unique among economists back then in mastering stochastic calculus, the challenging discipline that deals with modeling processes of change in continuous time when the underlying variables are nondeterministic (i.e., the calculus of an unpredictably behaving world). Employing impossibly complex tools with funny names (such as Ito's Lemma), Merton was able to solve the problem. In August 1970, he arrived at exactly the same formula as Black and Scholes (or shall we say, the special case of Sprenkle's formula). Pricing by dynamic hedging–fueled arbitrage had none of the cloudily semireligious feeling of CAPM-based pricing. It was instead based on the most advanced type of quantitative weaponry and the indisputably iron-clad arbitrage guarantee.

No wonder, then, that Merton's method took over. When Black and Scholes (after much hassle and lobbying by senior financial economics figures) finally published their paper in 1973, they essentially presented Merton's revised pathway to the formula, with a hat-in-hand inclusion of Black's original CAPM-revering derivation as an addendum. When people talk about the Black-Scholes formula they are basically referring to Merton's contribution, with no mention whatsoever of CAPM. What started as a CAPM-guided quest has passed into history exclusively as a dynamic hedging conquest.

Naturally, Merton's theoretical baby is not devoid of Platonicity itself (the assumption of a riskless rate of return is valid only if we can manufacture the replicating portfolio at all times and under the stringent conditions delineated), but at least its validity does not depend upon the validity of another theory. However, as will be analyzed in detail later in this chapter, Merton's Platonicity was to prove extremely disturbing and inefficient in real life throughout the years. Simply put, dynamic hedging has reliably proven both ineffectual and dangerous. Black's original analysis, in contrast, was, for all its softish naïveté, admirably harmless. It didn't commandingly direct traders to take very precise actions in the markets, and thus (unlike delta hedging) could not have an impact on the latter's turbulence. It is interesting to note that had Merton never showed up, the world would have had access to the same easy-to-use formula, delivering the same outputs, but without any of the collateral damage. In all fairness though, it is likely that the no-arbitrage argument decisively enhanced the tool's popularity among end users, as traders would be expected to be more comfortable with the notion of replicating the option through frequent stock transacting (after all, there is well-documented evidence that option players were familiar with some form of ad hoc delta hedging long before Black, Scholes, or Merton were even born) than with unfettered abidance by CAPM. In this light, Merton's contributions may have been the key to transforming the model from yet another obscure theoretical divination into an (at least initially) actionable construct endorsed by the real world. And not just brute pros. On endowing the model with the Nobel Prize in Economics in 1997, the granting committee cited specifically the dynamic hedging stuff (and the innovative way to price contracts that it enabled) as the very reason for the festivities.

Black and Scholes encountered enormous difficulties when trying to publish their paper. They were rejected by all major economics journals, which saw their contribution as too narrowly focused on a too unimportant issue. Academic establishment heavy hitters like Merton Miller and Eugene Fama (messiahs of modern financial economics who knew Scholes and Black and who loved their allegiance to the sacred scriptures of theoretical dogmatism) stepped in and sweet-talked the *Journal of Political Economy* into acceding. The formula became publicly available in May 1973. Merton was gentlemanly enough to wait until the duo went live before publishing his own derivation in detail.

We know that there were option pricing formulas (based on rigorous, accepted mathematical techniques) available well before BSM. In fact, we have seen how Black and Scholes unashamedly borrowed from Sprenkle, effectively making their formula look like Sprenkle's (under the special case of a risk-neutral world). We will expand on this substantially later in the book, but Sprenkle was not the only precursor. In 1964, James Boness, a PhD student at the University of Chicago, had a formula that was even simpler than Sprenkle's and even closer to BSM. Here the only unobservable involving human decisions was the stock's expected return, which he somehow tried to estimate from quoted option prices. Had Boness been more pragmatic, and less of a perfectionistic purist, he might have just selected the risk-free rate as expected return and would have produced the exact same mathematical beauty as BSM, almost a decade earlier.

Mathematician turned gambler turned hedge fund giant Edward Thorp partnered in 1965 with then fellow academic Sheen Kassouf to try their hands at warrant valuation. In their 1967 book *Beat the Market* they discuss market-neutral delta hedging, describing practical off-the-cuff approximation rules for rebalancing the hedge, without going as far as proposing continuous dynamic hedging that would remove all the risk all the time.

Thorp wasn't entirely satisfied from a quantitative angle, believing that more mathematical strictness could be added to the casual work already produced. In so acting, he soon churned out a formula (published in 1969) exactly similar to Sprenkle's but, crucially, took a leap of faith and assumed a risk-neutral world, thus yielding an identical BSM twin. He didn't think that enormous errors would be introduced by such reckless act of individuality and found the end result plausible. So much, that he soon began to use the thing for actual trading, as radar that could identify massively overpriced options. Also crucially, Thorp continues to talk about static delta hedging but points in the direction of a dynamic, superior alternative. He didn't, though, attempt to mathematize his way into dynamic territory, stating that *"The methods, technical details, and probabilistic summary are more complex so we defer the details for possibly subsequent publication."*

So if other very similar (or outrightly identical) constructs were already in existence, why did BSM establish itself, to this day, as the de facto option pricing tool? Such paradox is probably explained by a combination of factors. First, it had unassailably steely backing by the academic-theoretical financial economics establishment of the time, an unstoppably rising, Attila the Hun–style force (BSM results were widely and forcibly publicized as dogma backed by the highest academic popes, lending golden ivory tower legitimacy). Second, it could actually yield a result (all the ancient inventions demanded impossibly subjective, indelibly personal judgments on the part of users; Thorp was apparently more interested in moneymaking than fame, so had little incentive to spread the word of his second attempt). Third, its actual coming-out party coincided, like clockwork, with the inauguration of the Chicago Board Options Exchange (CBOE) and its listing of stock index options (in contrast, at the time of Sprenkle's or Boness's machinations, trading in equity options was a semimarginalized, limited, backstreets kind of activity).

The revolutionary aspect of BSM was not just limited to its original intent. Beyond simple option valuation, BSM took economics by storm by formalizing a way to enforce asset pricing through indisputable arbitrage. The buildup of a mirror replicating portfolio that is continuously matching was the true breakthrough concept, extended in posterior years to many other financial challenges. And yet it seems hard to conclude that the Merton-conceived arbitrage cruiser is devoid of leaks. In future pages we will analyze why dynamic hedging breaks down in real financial markets, but let's now consider a more general point.

BSM is built on flatly unrealistic assumptions, including the mathematical process it assumes the underlying asset to follow (lognormal random walk, whereby asset returns are supposed to abide by the Normal probability distribution that rules out extreme events), the posit that interest rates and volatility are constant, the tenet that asset prices don't jump, and the premise of perfectly liquid markets with no transaction costs. These assumptions were necessary for two obvious reasons: compliance with standard academic models, and the need to conceive of a world where dynamic hedging could operate unhampered. BSM has been repeatedly brought to task (though, as will be seen, not exactly harshly so) on account of such drawbacks throughout the years, with Fischer Black himself openly sharing his doubts about the model's unrealistic foundations. He was always unapologetically skeptical about Merton's eventually dominant insight, in part because of his devotion for CAPM-only solutions but in large part also because enforcement through dynamic hedging piles up the number of shaky hypotheses that need to be made at the outset.

Less talked about has been an apparently obvious, and undeniably weighty, additional motive to doubt the model. For BSM to be the market price, we unavoidably need people to enforce the nonarbitrage condition. That is, we need dynamic hedgers who follow the model's prescriptions. But not just a few—we need lots of them. BSM will be the true price only if everybody has read, understood, and implemented BSM. Otherwise how could they know that they have to do arbitrage and how to do it? Even assuming that the replicating strategy can actually work, it needs implementers. How can we be so sure that they will be out there, ready to play with delta? How can we be so sure that everybody has read, understood, and implemented BSM? The reliability of this particular piece of theoretical output depends on people being 100 percent aware, 100 percent of the time, of its tenets, understanding them, accepting them, and acting on them (even if the theory is understood and embraced, it may still not be acted on, be it because of implementation inconveniences or due to laziness). Unless people oblige, the theory won't be the practice.

How can we be so sure that the alleged BSM-aware, BSM-abiding arbitrageurs will be there and will be powerful enough to drive things towards BSM-compliant equilibrium? Other, more influential constituents not acting under BSM-hypnosis may outmaneuver them and drive prices away from theory. Imagine that the market price of a call option quotes at $10 when the BSM formula says it should be $9. According to the efficient market theory underlying BSM, this won't last as savvy arbitrageurs will go short the option and long the replicating portfolio (so as to capture an effortless $1 with no hassle), until both are worth the same. The BSM price thus becomes the market price. But this assumes that we are all dynamic hedging arbitrageurs. What if there are tons of players who not only ignore the existence of BSM, don't believe in it, or don't feel like delta rebalancing, but actually (and very much against the spirit of BSM) consider that their subjective judgments and opinions should play a role in the whole thing? These nonanalytical individuals may think $10 to be a pretty acceptable price because they expect the underlying asset to go up and up in the near future. The calls get bid up, without remorse, rendering the efforts of the theory-enforcing dynamic hedgers utterly unproductive, and perhaps taking the option price all the way to, say, $14 or $15. Far from descending into the mathematical arms of BSM, real prices would insultingly deviate.

It is obvious that humans are not born with BSM prewired inside their brains, and that BSM is not part of our DNA. We are not born ready and able to do delta hedging. By choosing the arbitrage path, BSM set itself a trap by entrusting its very feasibility to the existence of a huge army of flesh-and-bones BSM-adoring replicators. A first, foremost, and unassailable requirement for BSM to work is that people know about the model's arbitrage strategy and overwhelmingly decide to abide by it. For BSM to deliver on its promise, we must all be emotions-devoid dynamic hedgers. Sounds like a pretty ambitious assumption.

Thus, perhaps we should stop viewing BSM as a pricing formula. The market's price will be whatever the market wants it to be. BSM would rather be an arbitrage strategy that could be followed by those who believe in its foundations and are certain that delta hedging is feasible. If you are one of those loyalists and detect severe mispricing out there, you could make profits that are worth writing home about. But don't passionately expect your actions to determine prices for everyone else. That would a tad bit presumptuous. After all, not everyone else is like you.

Of course, players may use BSM as a way to obtain an option price *without* performing the replicating strategy in parallel. They may enjoy the conveniences of using a platform such as BSM (where the only parameter that needs to be estimated is the stock's volatility), but would totally shy away from full-blown delta hedging (don't believe it can work, too bothersome, too costly). They would be overly glad that the special case of Sprenkle's and Boness's formulas which makes it easiest to calculate an option price (risk-neutrality, which doesn't require subjective opinions and that comfortably limits the number of unobservables) is so conveniently justified on "scientific" grounds, but refuse to take the delta-express leap from those pioneer efforts to BSM. Under this scenario BSM may be the employed tool, but not for the reasons outlined by the model itself (which would certainly include CAPM, an even less plausible factor behind end users' actions). The model could then be seen as triumphant but its theoretical foundations would have suffered the bitterest of defeats: appallingly unmitigated indifference.

BSM is, crucially, not just the best-known financial economics scion but by far the most demonstrably powerful. BSM is the only theoretical finance construct that may have been actually and actively employed (in name at least) by hundreds of thousands of players around the world. BSM is the theoretical finance construct to have had the largest demonstrably tangible and impactful effect on real-life markets. Its powerfulness is particularly impressive when compared to its Nobel-endowed cousins. Neither Modern Portfolio Theory, nor CAPM, Miller-Modigliani, or GARCH can boast near the same level of influence. None of them can be massively found (again, in name at least) in traders' computer terminals globally, none of them has moved markets, none of them has caused a crash. Only BSM has been (most likely wrongly) credited with kick-starting a now ubiquitously essential segment of the financial arena. Such influence guarantees that no other mathematical model has done more towards helping establish and perpetuate the notion that modern finance is about math. No other tool has contributed more towards the academic PR campaign to have financial economics declared a science.

But there is another side to that coin. BSM has also been the most harmful of models, determinedly fueling the worst disaster in Wall Street history (the aforementioned crash, on October 1987) as well as bouts of extraordinary market chaos (such as the wild swings experienced by currency markets in the mid-1990s). More than any other famous theory, BSM is ingrained with the seeds of trouble, since its mathematical foundations encourage savagely trend-enhancing (as well as trend-reversing on occasions) position-taking by traders. Most taxing, BSM stands alone among its fellow theoretical icons as the only one which we know for sure has been rejected and declared unfit by the market. Mean-variance portfolio management and financial econometrics may have been considered less-than-appealing too, but we have no official market-dictated confirmation. Not so with BSM. Through something called "volatility smile" (more on this later), traders are unabashedly shouting their displeasure with the holy option pricing model, very illustratively indicating not only that they don't trust it but that they have collectively reached the conclusion of not employing it. While the BSM architecture may continue to be in use, the model's spirit has been purposefully manipulated into oblivion. Even when appearing to use BSM, traders have made sure that the tool is unrecognizable beyond its name.

BSM thus presents finance theory with a troublesome conundrum. It's not just that, as indicated above, the most glorified of constructs has displayed a tormentous capacity for havoc-wreaking or that traders obviously don't embrace it wholeheartedly. These have traditionally been relatively minor concerns, never obstinately challenging the perception that BSM is a successful theory (after all, the known episodes of market chaos have been few and apart, and many have traditionally viewed the volatility smile as a confirmation of the model's usefulness and popularity, not as a rejection). Unfortunately for BSM fans, something new has recently come up, a potentially much more damaging revelation. Akin to an apparently perfect son about whom you have been relentlessly bragging in front of the neighbors and who is later found out, after many years, of having indulged in all kinds of malicious vices. Once the disturbing truth is out, should you disown your offspring, reform him, or act as if nothing had happened? The BSM model has been "outed" as less-than-perfect by the intruding musings of two impudent rogues who, rather quite inconveniently, boast 30 years combined experience as option traders and understand the math. This time, the outing is real, not the typical mildish reminder that the model's mathematical foundations do not exactly hold in real life. Such timid disagreements never did any true harm to the model, its founders, its followers, or its modifiers. Much more critical, it never did much to diminish the perceived importance of BSM among naïve outsiders.

But things could change now that Nassim Taleb (20 years options trading experience at the highest levels, author of numerous articles on financial mathematics, author of the top book on option trading) and Espen Haug (15 years options trading experience at the highest levels, author of numerous articles on financial mathematics, author of the best-known book on option pricing formulas) have decided to let us know, Bastille-storming style, that BSM is in fact really not used, was not an original contribution, and was not needed in the first place. That is, the Taleb and Haug critique is even more impacting than having your favorite son unveiled as a misbehaving truant. It is akin to declaring that the kid never existed at all, exposing the parents as people who had been bragging about a ghost during all these years. In this light, what had been presented as the poster child of theoretical salubriousness may become an embarrassment. That which in the past gave you honor (a triumphant formula, a brilliant son) may be transformed into a black sheep. By having pegged your own reputation and identity so closely to the object of prior admiration, your reputation (as trustworthy theoretician, as reliable parent) inevitably suffers, too.

So how will academics react to Taleb and Haug? What should they do? Disown BSM? Reform it (once more)? Act as if nothing had happened? As much as ivory towerists and their Wall Street allies may distaste Taleb and Haug, they should not lose sight of the fact that these uncontrollable mavericks have presented them with a wonderful gift: a once-in-a-lifetime opportunity to prove that, despite the prolonged suspicions over the real-world applicability of abstract finance theory and the isolated inclusiveness of the professors, they in fact do care much about what practitioners have to say and about how the world really works. That they do not merely want to lecture birds on how to fly, but would actually lovingly welcome any clarifying contributions from the aves themselves. By embracing Taleb and Haug and kick-starting a serious all-inclusive debate on the real history of option trading and pricing, theorists would show that they are not the stubborn isolationists, unrepentant abstractionists, incorrigible obscurants that many had taken them to be.

The issue is particularly pressing because the Taleb and Haug critique is, as we know, by no means the only bad mark on BSM's report card. Even before, BSM already presented quite a challenging conundrum for the theorists. It is undeniable that the model has become an inconvenient source of problems for the theoretical establishment. BSM shows that theories can cause lots of damage in the markets, that they can be extremely inaccurate mathematically, that they may not have been needed whatsoever, and that they may not have been widely adopted at all. That is, that theories can be lethal, wrong, pointless, unpopular, and outrightly ignored. While the temptation to continue to brag about the Nobelist formula (and the justification it provided for the no-holds-barred unleashing of the mathematization of finance) may be hard to resist, theorists would be well advised to exercise some caution. Now that the son has been publicly revealed as a shadow of his former self, it may be time for the forebears to display some healing humbleness.

In November 2007, I published an article on the Black-Scholes model, detailing its limitations but at the same time highlighting what I perceived to be its number one competitive advantage (the reason why it is, purportedly, widely used throughout trading floors). With time, my position has somehow changed, and what seemed like a glorious vindication suddenly appeared as irrefutable rejection. The model's presumed advantage had transformed, to my eyes, into a symbol of its defeat. Though the change of opinion has been radical, in effect it only involves changing a few words inside the priorly held argument. Thus, I am going to reproduce the original laudatory article, with the necessary (limited, though crucial) clarifications to follow after. By operating like this, readers will most clearly appreciate the crux of the matter as well as the reasons why I modified my views and transformed Black-Scholes' triumph into its burial (and, to be honest, I very much like the way the original article turned out, so what the heck); they would also be exposed to the key concept of the so-called volatility smile, a market-created oddity that was not intended by the model's patriarchs. The number one purpose of this exercise is (by anticipating the most insightful insight from the Taleb and Haug critique) to make readers understand why BSM is, in truth, not actually used by the market.

Smiling at Black-Scholes

The volatility smile is a testament to the real-world usefulness of the Black-Scholes model.

The real-life existence of the so-called volatility smile for options is often offered as evidence of the uselessness of the Black-Scholes model. Unquestionable proof of its failure to reflect real-world realities. A clear message to its creators: you got it all wrong! In its pure version, Black-Scholes assumes constant volatility for a given underlying asset, so that the same number should be input under the volatility parameter when pricing a bunch of options on the same underlying with all the other relevant parameters (time to expiration, interest rates, spot level) constant. What this basically means is that the, say, three-month volatility of IBM stock that goes into the model should be identical under any strike level. After all, the real three-month volatility of an asset can only be one single number. The expected future fluctuation of IBM stock is of course independent of any particular option strike level. If we plotted implied volatility (the volatility

(continued)

parameter chosen by traders when pricing the options) against strike levels we should then get a straight horizontal line. If traders believe that IBM stock will fluctuate by 20 percent in the next three months, then all different strikes of otherwise similar IBM option contracts should show an implied volatility number of 20 percent.

However, in the real world we do not observe such straight lines. Rather, the market literally laughs at us by depicting a smiling shape. The volatility smile (or the less pronounced skew found in some markets) unequivocally shows that traders input a higher volatility parameter for deep out-of-the-money and deep in-the-money options. The goal, of course, is to make the prices of those options dearer than under the pure version of the model. Traders believe that Black-Scholes, because of its mathematical foundations, dangerously undervalues such contracts and thus fudges the volatility input so as to obtain new prices that are deemed more realistic. The result is a grin-like plot between implied volatilities and strike levels, with the former being progressively higher at the extremes, rather than uniformly equal across all strikes. Black-Scholes critics immediately take this graphical discrepancy as irrefutable evidence that the market does not believe in the model, and that this theoretical construct does not cut it in the wilderness of the trading floors-dominated real world.

I think this criticism needs to be reevaluated. Yes, the smile does convey an undisputable message of uselessness when it comes to Black-Scholes. But, perhaps paradoxically, it is not the model that is being deemed useless, but rather its assumptions. The volatility smile is a testament to the real-world uselessness of the model's assumptions but also to the real-world usefulness of the model itself: Practitioners won't trust pure results from Black-Scholes but they will continue using it because they can so easily fix it into delivering the results that they (and not some unrealistic theoretical device) deem appropriate. The smile very graphically shows how easily, in fact.

There is no denying that Black-Scholes is an edifice built on shaky foundations. Many of its assumptions are simply unworldly. Particularly bothersome is the assumption of lognormality, meaning that asset returns follow a Normal probability distribution. But there is also no denying that in spite of such drawbacks, derivatives players have embraced the model wholeheartedly and refuse to give it up. This is due to the fact that Black–Scholes comes with a built–in self–correcting mechanism that very conveniently lets traders manipulate the model so as to obtain the results that are deemed optimal from a practical point of view. Black–Scholes thus allows traders not to be hostages to the dictates of an unrealistic theoretical construct; it sets them free to express their opinions so as to arrive at a price that is deemed optimal given real–world realities. The way those opinions are expressed is, of course, through the volatility parameter, the only manipulable ingredient of the formula. The volatility smile is a reflection of those freely expressed opinions and of how Black–Scholes permits users to break free from its own mathematical straitjacket. Traders obviously love such freedom.

Thus, the smile is saying both things at the same time: "Black–Scholes is wrong, but it is right!" The model is mathematically wrong, but it can be easily righted through its built–in self–correction mechanism. When the right output can be obtained from the wrong model, then that model becomes the right one to use, after all. The message from the smile is very clear: Black–Scholes is a wonderful pricing model because it allows traders to have a voice and guarantees optimal outputs that make sense in real life.

Rather than create the need for newer, more sophisticated, alternative models, the existence of the smile is in fact a tremendous validation of the real–world usefulness of Black–Scholes. Look how easy it is to achieve optimal pricing levels by simple and straightforward manipulation of the model. The volatility smile is a testament to the market's acceptance of Black–Scholes. It's traders screaming "We don't trust this model, but we surely like it!"

In 1997, the Bank of Sweden granted the Nobel Prize to the model, but such recognition (though undoubtedly reputation–enhancing) may lag behind another type of much more relevant and previously existent endorsement: namely, the volatility smile, which can be seen as "practitioners' Nobel Prize" to the model.

Say Cheese

Let's assume that a Black–Scholes–employing trader believes that the "true" volatility number for a one–year option should be 25 percent.

(continued)

This is the market turbulence that he honestly thinks will take place. However, he knows that the resulting option price would not be right. Why? Because it comes out of a model that assumes Normality. In other words, a model that underprices the possibility of rare events. An adjustment needs to be made, in a way that includes a premium for outliers (or, in statistical parlance, "fat tails" events). A deep out-of-the-money put, for instance, should be more expensive than what the pure version of Black-Scholes says. Traders know that the real-life probability of such option delivering a payout is much higher than that implied by the thin tails-obsessed model. In order to correct for that fact, when pricing the put they would raise the volatility number to, say, 35 percent. Of course, they don't expect real volatility (market turbulence) to be as high. They still believe in the 25 percent assumption, but need to "lie to themselves" in order to sell the put at an acceptable price. On top of the honest future volatility estimate (25 percent) a substantial extra adjustment (10 percent) should be added, and the volatility smile/skew is born. When plotting strike levels and implied volatility, the deep out-of-the-money put strike would show a corresponding number of 35 percent, while those strikes close to at-the-money levels would show numbers around 25 percent.

Since in real life extreme market movements take place much more often than assumed under a Normal distribution, Black-Scholes prices need to be adjusted to reflect this fact. The only way to adjust the model is by manipulating the volatility number that goes into the formula. If the pure Black-Scholes price is judged as too low, then all a trader has to do is increase the volatility number and the option price will rise to the desired level. In order to obtain higher prices for deep out-of-the-money and deep in-the-money situations, that number is simply adjusted upwards (in this case, from 25 to 35 percent). Truly simple.

How do traders make such adjustment? In other words, what considerations go into the decision? The market's view of future volatility (i.e., true expected turbulence) is not the only ingredient that is used to "manufacture" a figure for implied volatility. A high level of implied volatility might imply the perception of high future real volatility, but it might also reflect the fact that traders consider that the option should be more expensive due to liquidity concerns. It may also reflect "crash-o-phobia" on the part of traders. Or particular supply-demand disequilibriums.

Traders would embrace a model that allows them to make those adjustments in a comfortable way and that yields reasonable-looking numbers, and which foundations are solid and make sense. Traders have embraced Black-Scholes precisely for those very reasons. They consider it a very good framework for "volatility fudging." In a way, then, Black-Scholes can best be viewed as an accepted platform from which traders can obtain trustworthy prices by twitching the volatility parameter. They trust it as a reliable platform where to perform their sacred rituals of conducting adjustments for liquidity, fat tails, and other key factors not rightly captured by unrealistic mathematical assumptions.

What the volatility smile is essentially telling us is that Black-Scholes became incredibly successful amongst practitioners because it easily made mathematics irrelevant. Given the limitations of mathematical modeling when it comes to the financial markets (which are only too well known to derivatives pros) this is indeed no insignificant feat.

The Limits of Mathematics

While there is no denying that quantitative modeling can provide a much-needed beacon of light to guide us through the treacherous waters of financial markets, it is far from clear that the markets can in fact be effectively modeled. At the very least, it can be argued that currently accepted methodologies present serious flaws.

The most widely used option pricing models assume lognormality—that is, that asset returns follow a Normal distribution. Such distribution describes a world where extreme market moves take place very seldom. Most of the probability is concentrated around the average level. The tails of the distribution are said to be thin. However, as was said earlier, in real life financial markets often experience fat tails events. Market crashes take place much more often than what the Normal distribution would dictate. According to such distribution,

(continued)

for instance, the 1987 stock market meltdown did not happen; it was statistically impossible. Of course, for real-world players the crash felt very much real. What good is a financial model based on mathematics that assume Normality? In principle, not very. But can we really trust alternatives that take into account certain market realities, such as the existence of stochastic volatility or sudden price jumps? We know that market turbulence takes place a lot, but how often exactly? What probability should we assign to a meltdown at any given time? What type of distribution can truly reflect market dynamics?

Perhaps the honest answer is that we just don't know. Modeling the markets right may simply be impossible. Why? Because in the financial markets, as opposed to the universe, distributions are man-made, and thus ever changing, ever unstable. Physicists have it good in this respect. They have to deal with God-made distributions, where explicit rules are followed mechanically. Financial modelers don't have such luck. The eventual distribution of asset prices will depend on the actions of millions of individual investors, constantly buying and selling. Can anybody honestly claim to be able to register such behavior with a few equations? Who knows why and when people would revert to dumping an asset, or to accumulating it? Can any type of math capture those wild spirits?

Black and Scholes: A Monument to Mathematical Irrelevance

Hold on a second. We just very strongly argued that math is not as relevant as conventionally assumed when it comes to the markets, but at the same time we know that possibly the most successful modeling effort ever to emanate from economic theory is the Black-Scholes formula, which is precisely used to value options. The math behind Black-Scholes is no joke, involving complicated things called partial differential equations, stochastic integrals, Ito's lemma, and the Girsanov theorem. The model also assumes lognormality. We forcefully said that in real-life markets show fat tails. Black-Scholes is of course widely used by practitioners, having been wholeheartedly embraced since its first public appearance in 1973.

So it turns out that in the real world derivatives wizards routinely employ a model that is both based on highly complex mathematics and that makes unrealistic assumptions. What is it then? Are sophisticated quantitative tools essential in finance or not?

Before fanatical quants start rejoicing and claiming the last laugh, let me make a very simple, yet bold statement. The very reason that explains Black-Scholes' success within the practitioner community is the fact that these players know full well that the markets can't be modeled and that they don't have the knowledge or patience for fancy mathematical trickery. Black-Scholes became the consensus pricing model because it allows traders to easily correct all nonsense behind its mathematical machinery and its wide-off-the-mark assumptions. Black-Scholes, in essence, is a model that lets people value options without having to rely on a dangerously untrustworthy model. A model that doesn't force you to trust the model. That's its true secret.

What am I exactly saying? Basically that, as we know full well, Black-Scholes contains its own self-correcting mechanism that allows traders to very conveniently obtain the price that they (not some unrealistic theoretical construct) consider to be optimal given real-world realities. While the model may have innate weaknesses (in particular, its Normalityness), it also provides a quick way to fix itself. Black-Scholes is a godsend for those who don't believe that markets can be modeled. A testament to mathematical irrelevance and to practical relevance.

Black-Scholes, in essence, gives traders "a voice," lets their views and opinions be fully expressed and reflected in the option's final price. Volatility will be changed so as to arrive at the price deemed more appropriate by market players, thus giving birth to the smile and the skew, shining symbols of the model's real-life usefulness.

This manipulation-friendly aspect of Black-Scholes allows traders to switch from Normality into non-Normality. With a single strike to the keyboard, a trader can self-transport from an imaginary world of thin tails to a real world of fat tails. Just like the spaceship in Star Trek could move from one dimension to another by the pushing of a button, option traders can use the Black-Scholes vehicle to instantly travel from an unrealistic mathematical universe into a

(continued)

practitioner-populated galaxy. The volatility smile is striking proof that such journey can successfully be taken.

This transformational characteristic is the single most important factor behind the model's real-world relevance. Practitioners don't trust Black-Scholes but they like it. They don't trust it because they don't trust its underlying assumptions. They know that they are not realistic by any stretch. And, clearly, a construct based on faulty components can never be trusted as a reliable guide. In this, Black-Scholes is of course far from unique. Markets, where untamable human spirits run rampant, cannot really be modeled with mathematics. It just ain't physics. What makes Black-Scholes different, though, is that its uniquely simple self-correcting mechanism is highly liked. Traders know that the model is wrong (they are not "fooled by the formula," in the words of legendary option expert Nassim Taleb), but they all use it because they have learned how to trick it into generating realistic and satisfactory results. The smile and the skew are the results of such tricking, the best-known testaments to the fact that practitioners don't believe in the model's inner mathematical machinery and thus apply the necessary corrections and adjustments.

No other derivatives pricing model allows practitioners to so comfortably get agreeable outputs. Dozens of new models have been developed through the years that tried to correct Black-Scholes' shortcomings and unrealistic foundations through the use of fancy mathematics. While the engineering behind these alternatives is more realistic and sophisticated, traders, again in Taleb's words, "tend to avoid them, despite the insistence of their research staff, in favor of the simpler Black-Scholes that they know how to trick." The funkiest models are simply not as easy to manipulate. It is much harder to obtain reliable prices. It is much harder to transform oneself away from mathematical unworldliness and into real life. That is why these complex inventions did not win the hearts of traders like their simpler cousin did. They can neither be trusted nor liked because unlike Black-Scholes they can't be easily stripped of any mathematical nonsense. Taleb sums it all up: "No experienced trader would willingly trade Black-Scholes for another pricing tool."

Black-Scholes thus shows that mathematics in derivatives matters most when they can be rapidly manipulated into oblivion.

> When traders' opinions can easily railroad any technical issue deemed inconveniently irrelevant. Black–Scholes, that carefully designed Nobel Prize–winning achievement, became the most popular financial model ever because practitioners know that in the markets mathematical devices matter the most when they can be made to matter the least. Nothing symbolizes this idea more graphically than the existence of the volatility smile.

Now that you are done reading the original, let me clarify. The volatility smile is, in fact, not smiling at Black–Scholes. It is rather frowning at it. Yes, the arguments about the built-in self-correcting mechanism are all valid. Yes, the model conveniently allows traders to erase any mathematical nonsense and obtain option prices that make real-life sense. Yes, that seems like a pretty good reason to use it. But the inescapable point is that by going through with those manipulations, traders are transforming the construct formerly known as Black–Scholes into something entirely different.

For you see, volatility fudging was never part of the original script, the authors never intended for people to produce the smile—in fact they explicitly forbade it by imposing the assumption that volatility is constant (one number and one number only). Neither Fischer Black nor Myron Scholes had volatility fudging in mind when designing the model. Volatility fudging goes directly against the very heart of the model, an insult to its core foundations, a direct violation of its founding principles. When you fudge and produce the smile, the model no longer is Black–Scholes. It's something else. What had previously been described (including yours truly) as BSM's number one advantage becomes its exterminator.

It was there for all of us to see, but sometimes the obvious refuses to be found. The volatility smile, rather than representing BSM's number one asset (the flexibility to allow traders to obtain desirable prices) represents in fact its demise. The smile, bluntly stated, is saying that the market is *not* using BSM. It may be using the architecture of BSM (i.e., the same formulaic expression) but the final result is not BSM-compliant. (In fact, as will be analyzed later on, by manipulating the volatility parameter, traders would effectively be embracing pricing models that were available

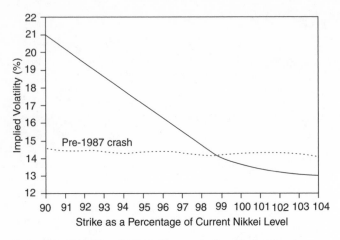

Figure 7.1   The Volatility Smile before and after Black Monday
Source: My Life as a Quant by Emanuel Derman, John Wiley & Sons, 2004, p. 227.
Reprinted with permission of John Wiley & Sons, Inc.

pre-BSM; that is, BSM architecture would be used to return to superior
pre-BSM formulas.)

So yes, the model would continue to be very enchanting to use and
to allow traders to break free from unworldly tenets. Those nice things
would continue to be nice. But not, as typically espoused, under the
Black-Scholes umbrella. The smile is not smiling at Black-Scholes. It is
proclaiming its death.

This is one of the few topics in this book that require some graphical
support, since visual reconnaissance is a must if we want to fully
understand why the birth of the volatility smile (after October 1987, as
will be detailed in a posterior section) renders BSM not-used.

Figure 7.1 plots the relationship between implied volatility and different strike levels for equity options (in this case linked to the Nikkei, since
the example is borrowed from Emanuel Derman, who reportedly first
heard of the smile while in Tokyo in the late 1980s; other international
stock markets smile in similar fashion, typically a tad more enthusiastically so in the United States). The horizontal line depicts how things
were before October 1987, in perfectly pure BSM-compliance: constant
volatility for all options on the same underlying asset, independent of
strike levels. The curved line represents the state of affairs post–October
1987, the volatility smile (actually a skew more than a matter-of-fact
smile, but this is customary in equity markets, for a variety of reasons;

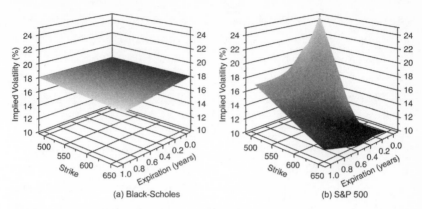

Figure 7.2   The Volatility Surface: Reality versus BSM

Source: My Life as a Quant by Emanuel Derman, John Wiley & Sons, 2004, p. 228 and 230. Reprinted with permission of John Wiley & Sons, Inc.

currency markets do experience full-blown smiles). Obviously, horizontal is not the same as curved. A curved line is a complete violation of BSM. Horizontal is not the same as curved. The end results are not BSM-compliant any more. It's not BSM. Curved is not horizontal. It's something else. BSM endorses horizontality. BSM negates curvedness. It can't be BSM. Curved is not horizontal.

Figure 7.2 (also from Derman; these ones are called *volatility surface*) tells the same story, this time operating in S&P 500 territory. Unadultered BSM (i.e., BSM) is flat as a pancake, same volatility for all strikes across all option maturities. Manipulated BSM (i.e., not BSM) is happy as a clam, with different implied vols across different strikes and expiration dates. If it's happy, it's not BSM. BSM was built to be exclusively sober. Something that's frivolously jubilant can't be BSM, even if a BSM-lookalike machine is being used to produce such shapely contentment. Particularly when a big reason for going from sober to content is to erase any traces of the machine's mathematical foundations and make sure that their unseemliness is not allowed to have a say in important real-life matters.

Let me provide what could be seen as a clarifying analogy. The Daiquiri cocktail was apparently invented by American engineer Jennings Cox in 1905. What could be deemed Cox's drink is supposed to contain 4.5 centileters (cl) of white rum, 2 cl of lime juice, and 0.5 cl of gomme syrup. That's what Cox had in mind when coming up with this invention. Those were the instructions. Very precise. Now, imagine that in real life you begin to observe that barmen all over the country are mixing it up differently. Depending on the room temperature, they would fudge the lime juice ingredient so as to obtain a more realistic output. If we plotted temperature and lime juice amounts we would get a smiling shape: the lime juice variable would be assigned higher values by barmen the more extreme the room temperature. That is, implied lime juice would smile at us. Could we still call such real-world daiquiris Cox's daiquiri? Of course not. Cox said nothing (I hope!) about fudging the lime juice figure. It was supposed to be constant, unaltered. If we do alter it, the final output can't be called Cox's daiquiri. It's something else (Hemingway's daiquiri?). If you are given a toy with very precise instructions and you choose to violate such instructions through shameless manipulation, you are betraying the original spirit of the inventors, so much that it no longer is the invention that those original inventors devised.

This is a very important issue that will be expanded upon when we discuss the Taleb and Haug critique of BSM. Suffice it to say, for now, that the smile is sending a very clear, and very theory-negating, message: The model that we believe option traders to be using can no longer be deemed Black-Scholes; traders' pesky manipulations have rendered a completely different monster, one that violates the original conception beyond recognition. It is not traders agreeably tweaking the model, it's traders killing the model. Obviously, this is a blow to established finance theory.

And it could be worse: The smile may in fact be indicating that no model (Black-Scholes or otherwise) is being used when pricing options, with staidly boring, good old supply and demand doing all the work. Under this scenario, the smiling shape loses none of its meaning, as demand for out-of-the-money options would be so large that if we used quoted market prices to backtrack the implied volatility figure from the (not in use) theoretical model, we would equally obtain the greatest numbers for those extreme strikes. Whatever the actual explanation (model fudging or no model), the inescapable truth is that, since at least October 1987, Black-Scholes is no longer in use by the market. R.I.P. legendary theoretical maven.

A fter completing the above section, I have become addicted to using old published material of mine to explain things relevant to this chapter.

Allow me, then, to satisfy my addiction. This time, the piece was run on June 2007 and it attempted to explain why Black-Scholes-inspired trading activities became the main factor behind the monstrous crash of October 1987 (the infamous "Black Monday"). Since I was as wrong about the true meaning of the smile as when I penned "Smiling at Black-Scholes" a few months later, this article concluded that amidst all the chaos caused by the model, theoretical victory eventually ensued as traders reacted by giving birth to the volatility smile, thus showing to the world what a fantastically flexible tool Black-Scholes was, a model that could correct its own mess. No wonder it is so popular, I mistakenly concluded.

Again, read and we will clarify things once you are done with the original piece (which, as before, I have tried hard to have included in the book, on account of very fond writing memories). Since we have already touched upon the true meaning of the volatility smile (dealt with here in slightly different terms than before), focus more on the narration of how Black-Scholes and its ideology helped cause the most devastating one-day loss in the history of Wall Street. The inescapable purpose of this effort is to show how destructive the side effects of BSM (and, thus, finance theory as an ideology) can be.

The Day When Black-Scholes Made Black-Scholes

The 1987 stock market crash highlighted the structural flaws of the model but it also unveiled its usefulness.

Imagine that you turn on the TV to check the latest news. Immediately, you notice something important is going on. The presenters are in a frantic mood, with many of them covered in sweat and white-faced. The word panic is regularly flashed in bright red colors. You begin to wonder if World War III has begun in earnest. Then you notice the little box at the bottom right of the screen, where stock prices are normally quoted. And now you finally understand what the fuss is all about. No wonder those pundits seem scared, you say to yourself, while feeling the fear creep inside. WWIII it may not be, but a drop in the Dow Jones of 3,000 points is surely a terrifying sight.

(continued)

To the untrained eye, this fictional story seems way too fictional. After all, the market simply can't tumble by 25 percent on a single day, right? Well, yes it can. In fact, a meltdown of such gigantic proportions already happened not so long ago. Only 20 years ago, to be exact. By the close of business on October 19, 1987, the Dow Jones had fallen by almost 23 percent. "Black Monday" was even graver in other parts of the world, with downfalls of close to 50 percent in some cases.

The October '87 crash is now part of financial markets legend. It was particularly important for the options markets. Bluntly stated, the crash showed that the Black-Scholes pricing model is wrong but it also motivated traders into showing why the model can be vastly useful. A Black-Scholes-demonizing event showed how reliable Black-Scholes can be in real life.

And not only that. Since it can reasonably be argued that the crash was decisively aided by Black-Scholes-inspired trading strategies (with the previous bubble and the subsequent free fall having been enabled and accelerated, respectively, by such strategies), it wouldn't be far-fetched to conclude that an event directly inspired by the inner dictates of the model, while generating bad press for Black-Scholes, also taught us why it continues to be widely loved by practitioners to this day. In effect, then, after Black Monday, and amidst the ruins caused by the model itself, traders unexpectedly learnt the true beauty of Black-Scholes.

How Black Monday Gave Black-Scholes a Black Eye

As it is well known, so-called portfolio insurance strategies (which were heavily employed at the time of the crash) have been widely blamed for at least accelerating the market's meltdown on that fateful October day two decades ago. According to several prominent and influential voices, without the sizeable trading activities undertaken by portfolio insurers, Black Monday would not have been as black (merely grey perhaps). While, in all fairness, some observers point to different causes, it is by now pretty much conventional wisdom that portfolio insurance is what really drove the market towards unknown depths.

What is perhaps more interesting to analyze is whether portfolio insurance contributed to propelling the market up prior to its dramatic fall (there can't be a crash without a previous bubble). In other words, did portfolio insurance help create the peak from which it could afterwards make the market nosedive to its trough?

The answer to this question is important when it comes to deciding how much blame should be placed on the Black-Scholes model as an instigator of Black Monday. Portfolio insurers, you see, were trading entirely according to the dictates of the model. To say that portfolio insurance was overly responsible for the crash (both enabling the bubble and fueling the downfall) is thus akin to saying that Black-Scholes was responsible.

Portfolio insurance was an attempt to synthetically replicate a short equity put position via Black-Scholes-inspired dynamic hedging techniques (which are, of course, at the very heart of the model's machinery). The goal was to provide affordable downside protection to equity investors at a time (early 1980s) when the availability of real (as opposed to synthetic) puts was quite limited. Portfolio insurance, which began to be marketed around 1981, became a tremendously popular industry in a very short period of time, with dozens of providers, hundreds of institutional clients, and assets under management estimated at over $100 billion right before the crash.

The dynamic hedging underpinning Black-Scholes is by nature trend-reinforcing. In order to replicate the sold option, dealers are asked to sell the underlying asset when its price goes down and to buy it when its price goes up. The fine print in the model assures us that such dynamic rebalancing will, in the presence of continuous trading and unlimited liquidity, guarantee a perfect match (i.e., hedge) to the dealer's short position. In sum, dynamic hedging allows one, in principle, to manufacture something that would behave similar to an option.

Following Black-Scholes, portfolio insurers proceeded to create computer-driven strategies that would replicate the equity puts sought after by concerned investors. Concisely enough, insurers would sell when the market fell and would have to buy when it rose. Assuming that the underlying assumptions of perfect liquidity and continuous trading held, clients would be synthetically protected from a market downturn.

(*continued*)

As the stock market embarked on a bull run at the beginning of the 1980s, portfolio insurers would have been forced to follow the herd upward. As the size of the portfolio pool being dynamically "protected" grew significantly (even the Episcopal Church pension fund reportedly adopted the strategy), the required buying would have become larger and larger. It would only be logical to assume that portfolio insurance quite likely provided a non-irrelevant push to the bullish market. In fact, plenty of evidence suggests that such assumption would be far from far-fetched.

Why can we say that portfolio insurance helped the market boom in the early-and-mid 1980s? On top of the dynamic buying required by the program (which, while eventually executed mostly through index futures, nonetheless boosted stock purchases by sending bullish signals to the market), several prominent studies point forcefully in that direction. The Brady Commission that investigated the 1987 crash, for one, concluded that the rapid rise in the popularity of portfolio insurance encouraged fund managers to invest more heavily in stocks during the rising market, as the promised cushion dispelled any concerns regarding the risks of a downturn. Insurers found that crash-averse customers who used to keep large amounts of cash were willing to commit those sums into equity once the synthetic protection became available. And while such new commitments may have been relatively marginal (when compared with the overall amounts of stock purchased in the years leading to the crash), another market-boosting influence was at play: As several other studies stated, portfolio insurance likely motivated insured investors to maintain existing equity positions that might otherwise have been reduced. Insurance gave institutions an artificial sense of security, in effect causing overinvestment in equities.

Such largesse on the part of insured investors may have prompted others to follow their lead, mistakenly thinking that the rising market was signaling fundamentally solid exuberance (rather than artificially created, fundamentals-neutral program trading). Ignorant of the extent of portfolio insurance programs, regular Joes may have thus been fooled into equities, providing yet another insurance-related push to the market.

In sum, we see that there are plenty of arguments that would allow us to credit Black-Scholes-inspired strategies for at least part of the equity boom leading to Black Monday (which was particularly intense in the 10 months just prior to October '87, mirroring a sharp increase in insured assets during that same period). Black-Scholes, we can half-confidently say, helped create the bubble. What is certainly less disputable is the assertion that Black-Scholes helped to crash that bubble.

When a serious correction in equities began to take place in mid-October '87 (with very sharp losses in the three working days preceding October 19), portfolio insurance-motivated selling helped drag the market to unknown depths. The recent price drops in the cash market demanded that insurers shorted a very substantial number of index futures. This, in turn, took stock prices further below. Much lower futures prices sent hair-raising bearish signals, prompting regular investors to dump stock. At the same time, index arbitrageurs went to work in earnest, like sharks smelling blood in the water. As future prices tumbled (the S&P 500 futures dropped by almost 10 percent right after the markets opened on Black Monday, reflecting the huge backlog of sale orders placed by portfolio insurers the prior Friday), a widening disconnect between index futures and stock prices took place. When this happens, arbitrageurs buy the (relatively cheap) futures and sell the (relatively expensive) stock. If stock prices fall as a result, more futures selling would be required of insurers, thus causing an even wider future discount, calling the arbitrageurs back into the action, and so on in a ceaseless downward spiral. Such vicious cascade is what took place during Black Monday. Investor perception about fundamentals triggered the original market declines, but the confluence of portfolio insurance and index arbitrage was what transformed those declines into a free fall.

In all, futures (which were supposed to track the underlying index as part of the replicating strategies) fell by almost 30 percent, some 10 points lower than the S&P 500 itself. Trading essentially became illiquid and discontinuous and dynamic hedging inevitably broke down. Many "insured" parties ended up with little or no protection from the ensuing mayhem. The synthetic puts turned out to be unreal after all, and precisely when they were needed the most. The crash thus unequivocally showed that Black-Scholes is built on shaky

(continued)

foundations. In the real world, perfectly replicating dynamic hedging is merely an illusion.

Was Black-Scholes behind the harshest market meltdown ever experienced? It certainly feels that way. Did Black-Scholes suffer severe reputational damage as a result of the crash? Without a doubt, yes. Not the best of days for the model, 19 October 1987.

And Yet, a Reason to Smile

But at the same time, something funny happened as a direct result of the crash. The currently ubiquitous volatility smile was born, a reflection of freshly developed crashophobia on the part of traders. After witnessing the massacre, it became clear to options pros that markets cannot be assumed to behave "normally" as the mathematics behind Black-Scholes (another big-time casualty of Black Monday) assumes, and that rare events do happen and can be truly criminal. In essence, traders realized that they had been hopelessly underestimating the value of crash protection. From then on, crash-protecting tools (such as out-of-the-money puts) would have to be priced upwards. Option traders' very survival was at stake.

To correct for the mathematical insanity of Black-Scholes and for the real-life difficulties of hedging an option book, now only too obvious, the volatility parameter that goes into the model (by definition, the only manipulable input) was artificially manipulated upwards so that the values of options with strikes at the extremes could be significantly pumped up, giving birth in the process to the smile. Prior to the 1987 crash, dealers had been content to charge the same volatility independent of the strike level, and the chart plotting implied volatility and strikes was more or less horizontally flat, exactly as the "pure" version of Black-Scholes would dictate. This, now we know, hopelessly underpriced out-of-the-money puts, providing scant compensation for the risks that dealers were taking. After a 20-sigma event on Wall Street (something deemed impossible by the Normal distribution), option pros decided to change tack and take protective measures.

The smile became such protection, and very graphically illustrated Black-Scholes's number one competitive advantage, the real reason why it is embraced and continues to be the most popular option pricing model: a built-in self-correcting mechanism that very easily lets users correct for any theoretical nonsense and deliver reliable outputs. By simply tweaking the volatility number, traders can obtain the price that they (and not some theoretical construct) deem practically relevant. No other model lets pros be in charge and impose their own law in such a way. Conveniently allowing traders to adapt the model to real-world realities (even those as earth-shatteringly unexpected as the 1987 crash), Black-Scholes proved its practical worth and earned its well-deserved preeminence.

In sum, the same event that highlighted the untrustworthiness of the model (which internal mechanics, arguably, contributed to the event taking place in the first place) helped underscore the reasons for its wild popularity. Rather than confine the model to the dustbin of history, a Black-Scholes-inspired disaster unveiled its unquestionable real-life usefulness. By producing the volatility smile following Black Monday, traders effectively rescued Black-Scholes from its self-dug graveyard.

Okay, let's clarify. After decisively contributing to the worst crash in the history of the equity markets, Black-Scholes was, in fact, not rescued by amicable smile-configuring traders, but rather it was left to die. Black Monday so outrageously exposed the shortcomings of the model's dynamic hedging spirit that there was little option but to do away with it. BSM was indeed confined to the dustbin of history. The previously model-compliant flat volatility smile abruptly became a glowing grin, as traders said enough is enough and sent the miserably failing construct packing. From that point on, they may still use the machine formerly known as Black-Scholes, but they would manipulate the volatility parameter in such a way that the final output would be something far different from Black-Scholes. As indicated in the prior section, another entirely possible possibility is that traders decided not just to manipulate the model into oblivion, but to actually stop using it (or to continue not using it, if that was the case before the crash) and to revert entirely to their animal spirits when pricing contracts. Learning from the mayhem, they would have pushed up the demand for extreme protection, making out-of-the-money puts costlier, which would translate into the smile when backtracking implied volatility from the model.

So it turns out that Black Monday signaled a double defeat for Black–Scholes, not a defeat followed by a healing restoration. The model was shown capable of causing the most harmful of pains (to its direct users and, worse, to plenty of innocent bystanders) and of not working properly when most needed, and it was utterly rejected, not fixed, by the market.

Now that we understand how black an eye Black Monday was for Black–Scholes, let's spend some time analyzing the exact dimensions of the financial carnage to which the poster child of theoretical dogmatism so decisively contributed. Yes, it has already been pointed out that Wall Street fell by almost 25 percent. But even that eerily creepy number does not in itself even being to capture the depth of the malaise. Black Monday signified not just a historically preeminent stock market drop. Black Monday posed a systemic threat to the continued well-being of the market's fabric. For an eternity-resembling few days, the system was seriously threatened. BSM almost brought the whole financial edifice down.

We could do worse than start by borrowing from the words of two of the most prominent actors in the drama, in reverse order of relevance. In October 1987, Eric Rosenfeld was a key member of one of the (if not *the*) most powerful trading groups in the world, New York–based Salomon Brothers' arbitrage desk. When asked to reminisce about the crashing day, he recalled *"Sitting at the trading desk and wondering about the end of the financial world."* Mark Rubinstein was (and is) a professor at the University of California–Berkeley who happened to have also initiated the whole portfolio insurance business, when he formed LOR Associates in 1981 with fellow academic Hayne Leland and marketing-maven John O'Brian. LOR, the biggest player in the field throughout, was by autumn 1987 covering around $60 billion (out of a total size for the portfolio insurance industry of some $100 billion). Right after witnessing Black Monday's debacle, he (justifiably concerned about his enabling role) entered into a clinical depression, fearing that *"The weakening of the American markets could tempt the Soviet Union to a challenge to the United States akin to the one that had provoked the Cuban missile crisis, and nuclear war might ensue."*

It didn't get to that. In the end, BSM did not provoke nuclear confrontation between the two Cold War foes. But a radioactive chill was most certainly felt in several corners of the markets. For starters, as night approached on October 19, 1987, it wasn't entirely obvious that the Chicago Mercantile Exchange (CME, the world's leading derivatives exchange) would open its doors the following day. According to some, not opening under such strenuous environment could have amounted to not being able to open again, ever.

The CME's concerns stemmed from the fact that its Clearing Corporation (the body that transfers sums from those losing money on a derivatives position to those making money; in other words, the body that makes sure that the exchange delivers and, effectively, functions as promised) was facing problems collecting from the vast number of players who had bet (spectacularly wrongly) on the U.S. stock market going up. Futures on the S&P 500 (the contract of choice for dynamic-hedging portfolio insurers) traded on the CME, and on Black Monday's evening those who had gone long (bought futures) owed those who had gone short (sold futures) about $2.5 billion, 20 times the typical amount. Unless such sums were secured before the start of business hours the following day, the CME would not be in a position to open and/or could face ruin. Clearly, an exchange that can't honor its commitments to its clients can't go on living. And concerns extended far beyond the CME's health per se. Failure to open would unleash nightmarish financial and economic havoc as contracts see their liquidity disappear into oblivion, causing huge setbacks to a large myriad of influential participants, from buccaneer speculators to corporate hedgers. The ramifications would be too life-threatening to contemplate, including massive liquidating sell-offs in all types of asset markets. Panic levels (unapologetically high as it were) would be exacerbated, potentially manifested in a cascade of bankruptcies, particularly among already-stressed-out financial institutions.

At 3 A.M. the CME was still short more than $1 billion, with Federal Reserve Board Chairman Alan Greenspan demanding an answer as to the CME's plans regarding opening. At 7 A.M., 20 minutes before regular business hours, the CME is still missing $400 million. In begging for the money, CME officials argument that nonpayment would result in the exchange going down the tubes and the United States entering into another depression. At 7:17 A.M., the wire transfer is suspensefully confirmed. Three minutes separate the CME from disaster.

But the system was still at risk. By lunchtime of that Tuesday, the New York Stock Exchange is about to stop trading, as activity has dried up almost entirely. Not even blue-chip stocks are spared, with trading in IBM shares ceased at 11:30 A.M. (so-called "specialists" who make markets in stocks were refusing to perform such role in the face of sharp, sudden credit restrictions and an avalanche of sell orders). Back at the CME, some may have regretted opening after all, as S&P futures dove 27 percent in the first couple of hours. At 11:45 A.M., the Chicago Board Options Exchange closed its doors, as there is little point to trading options when the underlying is not trading. Some minutes later, and faced with the likely closure of the NYSE, the CME eventually turns around and stops trading in S&P 500 futures. It seemed that only a miracle could now save the markets and the economy at large from untold, structurally impacting chaos.

At 12:38 A.M., the waters miraculously parted. Out of the bluest of blues, heavy trading in an obscure Chicago-based stock index future contract (the only one still operative by then) shook things up, brusquely awaking depressingly dormant spirits. NYSE specialists began to receive buy orders. No reason now to close the exchange, making both the White House (which had lobbied against the closing) and NYSE's chairman (who feared that closure, if chosen, may have been permanent) very happy. A cascade of reassuringly good news followed: The CME resumed trading on S&P 500 futures, and IBM shares were available again. Tuesday, October 20, ended up being a pretty good day. The next day witnessed one of the sharpest rises on Wall Street ever (decisively lending credence to the argument that portfolio insurance was the main force behind the previous Monday's crash, and naturally destroying the theoretically saintly assumption of "efficient markets"). The crisis was, incredibly fast, over.

So let's recap: A BSM-oiled unprecedentedly sized meltdown threatened the viability of the financial system, forced the closure of the world's most influential derivatives exchanges (coming within three minutes of bringing one of them down), and almost forced the (existence-menacing) closure of the world's most influential stock exchange; among the possible consequences of all this, economic depression and nuclear war were mentioned by the most relevant directly involved individuals.

Not even 9/11 yielded such negativity (neither the system's ongoing functionality nor the exchanges' survival were hampered, and depression was not seriously considered). When the widespread use of the Nobel-endowed crown jewel of financial economics can out-terror Osama Bin Laden, you know that something's not well in theoryland.

Unfortunately, October 1987 is not the only case of BSM-inspired market shoot-the-chute. Dynamic hedging techniques have contributed to other, if less noteworthy, troublesomely volatile episodes. A particularly extreme and headline-grabbing one afflicted the international currency markets, fueling the ire of one of the world's most legendary punters (now turned political activist) and encouraging a campaign to have certain types of options outlawed. While the actual and potential massacre was (to those at least not directly involved) much more trivial than Black Monday's, this was another grand hit to the safetyness of the model's mathematical engine. The dark paradox, of course, is that the exalted option pricing formula contributed to making the options family appear as criminally negligent, a clear and present danger to society.

In 1995 legendary financier George Soros publicly called for the banning of so-called "barrier options." Make them illegal, the Hungarian-American loudly proposed. They are the financial equivalent of crack cocaine, he proclaimed. Barrier option traders are havoc-wreaking evil-doers, he seemed to imply. What prompted the man who famously broke the Bank of England only a few years earlier to lash out at barrier options like that? What could possibly explain such anger? I mean, such a ruthless attack on the advances of financial engineering could be perhaps expected from a regulator or a journalist, but from an aggressive and sophisticated hedge fund manager like Soros? Really, George, what on earth ticked you off like that?

We might never really know the exact answer to that question (though some have ventured the hypothesis that the sage of Budapest might have suffered not insignificant losses due to market swings related to the trading of barrier options, which will be explained in just a bit), but we do certainly know the explanation that he gave then for his contempt towards barrier contracts. Simply put, Soros believed that barrier options (more specifically, the "knock-out" variety, vanilla options that can disappear if the underlying asset reaches a certain predetermined level during the life of the trade) should be outlawed because they cause too much undue volatility in the underlying spot market. Unexpectedly wild swings in exchange rates or stock prices, Soros's argument went, could be many times explained by the existence of large numbers of knock-out options having been written on those underlyings. Why? Because of the way in which the dealers that have sold these options to their clients (mainly corporate hedgers and investors) go about managing the risks derived from such activity.

Option traders, in general, use two basic methods when it comes to their own risk management: static hedging or our friend dynamic hedging. The former implies purchasing a portfolio of other options that, taken together, roughly replicate the behavior of the contract sold. By definition, this method is not market-altering as once the hedge is put on, no further action (or very limited) is required from the trader. The real volatility time bomb, naturally, lies with dynamic hedging. As we well know, this strategy involves continuous action on the part of the trader. The sold contract is also hedged with a replicating portfolio, but this time such portfolio has to be (pretty much) constantly rebalanced and adjusted so as to reflect new market realities.

The part of dynamic hedging that is of particular interest when discussing the possible destabilizing effects of option trading on the underlying spot markets is, certainly, delta-hedging. This is so because delta-hedging involves buying and selling the underlying asset on a continuous basis and in ever-changing and unpredictable quantities. Clearly, such activity, if significantly large, could disrupt the corresponding spot market, perhaps adding fuel to an ongoing trend, perhaps putting a break to such trend, perhaps creating a trend when none existed. In the case of vanilla options (simple calls and puts, like the ones being synthetically replicated by portfolio insurers), delta-hedging is trend-reinforcing, as traders are "required" to buy the underlying during a rising market and to sell during a tumbling market. Unsuspecting economic agents (not only hedge fund managers but many others, including governments) become witness to sudden market swings that cannot be explained by any fundamental reason. The yen may simply be rising too much in too short a period of time, the dollar tanking too harshly in too limited a space. In this light, it should not be surprising that players like Soros find delta-hedging activities bothersome. They could suddenly and dramatically derail spot positions carefully planned in advance and which make all the sense in the world if looked at from a fundamentally economical point of view.

While the delta-hedging associated with vanilla options can certainly enhance market volatility and drive people crazy, it is child's play compared to the tremors that can derive from the delta-hedging of barrier options. Dynamic hedging of barrier options is much more complicated for dealers than in the case of vanillas, for two main reasons: 1) the substantially larger amounts involved (a small move in the underlying can be the difference between owning a deep in-the-money option or nothing at all; thus, delta can be much higher); 2) the discontinuity of the deltas of barriers (for certain barrier contracts, delta can switch from negative to positive and vice versa). What this implies is that barrier options traders need to operate in the spot markets in much larger amounts and often with sudden brusque changes of direction. It is no wonder that such hedging activities have the potential of seriously altering the underlying markets. Additionally, of course, barrier options lend themselves to manipulation as the incentives for a trader to make the option knock out, or prevent it from knocking in, are just too large. Thus, a sudden and unexpected downward/upward trend in spot could be due to the fact that a group of traders are trying to make a knock-out option die. Unsuspecting spot traders might then suffer greatly (and, in principle, inexplicably) as a result.

Of all the members of the barrier family, so-called *reverse knock-outs* are likely to be the most destabilizing of all. As knock-out options, they are bound to be heavily manipulated and also involve large unwindings of now-unnecessary replicating positions by traders once the barrier is reached (and the option is thus no longer). As reverse (i.e., the barrier is in-the-money—that is, the contract would disappear at a time when it has a lot of value), they can present very large and sign-changing deltas. Also, given their relatively very low premiums, they might very well be among the most heavily used of all. As will be analyzed shortly, the type of market volatility witnessed in the mid-1990s that prompted Soros' rage was indeed caused by reverse knock-outs.

To illustrate the disturbing effects that dynamic hedging of reverse knock-outs can produce, imagine a reverse down-and-out U.S. dollar put/euro call with strike 1.00 and the barrier at 0.80 (the option will be in-the-money if the dollar is worth less than one euro, and will disappear if the dollar ever trades as low as 0.80 euro during the life of the trade). While the underlying is away from the KO barrier, the option's delta behaves like that of a vanilla put—that is, negative for the customer and positive for the dealer (if the dollar goes up, it's good news; if it goes down, bad news). In order to manage his delta exposure, the trader would have to create a negative delta position, so as to have a delta-neutral book (i.e., sell dollars if spot goes down). As spot goes down towards the barrier, things dramatically change. Now, the trader delta-hedging his short position has to buy, not sell, dollars: The dealer's delta has turned negative because decreases in the underlying are actually good news since they increase the possibility of the client being knocked out and releasing the dealer of any liability (that is, the barrier effect takes over the option effect when determining the sign of delta); to make a delta neutral position the dealer now needs some positive delta, which is obtained by purchasing spot.

This can influence the market because steadily asking for dollars stops down the spot movement towards the barrier and can in extreme cases prevent the barrier from being hit at all (this is the dealer's dilemma whereby the trader is "forced to going against himself"). On the other hand, if the hedger runs out of breath and downward market movement can't be stopped by the bank, then the option knocks out and the hedge is abandoned. Suddenly fewer dollars are being bought so that the down-ward movement of spot can be accelerated once a large barrier contract in the market has knocked out; plus not only have dealers stopped purchasing dollars as part of dynamic hedging, they now have to unwind their large long spot positions, greatly pushing the market down some more. This could lead to a chain reaction if large volumes of similar knock-out puts with progressively lower barrier levels have been written by banks.

The opposite situation can occur when traders hedge a reverse up-and-out call in which case dollars have to be sold when spot approaches the barrier. Say a 0.80 dollar call/euro put with a 1.00 KO (the option is in-the-money when the dollar is worth more than 0.80 euro and will disappear if it ever trades as high as 1.0 euro). Initially, with spot far from the barrier, the delta is like a vanilla—positive for the client, negative for the dealer (if the dollar goes up, it's bad news; you hedge by buying dollars and obtaining positive delta). As spot climbs towards the barrier, delta switches from negative to positive for the dealer (please, please, may the greenback rise and kill my obligation). To hedge this, the dealer is asked to sell spot (gain negative delta), which again works against his goal of seeing the option disappear. Such trading can severely disrupt a normal market rally perfectly explained by solid fundamentals. And if dynamic hedging does not carry enough force anyway and the barrier is breached, then there is a second opportunity for disruption as the dealer unwinds his heavy short position, thus providing undue acceleration to the upward dollar movement.

In other words, we see that BSM-inspired dynamic hedging of knock-out options can have two clear effects over the spot underlying market: 1) limit or even terminate the normal workings of market movements (force an upward market to stop going up or even start going down); 2) suddenly and perhaps dramatically accelerate the underlying trend (in case the barrier cannot be prevented from being breached).

This is not simply theory. If Soros is to be trusted, the foreign exchange markets in the early part of 1995 witnessed precisely the kind of knock-outs-induced roller coaster that is described in the previous, imaginary examples. What are two undeniable facts are that during a small window of time in the March–April period of that year the dollar experienced tremendously pronounced volatility against a group of key currencies, and that the use of reverse knock-out options had become widespread in previous months. The key question, of course, is: Were dynamic hedgers solely (or at least, mostly) responsible for such unruly market behavior?

The two currency pairs that famously suffered extreme volatility in the first quarter of 1995 were dollar/deutschmark and dollar/yen. Knock-out options, and barriers in general, had become quite popular in the preceding months (coinciding with the exotic options revolution that took place in the early years of the decade), and in both cases a large number of corporates had purchased reverse knock-outs with what seemed like improbable barrier levels as a way to obtain economical protection against a sinking dollar.

In early January 1995, with the dollar worth in excess of 100 yen, major dealers reportedly had on their books a substantial number of knock-out dollar puts with barrier levels between 95 and 85 yen. In late February, the yen began to appreciate sharply as the dollar, which had been sliding gradually for the past two years, suffered the consequences of financial unrest in Mexico and Argentina. On March 3, with the exchange rate approaching 95, Japanese and American monetary authorities jointly intervened in the currency markets, but to no avail. With the yen decisively moving towards the first knock-out levels, traders began to experience the kind of incentives capable of generating mayhem in the spot market. On the one hand, some dealers may have been tempted to manipulate the exchange rate in an effort to make the option die and free themselves of any contractual obligations. These traders would have started to massively sell dollars as soon as they smelled the possibility of spot reaching 95. On the other hand, dynamic hedgers, whose dollar-buying near the barrier (as a way to hedge their negative delta position) had proven incapable of stopping the downward trend, and had stop-loss orders requiring them to dump their accumulated long dollar positions at once following the breaching of the barrier. Moreover, the customers themselves would have been motivated to off-load their dollar holdings after being knocked out of a hedge.

The bottom line is that, given the large numbers of reverse down-and-out puts with barrier levels starting at 95, as soon as the dollar suffered a noticeable drop (in this case, yes, due to purely fundamental reasons) its fate was basically sealed, as the unleashed combined actions of manipulators, dynamic hedgers, and panicked customers would contribute to dramatically accelerating and magnifying the fall. Even worse, this would in turn make it much easier for the next (lower) barrier level to be breached, and so on. In this light, it shouldn't be surprising that the yen unstoppably strengthened all the way to 79.95 on April 19. This state of affairs was to be quite short-lived, though. By the following September (with all KO barriers in the market presumably having been breached and dynamic hedging forces thus quieted down), the yen was back to its normal level above 100, after a gentle recovery by the now-unconstrained dollar.

The story was quite similar in the case of the dollar/deutschmark market. Again, dealers in early 1995 had their books filled with reverse down-and-out puts with barrier levels in the 1.45–1.35 range. Since the dollar had steadily quoted in the 1.70–1.50 range for the previous year, end users felt confident with those knock-out strikes. Then in mid-February the German currency sharply rallied below 1.50 and in a matter of a few days it skyrocketed past 1.45 (late February), 1.40 (early March), until it reached rock bottom on, you guessed it, April 19 when the dollar was as weak as 1.35. Like in the Japanese tale, dynamic hedging most likely helped snowball things as barrier after barrier was hit. Also similarly, once the bottom KO was reached the dollar promptly and gradually recovered, hitting 1.50 again a few months later.

Now that we have a clear idea as to the real-life phenomena that angered and despaired Soros (who obviously did not enjoy the sudden ride in the foreign exchange roller coaster that he was forced to take), let's retake the crucial question that was posed some paragraphs ago: Was the mayhem mostly caused by the presence of knock-out options?

Was Soros justified in his calls for impeachment against these utmost symbols of financial wizardry? It is probably impossible to provide an exact answer, but it is also difficult to understand what else could have forced the dollar to move so sharply over such a short period of time. In the four trading sessions between March 2 and March 7, the greenback fell almost 10 percent against the yen and the deutschmark. On April 19, it hit record lows against both. And then, just like that, back to normal. During March and April 1995, the dollar suddenly disappeared from the radar screens, only to promptly return as if nothing unusual had happened. As if it had briefly traveled to another dimension but could not remember it upon its return. As if it had been temporarily abducted by aliens, only to resume its regular life after being reshipped back to earth.

What took place in the currency markets that had the equivalent dramatic effect of time travel or alien abduction? While it is true that coordinated action by as many as 12 leading central banks beginning in late May pushed the dollar higher and definitely contributed to a return to normalcy, this still does not explain why the record-breaking tumble in the dollar of a few months prior took place. Many people offered elaborate macroeconomic explanations but, while having some truth to them, it is not easy to accept that they fully account for such excessively and unusually violent market swings. Other factors must have been at play.

Soros, then, possibly had a point after all. It is quite reasonable to assume, now that we have fully exposed the mechanisms through which barrier traders can influence the spot market, that the presence of large reverse down-and-out positions did in fact cause the currency markets to go temporarily insane in the first half of 1995, particularly since spot levels promptly returned to normality once the lowest barrier strikes had been breached.

The episodes described above provide ammo to those skeptical about the propagation of mathematical guiding lights throughout the markets, and worried about their malfunctioning and their capacity for wreaking havoc. When it comes to the Black-Scholes methodology, the knock-out developments of the mid-1990s point to the capacity of math-inspired techniques to generate undue turbulence. But this doesn't mean that the financial products themselves should be thrown to the pyre, particularly when their existence is not dependent on the prior existence of complex pricing and hedging tools. Barrier options did not need permission from

BSM and its theoretical siblings before they could be traded, and it would be a huge mistake if quantitative failings turned people away from the obvious benefits of the products.

Even if barrier options can actually cause malaise in the spot market, this still would not justify taking the drastic actions that Soros advocated. Banning the use of barrier options would be a misguided step backwards to a time when risk management was both more expensive and less flexible. They represent a vastly significant improvement over the previous, vanilla-dominated state of affairs. No wonder that they quickly became the most popular and widely used of all exotic options. Having outlawed them more than a decade ago would have proven to be a painful disservice to the thousands of companies, investors, and public entities that have profited from their use through the years. Knocking out the knock-outs? Bad idea, George. Bad idea.

In a potentially revolutionary paper released at the end of 2007, veteran option traders and best-selling authors Nassim Taleb and Espen Haug made several very bold claims that strike directly at the heart of the Black-Scholes-Merton (BSM) option pricing model edifice. First, the duo argues, BSM was no original invention at all, as exactly the same formula had been available for a while. Second, it wasn't needed, as option traders had been doing fine without it for many, many decades. Third, most traders either price options using the pre-BSM models or using no model at all (simply via supply-demand interaction). In either case, the conclusion from this bottom-up analysis (drink from market evidence before you produce dictums, as opposed to the typical top-down academic approach) would be equally damaging for the Nobel-endowed construct: In real-life, pros don't use BSM that much after all and the arrival of the model didn't miraculously solve previously unsolved problems. When it comes to myth-busters, this one would surely be at the top of the rankings. By "sinking" BSM, Taleb and Haug could be taking finance theory as a whole down with it.

Let's briefly explain those three revolutionary assertions. Every text-book assumes as gospel that BSM enjoys paramount real-life success and is widely used by practitioners. Most journalists and outside observers would amiably concur. They all suffer from conventionalism blindness. How can they tell? Have they asked every option trader in the world?

THE BLACK-SCHOLES CONUNDRUM ■ 223 ■

Of course not. They assumed that BSM was used because a lot of other people were also assuming that. After Taleb-Haug, we can no longer assume so freely.

There are two main reasons why BSM is, frankly, not used. First, option prices (at least for liquid contracts) may be simply the result of supply-demand interaction, with no model involved at all. Taleb recalls that during his time as pit trader two decades after BSM was introduced to the world, he was surprised to see traders operate without recourse to any formula. As Taleb and Haug expose, many times options are priced via other options, through a simple conduit known as put–call parity (a key arbitrage relationship that allows one to obtain the price of a call from that of a put, and vice versa). No fancy mathematical modeling required, really. (It's frankly interesting to note that certain academics appear to have very recently embraced the notion that, shock of shocks, the price of an option may hinge on supply and demand forces. And not because after long periods of reflection it may have dawned on them that perhaps, just maybe, the fact that more people want to buy a contract than sell it, or vice versa, might have an impact on the contract's market value. No, they claim that the supply-demand factor should be looked at specifically because we now have good reason to suspect that the BSM-sanctioned theoretical formula for manufacturing an option may not work too properly after all, so poor devastated traders may be reduced to the decidedly barbarian chore of simplistically yelling "buy" and "sell." That is, academia would decide that supply and demand should matter when analyzing option pricing only *after* it has become convinced that theoretical alternatives are less than useful, not because the professors would naturally and instinctively take for granted, as anybody else would unfailingly do, that buyers and sellers should always be assumed to having a big say.)

One of the key implications of all this (there are many, including a questioning of the Nobel Prize in Economics) is that implied volatility, a ubiquitous element of the markets, would cease to make sense. In fact, it would cease to exist. Implied volatility (supposedly the number that traders are consensually inputting under the volatility parameter in the pricing model) simply can't exist in a world where option prices are determined by supply and demand. Implied volatility is 100 percent model-dependent. No model, no implied volatility. Rather than being the "market's expected future turbulence" or the "market's fear gauge," as conventional wisdom would hold, implied volatility would have proven itself to be nothing but a farce. A make-believe. A fairy tale. A nonexistent ghost.

Note that one of the unalterable beauties of BSM for the theoretical establishment is that even if option prices come from supply and demand, with no model used whatsoever, they can always match the market price to a BSM price through the implied volatility parameter, and thus claim that BSM is, in fact, widely employed. Say the humans–determined market price is 100 and that, given market parameters, you could obtain exactly that price via BSM by inputting, say, 32 percent in the volatility box. Academics would then victoriously stand up and yell "See, traders are using BSM and choosing a 32 percent implied volatility estimate. Theory wins once more!" Supply and demand may supremely rule the options world, and implied volatility may be an illusion, but BSM and its theoretical accomplices can be very resilient at hiding the truth.

Secondly, even when a model called BSM is used, it is not really BSM. Why? Because of our old friend, "volatility fudging." Prior to Taleb and Haug, conventional wisdom (certainly when it came to outsiders, possibly also when it came to many insiders) held that in spite of BSM's known flaws (highlighted often enough in earlier parts of this chapter), traders continued using it because they had learned how to trick it into conveniently delivering the right price. Traders, it was assumed, did not trust BSM but liked it because it was so easily manipulable (just change the volatility parameter and you can obtain your desired price, in a way erasing the bothersome unrealistic assumptions and obtaining an input more in tune with the real world). Haug and Taleb themselves admit to having held that belief for years as inhabitants of the trading floor.

Post Taleb and Haug, all that conventionalism would no longer hold. Fudging of the model, which was assumed to preserve the popularity of BSM in spite of its unworldliness, is (as has been already repeatedly discussed) in fact a complete negation of the model itself. Neither Black, Scholes, nor Merton had volatility fudging in mind when devising the model; volatility fudging is a complete violation of the model's original spirit. By fudging BSM one is actually (unbeknownst to him) ending up using a completely different (superior) model, and one that, Taleb and Haug show, had been already available under different authorships.

To me, this is the single most important insight from the paper. As Taleb and Haug state, traders use a formula called BSM without being aware of the irony that BSM couldn't be further away from what they are actually using. When it comes to option pricing and BSM, Taleb and Haug indicate, there has been a big "attribution problem" and they intend to do overdue justice to the truly worthy contributors. Perhaps, in the end, Fischer Black (who always favored practicality over dogmatism and who rejected academia for Wall Street) will be proven right, and the puzzling (to him) real-life acceptance of BSM would have turned out to be a misleading mirage. Not true, just imaginary.

Taleb and Haug claim that the truly used formula should be called "Bachelier-Thorp," in honor of turn-of-the-century French mathematician Louis Bachelier (who back in 1900 first invented the mathematical models underpinning security prices) and American gambler-mathematician-punter Edward Thorp (who in the late 1960s came up with a formula similar to BSM, which he actually used for trading before BSM was published, and every researcher in between that contributed with something valuable). Such approaches, according to Taleb and Haug, are more realistic because, unlike BSM, they allow for a broad choice of probability distributions (thus escaping the Normality straitjacket) and don't depend on (impractical) dynamic hedging techniques, whereby dealers are assumed to always be able to replicate an option through continuous trading in the underlying asset.

In a way, we are back to Bachelier-Thorp, notwithstanding the later BSM development: Traders manipulate BSM so that it becomes that which it tentatively replaced. Mathematically speaking, one would be using a Gaussian structure to produce non-Gaussian results, through modifications of the sigma parameter. In this light, the true role of BSM (at least since the crash of October 1987) would have been to act as convenient platform from which traders can recuperate pre-BSM pricing methods. Or put it much more drastically, BSM ends up doing exactly the same as Bachelier-Thorp but under a different nomenclature. One naturally wonders whether we needed all this theoretical trouble simply to end up referring to the same thing using different acronyms.

What's more, the model may have not been needed at all. Taleb and Haug show how, prior to 1973 (when BSM first made a public appearance), traders had very sophisticated knowledge about how options should be traded, priced, and risk-managed, even as far back as the 1600s. The long-held myth that we had to wait for BSM before options could be properly traded and understood thus flies in the face of historical evidence. Derivatives most certainly didn't have to wait for BSM before they could be traded. Free-thinking human beings agreed to begin transacting options with each other long before they received the mathematical authorization.

There is plenty of evidence of option usage hundreds (even thousands) of years ago. For instance, Joseph de la Vega described, in the seventeenth century, how options were actively traded in Amsterdam and even mentions the supposedly modern concept of put-call parity (a key method for pricing and risk-managing options). The late 1800s and early 1900s witnessed extremely sophisticated action in London and New York, including the publication of several practitioner-authored option treatises. Most prominent among those is *The ABC of Option Trading and Arbitrage*, published in 1904 by trader and arbitrageur S. A. Nelson, where put-call parity is once more described in detail (including references to even older work), and where there is plenty of evidence that traders knew how to statically (and even dynamically) hedge their positions, including an unmistakable reference to what is nowadays known as "delta" (one W. D. Gann is also referenced as having in 1937 discussed static and dynamic hedging). The funny thing is that neither put-call parity nor delta-hedging were supposed, if one listens to modern finance theory, to have existed that far back in time. Formal financial economics not typically including references outside of academia, put-call parity is assumed to have been introduced (by a theoretician, naturally) in 1969, while we were told that delta-hedging arrived with BSM in 1973.

Taleb and Haug also cite Herbert Filer, a trader who described a healthy options market in the 1920s and 1930s. After that, activity dried up significantly, as regulatory overzealousness in the United States combined with WWII proved too hampering. Options spent a long period in hibernation (London trading did not formally resume until 1958; New York activity remained distinctly underground), and this could partly explain the absence of recognition of past hands-on expertise on the part of 1960s–1970s theoreticians (though Taleb and Haug interestingly cite a 1961 New York Stock Exchange trader who described put-call parity not just in theory but as a widespread practice in those days). In any case, the point remains robustly clear that options markets did not have to wait for a formula before they could be. Ancient traders seemed to be doing fine without BSM, thanks very much.

Okay, but isn't it quite a coincidence that the starting date of the launch of the options business into the stratosphere conspicuously coincided with the arrival of BSM? Are we negating any positive effect of BSM over the revolution? We already know for sure that the CBOE (founded in 1973) and at least one major investment bank (Donaldson, Lufkin & Jenrette) endorsed the model from the start, and Fischer Black is also known to have had traders hire him to provide analytical support early on. Obviously, BSM must have had an impact, perhaps even an outstanding one (though options celebrity Martin O'Connell is quoted by Taleb and Haug as clarifying that the model was rarely used before the 1980s, with the modern options market well in full-swing mode).

But the birth of a salubrious modern option industry precisely in the early 1970s can be explained by a myriad of causes that are at least as plausible as the publication in an obscure academic journal of a paper full of mathematical notations that few traders could ever hope to master. For starters, it should be entirely reasonable even to equation fanatics that no one is going to go through the trouble of setting up a derivatives exchange just because some academics have solved a partial differential equation. Options trading is organized because there is a real need for the products, not because a mathematical formula is conceived. The idea of listing options on financial assets in Chicago was conceived years before either Black, Scholes, or Merton met each other.

By the mid-1960s life was tough at the Chicago Board of Trade (CBOT), then the world's foremost derivatives exchange. Though the reputation of the contracts had significantly recovered from insalubrious speculative incidents of decades past (options on commodities were banned in the United States in 1934, with only stock options being allowed to operate legally, if somewhat furtively), activity levels were in the doldrums, mainly due to yet more government intervention, this time in the form of food price controls that severely reduced the need for hedging, drastically hampering the CBOE's main line of business, the wheat futures pit. Such harsh reality prompted the exchange's honchos to start looking for alternative sources of income, and financial derivatives seemed attractive enough.

Next door at the Chicago Mercantile Exchange (the CBOE's main competitor back then), the mood was ripe for innovation, too. Having tried their hands at exotic commodity stuff (unsuccessfully with eggs and onion futures, more shiningly with pork bellies contracts), CME executives realized that a one-product line, no matter how diversified, was a dangerous business model. So in the later part of the 1960s the CME, too, began to consider financial derivatives. The gap in the market was certainly there for both the CBOT and the CME to exploit, since stock futures and options trading was at the time a decidedly illiquid affair, a shadow of its former glorious self in the pre-WWII era. Here was an opportunity to get in on the ground floor of a historic revival.

In 1968, the CBOE asked for legal opinion regarding the possibility of listing a Dow Jones futures contract, but they were discouraged (index futures would most likely had been declared akin to unlawful gambling). So they redirected their sights towards stock options, with the goal of replicating, on a massive scale, the backstreets, over-the-counter deal making taking place in New York. Meanwhile, over at the CME the obsession was with currency futures, and they enlisted academic superman Milton Friedman to assist in making the case to the authorities in late 1971. These efforts were fruitful and in May 1972 the International Monetary Market at the CME began listing currency derivatives (granted, futures, not options) one year before BSM was officially published. In April 1973, the CBOE, after its own enlisting of star academics helped assuage regulatory concerns, and its stock options made their debut.

The key reasons for all these developments were mainly two: First, the enhanced volatility in currency markets derived from the 1971-enacted end of the almost-three-decade-old Bretton Woods system of fixed exchange rates naturally generated an unavoidably urgent need to have access to currency hedging tools; second, exchanges were eager to expand their product menu beyond staid commodity contracts and to outrun the competition. It looks entirely unchallengeable that the financial derivatives that were unremittingly launched in the 1970s would have not been revoked of their birthright in the absence of a theoretical pricing model. Renewed volatility in the underlying markets after a very long dormant period coupled with innovativeness fever is what subliminally dictated the listing of the new products. As volatility continued to receive support (officially controlled monetary policy was disbanded at the end of the decade, unleashing unprecedented interest rate turbulence) and competition to heat up, things just got hotter and hotter, laying out the foundations for today's spectacularly splendorous derivatives industry. Yes, BSM may have helped a lot (and a former counsel of the CBOE during those critical days believed that *"Black-Scholes was really what enabled the exchange to thrive. . . . It gave a lot of legitimacy to the whole notions of hedging and efficient pricing, whereas we were faced in the late '60s–early '70s with the issue of gambling. The issue fell away, and I think Black-Scholes made it fade away. It wasn't speculation or gambling, it was efficient pricing. I think the Securities and Exchange Commission very quickly thought of options as a useful mechanism in the securities market and it's probably—that's my judgment—the effects of Black-Scholes."* Note, though, that this endorsement has a strong PR ring to it; it doesn't say anything about traders actually needing the model in order to move exchange activity along), but it seems hard to conclude that it was a requirement.

Taleb and Haug mention other factors that can be attributed with having truly propelled the derivatives juggernaut: the arrival in force of computers (which eased bookkeeping, processing, and technical support; they are not talking about computational finance models here), and the long stretch of peaceful economic growth and absence of hyperinflation. After all, the 1970s were a big computer decade with the arrival of the first consumer computers, the first microprocessor, and the floppy disk. And we can't exactly complain about the world's economic performance since 1972. Equally important for the derivatives revolution, I might add, has been the relentless process of "financialization" experienced in the last few decades (the end of Bretton Woods in mid-1971 could be reasonably seen as the catalyst for the unleashing of the new era), including the perennial rise in status of financial market professionals. Clearly, when being a trading floor guy or gal becomes increasingly cool and profitable, you know that the option business is going to flourish big-time. And remember, the golden finance decade of the 1980s took place just seven years after the CBOE was founded. The BSM coincidence certainly seems to have had a lot of fortuitousness about it.

Most damning, Taleb and Haug painstakingly produce a chronological list of technical and academic work on option pricing predating BSM, including basically identical formulas (including Thorp's). They pointedly remind us that the official economics literature never recognized many of those efforts, either because it didn't fit with someone's objectives or because of utter ignorance as to their existence. The truly important point is that of all the approaches (both theoretical and practitioners-enacted) available by the time that BSM was born, in the inquisitively clarifying words of Taleb and Haug, *"the only principle option traders do not use and cannot use is the approach named after the formula."* That is, the most impractical of all known methodologies was the sole one that turned out to be embraced by the theoretical community (and thus, encouraged by such encouragement, the world at large). In a shockingly puzzling development, we chose to adore precisely the one theory that couldn't work. Not exactly a triumph of viability here.

The pre-BSM existence of the Sprenkle, Boness, and Thorp formulas and the market's long-predating familiarity with (static, at least) delta-hedging are not, per se, the most damaging blow to BSM, bothersome as they certainly are. Yes, it is hard to endow a construct with the originality or pioneering labels when almost identical or exactly identical devices existed before, but, as we amply know, the way to get to the formula was indeed wildly innovative mathematically and theoretically speaking. So BSM was not an entirely redundant exercise.

The real problem with all that vast amount of prehistorical evidence is that it highlights two related discomfortingly anticonventionalism facts: one, there were better ways to obtain the same result; two, those approaches were actually implementable, in sharp contrast to dynamic hedging's headline-grabbing practical flaws (more on this further below). Put it bluntly, the discrediting threat to BSM is not so much that it has turned out to have had tons of older relatives, but rather that they were superior. As long as the memory of those elders is kept afresh (as Taleb and Haug have so forcibly done), we are forced to wonder why we needed the new, stochastic calculus–powered member of the family.

Sprenkle and Boness may not make things comfy by prying into our private lives and asking intruding questions about our preferences towards risk and our market forecasts, but intrusiveness does not equal implausibility. You can use those formulas. As long as you can express your opinions, you can get an option price, while fully complying with the model's fine print. Thorp is even more amiable, as you don't even need to spend time picking your own brain and listening to your heart—you just need to buy into Thorp's purportedly unharmful choice of the risk-free rate.

In loud contrast, BSM keeps you hostage to strict theoretical commandments, such as CAPM and continuous replicating portfolio–enforced non-arbitrage, that are not just realism-challenged but doubtfully implementable, and thus doubtfully trusted by pros. It is much easier to win a popularity contest among option traders if you allow them to express their opinions than if you forbid them from doing so and force them to show blind faith in modern financial economics and dynamic hedging. The mere existence of mathematical models that embrace the former alternative in itself stresses the inappropriateness of concoctions that promote the latter's.

It could be argued, as was anticipated in the earlier part of the chapter, that BSM did nothing more than provide iron-clad academic and technical justification for the adoption of special cases of the predecessor formulas that happen to be by far the most user-friendly. Obviously, the most convenient way to employ either Sprenkle's or Boness's mathematical scions is by assuming a risk-neutral world. Such nicety would deprive us of the taxing task of having to estimate risk preferences and expected returns, thus eliminating from the process hurdle-creating, entrenchedly subjective unobservables (clearly, each individual can potentially have differing takes on those two unknowns) and allowing us to concentrate all the "pricing debate" on just one, decidedly less opinionated, variable, namely volatility (and we know how useful volatility fudging can be). Traders would have loved to be able to insert that risk-free rate in those models (or, naturally, to directly embrace Thorp's) yet may have thought it too much of a self-serving stretch. An inexcusable act of unjustifiable self-indulgence.

But in 1973 there arose a contribution that said that the risk-free rate was the only possible solution and that you absolutely *had* to select it, all backed by the most sophisticated mathematical techniques and the most sacred of theoretical dictums. Who could now stop you from going risk-neutral? You may not even know what CAPM is or be even half-willing to embark on that weird-looking dynamic hedging thing, but you certainly adore their permission to go risk-free. For all of BSM's technical prowess, the only reason why traders may have embraced it is as a way to be able to go back to the past and use prior, less convoluted, formulas that don't demand your conversion to the financial economics faith or your engaging in troubling arbitrage. BSM's glorified analytical engineering becomes little more than window dressing for the use of older methods.

Of course, the alert reader would notice that we left out a third, critical reason why those oldies make BSM less than stellar by comparison: By not being embedded with the delta-hedging volatility time bomb, they cannot cause chaotic harm. When safer and implementable models are known to have trodden the Earth, the rationale for worshipping dangerous and far-from-robust machinations presents itself as less than enticingly compelling, in spite of comparatively grander technical brilliance.

So, if prior (and practically superior) models were abundantly in existence, why did BSM reign supreme, at least in theory? Because, Taleb and Haug offer, it complied with financial economics orthodoxy (such as the Capital Asset Pricing Model and efficient markets theory) in a very convenient way. BSM acceptance as the acceptable tool, thus, would be the result of an "academic marketing exercise," rather than the appearance of a wholly original, innovative piece of work. What allowed BSM to become accepted (or, in Taleb-Haug-speak, "palatable to the economics establishment") was the so-called risk-neutrality argument, which allowed one to price options without having to guess the asset's expected return, by assuming the risk-free rate as discount factor. But this holds only if continuous dynamic hedging is feasible in real life (or, per the original Black-Scholes collaboration, if CAPM holds). As it is not, BSM may be reduced to ashes.

"In an idealized fantasy world, dynamic delta hedging removes all the risk all the time, but what about the real world?" wonders Espen Haug in his history-challenging latest book. (If you have any doubts about the nonconventional, nonorthodox, nonacademic approach of Taleb's accomplice, perhaps the picture displayed next to the above text could serve to dispel notions: a tuxedo-wearing, black sunglasses–sporting, gun-toting Haug stands in James Bond-esque pose shoulder-to-shoulder with a scantily-clad, decisively not unattractive blonde female who is herself also packing heat; definitely no taciturn professor here.) His answer: no. The 10-year veteran option trader (who has made money for some of the world's top hedge funds and investment banks) alerts us that BSM-inspired dynamic hedging is far from robust in practice (we kind of imagined that after having read the part on the October 1987 crash). He generously notes that delta-hedging does remove a lot of the risk of an option position, but not nearly all of it. The concept of risk-neutrality is based on the notion that you can eliminate all the risk all of the time. If you can only perform elimination on some of the risk some of the time, then risk-neutrality becomes a suspect concept.

Perfect dynamic hedging (and the alibi it generates for BSM to differentiate itself from the identical formulas that were abundantly available before, and thus to exist) is only truly possible in a Platonic world of, in the words of Robert Merton, "dynamic completeness." While he has openly stated his belief that the financial arena will inevitably achieve such nirvana, Taleb and Haug opine that, if anything, we have spiraled away from it. There are several well-trodden reasons why those fastidious market realities conspire to sink the dynamic hedging vessel, but let's first clarify the degree of Platonicity that dynamic hedging (BSM) entails by reemphasizing an apparent oddity that was introduced earlier: A delta-hedging Wonderland is a place where demand for the product is assumed *not* to affect the price of the product whatsoever. If someone wants to buy the product, the market maker can borrow from the precisely precise mathematical recipe and, voila, manufacture an exact replica of the product. The cost of the product would then be dictated exclusively by such manufacturing costs, not by the savagery of the crowd's wishes.

In the words of respected academics, *"If competitive intermediaries can hedge perfectly, as in a BSM economy, then option prices are determined by no-arbitrage (aka delta hedging) and demand pressure has no effect."* Such quality is actually held in quite high esteem within the ivory tower: *"One of the major achievements of financial economics is the no-arbitrage theory that determines derivatives prices independent of investor demand."* Call me naive, but it seems to my nonmathematical mind that arguing (for almost 40 years) for a world where demand has no effect on prices simply because a mathematical lemma says so appears slightly overstretched.

For dynamic hedging to work, markets must be frictionless and continuous with unlimited liquidity and no transaction costs, a world where volatility is constant and short selling is not constrained. As soon as we have market jumps, liquidity gets drier, transacting entails expenditures, or it is hard to short-sell, dynamic hedging would break down, ceasing to be a perfect mirror of the replicated option. The end result can be a spectacular mismatch between the value of the option and the value of the "replicating" portfolio—or, in other words, a disastrously off-the-mark, very expensive hedge. Of course, those violations tend to present themselves quite often in real life. Many a trader attempting to hedge his book through large-scale dynamic hedging has seen himself walked out the door by oversized security guards not known for treating loss-makers kindly. October 1987 obviously highlights the fallibility of dynamic hedging in an outrageous way, showing what can happen when asset prices jump wildly and you can't find takers for your delta-dictated trading activities. But less dramatic events would also do the trick. Simply not being able to hedge every single day under normal conditions can produce significant mismatches (Taleb cites the example of a three-month option that is hedged only 50 times, producing a non-modest 10 percent error). No-arbitrage pricing may be food for the analytical brain, but it is not enforceable in the financial jungle.

In an honest display of honesty, Mark Rubinstein and Hayne Leland did warn (both before and after Black Monday) as to the potential fragility of BSM-inspired dynamic hedging out there in the cold hard real world. The analogy with true actual unquestioned insurance, they said as their portfolio insurance business was being lifted off in 1981, "breaks down if stock prices gapped downward, plunging discontinuously: there would not be sufficient time to adjust the replicating portfolio." Theoretically, such things could not happen. But these erstwhile academic recluses were now trying to make a buck in the financial jungle and had no option but to remove (even if just partially) the dogmatic blindfolds and admit to the unassailable evidence: Dynamic hedging would fail were the markets to be hit by a shock. In other words, dynamic hedging can't always hold perennially. We should not be able to get away with risk-neutrality under such paradigm.

Of course, the shock need not be external or monstrous. Dynamic hedging itself would do the trick, in a deviously successful exercise of self-reinforcement. The dogma would say that the adjustments to the replicating portfolio would not impact the underlying asset price, but as portfolio insurance became really big business the traded amounts became so large that the market did, in spectacular form, become exposed to the risk of an internal shock of potentially devastating consequences. Black Monday happened in October 1987 and not in October 1983 because by the former date the dynamic hedging requirements were sizable enough to take the market to hell at the first sight of a downward correction.

The fathers of portfolio insurance knew that to be the case, and seemed aware of the potential for snowballing were dynamic hedging to be widely embraced. "From the very first day I thought of portfolio insurance I said, 'Well, what if everyone tries to do it?' I didn't like the answer I came up with," stated Hayne Leland. Driven by such concerns, LOR did eventually try to refuse new clients, hesitating to bring the day of dynamic reckoning ever closer. "It was as if Pandora's box had been open," said Mark Rubinstein, "we could shut our doors but that wasn't going to stop anything." He was certain that the growing prowess of dynamic hedgers would enhance market instability. When the Dow Jones dropped by almost 5 percent on September 11, 1986 (biggest setback in 25 years), the authorities blamed it on fundamentals, but Rubinstein suspected the debacle hit closer to home and that the selling pressures by portfolio insurers had been the critical force. He couldn't prove it, but his gut prompted him to inform the regulators as to the insalubrious effects that the theoretical dream-world of dynamic hedging could have on the implacably undogmatic real-world. It is highly telling that the professors who actually ventured out of the ivory tower and tried their hand at implementing the alchemy behind BSM (the very reason why the formula is accepted, and the sole reason why it was awarded the Nobel) came to the unnegotiable conclusion that the beautiful mathematics lack miserably in the backstreets of finance.

All that BSM did, state Taleb and Haug, is rederive an already existing formula by using new (as we now know, quite fragile) theoretical arguments. They did not invent any formula. What BSM really is, add the traders-authors, is a thought experiment in a hypothetical world, an elegant argument that only works in a Platonic outer universe. In fact, within academic circles (including the Nobel committee), the prized aspect of BSM is actually the way in which they derived an already known formula.

What's more, BSM justified the risk-free rate on the grounds that it is possible (in its Platonic theoretical world, at least) to build a riskless portfolio made up of the option and the underlying asset through continuously rebalancing the delta, but Taleb and Haug argue that we didn't need to wait for such revolutionary-labeled discovery, as option traders had long before discovered a math-free way to hedge their positions, namely the oft-mentioned put-call parity technique, which allows you to statically hedge options with other options (you can manufacture puts out of existing calls, or vice versa). That is, the very (technical) reason why BSM was crowned as the chosen one was not really a new discovery from a practical point of view; traders already knew and employed hands-on techniques that allowed them to feel "risk-neutral"; they didn't have to wait for stochastic calculus-impulsed fabrications so that they could eliminate risk from their business. And with the crucial caveat, naturally, that while mathematically guided BSM-sponsored dynamic hedging does not actually work (and may in fact eventually increase, not reduce, your risk), insufferably provincial put-call parity seems to be stubbornly obliging.

Almost immediately after Taleb and Haug posted the first versions of the paper online, their campaign against BSM began to catch unremitting fire and gradually got more and more coverage in the nonacademic media and blogosphere spaces. Such popularization of Taleb-Haug is welcome, for a healthy debate regarding the real usefulness of BSM is certainly a necessity. However, some of the coverage has lacked depth, focusing on already well-known and familiar criticisms of BSM (which are mentioned almost in passing by Taleb and Haug, merely as an unavoidable part of the argument) rather than on truly path-breaking and innovative insights, which Taleb-Haug offers aplenty.

For a while now, everybody has known that BSM is a model built on shaky foundations. Its main assumptions simply do not hold: Financial prices do not follow the Normal probability distribution, tend to jump, and present a volatility that is not constant. The key strategy behind the formula (dynamic hedging) is sadly not really feasible in the real world. If Taleb-Haug, as some commentators seem to have implied, centered just on providing yet another laundry list of BSM's foundational faults, it would certainly have been wasted ink.

Fortunately, there is much more to Taleb-Haug. So much more, in fact, that their work does threaten to completely change the way we think about option pricing, financial academicism, conventional wisdom, and even the Nobel Prize. To recall, Taleb-Haug contains three innovative status quo–challenging dictums that do deserve wild popularization (if anything, as a way to get a widespread debate going). Pertaining to BSM, this is what the veteran players have to say: 1) It is not used (even by those who think that they use it); 2) It wasn't needed; 3) It wasn't original. Each one of these bold assertions is conventional wisdom–shattering. The three taken together in one devastating blow represent a (tentatively) deadly strike to the most famous construct to ever emerge from financial economics. While many had said many times that BSM is an imperfect model based on unworldly assumptions, no one had (at least, so forcefully publicly) said what Taleb and Haug are offering through their holy trinity of BSM-bashing.

In sum, the main contribution of Taleb-Haug is not that BSM is a hopelessly unrealistic model. We already knew that. What we didn't know is that it is not really used, it wasn't truly needed, and it wasn't entirely original. We could have known, though. All it would have taken is the courage and vision to question undoubted conventionalisms (perhaps by thinking a little bit, perhaps by talking to a few practitioners) and the scholarly spirit to research historical evidence. Thank God that Taleb and Haug chose not to be like the rest of us conformists.

Taleb's and Haug's bold statements, while a welcome contribution to the search for truth, cause us to become teary-eyed, nostalgic for a beautiful dream that has been unrepentantly shattered. Faced with the unavoidable heartbreaking truth, we yearn for paradise lost. Losing BSM would deprive us of something that seemed incalculably valuable. BSM, for all its flaws, offered quantifiable light where before there was only unknown darkness (prior related models contained, in general, too many unobservables and hurdles to implementation). By being deprived of BSM, we would lose such comforting, albeit misplaced, certainty. We thank Taleb and Haug for their veracity-seeking quest, but we loathe the loss of our innocent naiveté.

The most obvious certainty that the model offered was a precise number for the value of an option. This it did in a quite ingenious way. Everyone would tell you that an option should cost money because it gives you the right to enjoy a potentially large payout while limiting the possible losses if things do not go your way. But who ensures that that right has value per se? That value is supposed to come from the probability assigned to the option expiring in-the-money. So who guarantees that the probability of making money on the option is nonzero? Who can honestly claim to know the exact distribution governing financial assets? Pricing options based simply on probabilistic assumptions sounds a bit fishy.

What BSM innovatively did was price options through non-arbitrage arguments. It showed that (mathematically, at least) dealers could build a replicating portfolio of the underlying asset and borrowed money that would always mirror the value of the option. Non-arbitrage conditions guaranteed that the value of the option at any point should equal the value of the portfolio. Since the whole thing becomes riskless, we could assume a risk-free rate of discount, thus avoiding the need to guess the expected return of the underlying asset—a devilishly difficult task.

Providing a good rationale for why options should cost money and how much was not the only valuable quantitative contribution of BSM. The model also helped produce hard numbers for the risk parameters of options, the factors that can change the value of an option, the famous "Greeks." These Greeks would tell you exactly by how much the value of the option would be modified if the underlying asset moved ("delta"), if the volatility moved ("vega"), if time to maturity moved ("theta"), or if the underlying asset jumped ("gamma"). This is highly valuable information for any options dealer or speculator, as the Greeks could now determine with Swiss-like precision your mark-to-market exposure. BSM provided option dealers with a compass to allow them to risk-manage their options business and, in principle, help them confidently expand to include new clients and new areas.

In an ideal world, BSM would have thus been a sensational contribution, worthy of the admiration of any derivatives pro. Unfortunately, the world is not ideal, or rather BSM is not an ideal fit for the real world. The model itself relies on assumptions regarding the market's probability distribution that are plainly wrong (financial markets are not "normal"). More worrisome, the "dynamic hedging" behind the replication strategy is neither possible nor desirable because liquidity and transaction cost issues make the required continuous replicating impractical. Delta-hedging may be a mathematical beauty, but it is not an implementable tool.

Obviously if there is no model (i.e., if option prices come from supply-demand or from static, not dynamic, replication) then there are no Greeks. Delta, gamma, vega, and theta are 100 percent model-dependent; they have to be derived from a formula. There are no Greeks in supply-demand option pricing, so there are no precise numbers to guide dealers into how to risk-manage their positions.

Herein lies the tragedy. Quantitative finance produces mathematically beautiful devices that promise to tackle critical problems. Unfortunately, real life has a habit of relentlessly rendering such numerical applications useless. It would be great to be able to count on the certainties of BSM, but chaos-prone markets stubbornly refuse to allow their unpredictability and untamability to be ironed out. Perhaps the only certainty about the markets is that financial truth will always be determined by humans, however lacking in rigor, and not by precision-promising, nicely designed theoretical masterpieces like BSM.

In a big way, the shattered theoretical dream most glowingly symbolized by the BSM fallout highlights how naively eager we are to believe in the quantitative tooth fairy. We are so desperate for analytical certainties, that if the mathematical oasis turned out to be a mirage we would still drink the sand. For some strange reason, we are readier to admit to the infallible necessity of a model in order for things to work, than to succumb to the humble simplicityness that dictates that maybe humans are the only determining factor that essentially matters. We seem to need to believe that we need models for the financial world to turn. We are suckers for complexity, self-conned into the unquestioned dominance of unquestioned mathematical radars. I can wax so lyrically because I have suffered from the hallucination, and have seen so many with similar symptoms.

The funny thing about quantitative self-enslavement in finance is that it is highly aristocratic in nature: the ranks of those who blindly believe are dominated by highly educated, well-bred, good-positioned members of society (B-school professors, B-school students, journalists, regulators, financial pros, Nobel Prize committees). Those laudable qualities seem to make not a dent of difference when it comes to critically questioning the actual validity of the received gospels. How many hundreds of thousands out there still believe that the arrival of BSM was required for options markets to flourish, even exist? How many still believe that BSM was a superbly original pioneering piece of work? How many still believe that BSM reigns supreme in the markets? How many still believe that the engineering behind BSM functions decently well? How many still take all of the above assertions on unchallengeable faith? Based on my own observations, quite a lot.

When one realizes that even Taleb and Haug themselves held dogmatically conventional beliefs for many years, it becomes obvious that the power of theoretical finance lies in the low probability that someone, somewhere, would sit down and begin to drastically analyze the validity, applicability, usability, popularity, originality, and necessity of a particular theory, and, crucially, would not be shy about publicly disclosing the res/ults. Taleb and Haug's paper was a Black Swan for financial economics. A highly unlikely yet potentially devastating event. In this light, BSM had operated akin to a short option position, affording the theoretical community constant yearly benefits (in the shape of reputation, notoriety, and material for endless numbers of research projects) while negatively exposing it to the rare possibility that a couple of mavericks who have actually traded in the real world, who understand the math, and who later in life developed a profound skepticism towards quantitative indoc- trination would get together and decide to devote some of their time to analyzing whether BSM was needed, pioneering, or employed. Just like certain insurance companies operate in less-than-commendable ways and play the odds that no mistreated policyholder would contact a lawyer, finance theory crosses its fingers and hopes that no excessively thorough, high-profile attack is launched against it.

Now that the offensive has been dramatically propelled (articles on Taleb and Haug have appeared in the most prestigious and widely dis- tributed global financial media outlets), BSM has been effectively trans- formed into the Maginot Line of theoretical finance. The construct that had for many years allowed theoreticians to confidently proclaim the robustness and reliability of their contributions, to staunchly assert the superiority of their approach, is demonstrated to be less-than-fully clothed. Theory suddenly appears as shockingly much less reliable, much less successful, much less necessary. What was a symbol of strength be- comes a symbol of weakness. The symbol of might becomes the symbol of defeat. The symbol of impregnability becomes the symbol of fragility. By pumping up BSM so much during the good times, the fall becomes that much harder during harsher times. The Taleb and Haug blitzkrieg has been so notorious precisely because the other side had been so con- fident in its apparently unassailable fortifications. Therefore, a key lesson from the BSM debate is that theorists should lean towards more humble- ness and less sureness when it comes to their constructs. That way, when they are outflanked, they may be readier for the resistance.

Ideally, Taleb and Haug should serve as a catalyst for change within the theoretical community and those who voluntarily enslave themselves to the latter's doctrine (many times without having a clue what it's all about; qualifications-blindness at its worst, diploma-induced hypnosis at its most effective). BSM was published in 1973. Since then, thousands of intelligent men and women have received PhDs in Finance or Math- ematics and joined the ivory tower. Why did it take more than 30 years for someone to comprehensively investigate whether BSM was, as the classroom and the books indefatigably said, an unparalleled breakthrough that fueled the launch of the options business and that is daily used by enamored traders? Why did it take so long for someone to ask for opinions around trading floors? Why did the academics focus on minutiae mathematical details and not on the truly relevant big picture? Why didn't the academics consider the possibility that they may have been operating under completely unworldly assumptions, a parallel universe heavily in contradiction with historical and market realities?

It is entirely paradoxical that the toiling of two unabashed doubters of the academic scene's contributions would present ivory tower inhabitants with a golden opportunity: a once-in-a-lifetime chance for redemption, a unique avenue for relevance-obtainment, a not-to-be-missed guiding light towards salvation. Yes, a possible consequence (whether intended or not) of the irreverently critical paper would be the forceful put-down of theory and theoreticians, a devastating loss of reputation, a confinement to marginalized obscurity. But I, for one, would like to believe in a more hopeful unchaining of events. Faced with the ruthless efficiency of "amateurish" research efforts (Espen Haug's investigation of the history of option trading, pricing, and hedging surely is the most exhaustive such exercise ever), those with no practical experience and not in the habit of lemma-challenging digging could do worse than to take notice and assimilate that equation-scribbling without regard to mundane truths, both current and past, would not only be a futile labor but would expose them to highly publicized discrediting eye-openers down the road. And at the end of day, what finance scholar worth their salt would not be *personally interested* in how things really are (and were) in the action fields? Would it be too much to ask of academics paid to generate and spread knowledge and who can devote all of their time to such chores that they should demonstrate at least the same amount of curiosity as dilettantes who are not getting paid for their intellectual excavations and who have plenty of other occupations?

Taleb and Haug have shown that BSM is not as gifted as we had thought. The model's (truly pioneering) mathematical prowess is still there, intactly ready to continue to receive admiration from analytics-lovers. But all its other supposed strengths appear now indisputably diminished. The halcyon idol of mathematical finance now seems much less representative of a successful purportedly scientific discipline, while the latter's implicatively appears much less triumphant. So what? This wouldn't be the time for whining about paradise lost or, much worse, for stubbornly clinging to it in reckless defiance of contrarian evidence.

It would be the time to turn the page on the theoretical annals and unleash a new era of fruitful collaboration between those who do and those who don't do (but study a field where all that matters is the doing). Theoretical research would thus be filtered through the real-experience strainer, with anything too unworldly obfuscatory being discarded as impossibly unrealistic. We would all gain from that.

The alternative to theorists taking Taleb and Haug under consideration seems too tenebrous to contemplate. The pesky paper has presented academics with a unique opportunity, but also with a unique menacing challenge. Possibly never before have they been subjected to so much public scrutiny and so much pressure to do the right thing (i.e., learn to humbly learn from doers and to recognize theoretical defeats). Blatantly rejecting, even denigrating, Taleb and Haug's intromission would amount to a blatant disregard for truth and an irremovable oath to protecting and preserving theoretical orthodoxy no matter how impossibly off-target it may be. An undisguised declaration of independence from bothersome equations-doubting truisms. An irrevocable commitment to neglect theory-negating evidence. In sum, a fanatical manifesto that the financial world's reality will always take a backseat to their self-serving abstractions. I can't think of any other thing that would most gravely threaten the reputation of ivory towerists.

Conclusions

■ *Chapter 8* ■

Black Swan Deceit?

■ *The tired "perfect storm" alibi may be a facade* ■ *Indoctrinating clients and investors* ■ *The unseemly marketers of academic dogma* ■ *Do as I say, not as I do* ■ *Glorifying complexity* ■

This chapter is about how pros borrow from finance theory (even if convinced of its uselessness) to achieve certain practical, personal goals. In doing so, they may be not only betraying the spirit of the dogmas (perhaps a less than hurtful charge) but, most significantly, endowing the theories with respectability and wider exposure (perhaps an unintended, not directly sought-after effect). Theoretical ideology and mathematical edifices can be put to good use by self-serving, otherwise no-nonsense practitioners. They can act as convenient alibis with which to escape blame from bad news ("It's not my fault—according to the model, this could not happen"); they can be used to excuse venturing into certain trading and investment strategies ("The model says there's no risk, let's jump in"); they can be used to enhance one's reputation as an unassailable genius (while building stringent barriers to entry into the profession in the meantime); they can be used to help get business (aid with the obtainment of clients and investors); they can be used to dress up simple strategies and make yourself look more advanced and intellectual (enhance your aura of exclusivity); and they can be used to justify the existence of entire professions ("You need math, and only I know the math").

All those interested actions by no-nonsense pros go a long way towards helping cement in the public's psyche the notion that markets are amenable to quantification, that they can be modeled, that there can be theory-driven certainty. That is, academics and quants are not the only ones with clear-cut interests in promoting the view that finance is about math. Street-smart breadwinners roaming around trading floors can too benefit from the conventionalization of such assumptions. In this sense, a strange coalition is formed to push the theoretical agenda forward. We know who would benefit, but who would suffer? On top of the potential pain inflicted on the markets overall (i.e., all of us), the clients and investors of certain players may be doomed to doing badly. And there is no doubting the number one possible victim: truth.

During the turmoil-dominated credit crisis, we have witnessed financial professionals express their utter shock at the dimension of the mayhem that afflicted the markets. While the precise verbiage may vary, the central message remained unabated: Such violent and volatile movements were totally unexpected, totally unprecedented, and totally unpredictable. No one could see them coming, nor prepare for them. Thus, these pros seem to imply, do not be too hard on ourselves for having experienced losses in such a devilishly difficult environment.

Sounds familiar? It should. Very similar arguments have been heard throughout financial history. Take, for instance, 1998 (fall of mega-fund LTCM) and 1987 (Black Monday's crash). Both history-making events were deemed (and, curiously, still are in some quarters) a freak event, an outlier, the "perfect storm" that only takes place once in a million years. Most importantly, people referred to them as "completely outside any of our mathematical predictions, simply not captured by our models." Just like today.

If Goldman Sachs' CFO stands as the symbol of today's excusers by describing in August 2007 the latest bout of "irrationality" to hit the markets (and his firm) as *"25 standard deviations events several days in a row."* LTCM's −45 percent August 1998 returns were also described as a "13 standard deviation event," and the 23 percent drop in Wall Street on October 19, 1987, was memorably framed as a "20 standard deviation event." You don't need to be a statistician to understand what all these statements are trying to tell us: basically, that the probability of any of those three events taking place was negligibly small, zero for all practical purposes. No wonder that the models did not forewarn us of the risks, typically offer those who did badly as a consequence. Don't blame us too much, it was simply out of our control.

The problem, of course, is that those models are very wrong. Standard deviation as a measure of risk (dispersion of returns) only makes sense if the underlying probability distribution is Normal. Under such probabilistic construct, any move beyond three standard deviations is essentially assumed to be not likely to happen, so imagine 25, 13, or 20. "Never in the history of the universe," "a likelihood of 0,000 . . . 006 with 138 zeros before the 6," and "a 1,000-year hurricane" have all been offered as apt descriptions of such freakishims.

But in real life, as has been amply repeated throughout this book, financial markets can't be categorized as Normally distributed, if only because those one-in-a-million-years happenstances tend to take place rather more often than normally assumed. Many people much younger than one million years have witnessed several "rare events" in their lifetimes.

So why do financial pros keep returning to the old and tired standard deviation alibi when confronted with untold market chaos? Most of them are either old enough to have previously experienced one or two "impossible events" in their careers or informed enough to be fully aware of the previous and frequent existence of such events. And if all else fails, surely they must have heard of a book called *The Black Swan* by veteran trader Nassim Taleb where the argument for non-Normality (and the real-life habitual presence of rare events) is very forcefully made. The tome is a bestseller and has been profiled in every newspaper in the land. Why then the odd insistence on describing market crises as out-of-this-world improbabilities?

It is tempting to be naughty and to conclude that a bit of deceitfulness is taking place. That the joke is on us. Perhaps seasoned pros do know that the "Markets are normal" logo and the gazillion standard deviations stuff are utter useless nonsense. But they need to act a bit so as to be able to put on the market plays that they really want, safe in the knowledge that if things turn sour, the "perfect-storm" free get-out-of-jail card will always be available. So that you can afterwards say, "But this was an impossible event, one in a million, 25 standard deviations, no one could predict, outside the model, outlier, we relied on standard accepted Nobel-winning scientific methods . . ." In other words, pros may need to publicly dismiss the possibility of the Black Swan so as to be able to take Black Swan-exposed bets.

In this regard, the Normality assumption appears particularly handy, given that little has to happen in the markets for its dictums to be violated; that is, you don't have to wait for a really big tumble in order to be able to use your conveniently helpful scientific alibi. As soon as things deviate moderately and you begin to incur a few losses, the event can (courtesy of Normality) already be deemed a rare one and the excuse would be pleasantly on. Almost any setback could then be categorized as probabilistically very unseemly, and thus beyond your realm of responsibility. After all, can they really blame you for suffering from a risk that Nobel-endowed methods say would be beyond the 99 percent confidence interval? You can always say that you did the right thing, probabilistically speaking, by exposing your investors to losing money only if the odd, weird, strange 1 percent phenomena took place. Normality allows you not only to rationalize almost any losses, but also to appear as stringently cautious. Of course, for this to fully work you need investors who don't understand that what you call 1 percent might actually be something like 30 percent, and what you call 99 percent might actually be something like 70 percent.

Taking positions that could be destroyed if a large unfavorable move takes place and admitting that you were aware of the (huge) risks beforehand is certainly not politically correct. "You mean you knew that this could happen?!" is not what a money manager most wishes to hear from their investors and clients once mayhem has taken hold. Thus, you claim prior ignorance as to the real probability. According to your (industrywide-embraced) models, such things could never happen.

Such displayed "ignorance" allows you to confidently take subprime exposure, extra leveraged bets, and sell implied volatility. You can gain outsized returns for a while, and pray that the Black Swan will not take place. If the latter does unfortunately take place, swiftly borrow from the one-in-a-million script.

So it may turn out that all these players always believed in Taleb's theories (and doubted conventional finance theory), but can't say so in public. They believe in Taleb but don't want to be like Taleb, who rather than expose himself to a blowup prefers to patiently wait for the Black Swan to appear and benefit from it. This strategy (mainly implemented by purchasing deep out-of-the-money put options) entails suffering a constant stream of small losses before potentially enjoying a huge windfall. But many pros don't like that lifestyle. They want immediate, certain glory, not years of bleeding with the possibility of no glory at all. This means a stream of gains before potentially suffering huge losses. It also means having to (likely deceitfully) publicly deny that Black Swans may be on the horizon, in the process embracing (even if unbeknownst to these pros) core neoclassical financial economics.

Taleb, by being so open about his opinions, has condemned himself to not being able to take those kinds of bets (not that he wants to, of course). He spends all day telling us that they will blow up, and thus not many would give him capital to invest in those trades. He has condemned himself to bleed (before triumphantly triumphing). Those who may be hiding their true feelings when defending normality in public, on the other hand, condemn themselves to having to bet on the Black Swan not taking place (i.e., to having orthodox finance theory being proven right). After all, punting on something that you openly deem irredeemably improbable would not sound too prescient, would it?

Financial dealers make a lot of money by selling and arranging so-phisticated devices that can deliver nice returns for end users as long as markets don't turn awry. Collateralized debt obligations (CDOs) are the most recent example. For these dealers it is essential that the probability of the nasty scenario remains downplayed. After all, not many customers (not even the most reckless) would enter into a transaction where they face large odds of suffering a bloodbath.

The same logic would apply to hedge funds. Many of these high-profile players enjoy nothing more than taking positions that bet on the negative Black Swan (the crash, the meltdown, the defaults) not taking place. For instance, many punters seem to have traditionally been avid option sellers, a great way to generate tasty returns (in real-income form, to boot), but of course also a window to a potential devastating blowup. Here it is again crucial to downplay the possibility of disaster.

That is, for many pros it may have been practical to "indoctrinate" clients and investors into ardently believing that very nasty market sur-prises are the stuff of fantasy, not something to be witnessed in the real world anytime soon. The Black Swan must be presented and mar-keted as undeniably unlikely (these days, of course, such presentations become less convincing, courtesy of Taleb's incessant contrarian rooftop chatting).

Thus, the following paradox presents itself: Some masters of the uni-verse may have been doing the dirty work for orthodoxy-embracing financial economists, relentlessly marketing around the globe some of the key precepts that lie at the foundations of the discipline, such as the absence of Black Swans, the concept of diversification based on the statistical concept of correlation, the notion that risks can be quantified and measured.

It is often argued that, surely, sophisticated financial players must be fully aware that rare events take place quite often, that statistical devices are not to be entirely trusted, and that risks are not mathematically tractable in a precise way. There is no need for Taleb and others to point out that obviousness. Stop repeating what everyone already knows. Please, be more original.

And yet evidence unfailingly shows punters taking specific positions precisely because they would profit from the (entirely expectable, according to the position-builders) market's return to "normalcy." If such players were fully convinced of the existence of monsters lurking in the tails of the distribution and of the impossibility of prediction, then they did not walk the thought and chose instead to cheat themselves (and their investors) by taking the road that led to potential disaster. Such road can be irresistibly tempting. Rich pickings typically await those fortunate enough to see their pro-Normalcy bets ride a path that's eventually not compromised by fatal market mayhem. It is thus in many a fund manager's interest to exaggerate the normalness of "normal" plays, and to accentuate the exceptionalness of the alternatives. It seems easier to justify committing capital to trades that look very likely to succeed than to those that look very out-of-the-ordinary. Once you manage (possibly in accordance with prevailing conventional wisdom) to separate punts into normal and exceptional, it may seem smarter to offer yourself to investors as someone who will specialize in the former and repudiate the latter. You would most likely raise more money while providing a convenient hedge for later if things go wrong ("I did the normal thing").

It seems to be the case that in our world, a very good argument to categorize something as normal (or exceptional) is its confirmation (or rebuttal) by past evidence. Thus, an investment strategy that loses money only if something that has never (or very seldom) happened would be deemed normal, and as such worthy of backing by those eager to not have to wait for the "exceptional" in order to get richer. By backing such strategies, funds and investors are of course implicitly endorsing the most sacred tenets behind neoclassical financial theory and conventional quantitative risk management. More than that, they are helping spread the ideology. In fact, the most ardent of believers (or savviest of peddlers) may actively use the right theoretical aiding kit to endow their actions with analytical justification and to disarm any possible objectors.

People may overwhelmingly want to invest only in the inevitable. Thus, if you want their money you could do worse than propose trades that benefit from (perceived) normality. A theory that portrays such proposals as highly expected, and that rules out the converse, would obviously come in handy, particularly if it happens to boast a Nobel. If you want to appear as the champion of normal (i.e., most likely to be profitable) strategies, it seems only convenient to peddle investment proposals that do have, in principle, a decent chance of turning out okay (at least for a while) and, most important, that happen to be those that accepted, glorified, scientific methodologies would back. Needless to say, your marketing prospectus or business plans would predictably not fail to make mention of such reputable support. Academics and dealing room barbarians thus become strange bedfellows and accomplices.

Of course, financiers may be convinced of the dangers of such theory-backed strategies. They may be perfectly aware not only that rare events are not so abnormal, but that what really matters is the expected outcome of a trade, not so much its (pretty much, prospectively unknown) probability of occurrence. Were what's perceived as non-normal to materialize, clients and investors may be entirely wiped out, since when the Black Swan presents itself it does so with a vengeance. Financiers may also be aware of the fact that assigning quantitative measures to risk-detecting activities is utterly useless in the markets, that things like VaR or credit ratings are based on flawed methodologies and offer not-to-be-trusted outputs.

But even if deep in their hearts they wanted to be honest with outsiders and share their true feelings, can they really afford to? Those outsiders may actually want to be deceived. They may be so thirsty for belief that they may drink the sand if the oasis turned out to be a mirage. People may demand quantifiable certainty and the appeal of data-backed predictable normalness (the low VaR, the AAA rating, the small sigma). Pros may know that what's perceived as normal is not that normal, but what matters is that clients and investors *believe* it is normal, or can be easily made to believe that it is. Again, people may in general prefer not to bet on the perceived exceptional, so it's a piece of cake to convince them that the conventional normal is the normal thing (and, again, the theory helps in that respect, at least pre–Taleb). It seems harder to sell people on the idea that a 10-sigma event is likely. Thus, if you want business, you focus on peddling as normal the opposite plays, which luckily for you have respectable ivory-tower endorsement.

If customers and investors demand quantifiable certainty, then they may have to be lied to. If they need precise answers to questions such as "How risky is this?" you may have to hold your nose and borrow from the VaR or rating agencies script and oblige with a number or a letter soup. If such numbers and letters help the client or investor feel more comfy and thus aid and abet the transacting of business, it may seem understandable for fund managers or bankers to engage in a bit of deceit, once more theory-supported. If acting a bit more truthful instead and proclaiming that you don't know the risks or the probabilities, and that no one can know those things in the markets, will take you to the poorhouse, then it is a safe bet that openness would take a backseat. It appears easier (let alone more profitable) to provide the required measurements than to say that you just don't know. Another unseemly win for conventional theory.

Only by somehow managing to surround the possibility that subprime borrowers may default on their U.S. mortgages with the non-normal, exceptional mantle did the complex credit derivatives and securitization segments achieve the mind-boggling growth of the past few years. It also helped, of course, that rating agencies showed a palpable willingness to measure with confidence the potential risks of such activities (and that they did so with overall generosity). It is important to be able to talk about risk and return with confidence and precision, otherwise not much business may be captured. Quantitative finance could not be more pleased with such state of affairs. Finance theory emerges as the (unintentional) beneficiary of such matter-of-factly business practices.

A very interesting example of a trading strategy that was deemed normal (and its success therefore inevitable) on account of the guidance provided by past data is that of LTCM's volatility selling in the summer of 1998.

In this case, the endorsement of theoretical normality may not have been exaggeratedly deceitful, as LTCM of course housed not just believers, but the idols themselves (Robert Merton and Myron Scholes were partners).

In the early 1990s the so-called structured products market began to blossom in Europe. Investment banks, led by UBS's paratrooper-turned-trader Ramy Goldstein, began to offer investors vehicles that offered equity markets upside plus a guarantee on the money invested. In other words, the cost of the structure covered the purchase of a bond and an equity option, to which benefits the investor became entitled. Through the structured products market, dealers effectively became short long-dated equity index (call) options. Or, in option-speak, short volatility. Were implied volatility to go up a lot (i.e., were option prices to go up a lot), dealers could incur huge losses. You can try to hedge such risks through dynamic risk management strategies, borrowing from the famous Greek parameters (delta, gamma, vega). But this is in no way foolproof, economical, or convenient. Much better if you can find someone willing to take the other side of your exposure (i.e., sell you options to cover for the ones you had sold to investors).

Originally, the market for long-dated European equity index volatility was small, with few players. Thus, the opportunities for matching trades seemed limited. At this point, LTCM (traditionally a fixed-income arbitrage house) decided to explore the possibility of jumping in as volatility provider. The thinking was that at some point the price of long-dated call options would reach a sufficiently elevated peak (relative to historical data) for LTCM to make a very nice profit out of selling such overpriced contracts.

When long-dated implied volatility, steady at 16 percent for months, jumped above 20 percent (for the first time) in the fall of 1997 as a result of Asian crisis–originated stock markets turmoil, LTCM decided that the time was right to sell options to the banks. The fund became so eager to do so that it was soon nicknamed the "Central Bank of Volatility." With data showing historical volatility in European markets at 15 percent, LTCM deemed its actions irrefutably smart. It was selling volatility at 25 percent (in theory, historically very expensive), with a data-backed expectation that turbulence would soon return to its normal, much lower levels. If you sell options and implied volatility nosedives, you get nice mark-to-market profits.

Of course, were volatility to *rise*, not fall, LTCM would be in big trouble. Very big. Potentially wiped-out big. But, hey, the historical record said that 25 percent was already impossibly out-of-sample, an outlier, a freakishism, so nothing to lose, right? In effect, LTCM bet the ranch on the future being like the past. And in a very leveraged way: Precisely because of its newly found role as volatility provider (and the tasty returns that it purportedly guaranteed), LTCM decided in December of that year to give more than one-third of its capital back to investors, so as to be able to continue to report mythical returns (the lower your capital, the higher your return for any given profit made).

On August 17, 1998, Russia announced a combined ruble devaluation and default on its bonds. The financial world went mad. In early September, implied long-dated volatility on German, French, and other equity indices climbed above 30 percent. Suddenly, LTCM was being hit with aggressively large margin calls from its option counterparts. It has been estimated that for every one percentage point that volatility went up, LTCM was forced to hand over $100 million.

Soon, the few remaining long-dated equity options dealers were quoting implied volatility above 40 percent. LTCM simply run out of money to keep playing the game through margin (it was also simultaneously suffering bloody setbacks in the fixed-income markets), and that's why it had to be eventually rescued by a consortium of banks "encouraged" by the Federal Reserve. In all, LTCM's equity index volatility trades lost $1.314 billion (out of $4.6 billion total losses).

LTCM looked at the past and saw nothing to worry about. It looked at the present and saw "abnormal," "unexpected," "unimaginable" things. Based on that info and on a tightly held believe in Normality, it bet its existence on the notion that the perceived abnormal is nothing but an inconvenient outlier, an accident, soon to be short-lived, soon to be ironed out into oblivion by the unstoppable forces of inevitability. When the abnormal decided not just to remain around a bit longer but to actually enhance itself, LTCM died. Of course, from LTCM's point of view its volatility bet was free money. Its justification felt comfortingly adequate, both to PhD-holding Nobel-endowed insiders and to starstruck outsiders. It is far easier to argue (and to posteriorly defend) that volatility will revert to historical levels than to argue that anything can happen and no scenario is beyond-bounds in finance. LTCM bet the farm on the Black Swan not taking place. That farm is long gone.

Were LTCM's principals deceitful? Did they really believe in normality? Or did they play the very tempting normality bet because they knew that any mishap could be blamed on the "one-in-a-million-years perfect storm"? Housing so many Finance professors, did LTCM bet the farm safe in the knowledge that the theory alibi would be in hand if disaster struck? Maybe, maybe not.

According to an expert in LTCM, *"Armed with a computer presentation, core LTCM principals began visiting investors, explaining the previous summer's disaster as a once-in-a-lifetime event that was unlikely to be repeated."* This tells us what kind of message LTCM wanted to promote, but not exactly whether the effort was heartfelt or an act. Perhaps they knew that people have a tendency (a need even) to embrace the perceived normal and to abhor the perceived abnormal. That they are all too willing and ready to categorize as normal (and thus supremely expected) that which has not happened yet. That they are all too willing and ready to forgive those killed by abnormality, and to consider them as deserving of understanding and solidarity-filled warmth as those who lose their possessions as a result of an unpredictable earthquake or tsunami. That they suffer from conventionalism blindness and focus on (flawed) probabilities and not expectations. And that those probabilities are often provided by theories and mathematical constructs that conveniently assign a low number to the chances that trades like volatility-convergence would go berserk.

The inescapable truth is that the "perfect-storm" alibi survived the LTCM episode pretty unscathed. It didn't die in the Connecticut woods in late 1998. It wasn't refuted as self-serving hodgepodge, as dangerously inaccurate, as a deceit. So imagine that 10 years ago you had listened to LTCM's explanations of the downfall and studied a bit of the theory and, based on that, you had fully bought the 100-year hurricane stuff and thus concluded that, say, equity implied volatility cannot spike out of control, certainly not for a long while. Fully convinced, you decided to perhaps engage in a bit of option selling. Surely what happened in the summer of 1998 was a statistical aberration; it couldn't happen again. And then you went on to experience the dot.com bubble crash and (if you survived that unexpected roller coaster) the August 2007 shoot-the-chute (when Wall Street went down by 300 points only to go up by 250 points the next day, only to fall again by another 300 points) or the September–October 2008 insanity (with the VIX volatility index reaching almost twice its previously historically highest level). You are wiped out. Implied volatility did go crazy again, well before one million years. You feel cheated.

As we discussed in a prior chapter, none other than Warren Buffett may have (if only possibly partially) bought into the once-in-a-lifetime argument, because he has become an avid option seller of late. The sage of Omaha has decided to bet against the Black Swan, and dared to succeed where so many have failed before. In late 2007 and early 2008, Buffett sold large quantities of put options, collecting about $7 billion up front in premium money. In return, he is willing to bet that both the U.S. high-yield credit markets and mainstream international equity markets will not nosedive and/or become crazy. Will market "normalism" eventually rule the day and allow Buffett to reign triumphant? Whatever the final outcome, given his plainspokenness, openness, and folksiness, it is doubtful that the chairman of Berkshire Hathaway is trying to deceive anyone here.

A nother important lesson to draw from the LTCM episode is what could be called the "complexity disguise." That is, while conventional wisdom may hold that you are making (or losing) money through extravagantly, out-of-this-worldly complex, technology-driven, brain-intensive, PhD-enabled stratagems, in fact, behind the curtain, underneath the veil, you may be actually employing the simplest of tactics. Endowing yourself with the theoretical mantle helps a lot in this case. After all, surely a bunch of MIT PhDs won't be content with pursuing next-door-neighbor trading strategies; they *must* be doing something much funkier beyond the reach of mere mortals, right? Once more, theoretical and mathematical wrappings deliver wonderful benefits on the back of people's general case of conventionalism-blindness (also deemed intellectual laziness, or qualifications reverence).

Appearances are everything, even in the markets. If you have a PhD, have taught at prestigious universities, and manage to convince outsiders (journalists are especially valuable here) of your indomitable scientificness, then the world will sheepishly assume that you operate from a magically mysterious black box built upon the most sophisticated, latest quantitative techniques, no questions asked. The rocket scientist illusion becomes reality, courtesy of eager-to-be-impressed outsiders. Academic qualifications would then be used to disguise the staid and simple as turbocharged, ultrasmart complexity. Another convenient deceit aided and abetted by the glorification of analytics.

There is nothing complex or third-generation about selling vanilla options. Frankly, you don't need even a bachelor's degree for that. And yet that's exactly what LTCM did, in spades. A huge part of its overall portfolio consisted on a simple, easy as 1-2-3, tried-and-tested strategy (a third of its losses came through that conduit, as we've seen). Wait a minute—I thought that "the world's best finance faculty" could come up with more innovative things to do. Obviously, what looks ultracomplex is not always so.

A year before LTCM's demise, a very famous speculator lost his shirt by also selling equity (put) options. When the U.S. stock markets tumbled as a result of the Asian crisis disease, he had to close shop, ending many years of extraordinary returns. What's interesting about this story is that he, like LTCM's principals and employees, had also been considered by the outside (and inside) world as a brainiac genius who made vast amounts of money through the generous use of his brilliant, way-beyond-average intellect. The publication of his autobiography (an enlightened recollection of an intriguingly extraordinary life, full of allusions to high-minded nonfinancial stuff like music, poker, horse racing, sex, and science, plus his sharing of the fact that he seldom wears shoes or a description of his very notable academic and sporting achievements) only helped shape his image as a cut above the rest, a person gifted with magnificent skills (which in fact he is, just like LTCM's principals; that's beyond dispute). It just seemed unseemly to put such a man and naked vanilla option selling together. He just looked so much more sophisticated than that.

At least one observer pointed at the possibility of a facade. Best-selling author Michael Lewis, while conducting a review of the speculator's biography, put it like this: *"My guess is that . . . the story the author tells of his life in the market is very different from his actual behavior in the market. For whatever reason he does not want to explain the reasons for his rise in the world. He doesn't really want us to know them, or wants us to believe that they are something different and more complicated than they are. . . . Beneath all the bluster he remains ever so slightly ashamed of himself."*

The conclusion from these two stories is that one should never judge a player by its theoretical cover. "Intellectual" operators with an aura for genius brightness may in fact be concentrating their efforts on the simplest of strategies. The complexity disguise (which, while largely sanctioned by awestruck outsiders, was at least in part also clearly promoted from the inside by both LTCM and the famous speculator) may allow people to enhance their visibility and clout, and to raise more capital with which to make plain vanilla plays against the Black Swan not taking place. Once disaster strikes, it helps to have been perceived as complex. Forgiveness may be more at hand for those believed to have been the victims of sophisticated forces gone awry. It may be much more difficult to explain how you lost so much money on kindergarten-simple, ultraleveraged, unhedged plays. The "the black box malfunctioned as a result of unforeseen one-in-a-million-years events" excuse may sound preferable to the alternative: "I recklessly made a wild simplistic bet on markets not going turbulent, and by the way you don't need to hire a PhD for that."

Sometimes pros may appear to be embracing theoretically sanctioned certainties and dogma, while in practice acting in the opposite direction. That is, they would be matter-of-factly "deceiving" those that they had been trying to "deceive" verbally. A case of double deceit, if you'd like. This would be a situation where those who don't believe in the rarity of the 20-sigma stuff use the 20-sigma stuff as alibi for potential bad news while trying to make money by betting on the 20-sigma stuff taking place. This is not just saying "I will use conventionalism blindness to my advantage if things go sour"; this is going far beyond, to "I will use conventionalism blindness to my advantage if things go sour and try to make money on my deeply held conviction that conventional wisdom is badly wrong." In other words, I will borrow from theory to justify mishaps while actually betting real money against the theory.

The credit crisis (an unparalleledly abundant source of lessons-filled anecdotes) provides us with a highly interesting case. We will borrow here from the real experiences of a large Wall Street firm, which shall be named Bank X. In the summer of 2007, when some of Bank X's quant equity funds ran into trouble, bigwigs at the firm publicly dismissed such setbacks as the rarest of rare events, impossible according to Nobel-sanctioned statistical tools. That is, unless we want to play naughty and clamour "deceit!" we must assume that Bank X's execs believe in standard theoretical tenets and thus ruled out the possibility of the fat-tail event. And yet, deliciously paradoxically, one big reason why Bank X vastly outperformed its competition during the malaise-infected crisis is a big play, blatantly okayed by the firm's biggest cheeses, on the (statistical, if not commonsensical) rare event *taking* place. Bank X made billions from the "impossible," "negligible" event materializing itself, while publicly reminding the world of the utter rarity of such happenstances. It feels at least a bit ironic to bet on that which you apparently deem implausible. Almost an exercise in DAISNAID (or Do as I say, not as I do, apparently pronounced "daasnaad").

Of course, the shrewd observer may counter, I could be exaggerating things a bit. The zillion-sigma alibi was being used for equity markets situations, while the daring successful bet took place in the credit markets. More importantly, the latter might have been intended as a hedge for Bank X's previously built long positions in a healthy credit environment (i.e., as prudent risk management). But allow me some leeway in using this case as an example of a situation where the same pros appear to be embracing theoretical dogma with one arm while committing tons of capital against it with the other.

Bank X posted record profits in 2007, at some $12 billion. Let me rephrase that: During the year that saw the birth of one of the most dramatic financial crises in modern times, the firm called Bank X produced not losses or disappointments, but record positiveness. In contrast, rivals suffered severe setbacks, with one losing $10 billion during Q4 2007 (its worst quarter ever), other posting a net loss for the year of $8 billion, and a third one delighting its shareholders with an $11 billion meltdown in Q4 (deemed "the biggest quarterly loss in banking history") and a total $4 billion annual setback (its first ever). Bear Stearns, which of course was subprimed into oblivion just a few months later, very narrowly missed reporting its own first-ever yearly loss.

What explained Bank X's shiny exclusivity? In large part, the $4 billion in profits generated by a tiny group of traders who had the audacity to bet, late in 2006, on the unexpected (at least according to mathematically and data-intensive things like VaR and credit ratings, and overall conventional wisdom) taking place: that the U.S. mortgage market would shortly unravel dramatically. Like the journalist who best covered Bank X's contrarian profit-making said in late 2007, *"As recently as a year ago, few on Wall Street thought that the market for home loans made to risky borrowers, known as subprime mortgages, was heading for disaster."*

In December 2006, Bank X's CFO summoned his firm's structured credit trading honchos and encouraged them to take a bearish bet on the

U.S. subprime mortgage market. He was looking for a hedge to bullish bets made by other departments. Since the latter were firmly grounded on the assumption that the rare event would not rear its ugly head, the CFO was essentially trying to be net Black Swan–neutral by pushing a small group of maverick traders to be heavily pro–Black Swan. If the normality tale seemed fitting for those CDOs held by Bank X itself and by its clients, it was time now to switch intellectual gears and to embrace antinormality plays.

The traders naturally obliged and proceeded to bet big on the risky home loans collapsing by essentially buying protection through a short position in an index made up of credit default swaps referenced to very low credit ratings. Were that index to go south, Bank X would make boatloads of profits. And south it went. Just a few days after the traders began their pro–rare event punts, the index fell from 95 to 90. By late February it was down to 60, reaching the mid-70s one month later. With the subprime market experiencing a relentless bloodbath in the fall of 2007, the gains reached several billions of dollars. The Black Swan had shown up, mercifully for the segment of Bank X that decided to bet in its favor. Not so mercifully, certainly, for those inside the bank that had been betting against rarity, and for the bank's customers who had dabbled in turbulence-abhorring long CDO positions.

Some commentators accused Bank X's bigwigs of unfettered hypocrisy by playing both sides of the fence. How could you encourage pro-rarity trades with one hand and peddle antirarity trades with the other? Yes, a bit of DAISNAID may have been going on. But let's not be exhaustingly critical. Let's not raise hell when different members of an institution hold differing points of view and decide to act on them. Unmitigated, unbreachable group-thinking should not be a requirement for a financial institution. Some people may have positive thoughts about a certain market, while others may foresee more gloom. That's fine. As for the bosses suddenly working the other side of the street, going from (purportedly) subprime bulls into (real) bears, well even executives of large banks should be allowed to change their mind. If anything, one could argue that Bank X's CFO showed commendable vision and laudable initiative by prompting some of his gladiators to hedge the firm's prior adventures, six months before the latter's market value unraveled into Armageddon. Such prescient commands prevented lots of sorrow, including perhaps an irreparable descent into the kind of chaos that saw some of Bank X's peers glide into bankruptcy and oblivion. Yes, he borrowed from the standard deviation alibi aplenty when bad news set in while concurrently pushing a few key operatives into a Black Swan love-fest, but perhaps, just maybe, we should be understanding this time around.

I became obsessed with derivatives about 10 years ago. The late 1990s were a booming time for financial engineering. Swaps and exotic options having become consolidated, new funky markets were emerging. I became irremediably intrigued by this sector of the financial markets where extremely smart and mysterious individuals seemed to be making millions. I began to devour everything with the word *derivatives* on it.

As is probably the case with most outsiders (i.e., people whose jobs do not involve derivatives), I immediately concluded from my readings that the derivatives industry was dominated by mathematical geniuses and that a PhD in computer science was needed to get in the door. I imagined that derivatives professionals spent all day solving stochastic differential equations and programming funky models in C++. This notion, in fact, is what pushed me into doing a Master of Science, rather than the more common MBA, at New York University's Stern School of Business. If I really wanted to make it into derivatives, I had to learn some quantitative stuff, didn't I?

While I don't regret for one moment having pursued a quantitative graduate education (well, that stochastic calculus class was murder), the truth is that I later came to realize that I had perhaps been a bit naive regarding my perceptions of the derivatives world. In early 2001 I joined a bulge-bracket investment bank that was particularly famous for its financial engineering expertise, and I remember going around asking traders and salespeople about Ito's lemma, GARCH, and implied volatility trees. By far, the most usual response was puzzlement, followed by the (forceful) advice to "pick up the phone and start doing some business."

Now, it's not just that these people were eager to remind me of the sole reason why they had hired me. Or that they wanted to brusquely (but necessarily effectively) exorcize out of me any intentions that I may have had to engage in "thoughtful" activities. I honestly believe that those guys (and gals) simply had no idea what I was talking about. I have to assume that they didn't know who that Ito fellow was (Japanese soccer player?), what GARCH stood for (new computer game?), or why implied volatility trees should matter (something to do with forestry?).

During a restroom encounter with a very senior derivatives manager with a very quanty background, I naively mentioned that I had taken stochastic calculus at B-school; he grabbed my arm, took me back out into the trading floor, and began screaming from the top of his lungs "Look people, this guy knows stochastic calculus, he knows stochastic calculus!" Everyone looked funny at me. On another occasion, the head of the equity structuring unit gave me a passionate speech as to how maths and theories don't count that much, otherwise she would hire professors, not their students. All in all, my notions of a rocket-scientists-fueled derivatives business were quickly shattered. (This in no way implies that derivatives pros are not very smart and competent; many of them are, it's just that the nature of their work simply does not demand that they know or perform any advanced quantitative stuff.)

So it was with more than passing interest that I queried my fellow derivatives bankers at the year-end dinner, held at a high-end Lebanese restaurant in London. "Why is it that the outside world thinks of derivatives as the exclusive domain of mathematicians and physicists?" I pondered. "Why is it so advertised that you need lots of advanced quantitative skills just to have a chance to get in the door? I mean, I have never seen any of you solving equations or coding computer software, and I certainly have not had to do it myself. What's the deal here?" My then-colleagues stared at me, half-boringly, slightly bothered that I would bring up such an unexciting topic of conversation (after all, many of those present were celebrating a year full of tasty income-bringing transactions), but, possibly out of misplaced politeness, took turns to answer. "It's all barriers to entry, to make it difficult for people to join in," offered one banker. "As far as I am concerned, it's all good; I get to tell people that I am one of those derivatives geniuses, a rocket scientist," celebrated another. "The real world is never like the theoretical world," assured a third pro, who happened to be endowed with a math PhD from Harvard.

Six years (and hundreds of graduates from quantitative finance programs) later, things might have substantially changed, but I somehow doubt it. Derivatives, like finance in general, is, above all, a business. It is not a subdiscipline of mathematics, probability theory, or computational physics. Take a peek inside any trading floor and you won't find derivatives traders and salespeople dressed in white robes solving mathematical problems on their yellow pads. They are too busy doing the only things that directly generate revenue for the bank: closing deals with clients, designing new products, and taking positions in the market. (Of course, there is a small group of derivatives professionals who do hold PhDs and who do spend all day solving equations and programming advanced computer code. These quants are also inhabitants of the trading floor and their inputs are extremely important, and they, too, make very good money; but their role is pretty much a supportive one for the players who do bring the bacon home.)

And yet, for those non-math-performing players, the temptation to be seen as rocket scientists may continue to be as mouth-wateringly as it has traditionally been. While many of today's pros may in fact have been familiar with Ito's lemma and GARCH at one (earlier) point in their lives, they may soon realize that those terms belong to a parallel universe, different from the one in which they get their hands dirty every day. And as such, conveniently forgotten, expediently ignored. But that doesn't mean that you have to claim ignorance or gratuitously explain the real facts of life to those outsiders eager to label you a genius, one of the chosen few. Surely, such perceptions can only help. Not just from a social-standing point of view, but also from a professional one. More opportunities are certainly available to those deemed intellectually superior, a rare breed.

In this light, the existence of ever more complex finance theories (which help shape outsiders' perceptions of brilliantness) acts as welcome aid for those masters of the universe who likely don't believe in or even know about the existence of the models, but glorify the complexity that allows them to appear as math geniuses. In other words, there might be strong personal reasons that prevent those who know the markets best from speaking (too loudly) against those who try to model those markets from isolated outsideness. Needless to say, this would be music to the ears of theorists. When those best armed to criticize your work refuse to take part in the debate, your chances of victory get drastically enhanced.

Leading risk manager and famed quant Ricardo Rebonato's latest book introduces, almost in passing, a very damning argument against some of those professionals who promote the view of finance as a field that is mathematically tamable. Rebonato details the real-world limitations

of conventional quantitative financial risk management. His main con-
tention is that things have got way out of hand when it comes to using
mathematical and statistical techniques in the markets. Very precise measurements are assigned to risks about which we may truly know very little
through the use of complex computations that purport to understand the
probability distributions governing the human-driven markets.

But, most interesting, Rebonato also touches upon how quanty types
inside banks, consulting firms, and software companies prefer more complexity to less complexity when it comes to dealing with risk. The more
difficult risk taming is made to look, the more indispensable the inputs
of those with PhDs in physics, math, and computer science appear. Too
many people simply have too many vested (and very material) interests
in convincing the rest of us that financial risk management is exclusively about extremely sophisticated quantitative techniques, which they
just happen to uniquely master. In other words, the intimidating peddling would go, if you want to control your risks you better hire quants,
grant contracts to specialist consultants, and buy the software packages
incorporating the latest statistical gizmos.

As Rebonato says, whether quantitative risk management is a pure or
an applied science has ceased to be the relevant debate. What it truly has
become is big business, with tasty monetary and professional gains for
all those purported as experts. It seems only logical that the quant lobby
would work very hard at trying to perpetuate the notion (now almost
conventional wisdom) that financial risk is about equations and high-
powered computational models. In other words, about measurement
first and foremost.

The problem with all this is that it is expected that many peddlers of
the quantitative snake oil would be perfectly aware of the unworldliness
of some of the solutions. Of their meaninglessness. Perhaps even of the
danger that they pose (nothing could be more dangerous than operating
in the markets under faulty radars, and VaR has already caused more than
its share of trouble, essentially helping increase, not tame, risk). By continuing to sell their wares, they would be incurring an intellectual fraud.
For people endowed with prestigious doctorates from the world's leading
universities, and who might have previously dreamed of academic glory
and yearned for the pure discovery of knowledge, the moral dilemma may
prove taxing. They would be corrupting their beloved and sacred scientific methodologies in the pursuit of material comfort. They would be

(knowingly) contributing to a lie that clouds understanding and that may put the world at large in undue danger. They would have contributed to transforming advanced mathematics and statistics into misleading sales pitches in search of a quick buck.

Some may argue, so what? Don't people in finance lie and cheat all the time anyway? Shouldn't PhD-holders who make it into the game also be allowed to do so? This rationale would not be entirely correct (and not only because not all people in finance lie and cheat). A bond salesman may sometimes act economical with the truth when peddling some security to a client, but the bond is nonetheless real. It is a real security. It exists. Same with someone who buys a share on the Nasdaq or a call option on gold from a Wall Street dealer. The selling pitch may have been a bit too sugarcoated, but there is no doubt as to the full soundness of the final product. Not so with modern quantitative risk management. Those peddling it must be (surely) fully aware of the deep unrealism of the product, of its inextricable meaninglessness, or its unavoidable fraudulence.

That is, the biggest deceit concerning less-than-truthful endorsements of finance theory may be not that committed (quite innocently in many cases) by street-smart executives and traders who would still have made a financial career for themselves in a models-deprived environment, but the one committed by some of those former scientists who crawled towards Wall Street in search of a life previously unimaginable and unreachable, and whose original attraction towards the tools was entirely dictated by a love of science and the quest for knowledge, not as means of holding on to jobs that require the utterly improper and fraudulent use of such tools.

Chapter 9

An Unhealthy Yearning for Precision

■ Dangerous voluntary enslavement ■ Let freedom ring ■ Normality can kill you ■ A VIXing issue ■ Protect those derivatives ■

Most of us hate uncertainty. The unknown, the dubious, the inscrutable. Most of us despise the unmeasurable. We dislike living in a world where unquantifiable vagueness can roam freely. We abhor the nonconcreteness of things. We yearn for precision, for unequivocal tangibility. We can't stand the darkness of impreciseness. More than anything, we fear it. We thirst for numerical guiding lights, we need concrete measures attached to things, we demand precise diagnosis. We can't bring ourselves to accept that our surroundings may be completely dominated by unscripted chaos. We want to dream of an orderly environment where one can assign familiar digits and symbols to the elements that shape our existence. We refuse to admit that our future paths may be plagued with indecipherable fogginess; we want to believe that it is possible to forecast. In other words, we are total suckers for quantitative snake oil peddlers.

When it comes to the financial markets, our fear of the dark is particularly stringent. We don't want to conceive of a reality devoid of inalterable truisms. We can't operate absent the knowledge that it is possible to ascertain the future behavior of asset returns, that we can quantify risks, and that we can assign probabilities to events. We can't accept that wild randomness and utter chaos may be all there is to it. We seek the comfort of order and con ourselves into believing that someone, somewhere must have the answers, down to the third decimal. We don't want to walk the financial street alone; we seek expert guidance.

Thus are born the professions of market analyst, rating agent, financial reporter, and, naturally, finance theoretician. These people exist out of our need to have our hands held, to be cuddled and sung comforting lullabies amidst the vast unknown. We need to be told whether we should buy or sell, whether the stock price will be \$4.57 or \$4.73, whether the structured credit vehicle is AAA trustworthy or BB crap, and whether expected volatility is 30 percent or 40 percent. Yes, yes, deep inside we may be fully aware of the utterly blatant inaccuracies that such statements typically contain. After all, how many times do analysts get the call wrong? How many times did the stock drop when it was supposed to rise? How many times did the AAA paper end up worthless? How many times did "risk" underestimate true danger? How many times did "uncorrelated" assets tank together? And yet, even for those slightly savvier, self-enslavement to perceived expertise runs rampant, an incurable addiction. We never cease to unremittingly require our regular fix of precision-promising exactness.

Interestingly enough, our unconditional servitude may be most unfettered in the case where the promise of darkness-combating may be least fulfilled. It is undeniable that analysts and rating agencies have proven less than reliable on many occasions, and we wouldn't deserve the lunatic label for affirming that both have behaved in inadmissibly fraudulent ways in the past. Internet stocks, Enron, and CDOs will forever remain indelible stains on the reputation of those whom we trust for diagnosis on the health of companies and creditworthiness of securities. But at the same time, we average Joes can't be expected to develop such views entirely on our own, if only because we tend to have other things to do in our daily schedules; it thus makes sense to have people get paid to provide some guidance as to a firm's prospects or a bond's probability of default. And not all analysts and all rating agents fail all the time. Obviously, we would require that those would-be guides be honest, impartial, and truly knowledgeable, attributes that have been lacking of late. So it would make sense to keep in place those two subsets of purported experts, provided that unabashed reform takes place (this would naturally be particularly pressing in the case of the rating agencies, following the credit crisis debacle; analysts would have already gone through a beatifying cleansing following the dot-com mess of a few years ago).

The usefulness of finance theory is, unfortunately, much less justifiable. It doesn't seem far-fetched to argue that we could continue trotting along without über-Platonic models whose validity depends on the fulfillment of assumptions that are unfulfillable on Earth, without risk measures based on scandalously unworldly probabilistic tenets, and without forecasting machinery that borrows unrepentantly from the past. Here, the middle ground appears less feasible. The "Okay, we need it, but reform it" motto looks much less suitable. The issue here is much more structural: What's the point of theory when it comes to the markets? You may be able to thoroughly analyze a company's reported quarterly results, you may be able to dissect the credit quality of a security's issuer into a nice-looking letter soup, but you can't mathematize human financial action. Theory can't deliver us from the dreaded unknown.

But it is precisely theoretical developments that we hold in the highest awe. We surround them with an aura of purity that we never regale sullied financial professionals with. We castigate analysts, rating agencies, and traders with vilifications that we would never dare throw the academics' way. There are a few good, noble reasons for such conduct on our part. One is the respect and reverence that we overall show towards professors and educators (it is much harder to criticize the theoretical explorations of your former teacher, or of someone associated with your alma mater). Another is the undoubted brainpower of the theory concocters (we all know that it's not easy to get admitted into Harvard's or MIT's Finance PhD programs).

In the end, though, it all probably overwhelmingly boils down to qualifications-blindness run amok. The university is simply one of those institutions at whose altar humans have historically tended to bow. We take for granted that whatever is churned out of mythical campuses must be unalterably dependable. Redoubtable group-think may be hard at work here: You don't express doubts about a Harvard-nurtured theory for fear of being deemed a brutish hick by your mates, who in turn oblige motivated by similar concerns. The equations help, as we can abruptly kneel in nonnegotiable submission when presented with complex lemmas and analytics ("They look so intelligent that they must hold true; who's to interfere with such wisdom?"). Endorsing prestigious academic theories (Nobel-endowed ones preferred) becomes a way to present yourself as a sophisticated member of society who is in tune with accepted, diploma-sanctioned erudition.

That is, financial academicism becomes the perfect type of expert guidance. Its ivy-clad reputation and Nobel endorsement can be waved in the face of doubters (or one's reflection in the mirror), our intellectual surrender having been proclaimed way in advance. Once we throw in the quantitative production that goes on internally at banks and funds, we have a powerful theoretical beacon to worship. We trust quantitatively flavored constructs (VaR, Black-Scholes, CAPM, Gaussian Copula) to escort us away from the gloom of immeasurable uncertainty and into the light of secure concreteness. We endow the theories with the power of relieving us from the unbearable sense of loss evoked by a precision-less reality.

And yet, in embracing quantitative finance as a bridge towards endurable order, we may be sowing the seeds of market chaos. The theory-aided search for certainty may yield untamed, out-of-control uncertainty. By looking for precise knowns through analytical machinations, we may be condemning ourselves to plunging into the deepest of unknowns. Our self-enslavement to theoretical dictates may result in forced enslavement to misery and turmoil.

Consider the recent months and what we have witnessed: the disappearance of the independent investment banking industry; the fall of three of the world's leading investment banks and the shelter-seeking rushing into regulatory arms of the top two; the outright nationalization of mortgage lending giants; the almost disappearance of the world's largest insurer; historic freezing-overs in the interbank lending market; the lowest (essentially zero) yields on U.S. government securities in peaceful times; untold stock market turbulence. The developments that led to the crisis that led to such eerie consequences were founded, in large part, on theory-supported quantitative certainties. The abided-by risk measures provided an enormously valuable alibi for highly leveraged punting on real-estate variables through very complex positions. The chosen valuation models also encouraged such risk-taking by downplaying the possibility of rare events, endowing analytical credibility to the whole affair, and, most crucially, facilitating the obtainment of satisfactory, deal-enabling, complacency-building credit ratings. Precrisis, the system appeared under quantitative control. What was forgotten is that the price of enjoying such illusion was the facilitating (even tacit encouragement) of actions that would in due time annihilate and vaporize any notion of control in the markets, and unleash the worst kind of mayhem. Theoretical self-enslavement (more cynically self-serving in the case of pros, more insultingly vassalish in the case of outsiders and regulators) did not end well. Perhaps, with the financial system in tatters and the global economy subsequently imperiled, it's high time to realize that we should fear Platonic quantitative preciseness much more than we fear earthly vagueness.

Finance theory can thus present us with an insurmountable case of what Nassim Taleb deems "Iatrogenic Risk," or the healer killing the patient. We embraced theory so that it could cure our fear of the dark, only to find ourselves immersed in the bleakest, deepest of obscurities. We trusted the quantitative doctor with our health, and he killed us.

It is important to keep firmly in mind that arguably the worst financial crises since the 1929 crash were all linked to finance theory, either as direct executioner, abettor, or justifier. Dynamic hedging directly caused Black Monday in October 1987 which, as we saw, came very close to bringing the entire financial system to a halt. The LTCM episode, which required a government-sponsored rescue mission so as to save the system, was fueled by dogma-adoration and by VaR. The more recent credit meltdown, which nasty ramifications need no further reminder, was aided by mathematical modeling and by VaR. Blind belief in the power of quantification played a substantial (when not entirely causational) part in all those debacles. Self-enslavement to equation-laden dictums and to diploma-waving wisdom propelled the mayhem vessel to its destination.

In the case of portfolio insurance, not only would the whole thing not have existed without the prior existence of the Black-Scholes model, but it is highly likely that it wouldn't have taken flight and reached the mountainous dimensions that it did had the backing argument not been a prestigious theoretical model and had the sponsors not been acclaimed academics sporting notorious doctorates. Potential customers would have been in awe at the unchallengeable ivory tower–charged firepower, defenselessly hypnotized by the inalterably impressive math and the augustly framed diplomas (remember, this took place at a time, the early 1980s, when financial pros were not used to such display of analytical prowess, and thus made for more receptively starstruck patrons). Leading peddlers of portfolio insurance magic defended the put option–synthesizing strategy by arguing that *"It doesn't matter that formal insurance policies are not available. The mathematics of finance provide the answer."* The "mathematics of finance" taken as self-explanatory gospel. Of course, certainly, naturally. How many of those portfolio managers who contributed to the portfolio insurers' money pot took such assuaging scientifically sounding sales pitch on unbreakable faith? Had theory-skepticism been more prevalent, any strategy built entirely on the validity of theoretical notions may not have been allowed to grow to the point where the breakdown of the theory could cause biblical destruction.

In the case of LTCM's fall in 1998, the actual role of convolutedly quantitative techniques is not as straightforward (some of the strategies, though grounded on the theory-conforming notion of Normality, looked decidedly simplistic), and the support of the fund by investors and other financial institutions certainly owed a lot of its enthusiasm to the outstanding track record of LTCM's principals, who at one point during their prolonged stint there in the 1980s generated all of Salomon Brothers' profits. But it still seems plausible to make the case that qualifications-blindness played a decent role in the whole affair. In spite of the extraordinary performance of the (mostly PhD-holding) former Salomon team, it may have resulted just a tad harder to enlist partners and strike the awe of the general public without the presence of academic superstars Myron Scholes and Robert Merton in the roster and without the fund's claim to be "the world's best finance faculty." Such ivory-towerish mystique added cherry on top to the glorious antecedents of the (pretty ivory-towerish in themselves) traders. Outsiders looked at the MIT diplomas and at the co-founders of that famous formula and dropped to their knees, begging to be let in and participate in the unimperilable, theory-guaranteed success. It is not clear how decisive the quanty factor was (versus the track record factor) in securing funding and admiration, but it must certainly have been non-negligible. It seems an easy bet that people got blinded by LTCM's moneymaking skills but also by its academic pedigree, with its promise to quantify uncertainty into oblivion. Crucially, such apparent scientifically backed infallibility may have irrevocably encouraged other punters to copycat LTCM's punts and business strategy, fueling a process that was to prove ultimately disastrous and crisis-enabling (as liquidity dried up in those markets where the fund was active, the result of unison unwindings by those who had bet alike the exalted brainiacs; the number one reason, as will be analyzed in a second, why the fund was eventually rescued was the damage that its sudden liquidation could do to the myriad of banks that had engaged in copycatting).

Much less debatable is the role that VaR played in the mayhem, and the role that fanatical submission to quantification played in establishing VaR as the de-rigueur risk-measuring apparatus just a few years prior to the disappearance of LTCM. It wasn't until 1997 (Asian crisis) and 1998 (Russian-LTCM crisis) that the dangerous side of VaR (widely adopted by financial institutions in the early part of the 1990s and sanctioned by regulators in 1996) was made abundantly obvious to people. Those episodes mark the very first time when the theoretical monster inside of VaR arose in uncontainable fury and unleashed hell unto the financial landscape, claiming an insatiable number of victims (including lots of puzzled VaR-lovers). Just a few years back, VaR had been adoringly endorsed by regulators, who enthusiastically clapped at the born-again-scientification of bank executives and the rigorousness they had shown by replacing boorishly antiquated risk-management policies (time-honored stop-loss orders and the like) with academically compliant quantitative methodology full of standard deviations, correlations, bell curves, and confidence intervals. Now, policy wonks (which had been enchanted so much by VaR that they had allowed banks to calculate capital charges based on it) had to contemplate in faith-shaking disbelief how the analytical Dr. Jekyll came inevitably joined at the hip by the mischievous Mr. Hyde.

After two initial years of hefty returns (by the end of 1995, a dollar invested at launch date in February 1994 was worth $1.61 net of fees), LTCM began to experience a slowdown in 1997. The fund was still earning good money (almost $1 billion, not too far from the $1.65 billion made in 1996), but supported by a lot more capital, as new investors had frantically joined the party. That is, annual returns climbed down significantly, to a mere 17 percent (dismal when compared to the 31 percent posted by the S&P 500).

LTCM found itself in a bind. Its sole reason for existence was the generation of mythical returns, and its $7 billion capital base suddenly appeared as a huge impediment to that goal. So in December 1997, LTCM decided to return almost $3 billion back to investors. It has been argued that VaR helped in making such (eventually quite fateful) decision. While LTCM, as an unregulated hedge fund, was not required to oblige with regulatory-sanctioned VaR limits and capital charges, the fund decided to use it nonetheless. And their VaR was telling them that expected maximum losses should be modest, around $300 million monthly with a 99 percent confidence interval. Perhaps this comfort blanket proved decisive when deciding to significantly trim down capital. When you are mathematically assuaged that nothing can go terribly wrong, it could make sense to enhance your leverage so as to safely enhance your returns.

Normality-revering theory provided assistance in another key way: Myron Scholes and Robert Merton (two big time Normality-endorsers) believed in a world of negligible capital and abundant leverage, where equity was not needed because financial engineering would guarantee that risk is consistently tamed through the buildup of perfectly replicating portfolios that require only borrowed funds as lubrication. Under such assumptions, capital becomes only a source of diminishing returns and pesky shareholders. For such world to truly exist (and LTCM may have managed to make it true for at least a while), markets must behave. When they don't and ruthlessly unravel, the machines break and the need for capital becomes dire. And if you no longer have enough capital, you sink. Which is, naturally, exactly what happened to LTCM amidst untold market chaos in late summer 1998.

VaR fueled the chaos. After the Russian government defaulted on its bonds in mid-August, financial institutions all over (everyone had punted on Russia) saw their VaR numbers spike. As tends to happen whenever turmoil strikes, VaR limits got breached. According to regulatory rules, if you are breached several times you must put up more capital or cut positions. Given the limited equity amounts typically held by investment banks (the credit crisis just provided a very graphical reminder of that fact), the decision was made to off-load stuff (not just Russia-related assets) into the markets. The same thing was happening at those hedge funds that had chosen to comply with the rules. To top it all, banks began asking their institutional clients to put up more capital, which had a similarly deleveraging effect. In sum, a lot of big players obediently abiding by VaR began to concertedly dump a whole spectrum of securities. Prices, naturally, went down (as liquidity is of course never perfect, and as a lot of people were selling the same assets). VaR, as a

Normality-based tool, assumes (just like dynamic hedging, that other famous scion of Normality) that markets are eternally liquid and continuous and that the actions of the theory-abiders will not change that. VaR's fine print says that if you have to cut back you can always do it in an orderly, non-market-impacting, harmless way. That is, VaR-guided risk-reduction is supposed to always be to your benefit, never to end up actually destroying you (and your friends).

August 1998 showed that not to be exact. If people use the same flawed machine, there is a big chance that they will all consensually sink the market (and each other) when the machine predictably malfunctions. Had Normality not been selected as the machine's spiritual core, such malaise would tend to happen much less often, as users would not be forced to dump stuff at the slightest piece of bad news. It would take a much more severe development to break a non-Normal measure.

A lot of players had copycatted LTCM's complex arbitrage plays. Now, pushed by VaR, everyone was trying to shut them down. Naturally, this created humongous markdowns for LTCM, which held eye-popping massive positions in those areas. That which LTCM was long in went down in value, and that which LTCM was short in went up in value (the result of an indiscriminatingly abusive flight-to-quality). The assumption that certain assets were uncorrelated (essential in VaR-land) proved terribly misguided, as plenty of previously uncorrelated stuff began to dive all together. By the way, the very theoretical notion of correlation is only valid under a Normal dream.

Of course, as markets became increasingly poisonous, VaR limits became increasingly violated, demanding yet more liquidations, and so on and so on. When LTCM finally threw in the towel in early September (incapable of meeting the calls for collateral emanating from all that nastiness, and suffering a final blow from yet another huge Normality-grounded strategy gone dismally bad, equity option selling in this case), the entire financial system was put in danger, and a government-sponsored rescue plan had to be put in place. The VaR virus had made amply certain that a non-immensely critical happenstance in a faraway corner transmuted itself into a system-threatening debacle, by forcing institutions that had been allowed by VaR to be hugely undercapitalized to engage in a rabidly lunatic fire sale.

What about the credit crisis? Would it be reasonable to say that adoration towards quantitative finance brought the financial industry to its knees? That the crisis would not have happened had we never embraced theoretical utensils? Well, the point of genesis took place in the decidedly unsophisticated, absolutely non-ivy-league world of the shaky, door-to-door, subprime American home loan (down) market. No PhDs there. No Nobel Prizes. No stochastic calculus. The math began to play a role once those dubious mortgages began to be packaged and traded as part of latest-generation derivatives toys. Once the game moved over to the trading floor side of the fence, the math began to have a serious impact as friendly enabler. Valuation models (most notably of the Gaussian Copula type) decisively contributed to enticing punters, by delivering the right credit ratings (senior tranches) and the right prospective returns (equity tranches). Risk measurement techniques (VaR) propagated the comforting idea that everything was calmly safe for credit transacting to proceed unfettered. Capital-charge-determining analytical tools (VaR again) gave permission for the buildup of you-only-live-once leverage. If you wanted to play the structured mortgage-linked credit derivatives attraction in earnest, you had a loyal friend in quantitative finance and those who peddle its virtues.

It is thus possibly non-incoherent to argue that theory contributed massively to the crisis by contributing extraordinarily to the nuclear-race-style amalgamation of toxic securities on banks' balance sheets. After all, bank losses are what the crisis is truly known for. The key question is, was the quant stuff an absolute requirement for such wild-eyed behavior? Was the math the only conduit through which the craziness could have been enacted? Not really. After all, Moody's and Standards & Poor's could have assigned AAA nomenclatures using some other kind of alibi (maybe a "Subprime is Sublime" tagline), market valuations could have reached similar levels through rough-and-tumble, and regulators may have allowed similarly generous capital terms via simple man-to-man handshakes. The net effects would not have been abominably indistinct. Unlike in the case of portfolio insurance where abidance by a very precise mathematical recipe defined the thing in itself (note that the same argument would be valid for the delta-revering strategies that led to the 2005 correlation meltdown), in the case of the credit meltdown that first reared its ugly head in mid-2007 there were several other plausible, nontechy, paths towards resembling outcomes.

Having said that, the main point remains that the quant stuff was unalterably responsible. It is true that by deciding to endow the entertainment with scientific cred, credit players and regulators condemned quantitative finance to be shamed for developments that might have happened anyway. But there is a sea of difference between the might-have and the did-have. Quant embracement definitely guaranteed that the ought became the is. What might have anyway been AAA was made to be AAA by quant embracement. What might have anyway been a highly permissive risk radar was made to be a highly permissive risk radar by quant embracement. What might have anyway been a collaborative credit charge was made to be a collaborative credit charge by quant embracement. Naturally, savvy pros are only too aware of all this, and that is quite likely a big reason why the often-puzzling backing of the math by otherwise no-nonsense operators suddenly appears less puzzling.

The late part of the twentieth century and the early part of the twenty-first century thus irrefutably show how human welfare can be immodestly hampered by a desire to tame uncertainty into subjugation via waving of the quantitative magic wand. And the malaise has only gotten worse with the passage of time. The theoretical hospital continues to churn out rampant medical malpractice, doggedly refusing to reform itself or to punish the malfeasant doctors. The patients who through the years went in there tempted by the loudly peddled claims to have found a cure for impreciseness continue to suffer devastating infections at the physician's table. The iatrogenic atrocities keep recurring, the hospital remains open for business, unremittingly sticking to its perennial marketing pitch. One naturally wonders, where are the health authorities? Busily promoting the iatrogenists, that's where.

If history is any guide, qualifications-blinded officials likely won't be the ones to do something about the rot. The only sure way to close down the inmate-decimating quantitative infirmary is for would-be patients to stop registering there, no matter how irresistibly enchanting the sophisticated uncertainty-ending cure prospectus may look.

After having devoted an entire book to shedding light on the wrongness that finance theory can entail, it is perhaps high time to try to offer a way out, a solution, a remedy. In doing this, allow me to be Washingtonian rather than King Georgian and to propose a bottom-up popular revolution rather than top-down dictatorial imposition. For you see, it is not just our most elementary freedoms that can be obtained through the struggle of the many. Our unchaining from the insalubriousness-inducing shackles of quantitative finance also starts with us, is entirely in our hands; no need to sheepishly wait for a single high command emitted by an all-ruling deity. It's really simple: As long as we take the brave step to remove the self-imposed blindfolds, we won't be fooled again.

It is not a requirement that you indiscriminately conclude that all finance theory is dangerous or shamelessly useless. It is more than enough if you enlist yourself in the army of relentless skeptics, forever refusing to slavishly bow at the altar of analyticalness. Don't take quantitative stuff at face value ever again, at least not before an inquisitive look under the mathematical hood. Don't let yourself be milquetoastedly intimidated by sober equations, credentials, and prizes. Untimidly analyze what's truly behind all that bluster (which, usually, can be easily summarized and understood) and decide for yourself whether it makes sense or not, whether it can cause danger down the road, and whether it should deserve your unimposed endorsement or not.

When average investors, shareholders, taxpayers, students, pensioners, insurees, and assorted observers stop giving theoretical concoctions a free pass simply on account of its theoreticality, it becomes that much harder for bad theory to infiltrate the markets. The until-now very comfortable stay of horrendously lacking theory in the real world has been built entirely on its being unopposed by the populace at large. Borrowing from a well-known popular dictum, all that is needed for bad theory to triumph is for average men to do nothing. If students revolt upon learning that markets are supposed to be Normal, economic agents rational, and dynamic hedging feasible, the theories that spread such (demonstrably harming in practice) tenets would cease to be presented in the classroom as anything other than poster children for the danger that unworldly dictums can pose. If shareholders and investors revolt upon learning that institutions are managing their risks through devices that rule out even the slightly rare event, that painfully fail when most needed, and that have been proven time and time to wildly disappoint under stress, standard statistical machinations won't again be trusted as warning signals. If employees revolt upon learning that their hard-earned pensions are being gambled on convoluted securities which calculated creditworthiness is based on the use of faulty mathematical models, rating agencies won't be able to keep up the racket of "scientifically" AAA-ing impossibly toxic stuff. If day traders revolt upon learning the meaning of the volatility smile and that Black-Scholes is not used, journalists won't be able to continue describing implied volatility as the market's expected future turbulence. If voters revolt upon learning that the reason why they have to foot the bill for a billionaire bailout of speculators-gone-wild is that the latter were allowed to build unfenced leverage thanks to the regulators-permitted use of deeply unrealistic models, VaR will no longer be used to set capital charges.

We, the people, can help create an atmosphere that is no longer tolerant of perniciously impractical mathematical wizardry. When resistance to quantification is active and popular at the base, it becomes much harder to impose quantification from the top. The message that, going forward, theory won't be unnegotiably revered and will be unnegotiably second-guessed must filter every pore of the system. Instinctive, automatic skepticism towards attempts to mathematize finance must become an ingrained part of our mind operandi. We must resist out-of-control, unchecked, uninhibited quantification with the same ardor for self-preservation that we display when resisting fraudulent accounting practices or unsavory lending policies.

We need to stop taking quantitative things so seriously, and start to take the perilousness of quantitative things more seriously. We need to stop serfishly adoring the Nobels, and start to wonder how the granting of the prize to a particular piece of theoretical production can affect the stability of the markets and the economy. We need to stop unconditionally venerating the PhDs and start to consider the havoc that such skill set can wreak. We need to stop shying away from declaring a theory unfit and inappropriate, notwithstanding the technical brilliance of the gadget. Our reluctance to unquestioningly admire the equations is the best defense against the seemingly unavoidable future carnage. It's very much in our own interest to de-deify theories and to judge them for what they really entail, past the intimidatingly complex mathematical veil.

The heavy metal band Accept (famously fronted by a camouflage-clad, height-challenged, histrionic singer) sang in the 1980s that "Wrong Is Right." Quantitative Finance has for too long also espoused the wrong-is-right melody when defending its own application, typically to the same approving roar of the crowd as head-banging rock stars. We may not know expected returns but the theory is okay; we may not know the correlations but the theory is okay; standard deviation may not be a proper measure of risk but the theory is okay; we may not know the probability distribution but the theory is okay; we may gravely underestimate the occurrence of rare events but the theory is okay; dynamic hedging may not be feasible but the theory is okay; the volatility smile may negate Black-Scholes but the theory is okay; we can't forecast but the theory is okay. It's time to end this charade and for once state the obvious: Wrong is wrong. If we can't know expected returns or correlation, then the theory is not okay. If rare events happen very often, then the theory is not okay. If dynamic hedging is not feasible, then the theory is not okay. If we can't measure risks statistically, then the theory is not okay. Stop giving the wrongers a free pass by allowing them to claim rightness in the face of inundating wrongness. You don't need to find loud hard-rock bands with a taste for military gear distasteful in order to understand that, frankly, wrong is not right.

Overall, we need to be inexhaustibly irreverent towards the assumption of non-street-smart knowledge. We need to cease to assume the existence of non-street-smart experts. We need to develop an unremitting disdain for the notion that we can quantify, that we can measure, that we can understand. We need to instill in the fabric of our society an overarching sense of incredulity, a religiously fanatical atmosphere of quantitative agnosticism. We need to stop prospectively endowing the university with unlimited respectability and unlimited credence, and to stop surrounding its productions with an aura of undismissible infallibility. We need to release our common sense from the state of diploma-hypnotization to which we have condemned it, and which has forced us for too long to unoppose the validity of academic tenets that may have been utterly rejected as impossibly unseemly had our senses operated hypnotism-free. It is entirely possible that had the most famous finance theories been produced by amateur nonacademics, they may have been outrightly dismissed as the awkward mumblings of a group of hopeless (yet mathematically quite skillful) cranks. But endow the authors with degrees from the best business schools in the world and, voila, the dictums are not only accepted and embraced but rewarded with the highest honors. From such unassailable platform the models are released unto the real world, and we know what tends to happen afterwards. So beware your blind, common-sense-denying reverence towards anything endowed with the ivory tower stamp.

Place the burden of proof mightily on theoretical peddlers; make them feel doubted and suspected until they can show us that their discoveries can indeed be valuably applicable and, most critical, harmless. Enforce the tyranny of unknownity and save the world from the perils of mathematically driven hubristic presumptuousness. Inscribe into law the chaos-preventing accolade that vast uncertainty and complete unforecastability are way superior (and more wholesome) than monstrously misguided precision-seeking implements. By admitting that no one knows anything, we can prevent the mayhem that can ensue when we believe ourselves (and the often-failing technical tools that we have invented) to be all-knowing. No-theory is better than a bad theory. No-model is better than a dangerous model. No-math is better than a perilously underachieving math. No-knowledge is better than wrong (sometimes, not even wrong) knowledge. Uncertainty is better than Platonic certainty. Darkness is better than Faustian light.

The physicist Ian Hughes once commented, on discussing the limits of his discipline, that *"Science continues to be represented by some as the means by which infinite knowledge may be obtained. . . . We are told that theory would ultimately allow us to know the mind of God. Such an idea is deeply appealing. . . . We yearn for certainty in an uncertain world. But is it not the legacy of [legendary Danish physicist] Niels Bohr that such a quest for certainty is an illusion? . . . Rather than providing certainty, every major scientific advance has increased our uncertainty, reduced our status as a species and undermined our sense of purpose. . . . The true lesson of science may then be that we are like sea urchins on the seafloor: using our limited sensory inputs to make sense of our environment and in awe of our intelligence at being able to so do, all the while sensing only a tiny fraction of what is."* If such a divine field as physics can be limited in what it can explain about the (law-obeying) physical universe, what hope is there for a discipline bent on trying to quantitatively explain the (anarchy-revering) financial universe? Perhaps the only solution, in both arenas, would be unconditional humbleness. Bohr reportedly said that "It is wrong to think that the task of physics is to determine the nature of reality. Physics concerns what we can say about nature." That is, we will find out as much about reality as our own intrinsic intelligence would allow, which may not be enough to cover everything. Hughes finds salvation in admitting our limitations, however taxing that may result, *"This dangerous idea threatens to knock away our only remaining prop—our belief in our own intelligence. Without that belief, stripped of the security blanket which science is providing, we would be forced to stand naked before ourselves and face the limitations of our knowledge as a species. Then, secure in the knowledge that we cannot know, we could at last let our minds be at rest. Perhaps this is what it means to grow up."*

If hard scientists, on the heels of an endless number of successful discoveries, can admit to their knowledge shortfalls, why can't financial economists? When hard scientists pronounce unvanquished uncertainty to be the only certainty in the physical world, shouldn't we do the same when it comes to the notoriously less-tamable financial world? If hard scientists are willing to remove their absolute-wisdom chains, shouldn't we remove our quantitative-finance shackles? When hard scientists wish for peace-granting atonement, shouldn't we, too? Let's then join Ian Hughes and save ourselves by enthusiastically proclaiming that we don't know, we can't know, and we won't quantify. Let's, indeed, grow up.

T he often-embraced assumption of Normality by finance theory has faced defiant criticism throughout the years. Many have described it as naively unrealistic, conveniently self-serving, and insultingly inaccurate. Those complaints, certainly, are not inappropriately off-the-mark. By themselves they are more than enough ammunition to justify the consignment of the Normality dictum to the trashcan of unbearable practical irrelevance. However, they are not the harshest indictment that one could throw at Normality. For those eager to slap theory on the face, a much more devastating accusation is possible.

To put it bluntly, the assumption of "normal" markets can deliver abnormally chaotic markets. By dreaming up a mathematically convenient tame world, financial economics can unleash raving unquietness. In modeling an analytically tractable timid universe, quantitative finance is exposing the markets to around-the-corner venomous precariousness. By assuming peaceful conditions, you get casualties-infested war. Normality, in brief, can kill us.

When you assume that markets are normal, you are ruling out the possibility of extreme events. This will yield metrics that breed complacency. The theoretical guiding light would be telling you that potential future market movements will be of a limited dimension. We have seen in this book that such assertions can lead to outsized confidence in influential things like (modest) risk measures, (modest) capital charges, CDO tranche pricing, or dynamic hedging. Normality can lead to unseemly low loss expectations, capitalization levels, correlation factors, and option prices. This in turn can lead to inappropriately exaggerated risk-taking,

devastatingly pronounced leverage, perniciously optimistic credit ratings, and dangerously widespread portfolio insurance programs. In other
words, to volatility time bombs ready to make boom at any point.

By assuming placidity, finance theory has endangered us for way too
long. Markets became way more turbulent and disastrous than they would
otherwise have been. The negation of rare events, and its adoption as
gospel by those pushing the quantitative agenda, has been a decisive
driving force behind three of the four biggest crises in the modern
history of financial markets. Dynamic hedging is built on Normality,
VaR is built on Normality, Gaussian Copula is built on Normality. The
portfolio insurers who sank Wall Street in October 1987 abided by
Normality. The LTCM brainiacs who threatened the system in the fall
of 1998 and their complicit colleagues abided by Normality (as was amply
discussed earlier). The rating agencies that peddled trash as gold during
the pre–credit meltdown days abided by Normality. The regulators who
enabled the unfettered leveraged speculative orgy that vaporized the
investment banking industry in 2008 abided by Normality. The Nobel
Prize committee that provided iron-clad legitimacy to the Normality-
abiding theories abided by Normality. The professors who indoctrinated
many of those involved in the carnages abided by Normality.

Regular exercise, a healthy diet, and sexual activity are widely recom-
mended as pathways to a better, safer life. Let's add the demolition of
the Normality assumption to that list of beneficial factors. Endowing a
black-swanish world with the Normality attribute is hazardous for our
well-being. Normality will bring freakishness. The negation of the rare
event will cause the rare event. This certainly has got to be the most
shocking contradiction of finance theory.

Some realized this long ago and took preemptive and preventive measures. The volatility smile is testament to the fact that traders decided to
stop believing in the salubriousness of the Normality tenet when faced
with the decidedly nontimid crash of 1987. They abolished Normality
from the premises as a rotund way to protect their livelihoods and business (as we saw in earlier chapters, dynamic hedging–fueled portfolio
insurance did end up putting the ongoing viability of exchange-traded
derivatives in jeopardy; that is, Normality came close to destroying the
derivatives market).

In 1991, the Options Clearing Corporation (OCC, the collective
clearinghouse for all U.S. options exchanges) decided to change the
probability models employed to calculate margin requirements. This was

as a direct consequence of Black Monday, and as means to avoid such freakishness from happening again. The OCC switched to a so-called Levy distribution, which is a distribution that endows rare events with a much higher chance of existence than the prohibitive Normal distribution. A Levy distribution is one that allows for the existence of *wild* randomness, not simply mere randomness. The OCC liked the fact that under a Levy regime, a 99 percent confidence interval would shelter five or six standard deviations (recall that under Normality the corresponding figure would be less than three sigmas). This was desirable not just on account of "representation fairness" (as markets err on the side of wildness when it comes to randomness), but as a survival mechanism for the OCC and the individual exchanges that cleared with it.

What would be deemed extremely extreme under Normality is considered only slightly noticeable under Levy-ty. By basing margin requirements on such probabilistic map, you essentially guarantee much more stable margin levels, and thus less room for margins-fueled disruptions. Here is how: When something drastic happens in the markets, margin requirements would not go up that much because the distribution (with its infinite variance assumption) is familiar with such scenarios and does not get scared easily. No need for a whole lot of extra cash to provide shelter from the storm, as our Levy tool would not consider those developments truly stormy. Conversely, if calm reigns supreme, margins would not be reduced scandalously because the probability of tail events would nonetheless remain non-negligible. That is, under Levy the tails are always thicker, but extremely so.

Why is this important for the stability of the world? Simple. If, after a moderately impacting event, you force players to suddenly come up with lots more dough (as your Normal guide would be screaming "Danger, danger, untold mayhem, utter chaos, need more cash for protection!"), you may kick-start a snowballing liquidation party that may lead to another Black Monday or another LTCM-Russian crisis. Under Levy, in contrast, the demands would be much less brusque. Similarly, under placidity Normal margin requests may prove too little, building risk-encouraging complacency, while Levy-based requests would be immodest enough to keep people on alert. That is, compared to its predecessors, the Levy distribution makes punting preemptively costly during peaceful times and wisely economical during turbulent days. Not a bad way to avoid chaos. While the assumption of Normality, in a sinister contradiction, can unleash wild randomness, the assumption of wild randomness can keep wild randomness in check.

Will similar Normality-banning efforts take place as a result of the credit crisis, a decidedly much more impacting trauma than even Black Monday? A quick look at the battlefield littered with the bodies of the investment banking crème de la crème and a gravely wounded financial system in hasty retreat would seem to indicate that yes, Normality has to go, once and for all. Credit traders appear of late to have reached the same Normality-abhorring conclusions as their equity or foreign exchange counterparts did 20 years ago and have given birth to their own smile, tentatively indicating that extreme events (turbocharged correlations in this case) should be considered more regular. It is likely that as a result of the crisis, that smile will grin ever happier (assuming that the credit correlation market continues to exist, that is).

But more needs to be done. VaR has to go, once and for all. An unabashed VaR critic, inconsolably wondering why Black Monday plus LTCM (the occurrence within 11 years of two events deemed unimaginably improbable by the Normal distribution) had not resulted in the unpostponed burial of VaR, concluded that only a new severe market crisis could finally bring people to their senses and stop employing a tool that produces nonsensical results. Now that the crisis is here (and more severe than anything that could have previously been imagined), will he be proven right, or will he again be left in hopeless disbelief?

VaR is a tool that transforms low volatility into higher risk. A mechanism for transforming stability into mayhem. Through the frenetically unrealistic gadget, good times are converted into bad times. Insanely but true, a relentlessly misguided mathematical device is permissively let loose to take us from safeness into trouble. We have seen how this works: As VaR is calculated from past market action, a recent track record of nonturbulence yields a low risk estimate, thus giving carte blanche to increased speculation through enhanced leverage. This is exactly what happened pre the credit crisis, which was of course elevated to historical legend by unapologetically excessive punting on complex securities on the back of tiny capital levels, and on the heels of a prolonged prior quiet period. VaR is a perennial havoc-enabling mechanism, whose corruptive influence can be the most damaging the more peaceful things have been. The more normal things truly appear to be, the more abnormal they can be made to be, thanks to VaR. The ubiquitous presence of Normality-founded VaR makes crises much more likely.

Why do regulators persist in adopting such a corrosively corrupting influence? Is it really that hard for officials to realize that markets are not normal, and that such assumption breeds voluptuously sized tribulations? I mean, while many traders retire quite young and may withdraw themselves into a deserted beach upon hanging their hats, most regulators are pretty advanced in years and have thus seen it all. While few (if any) of today's traders remember (let alone experienced) Black Monday or even LTCM, a lot of policy makers do. They are aware of the disrespectfully exaggerated unseemliness of Normality when it comes to finance. They are aware of the bloodbaths caused by Normality-credence. They must understand that VaR will inevitably be violently breached, leading to potentially devastating liquidations. They must comprehend that VaR will inevitably lead to thin capital bases. They must register that VaR will inevitably encourage excess punting. If you have witnessed and analyzed the credit crisis (and, likely, also LTCM and Black Monday), how can you not reach all the above conclusions? And if so, how can you continue to participate in high-level VaR peddling? The sad obviousness is that regulators have been acting like health officials who not only don't prevent the iatrogenic quantitative doctors from hurting the patients with their abominable instruments but actually enforce the use of such instruments in their medical best practice manuals.

Voluntary self-adherence to the products of quantitative finance can be so powerful as to manifest itself even when the theoretical device is utterly misunderstood and misinterpreted. That is, the theory would be adopted and acted on under completely false pretenses. People would be told that the analytical stuff means something that it clearly does not, and still wholeheartedly abide by such politically correct, yet false, assumptions. Such scenario, clearly, would reveal a particularly dangerous side of quantification-revering: The obedience and allegiance to the mathematical guidance would be so submissively blind and unconditional that the bowed-to construct would not even have to actually mean what it is assumed to mean. Simply put, such cases would mercilessly indicate that people would believe anything that they are told about a theoretical gadget, a self-delusion only explained by the slavish submission to anything involving equations and formulas. This reality can be extra harmful, as such misinformed following of the quant stuff could manifest itself into weird (and potentially chaotic) market activity. The key message is that we can't have wildly misunderstood, influential theoretical devices running loose throughout the financial landscape.

The VIX "volatility" index is a very good (and very real) example of a quantitatively conceived tool that is widely misinterpreted and widely influential. The insatiable thirst for precision (in this case, the search for a precise window into future stock market volatility) directs us en masse towards allegiance to a math-derived device that we are ceaselessly told stands for that which we are so eager to measure. The problem is that the device does not, in truthness, represent such variable. Our yearning for concreteness leads us to endow the theoretical scion with a significance that it actually does not possess. In our desperation for uncertainty-erasing measures we in fact create a ghost, make up a story that satisfies our hunger. This we do, not after thorough analysis of the mathematics, but entirely based on the interpretation of "experts." We are told that the VIX stands for something and we, compliant slaves, inescapably oblige. This would be of limited importance if the matter was just of a philosophical nature (so what if we decide to delude our minds so as to sleep better), but unfortunately its reach extends very much to the practical. The VIX actually influences the actions of lots of people out there. In our desperation for reliable guidance we have allowed a ghost to influence markets.

The VIX has always been widely followed, but it became really fashionable during the credit crisis to talk about the Chicago Board Options Exchange–quoted index. On several occasions during that period, the VIX exploded upwards, reached peak-setting levels, milestones never conquered since a new, more complex method of calculating the VIX was introduced in early 2004. Pundits, analysts, and financial pros, as many times before, unrelentingly directed their attention to the index as a not-to-be-missed indicator.

With the return of "VIX-speak," inevitably came the return of "VIX-misspeak." The VIX has established itself as a predominantly ubiquitous figure in modern markets, with many endowing it with highly influential powers, from reflecting players' state of mind to forecasting future movements in stock prices. To top it all, there are now derivatives on the VIX itself available, futures and options contracts whose payout and market value depend purely on the levels of the index. In other words, the VIX is one of those things where misinterpretation and confusion can have critical real-life consequences. And yet the inescapable fact is that the VIX has been consistently misunderstood, misrepresented, and misspoken about.

Conventional wisdom has it that the VIX stands for expected future stock market volatility, purportedly estimated from the market prices of liquid equity options. That is why it tends to be described as investors' "fear gauge." A high VIX is consensually characterized as corresponding to enhanced worries on the part of option players. The conventional wisdom (espoused by the world's leading financial media outlets) is that the VIX equates expected movement in the S&P 500 index over the next month. For example, a VIX of 30 would typically be seen as irrefutable evidence that the options market expects the S&P 500 to move up or down by

$$30 \div \sqrt{12} = 8.66\%$$

(VIX is quoted on an annualized basis) during the following 30 days. There are several reasons why all this is not exactly right. To illustrate, let's briefly revisit the VIX's lifeline.

In 1993 the CBOE introduced the VIX, with the noble idea of making it the overall accepted benchmark for market volatility. In order to perform such function, the original VIX was made to reflect the levels of implied volatility for one-month S&P 100 at-the-money options, assuming that traders are using the Black–Scholes model when pricing those options. That is, for every quoted market option price, a corresponding implied volatility level could be obtained by reverse-engineering the Black–Scholes formula (i.e., the number that traders are assumed to be inputting under the formula's volatility figure).

This original approach presents two big problems. First, implied volatility is not the same as expected future real volatility. Many people seem to continue to believe so, essentially assuming that the number traders consensually input under the volatility parameter is their consensual expectation of future turbulence. However, this is not exactly accurate. Implied volatility would rather be simply a conduit used by traders to arrive at the desired price of an option, a catch-all that would include all aspects deemed relevant by traders, and which are not fully captured by the (famously imperfect and unrealistic) Black–Scholes model. It is likely that traders would include some view on future turbulence when deciding on the implied volatility figure, but a host of other factors would also play a large part. For instance, the fact that traders consider that the option should be more expensive due to liquidity concerns, and bump up the volatility input (the only manipulable input in the formula) accordingly. It may also reflect crash-o-phobia on the part of traders who, fearing a market meltdown, ramp up the volatility number for the options that they sell to others as protection so as to obtain a cushion in the form of higher premium up front. Particular supply-demand disequilibriums could similarly play a significant role; if supply is dramatically restricted for certain contracts, then the value of those contracts (and thus the quoted implied volatility) would naturally shoot up.

Any unseemly factor could alter implied volatility. For instance, during the famed LTCM episode of late 1998, equity options counterparts to the fund reportedly marked the volatility parameter up by a lot, not because they expected turbulence to be that high, just as a way to protect their interests. A naive observer might have looked at the 40 percent figure and concluded "The market is surely forecasting a wild ride!" ignorant of the fact that there was so much more behind that staggeringly large number than a simple volatility forecast.

That is, implied volatility is not a good mirror into expected real volatility. The existence of the volatility smile, which shows traders assigning different implied volatilities depending on the strike level of otherwise identical option contracts, is a glowing testament to that (as, clearly, the market's consensual volatility expectation for a given underlying asset cannot be more than one number).

A bigger problem is the assumption that traders use Black-Scholes when pricing options. As we know full well, recent groundbreaking research by veteran option traders and intellectuals Nassim Taleb and Espen Haug casts serious doubt on such assumption, essentially claiming that many times the prices of options come straight from simple supply and demand interaction, with no mathematical model involved. Since the concept of implied volatility is 100 percent model-dependent (you can't have implied volatility if option prices are not derived from a formula), the old VIX would be nothing but a make-believe fairy tale, not even a reflection of implied volatility, let alone real expected volatility.

We see then that the old VIX did not live up very well to its billing as mirror into the market's forecasted mayhem. Maybe it was implied volatility (if prices came from Black-Scholes) and thus reflected traders' opinions about something, but it wasn't exactly expected turbulence.

What about the new shiny VIX, introduced a decade later? Well, the idea was to reflect advances in option theory and market realities (such as the volatility smile). The index is now based on options on the S&P 500 and uses a weighted average of many different option prices across different strike levels, including deep out-of-the-money and in-the-money strikes.

The new VIX does not assume the use of Black-Scholes in real life, and does not reverse-engineer from a model. But the CBOE stubbornly continues to call it "implied volatility" and "a measure of volatility expectations." Almost everybody else continues, too, to follow that tagline. But they seem to continue to be wrong. The new VIX calculation is based on very complex mathematical ruminations pertaining to the pricing of newish complex derivatives known as "variance swaps." In order to understand where the new VIX figure comes from, one has to take a concise look at a devilishly complex paper put together by Goldman Sachs quants in 1999. It is almost understandable that many would shy away from such burdensome task and instead hang on tight to the conventional tagline.

The Goldman paper (referenced by the CBOE on its VIX web site) attempts to find a theoretical price for variance swaps, a contract where one makes or loses money depending on the future value of the realized variance (standard deviation, or volatility, to the second power) of stock prices. Such theoretical, or fair, price is defined as being equal to the stock's expected variance during the life of the transaction. The quants then proceed to use advanced probabilistic arguments and fancy stochastic calculus to quantify such expected value. By doing so, they find that expected variance depends, among other things, on something dubbed a "log contract," which happens to be replicable by a bunch of plain vanilla call and put options, as many as feasible. And this is how, voila! the theoretical expected variance gets to be linked to, among other things, the market prices of a wide range of standard options across many strike levels. Future volatility (of the theoretical kind) would thus be made to depend on the prices of options simply by means of a mathematical sleight-of-hand, as if by accident.

Obviously, one could not imply from such exercise that those prices, set in the market, are necessarily implying anything about expected volatility.

The VIX (the variance swap's fair price) would change when option prices change, according to the formula inspired by Goldman's work, but this is not the same as being implied. The mathematical construct does not allow us to make any link between traders' volatility expectations and the VIX. There is no reverse-engineering here. All we can say about the VIX is that it will change when the prices of a bunch of one-month S&P 500 options with many different strike levels change. But who is to say that those prices (especially if model-independent) would contain any expected volatility component at all? And in what amount? Option prices could perfectly go up, taking the VIX upwards, even if volatility expectations did not go up at all. Even if there are no volatility expectations at play.

That is, the new VIX is not implied (much less, expected) volatility, either. The link with option prices is accidental, not uniquely direct. Implied volatility as we've always known it is not supposed to be accidental: Traders are very much assumed to be thinking about volatility when setting prices. In the new VIX, option prices will impact theoretical expected variance but it doesn't necessarily mean that those prices include precise thoughts about future variance. The only sure way to go from quoted option prices to expectations is if traders are using a pricing model with a volatility parameter that they use to express their views about future volatility (among other things), and which can be, and is, reverse-engineered into something called implied volatility. If we are not outrightly reverse-engineering, as is the case with the new VIX, then we cannot indisputably claim to be obtaining implied volatility or expectations. At least with the old staid VIX we could fantasize that such claim held ground, as long as (as was widely believed prior to Taleb and Haug) traders were consensually using the Black-Scholes model.

So why exactly does the new VIX go up or down? The way the VIX is calculated, we can roughly say that when option prices go up (on average) the VIX goes up, and when they go down (on average) the VIX goes down. Since the VIX is now linked to option prices across a wide range of strikes, we could roughly say that the VIX reflects the level of the volatility smile at any one time, rising if the smile becomes (on average) happier, falling if the smile becomes (on average) sadder. Were option prices to be determined via Black-Scholes, one could assume that the prices of the options used to calculate the VIX would contain an implied volatility component, which in turn may contain some degree of real volatility expectations. In that scenario, it might be valid to ascertain that the VIX does reflect implied volatility (and thus, perhaps, volatility expectations) in some manner. But not, again, in a reverse-engineered type of manner. And who is to assure that traders are using Black-Scholes? Or that they are thinking about future volatility when pricing options? That is why the best way to view the VIX is as a measure of option costliness (across the full volatility smile), not a measure of implied or future volatility.

What does all this mean for the reputation of the VIX as a relevant indicator? That it probably has been exaggerated, on top of being misunderstood. We think that the VIX is about volatility when it most likely isn't, so adopting it as guiding light is bound to be harmfully counterproductive. And volatility forecasting may not be the only power of dubious merit with which the VIX has been endowed. The index is also seen by many as capable of signaling market direction. According to this logic, if the VIX is so, the markets will move this way, and if the VIX is not so, the markets will move that way. It used to be that a low VIX meant that markets were going to be stable (i.e., you can buy safely), while a high VIX meant panic-fueled upcoming trouble (you better sell). These days, so-call contrarians send, well, a contrarian message: Low VIX equals dangerous complacency (sell!), high VIX means players bailing out driven by excessive fear-driven conservatism (buy!).

How reliable are such statements? Should investors run to the hills in the presence of a sky-high VIX or rather accumulate cheap offerings? Is a low VIX an opportunity to get in the market or a dire warning? The only message that the VIX indisputably displays, as we stated earlier, concerns the affordability of equity options. A high VIX means that options are, on average, dearer. A low VIX says that options are, on average, cheaper. Can we translate option prices into forecasts for market direction? Maybe. A high VIX can mean three things: that all the options included in the calculation got more expensive, that the put options got more expensive, or that the call options got more expensive. While the first option would indicate neutrality, the second may indicate bearishness (people buying puts believing that the market will tank), and the third may indicate bullishness (people buying calls in the belief that the market will soar). So if you think that behind a high VIX lies a disproportionate demand for put options (or a supply restriction on such contracts), you might safely assume that option pros are forecasting a meltdown. But for those who think that call buying is truly behind the bump in implied volatilities (perhaps traders stocking on out-of-the-money calls in the expectation of a rally), the signal from the VIX would be bullish.

Similarly, a low VIX may indicate low demand for puts (bullish signal), low demand for calls (bearish signal), or low demand for all types of options (no signal, really). The main point is that it's difficult to read the VIX when it comes to market direction. In the end, neither traditionalists nor contrarians may have it right, and the daily level of the VIX (as a nonindicator of expected volatility estimates) may not be much of a reliable crystal ball into the future for equities.

Of course, all this could change if enough players buy the VIX-as-direction-signaling slogan, which is the same as saying that they buy into the VIX-as-volatility-forecast slogan only that with different diagnosis. Imagine that a substantial number of investors bought into one of the schools of thought and thus assume an unquestionable mechanical relationship between the markets and the level of the VIX. If the VIX goes up or down, a whole bunch of supposedly sophisticated investors would buy or sell (or sell or buy) simply because the gospel-like assumed mechanical relationship says so. Clearly, in such scenario the VIX would have the power to move markets, simply because people chose to voluntarily enslave themselves to a certain theory, itself based on a deeply misinterpreted theory.

This could be dangerous. The assumed predictive powers of the VIX could become a self-fulfilling prophecy. Instead of going up or down because of fundamentals or even pure gut feelings, stock prices would vary according to dubious signals from option traders, who may or may not be sending the messages that VIX theorists and their obedient followers assume they are sending. Rather than following economic news, company results, and other meaningful variables, stocks (which play such an important role and affect the incomes of so many businesses and individuals, and which have the power to move a myriad of other financial assets) may become slaves to the mysterious, impenetrable, and possibly completely unrelated implied volatility figure. In this sense, the unhealthy yearning for precision could lead to incorporating untold levels of unwarranted tumultuous noise into the markets and the disrupting disruption of the natural flow of things. People's embracement of a misleading theoretical volatility measure may produce untold real volatility. People's abysmally unquenchable demand for a tangible quantity may come back to haunt them—hard.

Derivatives, naturally, have ferociously fronted the headlines in recent months (or shall we say, recent years?). Their reputation, already tarnished in many quarters, has taken a huge blow following the credit derivatives–enabled credit crisis. This is an overall unfair development, for derivatives have provided lots of value in many areas and to many end users (not just speculators) throughout history. Yes, derivatives can, believe it or not, deliver positive things. The value added by interest rate, currency, energy, or commodity derivatives to companies, asset managers, pension funds, governments, retail investors, and insurance companies all around the world has been extraordinarily positive.

Beyond the familiar economic arguments for the adoration of derivatives (notwithstanding the untold malaise caused by a rather deleterious member of the family), there is an additional key, more philosophical, reason why we should learn to love them and yearn to protect them. Simply stated, derivatives are the tools that made uncertainty irrelevant. Derivatives miraculously allow us to plan ahead without having to forecast. Thanks to derivatives we don't have to care about uncertainty. It can't hurt us, it can't worry us. At least when it comes to the financial markets (and even beyond), the existence of a healthy derivatives industry shelters us from the darkness of the unknown. One would be hard-pressed to think of a more valuable contribution.

Financial markets are, clearly, unforecastable and volatile. We just can't predict. We are simply not smart enough to guess what others are going to consensually do, and thus anticipate future prices for stocks, bonds, or currencies (or, painfully obvious of late, credit events). But there is something we can very much do. In fact, we have been doing it for a long time. We can hedge the unforecastable uncertainty into oblivion, through derivatives. It turns out that we are smart enough to trade uncertainty.

That is, we shouldn't care if the world is a scarily uncertain place. We should only care that people are willing to make a viable and liquid market in future events. Once that market is a reality, uncertainty becomes irrelevant. Harmless. As long as there are derivatives, there is no need to forecast (i.e., no need to be right in our forecasts).

In fact, uncertainty and volatility become somewhat welcome, for their very existence is what drives the birth and evolution of the derivatives business in the first place. For derivatives to exist, turmoil must be first present. No one needs a hedge if there is no volatility. It is hard to make a liquid market if few players want/need to participate. That is precisely why post–WWII Keynesianism guaranteed a dormant derivatives scene. With exchange rates kept fixed (Bretton Woods) and interest rates under official control (interventionist monetary policy in search of full employment) there was no need for currency or interest rate derivatives. These now–essential members of the derivatives family (in essence, the two largest members) only began to show up in force in the mid-1970s, as asset prices were allowed to float freely in the markets.

So derivatives not only make uncertainty irrelevant, but also feed on it and fight it back: The more volatility, the easier it is to create an efficient derivatives market with which to hedge the mayhem into oblivion. In a sense, through the derivatives conduit more uncertainty makes uncertainty irrelevant. Once derivatives are in place I can plan about the future in spite of rabid uncertainty. And I can plan precisely because uncertainty is so rabid. Take weather risk. Climate change creates more uncertainty for those whose bottom lines are weather-dependent. Such concerns push the weather derivatives market forward, dramatically enhancing liquidity and attracting new players, making weather hedging a viable alternative for everyone, finally erasing age-old weather-related uncertainties for businesses and governments throughout the world.

To those out there concerned about the future and how to prepare for it, the message should be loud and clear: Don't invest in devising ever more complex (and predictably disappointing) forecasting tools, invest instead in developing mature and liquid derivatives markets. If you want to operate amidst untold chaos, don't engage in the fruitless act of forecasting. Use derivatives, and submit uncertainty into irrelevance.

But don't just use derivatives. Protect them eagerly from any threats to their well-functioning or even mere existence. And a major threat, in that respect, may lie in some of the complex quantitative techniques that have bullied their way into financial theory and practice in the past decades. Nassim Taleb has declared that the scientification of finance makes market crises more probable. As we have seen in this book, there is no doubt that he is not exaggeratedly off-the-mark. Malfunctioning models and measures that provided a false sense of security have on many occasions encouraged misguided actions that have yielded mayhem and chaos. As long as theory continues to display massive unworldliness and continues to be adopted into the markets, those nasty episodes would recur.

If derivatives, as tends to be the case, end up carrying a large share of the blame and suffering a public relations meltdown (as a result of the credit crisis, undiscriminating anti-derivatives songs have been loudly sung, and derivatives dealing in all areas will consequently become more cumbersome), we may witness a drastic reduction in their use as clients shy away from such conflictive tools, dealers retreat from business areas, and regulators begin to seriously meddle. All this would be disastrous news for the fight against unpredictability. We must not allow those mathematically charged fake subduers of the unknown to deprive us of the genuine, time-tested, true uncertainty-tamers.

Chapter 10

We Need Fat Tony

As we have amply discussed throughout this book, the three-decade-old process of quantification, mathematization, and theoretization of finance has blood on its hands. Severe market trouble has been directly caused or indirectly enabled as a result of the embracement of analytical constructs and dictums. A potentially lethal culture of numerically justified overconfidence and false security has impregnated vast regions of the financial universe. Reckless actions by otherwise no-nonsense pros have been excused and alibied via lemma-filled technical exonerators. What's more, the theory and its endorsers are not content with having contributed to monetary, economic, and institutional destruction. They also want to commit actual murder. They want to annihilate a two-legged target. They want to kill Fat Tony.

Who's Fat Tony? He is a Brooklyn-born, highly successful, non-nerd, former bank clerk who made a fortune by purchasing undervalued properties on credit. He wears Italian tailor suits and a gold wrist chain. He has a happy predisposition and leads a gregarious existence. He exudes street-smartness and is somewhat IQ-challenged. He is not the least scientific, in the generally accepted sense. He is obviously overweight. And he is a fictional character invented by Nassim Taleb.

Fat Tony embodies those people who don't take crap, call things as they see them, are 100 percent practical, and are not enslaved one bit to dogmatic or theoretical sanctities. In sum, the epitome of thinking outside the box. The complete opposite of your typical "scientific," modern-day, quantitative finance professional (represented by Fat Tony's nemesis, Dr. John). As Taleb says, Fat Tony is the kind of guy who would assign no more than 1 percent chance to obtaining tails from flipping a coin, once we know that heads have previously come up 99 consecutive times (obviously, the coin's "gotta be loaded"). Dr. John, in contrast, would trivially assign 50 percent probability (predictably impervious to the possibility that anything beyond hard statistical rules could be a factor).

Why would (some) quants and theorists want to exterminate Fat Tony? In the context of this book, Fat Tony represents those financial pros and thinkers who refuse to employ high-tech quantitative stuff or are at the very least open and willing to severely question its applicability. He represents math-devoid decision making. A world where humans (borrowing from their own experience and decades, even centuries, of accumulated practical knowledge), not models, rule. A world where a PhD-holder doesn't need to draw on his doctoral wisdom in order to be able to make it in the markets. A world where addition, subtraction, multiplication, and, maybe, division are all the analytics you would ever need. A world that recognizes that prices are ultimately determined by emotions, supply, and demand. A world, in effect, that may appear to many today as unacceptably backward and illiterate.

Fat Tony is both a menace and a target for the theorists. He and his kind threaten their very existence and their view of the financial universe, and must thus be erased. Fat Tony is a man who can very loudly (maybe while wearing loud silk shirts half-open to the chest and puffing a large cigar) point at the ridiculous unworldliness of many of the theories, from the vantage point of a non-intellectually-pretentious amicable chum who has spent his entire life around the block. A man who is completely unchained to the iron ball of qualifications and classroom-obtained erudition conventionalisms. A man not the least impressed and subdued by academic diplomas and equation-solving prowess. A man enslaved only to the deity of common sense and pavement-honed encyclopedism. Fat Tony is a man who can try to ban the nerds from the premises. The most dangerous kind of threat.

Of course, since Fat Tony is not a real character, real murder is not an option for his detractors. Rather, they would attempt to forever extirpate his stigmatic spirit from the four corners of the financial industry (note that any resemblance of Fat Tony was long ago exiled from the academic arena). How? Through a breathlessly relentless propagandistic putsch. Advanced quantitative stuff must be endlessly portrayed as an essentially necessary part of finance, unavoidably required. Anything slightly nontechnical must be categorized as ineludibly antediluvian, perilously nonrigorous. Only those with the scientific PhD should be allowed in, unreturnably crowding out those ancient fossils who uncouthly let themselves be guided by unbearably softish common sense.

Needless to say, much of this has already taken place. Consider risk management, or even some trading these days (quant work, by its own nature, requires technical people; no Fat Tony-desecrating here—not that Fat Tony would ever want to do quant work). It is currently basically inconceivable that anyone hired for such occupations would not hold a highly quantitative PhD or Masters, and that the job interviews (and skills required) would not center universally on mathematical, statistical, and computational themes. Measurers and modelers have completely conquered, appropriating highly critical roles that were once the preserve of C++-illiterate, Ito's Lemma-ignoring, Gaussian Copula-uncognizing non-nerds who would never have imagined that Monte Carlo would stand for anything else than a sun-drenched gambling den where attractive women seem to be puzzlingly turned on by those exotic Brooklyn, New Jersey, or Cockney accents.

The quantification of finance personnel carries heavy baggage. It's not just that people whose number one contribution would be the application of analytical tools of doubtful practical validity and possible harmful effects (here, once more, we are not including the unlimitedly valuable chores of software development and computational assistance) are taking over. The whammy is very much double, because the presence of mathematical people implicates, by direct elimination, the nonpresence of nonmathematical, commonsensical people. Every time you hire a quanty PhD to manage risks, you are not offering his desk to a less technical, but possibly more street savvy, individual. If you choose to go with Dr. John you are obviously abruptly discarding Fat Tony with the same stroke.

In other words, it's personal. The invasion of the equations and statistical precepts means that a certain type of people (theoretically dogmatic, exam-taking, studious) dominate in certain areas over another type of people (open-minded, skeptical, intuitive). The former are likelier to devoutly abide by a few mathematical precepts and to never question their preeminence. After all, that's the world they know. If you have devoted your entire youth (and even post-youth) to studying and researching quantitative models inside a university building or laboratory, chances are that you would have more than a passing belief in the supremeness of the tools. And even if you had somehow become agnostic after deciphering one too many lemmas, you are fully aware of where your skill set lies and what kind of expertise and knowledge you have to peddle in order to make a living. The most agnostic of quantitative folk may suddenly become reconverted when competing for a generously paid, math-demanding position in the interview room of an investment bank or hedge fund.

The predominantly abundant presence of quantitative apostles inside trading floors in turn helps convince influential outsiders (such as journalists, regulators, and academics) that advanced math counts a lot in finance these days. Such convictions, fueled by a willingness to fall victim to what appears to be unchallenged conventional wisdom, in turn reinforces the message that analytical stuff is key, further encouraging the hiring of quant folk, the enacting of math-driven regulations, the spreading of the gospel to the masses, and the indoctrination of young, impressionable minds. And so on, and so on, until the specter of Fat Tony becomes unremittingly eradicated.

We all stand to lose from the eradication of Fat Tony–like characters from financeland. They can protect us from trouble by making sure that financial institutions do not do weird things on the back of scientifically sanctioned methodology. It is highly unlikely that Fat Tony would have allowed exposures to be measured via such a defective tool as VaR, let alone allow capital charges to be determined by it. It is highly doubtful that Fat Tony would have bought into the delta ratio mathematical guarantee that drove so many into the equity-mezzanine play. It is highly improbable that Fat Tony would have embraced portfolio insurance–style dynamic hedging programs. Had Fat Tony been in charge of global risk management, trading, or (why not?) regulatory policy making, the several crises that we have analyzed in this book might not have taken place at all. Once we substitute blind theoretical adherence with non-nonsensical, practicality-seeking, fiercely skeptical out-of-the-box-ness, we can save the world a lot of pain. Once rashly "irrational" intuition is allowed to dominate, financial decision making is bound to improve.

Some may argue, what guarantees that Fat Tony would do a better job at managing risk? After all, doesn't he look kind of funny, and didn't his school grades stink? Granted, there is no guarantee that Fat Tony and his peers would perform satisfactorily per se. Their street smarts and nondogmatism sound like positive assets in principle, but they could backfire in practice, somehow. But by embracing Fat Tony we would at least have incontrovertibly achieved a very laudable goal: the assurance that bad practices won't go on, notwithstanding the technical brilliance behind the machinations. When it comes to Fat Tony, a theory-abetted meltdown cannot be an excuse for remodeling the tools or for dreaming up even more complex alternatives, but rather an unapologetic catalyst for the complete abolition of such tools as well as the all-across-the-board, hold-no-punches questioning of the role of analytics in finance. That is, by telling you what *not* to do, Fat Tony (just like his progenitor Taleb) would already be doing us a tremendous service.

It may sound moronicly simplistic, but by simply convincing people not to take things on theoretical faith the improvements could be huge. If a rating agency assigns a triple-A rating to a complex mortgage-backed-securities-based CDO structure, you can (as most do) take it unquestionably on faith, or you can skeptically dig deeper. Fat Tony would tell you to investigate who exactly are the mortgage borrowers and how exactly they were approved for the loan (in American political terms, this would equate to Fat Tony having rushed to learn more about Barack Obama's past Chicago activities or Sarah Palin's Alaskan record before casting his vote, rather than slavishly and conformistly buying into the "change and hope" or "exemplar mother of five" taglines). Once you hit the streets and learn of NINJA financing and of vast overstatement of personal incomes on the applications, you may conclude that the ratings coin "gotta be loaded" and that the risks of clustered defaults are hugely above those suggested by the three letters.

Now the yield offered by senior tranches (purportedly calculated by a computer model) appears as way too low, so you detect an instant opportunity to buy protection; you are more than willing to pay small regular amounts of money in exchange for receiving a very large one-off sum once disaster inevitably strikes. In fact, you are quite glad that everybody else is blindly following the unchallenged holy opinion of the agencies and that the model churns out low default probabilities. Lots of market participants would rush to sell protection, reveling in the prospect of attractive "riskless" returns, thus bringing down the price of buying protection, and dramatically enhancing your potential returns. Once more, Fat Tony and his followers would have made a killing by being overly curious about the texture of reality and discovering undervalued opportunities, while the theoretical crowd is complacently bowing to the altar of mathematically sanctioned certainties. Dr. John, taking for granted that ratings are based on sound methodology employed by PhDs from the top universities and that no further introspection is needed, would have contrastingly sold protection, naturally ending in the cleaners.

Or take VaR. Fat Tony would have taken a look at those low numbers being reported before the credit crisis and would have understood that such placidity was entirely based on historical data that included negligible activity in the very (high-risk) areas where banks had been aggressively diving into for the past few years. He would have understood that the numbers were meaningless (don't get him started on Normality!) and that they were encouraging dealers to accumulate funky exposures in a highly leveraged way. Consequently, he may have shorted banks' stock. Dr. John, on the other hand, would have seen only prudently scientifically managed portfolios that didn't seem to forebode malcontent, instantly contacting his broker and buying some Bear Stearns, Merrill Lynch, and Lehman Brothers shares.

The financial world was once entirely dominated by Fat Tonys. It still, to a large degree, largely is. There are tons of important areas that have not succumbed to quantification. But when it comes to undeniably influential roles such as risk management and (some) trading, Dr. John types and Dr. John ideology have taken over. The conventionalism that market activities require rocket science has, after three decades of hammering down the message, become stringently unassailable in plenty of quarters.

We need a new approach. The adoration of unworldly theories and their implementation have caused too much mayhem. We need to stop treating quantitative constructs as reliable doctrine, and start to reconsider the competitive advantage of experience-honed human common sense and intuition (academics could play a key role in this respect, by internally reexamining their own Taliban-like adherence to analyticness). Financial decision making would benefit, if only from the nonadoption of the harmful lemmas going forward. We need to hand over the keys to the risk kingdom back to free-thinking, gumption-honoring, innumerate chums. We need Fat Tony.

■ *Finale* ■

Should the Nobel Prize in Economics Be Eliminated?

T he International Association of Culinary Professionals lavishes awards on, well, culinary professionals every year. Now, imagine that annum after annum the recipients of the prize for excellence in the field would irrevocably turn out to be people who have never cooked. They are not chefs, they are not grill men, they are not pizza makers. They have never cooked. They are not, and have never been, in the cuisine business. They are "cuisine theoreticians"—they theorize about cuisine.

The award is justified on the basis of some complex recipes that those nonchefs have come up with using sophisticated quantitative tools. At first sight, the recipes look somewhat weird, not exactly accordant to the realities of the cuisine arena, but this seems not to have bothered the awarding committee too much, as year after year they praise such contributions, gloriously applauding the arrival of rigor and scientific methodology into the otherwise hopelessly "anecdotal" and "institution-alist" culinary world. The fact that some of those recipes eventually end up causing widespread nausea and assorted sicknesses in naïve consumers (who embraced the rigorous innovations precisely as a direct result of the reassuring backing of the award committee) appears not to have made a dent in how the prizes are awarded. The same type of recipes, complex if nor exactly real-life-compliant, keep being magnificently crowned. Even more important, and as if to dispel any doubts that the chosen approach is the only valid one, no real hands-on, kitchen-inhabiting cook has ever been considered for the award, let alone honored.

Were we to present this hypothetical state of affairs to regular folks, what kind of feedback would we obtain? Naturally, the whole idea would be dismissed as unchecked lunacy. A wholly unseemly conjecture, an annoying implausibility. Clearly, no one in their right mind would ever conceive of such an award-granting strategy. Who would want to lavish cooking awards on noncooks whose recipes can cause ill? What would be the point exactly? Perhaps a naughty exercise in blatantly and insultingly openly disregarding actual practice by adoringly cuddling its nemesis, unrepentant abstractionism? A sheepishly docile submission to the dictates of those who scribble food equations, and an unfettered dismissal of those brute vulgarians who actually work with food? Maybe the award committee simply hates the culinary art and its practitioners, and this is payback?

For those taking excessive comfort in the idea that such a hypothetical story could never be reproduced in the real world, allow me to throw in the reminder that since 1969 a very distinguished award dealing (in name, at least) with a discipline that, like the culinary one, is only practical and only human-action-shaped, has been unremittingly lavished on people with zero practical experience in the field and for contributions that are entirely theoretical, that on occasions have resulted in dramatically negative real-life outcomes, and whose awards-sanctioned lauding can encourage unsavory behavior. This is not to deny that great contributions of vast use to practitioners may have been among the awardees, but rather to expose in as graphical terms as possible the essence of the matter.

What's more, the above-mentioned discipline is the only one of a group of six disciplines, for which awards are handed out under the same umbrella, where the honor always and invariably goes to nonpractitioners in the field. The other disciplines, by definition, are religiously practice-oriented, and those who toil there are nothing if not practical. They are, by definition, the practitioners in those areas or at the very least engage in discoveries that exclusively aim to achieve empirically valid, applicable, actionable results. Their actions and work thus constitute or at the very least decisively help shape the very practice of that field. The discoveries that are awarded are always practice-altering and practice-shaping. The nonnegotiable goal is to find an implementable solution to a (previously unsolved) practical problem. In other words, those people are 100 percent hands-on. They may make theory, but it's the type of theory that unveils laws and principles that firmly hold in practice. The type of theory that is not only enthusiastically welcomed in practice, but whose unassailably natural ultimate destination is practice, as has been for ages. That is, a theory that invariably works.

Not so with the other, rather odd sixth discipline. Those who belong to it are not the ones practicing what's under study. They are not, by any stretch, the practitioners of that area. Other people are doing it in the real world. Their discoveries are empiricism-challenged, and the dictums are rewarded without regard for practical validity, simply on account of the analytical techniques employed. Here there is a huge dichotomy between the theory and the practice. Theoreticians do not (can't) produce laws and principles that will always hold in practice; the field is simply not amenable to scientific taming. As a result, most (all?) of the time the theory is entirely ignored in practice, deemed inapplicable or outright unworldly. Here, the theory doesn't work. In fact, it may be entirely desirable that theory does *not* get translated into practice, as the potential for negative impacts is demonstrably large (those sickness-inducing recipes . . .).

We are, certainly, talking about the Nobel Prize in Economics, and its Physics, Chemistry, Medicine, Literature, and Peace siblings. It goes without saying that in the case of the latter two, awardees can be nothing if not direct practitioners. You may personally disagree with the merits of this or that particular honoree, but the undeniable fact is that writers are the ones who do literature and "pacifists" are the ones who engage in "peaceful" actions. Neither Mother Teresa nor Gabriel Garcia Marquez are "peace theorists" or "literature theorists"; they are über practitioners.

The same logic would apply to the hard sciences. For someone to get the Medicine, Chemistry, or Physics Nobel the discoveries must be empirically valid (i.e., the organs, cells, antibodies, nerve fibers, immunity systems, gases, atoms, semiconductors, wave functions, photoelectric effects, proteins, molecules, hormones, or isotopes must function and operate in reality exactly as the scientists posited), and thus intransigently applicable and actionable. And, of course, must provide a new way to solve an old problem.

When it comes to Economics, well...let's just say that things are not that empirical, that real, that actionable. It is one thing to make up a theory about how human begins should act and another to have that theory validated by real-world happenstances. There can't be eternal laws when dealing with human economic behavior. Talking specifically about financial economics, the theorists couldn't be further removed from the practice. They are not traders, corporate financiers, chief finance officers, treasurers, venture capitalists, asset managers, loan officers, risk managers, salespeople, investment bankers, or finance ministers. They don't even generally attempt to describe what those living objects of analysis are doing, but rather presumptuously assume from the isolated confines of a darkly lit university office.

And they tend to assume quite unrealistically. The Nobel awards for work in finance theory make for a nice recollection of utterly inapplicable, utterly unactionable, utterly unempirical ruminations. Among those tenets being rewarded with the $1 million windfall, we can underline the assumptions that we know the market probability distribution, that we know the expected asset returns, that we know the correlations among asset returns, that markets behave normally without experiencing rare events, that past data can be used to forecast the future, that agents are rational, that markets are perfectly efficient and Warren Buffett doesn't exist, that markets are in heavenly equilibrium, that markets are always frictionless and perfectly liquid, and that we can measure risks. Not a single one of those assumptions holds in the real world, and yet the Nobel committee decided to honor them all. Not a single one of those assumptions has demonstrably helped solve a previously unresolved problem (among other things, precisely because the theories are not implementable), and yet the Nobel committee decided to honor them all. Can you imagine something similar taking place in the hard sciences arena? It seems obvious that, for whatever reason, Economics gets a free pass with respect to its Nobel cousins, and empiricism and applicability are ruthlessly tossed aside, steamrolled by the only consideration that is shown to have mattered: technical wizardry for the sake of technical wizardry. It doesn't matter if the new recipe can't be transformed into a meal that people may wish and be able to consume (safely); all that matters is that the instructions are quantitatively convoluted enough.

Should we care that noncooking economists are being awarded high-profile cuisine trophies? Is there something intrinsically wrong with that? Can we get hurt? Should we protect ourselves?

In physics, chemistry, or medicine it is possible to make valuable discoveries that truly help us understand the world better and develop highly useful practical applications. This is because the objects of analysis (molecules, atoms, animal anatomy, the human body, the planets) are not free-thinking entities that can change their opinion. They display predictable and regular patterns of behavior, once you have unlocked (through your analysis) the key to such well-enscripted knowledge.

Not so in the financial markets. The objects of analysis are free-thinking agents that change their minds all the time for an infinite number of possible reasons and that don't follow lawful behavior. No celestially predictable or regular patterns here. So, where physicists, chemists, and doctors have to be extremely gifted individuals (as unlocking God's laws is no easy task), those capable of taming the untamable financial beast would have to be assumed to posses much more impressive powers, as the chore appears monstrously harder. A scientist of good repute could be reasonably expected to unlock a creature's DNA or to land a rocket on Mars, as we know that the secret information that needs to be deciphered is definitely out there, pristinely well-kept and safe-guarded, eternally preserved and unmodified. Getting to it may be hard, but there is no doubt as to the certainty of its existence and availability. God may have played a bit of hide-and-seek, but he didn't fail to place all the necessary pieces around. But what about those God-less markets? How do you find the DNA of something that keeps mutating ceaselessly? How do you detect immortally eternal laws in a lawless planet? You would need to be of divine caliber to get it right.

And that is exactly what financial economists are demanding of themselves. Friedrich Nietzsche famously talked about an "übermenschlich," a superhuman that would overcome regular man and eventually look down on him as a laughingstock or an embarrassment. In awarding the Nobel in Economics, the Swedish Central Bank is playing German philosopher and endowing honorees (and their colleagues) with übermensch-ness, very publicly endorsing their capacity for beyond-human actions such as mathematically predicting and modeling the markets.

So, are the Nobelists superhuman individuals who have overcome the rest of us pitiful men and women? They are highly intelligent (their qualifications and intellectual production attest to that), hardworking, resilient, ambitious, well-spoken, admired by their peers, respected by the world. But perhaps, after all, they are more like the rest of us than a different kind of Nietzschean species. A cut above the rest of us quite possibly, but not a race above the rest of us. Just IQ-unchallenged, over-achieving accomplishers faced with the impossibly insurmountable tasks of divining what people like you and me are going to do in the markets tomorrow and, even less plausible, trying to tell deviously unruly people like you and me what we *ought* to be doing in the markets tomorrow. Perhaps those Swedes slightly overestimated the capacities of the extraordinarily gifted theoreticians.

There is, of course, a crucial caveat. Nietzsche had his übermenschlich firmly planted on Earth. The Nobel committee forgot to footnote that the economists' powers genuinely applied only to a parallel, radically Platonized universe. There is no doubt that over there, in that faraway galaxy, the masterfully crafted tenets do gloriously hold true. Over there, we can really know (ex-ante) the expected return and volatility of any asset, we can really know the correlation between assets, we can really know the probability distribution reigning in the markets, we can really use the past to predict the future of the markets, delta-hedging is always continuously possible, everything is in perpetual equilibrium, no one can beat the market (no pesky Warren Buffetts), agents are rational optimizers. In this light, it may not be entirely inappropriate, as will be expanded on later, to recommend that the Nobel be changed into something like the more fittingly worded "Nobel Prize in Platonic Economics." That way, no one (not even Nassim Taleb!) could ever doubt the practical validity of the theory in the environment for which it was unfeignedly designed.

Short of the award undergoing such a change in nomenclature (but without discarding this option entirely), we could, rather more somberly, humbly question the rationale for rewarding on Earth tenets that may feel more at home galaxies away. We wouldn't be alone in that, frankly. No less a figure than Peter Nobel (yes, a direct descendant of the man himself) has called for the immediate abolition of the Economics aberration. For him, it's personal. He believes that the Economics award is a stain on his family's legacy, given that Alfred Nobel (whose brother Ludwig was Peter's great-grandfather), as we all know, never intended for it to happen and that it represents an utterly inadmissible betrayal of his spirit.

Now, to be perfectly honest (and though I am not quite sure that economists would appreciate my spreading of the word), the "Nobel in Economics" is *not* a real Nobel Prize. For one good reason: Peter Nobel is right. His ancient philanthropic relative never said anything about a Nobel that didn't cover the fields of physics, chemistry, peace, medicine, and literature (the holy quintet). It was only in 1968, 67 years after the awards began to be disbursed, that Sveriges Riksbank (Sweden's Central Bank) decided on its own accord, and in celebration of its 300-year anniversary, to establish the "Sveriges Riksbank Prize in Economic Sciences in Memory of Alfred Nobel." The prize is funded by an endowment from Sveriges Riksbank and is awarded by the Royal Swedish Academy of Sciences.

Although it is not one of the five Nobel Prizes established in Alfred Nobel's will, Nobel Prize rules are followed regarding nomination of candidates, adjudication, and award presentation. The Prize Award Ceremony takes place on Nobel Day on December 10 each year and the prize amount equals that of a Nobel Prize for the same year. In other words, it's not *really* really really a Nobel, but it walks like one and quacks like one. Everybody deems it a Nobel and it is announced as such (for instance, witness the *New York Times* headline on October 15, 2007: *"[Three] Americans to Share Nobel Prize in Economics: The Nobel Prize in economics was awarded today to three Americans for their work in mechanism design theory, a branch of economics that looks at . . ."*). The Nobel Prize organization does not (it can't) call it a Nobel on its web site (it calls it "Prize in Economics"), but this in no way implies that the award is belittled or hidden in shame. Quite the opposite. As of September 11, 2008, if one visited www.nobelprize.org, they would notice that the front cover was entirely dominated by, you guessed it, all-dominating references to the "Sixth Prize," including glossy pictures of a few past winners. No irrelevant afterthought, this "Nobel," certainly. And that is what irked Peter Nobel. He demanded that the Nobel term be for eternity disassociated with the Economics impostor. If the Central Bank of Sweden wants to flatter a bunch of economists, they should do it entirely on their own.

Now, while we wish him good luck in his quixotic quest, and to be perfectly honest, for the purposes of this book nomenclature nit-picking is, per se, less than fundamental. The main issue for us is not whether the Economics award is, like a Peruvian infant lovingly adopted by a Swedish couple, endowed with the Nobel surname or not. What matters is the exposure and the exercise in legitimization that the award concedes. Granted, as long as Alfred Nobel's memory continues to be betrayed, the PR exercise would probably be further-reaching than otherwise (a Nobel-less Sveriges Riksbank affair sounds less intriguing, in principle). But even if the disgruntled Nordic heir has his way, the award could continue to successfully tag along as the inheritor of the legendary Nobel in Economics tradition, without a discernable loss of reputation and admiration. (However, as will be noted later, a change in name *accompanied by* an eye-opening, clarifying disclaimer could in fact be very helpful to our cause.)

What should concern us about the Nobel-or-whatever in Economics is how its whiter-than-white mantle can encourage the spreading and adoption of theoretical dictums that may contain the seeds of destructive market chaos. Given the incurable prevalence of qualifications-blindness among the populace (including all levels of informedness), a high-profile, officialdom-stamped coronation can make wonders for the perceived unassability and unquestionableness of a theoretical construct. After all, only an unmitigatingly rube individual would dare challenge the validity, soundness, and salutariness of a theory that is held in such high esteem by such highly esteemed institutions. Right?

It is obvious that getting the "Nobel" in 1997 decisively assisted Black-Scholes-Merton in being abundantly seen as the "it" option pricing model, even after having experienced the debacle of October 1987 and the soon-after-the-Nobel LTCM tragedy. In fact, the Nobel plumage helped override any concerns that those two episodes (among many other, less headline-prone, negative happenstances) may have cast over the smartness of continuing to rely on the model ("How can you doubt BSM? They got the Nobel, didn't they?"). Such camouflaging had three less-than-salubrious effects: one, it contributed to the misleading presentation of finance as a scientific field where things can actually be accurately measured and are mathematically tamable, encouraging the future embracement of hopelessly off-target theoretical concoctions; two, it contributed to exposing a misinformed world to a device in which name grand turbulence has been created and could again be created; and three, it contributed to hiding truthfulness from the world (in the name of scientific accomplishments, no less) by portraying BSM as a widely employed, crazily popular success, when the fact of the matter is that the model has at the very least been openly deemed untrustworthy by its supposed users (for at least a decade prior to getting the Nobel) and, at the very worst, been openly manipulated into oblivion by those same supposed users. That BSM received the award when the volatility smile had been glowingly reigning supreme in the markets for 10 years is, frankly, a testament to the Nobel committee's abrasive disregard for practical affairs. By honoring a model that has been so flagrantly rejected (notwithstanding the mathematical creativity behind it) by its customers, the committee very clarifyingly lets us know where its preferences lie, in the process highlighting the harm that its decisions could inflict.

Let's take an illustrative rearview-mirror at the Nobel committee's reasons for enthroning BSM. The stated main reason for the choice was enshrined as *"for a new method to determine the value of derivatives."* Okay, fair enough. The method was in fact different from the many option pricing models already available previously. The capital asset pricing model (CAPM) and dynamic hedging justifications for going risk-neutral were one-of-a-kind, as were some of the technical tools innovatively employed.

What else? *"Robert C. Merton and Myron S. Scholes have, in collaboration with the late Fischer Black, developed a pioneering formula for the valuation of stock options. Their methodology has paved the way for economic valuations in many areas. It has also generated new types of financial instruments and facilitated more efficient risk management in society."* Okay, except for the first and the last part. Pioneering the formula really wasn't entirely, the committee could have easily found this out. The methodology was pioneering, not the final result. Secondly, are you sure that new types of financial instruments that would not have been created otherwise were created exclusively because of the appearance of BSM? Of course, the Nobel committee is doing nothing more than toeing the official, conventional-wisdom-following, line: BSM invented the options industry. But you see, a Nobel committee should be expected to dig a little deeper than the average official-line disciple.

As we have analyzed in this book, it is extremely likely that today's imperial derivatives market would have evolved exactly the same in the absence of BSM. And, by the way, if we can credit BSM with the derivatives revolution, why can't we credit some of its predecessors? Why can't we credit James Boness's formula, which becomes 100 percent identical to BSM if we select the risk-free rate of interest as the stock's expected rate of return? How can we be sure that the post–1973 market was excitedly using BSM and not Boness (available since 1964) with the riskless rate as the selection of choice (not an insanely odd choice, actually)? Boness's formula was published in a top-notch academic journal for all to see and implement. If we are to credit a mathematical theory with the development of an entire (rather nontrivial) business, why slavishly select the 1973 one and not the easily identical 1964 cousin? As for more efficient risk management, I guess the biggest Wall Street debacle ever doesn't count in Scandinavia.

But let's dig deeper, the best is yet to come. *"Attempts to value derivatives have a long history. As far back as 1900, the French mathematician Louis Bachelier reported one of the earliest attempts in his doctoral dissertation, although the formula he derived was flawed in several ways. Subsequent researchers handled the movements of stock prices and interest rates more successfully. But all of these attempts suffered from the same fundamental shortcoming: risk premia were not dealt with in a correct way,"* admitted the committee, adding that *"Assigning a risk premium is difficult, however, in that the correct risk premium depends on the investor's attitude towards risk. Whereas the attitude towards risk can be strictly defined in theory, it is hard or impossible to observe in reality."* Well said.

And now for the bombshell: *"Black, Merton and Scholes made a vital contribution by showing that it is in fact not necessary to use any risk premium when valuing an option. This does not mean that the risk premium disappears; instead it is already included in the stock price."* That is, the entire justification for the award is the removal of the need to calculate expected return afforded by the dynamic hedging-supported assumption of risk-neutrality. Of course, the methodology counts: BSM would not have obtained a prize if they had just said "How about we just put the risk-free rate in there—kind of cool, isn't it!" They provided a theoretically and mathematically rigorous and brilliant alibi.

So let's recap: BSM was given a Nobel for the way in which they derived a formula that was already pretty much known (derivatives and option theory guru Mark Rubinstein summed it up well: *"The real significance of the formula to the financial theory of investments lies not in itself, but rather in how it was derived. Ten years earlier the same formula had been derived by Case Sprenkle (1962) and James Boness (1964)."*). Wow! I guess that derivation must have been some kick-ass stuff. I mean, how rock-solid a derivation method has got to be if it earns you a Nobel Prize for coming up with something that was already known a decade earlier!

Unfortunately, we know after reading this book (hey, don't blame me and don't call me whistle-blower; I quote plenty of expert witnesses) that the methodology, the alibi, does not work here on our beautiful blue planet. Risk-neutrality in the fashion that BSM excused it is only possible in a Platonic environment, but not in the financial markets.

Which brings us to a particularly loaded complaint: Why wouldn't the Nobel committee care that the very specific technicality that was being prized is ineffectual in real life? It wasn't a secret (remember October 1987 . . . I am kind of getting Black Monday fatigue already), they could have asked around trading rooms. Or is it perhaps that when it comes to the Nobel in Economics, practicality and applicability entail an oxy-moronic conversation? Did the Nobel committee fall in love with BSM's mathematical derivation *per se*, without regard whatsoever for its possible use? Is working under a self-imagined, unfailingly abided-by, Platonic world the all-conquering requirement for a theory to titillatingly seduce the committee?

We covered in Chapter 5 that BSM presented finance theory with a conundrum: Keep embracing as crowning achievement a construct that has demonstrably failed in real-life, or humbly admit fallout and reform. It turns out that BSM is also a conundrum-provider when it comes to the Nobel. BSM may expose like no other awardee the shortcomings of the whole affair. Does it reward theories for the sake of their theoreticalism, or does practical relevance (in a field of study that is *only* practical) matter? Does it thoroughly search for historical precedents? Does it consult with practitioners to check the non-nonsensicality of the theory? Is it an entirely Platonic affair? Would the committee be willing to reform its ways? Does it believe that practical relevance should count? Does it believe that the reality of a field that is nothing if not practical should count? Or will it tie itself to the mast of business-as-usual, perhaps even wax its ears too?

It gets worse (the imprudent side of me wonders if some committee member reading this is by now wishing that BSM had been honored in a slightly different way). In the particular case of BSM at least, not even the (inapplicable) specific technicality for which an already-known, dubiously-employed, trouble-making theory was given the Nobel solved a previously unsolved problem. Dynamic hedging was not needed for option traders to remove risk out of their bread-winning activities. As Taleb and Haug forcefully hammer down on us, staid, noncomplex, unpretentious put-call parity can suffice. And, dare I reminisce, put-call parity has been known to traders since at least the seventeenth century. And, dare I re-reminisce, put-call parity seems to actually work.

So let's now complete the accurate (critical) definition of what the Nobel committee chose to enthrone: a specific technicality that allowed you to obtain a formula already available for many years, which (the technicality) mathematical foundations break down in real life, and which (the technicality) purported to find an innovative solution to a problem that in fact had already been efficiently solved centuries earlier. And, lamentably, it gets worse again. At the risk of putting the reader to sleep through unabashed repetition, the new technicality brings with it a ticking volatility time bomb, potentially enhancing, not eliminating (as advertised), risks for its users and with the capability of unleashing untold mayhem unto the markets. In other words, on top of not working properly and not being necessary, the Nobel-caliber device can cause lots of painful troubles.

In light of all this, should BSM be revoked of its Nobel? No, in my very humble opinion. The authors do deserve ample recognition, but it should come with a big-letter caveat. The Nobel should come cleaner about what it awards, how, and why. Particularly when the prizes tend to come well after the theory has been around, and thus a sensible process of analysis and testing has most likely already taken effect, and expert feedback is too widely available. In other words, Nobels tend to be awarded to theories that already have a record. It is entirely possible to know whether the theory has been applied in the real world or not, whether practitioners have embraced it or not, what have been the consequences of such embracement, and whether the math does make sense out there. By being stratospherically explicit about its intentions, the Nobel committee can avoid the unpleasantness of being caught with their hands in the cookie jar of irrelevance-honoring, once the prize is handed to a construct that possesses a mile-long rap sheet of demonstrable unwordliness, unpopularity, and havoc-wreaking.

Better to be incommensurately honest from the start. Rename the award in a disclaimer-incorporating manner. Let's be hopelessly idealistic and assume that Peter Nobel finally gets his Dulcinea and that the Economics trophy is forced to unattach itself from the main body. Since this book concerns itself with financial economics (let's leave the micro/macroeconomics stuff to others; that's a tough enough fight in itself), let's imagine a separate subfield-specific award. Taking all these considerations into account, we could suggest the following rechristened, fully disclosing substitute for the current prize:

The Sveriges Riksbank Prize in Platonic, Potentially Lethal, Typically Impractical, Financial Economics*

*Warning: This prize exclusively rewards the capacity to devise complex theoretical/mathematical concoctions that are related in name to the practical-only field of financial activity; no practical relevance, practical use, and practical applicability is required. The ability to offer a solution to a previously unsolved real-life problem is not required; the techniques are not required to make sense or be replicable in real-life; feedback from financial practitioners is neither required nor important. The fact that a particular theory under consideration may have already caused lots of trouble in the markets or may have an obvious capacity to potentially do so will not, under any circumstances, count against its possibilities to obtain the award. The fact that the soundness of a particular theory may have been demonstrated to be negligible by market events will not, under any circumstances, count against its possibilities to obtain the award. The single most decisive deciding factor when selecting a winner would be technical prowess per se and the awe in which the theoretical community holds that technicality. Prior awardees have been known to have proven impractical, unpopular, and inapplicable, with mathematical dictates that break down in real life and that are not immune to the charge of market-turbulence-stirring. It wouldn't be far-fetched to posit that by providing high-profile legitimacy to the use of abstract quantitative techniques in finance, the award aids and abets the development among market practitioners, observers, and regulators of a dangerously false sense of security grounded on less-than-entirely reliable, "certainties."

So let's not eliminate the Nobel; let's adequately rename it. I don't think we should be telling people not to award prizes to whomever they see fit. Who am I to prohibit some descendents of Eric the Red from lavishly regaling the theoreticians? These people obviously love their math—let them crown it!

But libertarian as I want to force myself to be, I also live by the motto that others' freedoms should be prevented from causing my death. Finance theory run amok can, as we have discussed throughout, kill. Thus, we should attempt to protect ourselves as best we can. Adding a big disclaimer onto the Nobel that regularly endows the theories with a far-reaching seal of approval would be a reasonably healthy step. By proceeding down that path, we would be not only welcomingly shedding light on the true meaning of the award and on the true nature of the honorees, but in the process also adding an extra layer of concrete to the fortification that keeps menacing, unworldly, quantitative dogma at bay. In classic jiu-jitsu style, the phenomenal reputation and global reach of the award would be transformed from foe into ally for those concerned about the prize's collateral damage.

By coming clean about its past actions and philosophical guiding light (perhaps along the lines of my above suggestions), the Sveriges Riksbank Prize could be the catalyst that makes people solidly understand that recondite theorems concerning human behavior in the financial markets can do harm, and so it is in our best interests to always be inalienably skeptical and watchful about quantitatively adorned gadgets making their way into practice. Deliciously paradoxically, the "Nobel" could end up diminishing, not fortifying, the qualifications-blindness and self-enslavement to equations-laden dictums that, fifth-columnist-style, pave the path for our sacrifice at the altar of misplaced concreteness.

■ *Notes* ■

Foreword

Page XIII: Well, Espen Haug and I. Coincidentally, our paper introduced the metaphor: "lecturing birds how to fly."

Preface

Page XXI: The *FT* op-ed. "The Pseudo Science Hurting Markets," *Financial Times*, October 23, 2007.

Page XXVI: Models...rely on. "Blame Your Business School Professor," *Economist,* April 3, 2008, www.economist.com/blogs/freeexchange/2008/04/blame_your_business_school_pro.cfm#list-comments.

Mathew Gladstein's Complaisance

Page XLIII: A year earlier, Mathew Gladstein from DLJ's. Robert Merton's Nobel Prize autobiography, http://nobelprize.org/nobel_prizes/economics/laureates/1997/merton-autobio.html.

Page XLIII: A source details how DLJ was anxiously. Donald MacKenzie, *An Engine, Not a Camera* (MIT Press, 2006), 158.

Page XLVI: Other times quant. Ibid.

Chapter 1   Playing God

Page 4: It's not that physics is better. Emanuel Derman, *My Life as a Quant* (John Wiley & Sons, Inc., 2004), 266.

Page 4: No mathematical model can capture the intricacies. Emanuel Derman, "The Boys Guide to Pricing and Hedging," *Risk*, January 2003.

Page 5: As a physicist, when you propose a model. Derman, *My Life as a Quant*, 267.

Page 6: There is an almost religious quality. Derman, *My Life as a Quant*.

Page 7: Neoclassical economics works really well. Chris Farrell, "Economists Suffer from Physics Envy," *BusinessWeek* interview, February 20, 2006.

Page 7: We weren't widely warned as to. Bruce Jacobs, *Capital Ideas and Market Realities* (Blackwell, 1999), 98.

Page 9: In the Mediocristan world of sports. www.yaronkoren .com/blog/?p=94.

Page 10: If the U.S. Food and Drug Administration. Eric Gelman, "Fear of a Black Swan," *Fortune* interview, April 3, 2008.

Page 10: Trying to model something that escapes modelization. Ibid.

Page 14: In the beginning, when I knew close to nothing. Nassim Taleb, *Fooled by Randomness* (Texere, 2001), 97.

Page 16: The hurricane is not more or less. Richard Bookstaber, *A Demon of Our Own Design* (John Wiley & Sons, 2007), 112.

Page 20: VaR, stress tests and other risk measures. Christine Harper, "Death of VaR Evoked," *Bloomberg*, January 28, 2008.

Page 21: In one study of U.S. banks. Jeremy Berkowitz and James O'Brien, "How Accurate Are Value at Risk Models At Commercial Banks," FEDS Working Paper No. 2001-31, July 2001.

Page 22: The only function of economic forecasting is. http://en.wikiquote.org/wiki/Economics.

Page 22: Economists have never had much luck. John Faust, John Rogers, and Jonathan Wright, "Exchange Rate Forecasting: The Errors We've Really Made," Board of Governors of the Federal Reserve System, International Finance Discussion Papers, December 2001.

Page 23: In 1999, Washington, D.C.–based Heritage Foundation. Heritage Center for Data Analysis, "How Reliable Are IMF Forecasts?" August 27, 1999.

Page 23: In 2001, the RiksBank (Central Bank of Sweden). Riks-Bank Monetary Department, "How Good Is the Performance of Major Institutions?" *Economic Review,* March 2001.

Page 24: Perhaps the most illustrating analysis of how. Spyros Makridakis and Michele Hibon, "The M3-Competition: Results, Conclusions, and Implications," *International Journal of Forecasting* 16 (2000).

Page 24: "Pure theory and elaborate methods are of. Ibid.

Page 26: Renowned journalist John Cassidy once wrote that. John Cassidy, "The Decline of Economics," *The New Yorker*, December 2, 1996.

Chapter 2   The Financial Economics Fiefdom

Page 31: Like academics Warren Bennis and James O'Toole mentioned. Warren Bennis and James O'Toole, "How Business Schools Lost Their Way," *Harvard Business Review*, May 2005.

Page 32: You would probably be scared to death. Peter Hahn, "Lessons from School of Life," *Financial Times,* May 7, 2008.

Page 32: The real world simply does not offer. Pablo Triana, "Those Who Can Choose to Teach at Business Schools," *Financial Times*, January 10, 2008.

Page 34: had to do with Federal Reserve policy. Peter Bernstein, *Capital Ideas* (John Wiley & Sons, 1992), 42.

Page 34: During the past several decades, many B-schools. Warren Bennis and James O'Toole, "How Business Schools Lost Their Way," *Harvard Business Review*, May 2005.

Page 34: the high prestige of the natural sciences. Richard Whitley, "The Rise of Modern Finance Theory," *Research in the History of Economic Thought and Methodology*, April 1986.

Page 35: No wonder that the focus of business academics. "Our History," Tuck School of Business at Dartmouth, www.tuck.dartmouth.edu/about/history/history2.html.

Page 35: Among the goals that the Foundation deemed. Richard Magat, "The Ford Foundation At Work" (1979), 107, www.fordfound.org/archives/item/0173/original/103.

Page 35: One of the few criticisms of the program. Ibid., 107.

Page 36: questioned the proliferation of narrow, excessively specialized. Jerold Zimmerman, "Can Business Schools Survive," September 5, 2001.

Page 36: For the first half of the twentieth century. Bennis and O'Toole, "How Business Schools Lost Their Way."

Page 36: institutional arrangements, legal structures, and long-term. MacKenzie, *An Engine, Not a Camera*, 37.

Page 37: Well, Dewin's era-defining magnum opus. Ibid.

Page 38: Friedman's essay became a very convenient alibi. Ibid.

Page 38: Around here we just sort of take for granted. Ibid.

Page 38: While some financial economists cared somewhat more. Ibid., 12.

Page 38: In finance, one can almost sense. R. A. Kavesh, "The American Finance Association 1939–1969," *Journal of Finance* 25:1 (March 1970).

Page 39: Some of these bright young men spent. H. Sauvain, "The State of the Finance Field: Comment," *Journal of Finance* 22 (December 1967).

Page 39: The new finance men have lost virtually. David Durand, "The State of the Finance Field: Further Comments," *Journal of Finance*, December 1968.

Page 39: one foot on the ground. Ibid.

Page 40: The economics camp responded by developing. MacKenzie, *An Engine, Not a Camera*, 40.

Page 40: Although few B-school faculty would admit it. Bennis and O'Toole, "How Business Schools Lost Their Way."

Page 43: These academics couldn't understand the fact. Michael Lewis, "In Nature's Casino," *New York Times*, August 27, 2007.

Page 43: Management school faculty often focus on. Richard Schmalensee, "Where Is the B in B-school," *BusinessWeek*, November 27, 2006.

Page 44: The current model of business school education. William Holstein, "Are B-schools Failing the World," *New York Times*, June 19, 2005.

Page 44: A management professor who publishes rigorously. Bennis and O'Toole, "How Business Schools Lost Their Way."

Page 47: I thought he was the best teacher I had. "Student Life," Washington University, April 2008.

Page 47: **I think Olin is trying to get their name.** Ibid.

Page 47: **I absolutely think the University made a mistake.** Ibid.

Page 47: **Admired is the understatement of the year.** Ibid

Page 47: **Zach is a shining example of the lecturers.** Ibid.

Page 47: **In 2007, Zach was awarded the.** Ibid.

Page 48: **Zach is a very good researcher.** Ibid.

Page 48: **don't understand the role that research plays.** Ibid.

Page 48: **Students do not mindlessly attend Zach's class.** Ibid.

Page 48: **The administration is blatantly saying that the students'.** Ibid.

Page 49: **Prove to us that teaching quality** Ibid.

Page 53: **his stubborn and meticulous devotion to clarity.** Derman, *My Life as a Quant*, 167.

Page 53: **seemed to consist of unafraid hard thinking.** Ibid, 168.

Page 53: **he like to describe the financial world.** Ibid, 168.

Page 53: **Certain economic quantities are so hard.** Ibid, 171.

Page 53: **In the end, a theory is accepted.** Ibid, 268.

Page 54: **The basic problem with research in business.** Perry Mehrling, *Fischer Black and the Revolutionary Idea of Finance* (John Wiley & Sons, 2005), 301.

Page 56: **No less a figure than Steven Levitt.** Steven Levitt, "Let's Get Rid of Tenure (Including Mine)," *New York Times*, March 3, 2007.

Page 57: **innovators and tinkerers who showed us.** Peter Bernstein, *Capital Ideas* (John Wiley & Sons, 1992), 6, 14, 306.

Chapter 3   Quant Invasion

Page 62: **Traders didn't quite know what quants.** Satyajit Das, *Traders, Guns, and Money* (FT Press, 2006), 184–187.

Page 63: **Some of the future most powerful members.** Victor Haghani and Larry Hillibrand.

Page 64: **He was (on occasion at least) not above.** Mehrling, *Fischer Black*, 248.

Page 65: **building up the quant side of its operation.** Ibid., 243.

Page 65: **They had maybe 10 or 20 people.** Emanuel Derman, interview by Adelle Caravanos for the New York Academy of Sciences, www.nyas.org/publications/readersreport.asp?articleID=63.

Page 65: "You know," Derman was explanatorily told. Derman, *My Life as a Quant*, 9.

Page 67: Watching quants pursue sacred laws for the. Ibid., 15.

Page 67: The mathematics of economics is so much. Ibid., 15.

Page 68: It's common to imagine that physicists. Emanuel Derman, "A Physicist's Guide to Quantitative Finance," speech presented at the American Physical Society, April 2002.

Page 69: At Goldman Sachs, despite the models we build. Emanuel Derman, "The Future of Modeling," speech presented at the Risk Tenth Anniversary Global Summit in London, November 19, 1997.

Page 69: Former quant Mark Joshi concurs. Mark Joshi, "On Becoming a Quant," May 20, 2008, www.markjoshi.com/downloads/advice.pdf.

Page 71: I think a model works (serves its purpose). Emanuel Derman, "Roundtable: The Limits of Models," derivativesstrategy.com.

Page 72: In the real world there is, as derivatives. Ibid.

Page 73: If we take a look at the models. Derman, "The Limits of Models."

Page 76: An investment process is fundamental. Frank Fabozzi et al., "Challenges in Quantitative Equity Management," CFA Research Foundation, April 2008, 20.

Page 76: Then both the inputs and the forecasting. Ibid., 21.

Page 77: We read annual and quarterly reports. Ibid., 22–25.

Page 77: We don't use fundamental overrides. Ibid.,26.

Page 77: Presently, only a small percentage of. Ibid, 27–30.

Page 77: A survey of market participants and assorted. Ibid., 26.

Page 77: Certain specific advantages of quant versus traditional. Ibid., 32.

Page 77: There are perhaps 10 years of active records. Ibid., 18.

Page 78: Because quant funds are broadly diversified. Ibid., 43.

Page 78: Chicago-based Citadel ($20 billion under. Katherine Burton, "Citadel Returns 26 Percent, Breaks Hedge Fund Mold, Sees IPO," *Bloomberg*, April 29, 2005.

Page 78: By 2006, the stock market went back. Fabozzi et al., "Challenges." 59.

Page 79: Quants, as a group, were found. Ibid., 65.

Page 80: This characteristic of quant funds may be. Zubin Jelveh, "How a Computer Knows What Many Managers Don't," *New York Times*, July 9, 2006.

Page 80: It is harder for a computer. Fabozzi et al., "Challenges,"

Page 80: Even when recognizing that human behavior. Ibid., 2.

Page 80: There is a clear advantage of a quant approach. Ibid., 40–42.

Page 84: One source estimates that during 2000–2005l. Ibid.

Page 84: Another indicated that between 1998 and 2007. American Century Investments, "A Trial Endured and Lessons Learned," July 2008.

Page 84: Many of the new entrants apparently. Ibid.

Page 85: It is important to note that many. "Quants Tail of Woe," *Risk*, October 2007.

Page 85: It was the first time that it. Ibid.

Page 85: One lesson from the events of July–August 2007. Fabozzi et al., "Challenges," 43.

Chapter 4   Copulated Nightmares

Page 93: Having a risk number is not trivial. www.fooledby randomness.com/notebook.htm.

Page 99: Quantitative models should be added to the list. NINJA stands for "no income, job, or assets," referring to the lack of qualifications required to receive one of these loans.

Page 100: Once we know the marginal (i.e., individual. David Li, "On Default Correlation: A Copula Function Approach," *Journal of Fixed Income*, September 1999, 12.

Page 100: The default rate for a group of credits. Ibid., 11.

Page 101: Believing that "Default is like the death. Mark Whitehouse, "How a Formula Ignited Market That Burned Some Big Investors," *Wall Street Journal*, September 12, 2005.

Page 102: However, data about asset price correlation. Arturo Cifuentes and Georgios Katsaros, "The One-Factor Gaussian Copula Applied to CDOs: Just Say NO (Or, If You See a Correlation Smile, She Is Laughing at Your "Results")," *Journal of Structured Finance*, October 2007, 5.

Page 102: In fact, one of the attractive things. Ibid., 9.

Page 102: Given that Gaussian copula assumes a stable. Nomura Fixed Income Research, "Correlation Primer," August 6, 2004, 5.

Page 102: By being erected on Gaussian foundations. Ibid.

Page 104: The following table gives quoted parameters. Ammar Kherraz, "The May 2005 Correlation Crisis: Did the Models Really Fail?" June 19, 2006, 17.

Page 104: This ratio can be interpreted as the sensitivity. Ibid.

Page 105: As credit spreads shot up. Ibid, 18.

Page 107: Both implied volatility and implied correlation. "Credit Model Meltdown," *Risk*, November 2006.

Page 107: During the crisis, implied correlation on the iTraxx. Mohamed El Morsalini, "Correlation Trading: Facts and Challenges," September 2005.

Page 107: Take the Dow Jones CDX North American. "Crisis of Correlation," *Risk*, June 2005.

Page 107: The so-called correlation curve, which can be. Kherraz, "The May 2005 Correlation Crisis."

Page 108: Dealers (i.e., investment banks) had apparently. Mohamed El Morsalini, "Correlation Trading: Facts and Challenges," September 2005.

Page 108: This sudden accumulation of long mezz trades. "Crisis of Correlation," *Risk*, June 2005.

Page 108: We can also see how index reference spreads. Kherraz, "The May 2005 Correlation Crisis."

Page 111: UBS also lost $800 million through its. 6-K, February 14, 2008, 17–18.

Page 111: In Q1 2008, UBS lost another $5 billion. 6-K, May 6, 2008, 9.

Page 111: The second quarter of 2008 yielded respective. 6-K, August 12, 2008, 20.

Page 111: It recorded losses on its super senior subprime CDOs. 10-K, February 25, 2008, 37.

Page 111: $1.7 billion in Q1 2008. 10-Q, March 28 2008, 77.

Page 111: $3.5 billion in Q2 2008. 10-Q, August 5 2008, 86.

Page 111: The differences between the agencies' methodologies. Gunter Meissner, Tim Garnier, and Tobias Laute, "A Comparative Analysis of Fitch's, Moody's, and Standard & Poor's CDO Rating

Approaches," Chapter 19 in *The Definitive Guide to CDOs* (Risk Books, 2009).

Page 112: The probability of both few defaults and many. Ibid.

Page 113: Ratings played a key role in the very birth. Arturo Cifuentes and Georgios Katsaros, "CDOs and Their Ratings: Chronicle of a Foretold Disaster," June 4, 2007.

Page 113: at least one notable source suggests that. Arturo Cifuentes, testimony before the U.S. Senate Committee on Banking, Housing, and Urban Affairs, April 22, 2008.

Page 114: Ninety percent of the CDOs that were downgraded. Ibid.

Page 114: On the other hand, capital charges can. Cifuentes and Katsaros, "CDOs and their ratings."

Page 115: The disagreements were exaggeratedly accentuated. Ibid.

Page 115: At the time, the demand for BBB. Michael Crouhy et al., "The Subprime Crisis of 2007," July 9, 2008.

Page 116: In October, S&P downgraded residential ABSs. Ibid.

Page 117: In all, between Moody's, S&P, and Fitch. "A Matter of Trust," *Risk*, March 2008.

Page 118: In a particularly poignant case. Nomura Fixed Income Research, "Rating Shopping—Now the Consequences," February 16, 2006, www.adelsonandjacob.com/pubs/Rating_Shopping.pdf.

Page 119: The most common argument that we have heard. Cifuentes and Katsaros, "The One-Factor Gaussian Copula."

Page 122: Some credit models have not done terribly well. "Tails of the Unexpected," *Risk*, June 2008.

Page 123: You're making a brave assumption that. Ibid.

Page 123: With hindsight, if we look at the peaks. Ibid.

Page 123: As a practical matter, introducing frailty factors. Ibid.

Page 124: The probability of extreme default losses. Darrell Duffie et al., "Frailty Correlated Default," January 27, 2008, 1–2.

Page 124: Our approach is to directly allow for unobserved. Ibid., 3.

Page 124: The results show that all factors. Ibid., 18.

Page 125: Once this econometric intelligence is gathered. Ibid., 19.

Page 125: For instance, for the period January 1998. Ibid., 1–2.

Page 125: This paper finds significant evidence among. Ibid., 33.

Chapter 5   Blah, VaR, Blah

Page 128: Risk management is the air bag that must. Aaron Brown and David Einhorn, "Private Profits and Socialized Risks," *GARP Risk Review*, July 2008, 12.

Page 130: Now we understand why investment banks held. Ibid.

Page 130: In the current crisis it has turned out. Ibid.

Page 130: In what some have salaciously deemed. Ibid, 13.

Page 135: In all, Lehman Brothers revealed 3 exceptions. "A VaR, VaR Better Thing?" *Risk*, February 2008.

Page 136: Someone has compared them to winning. Kevin Down et al., "How Unlucky is 25-Sigma?" *Journal of Portfolio Management*, Summer 2008.

Page 137: VaR has inherent limitations, including reliance. 10-Q, February 29, 2008, 77.

Page 137: On February 29, 2008. Ibid.

Page 138: The firm attributed this to substantial losses. Ibid., 78.

Page 138: Similar alibis were previously employed. 10-Q, August 31, 2007, 62.

Page 139: By late summer 2007, Bears' balance sheet. 10-Q, August 31, 2007, 5; "Private Profits and Socialized Risks," *GARP Risk Review*, July 2008, 16.

Page 139: These (VaR-supported) leverage and illiquidity excesses. 10-Q, August 31, 2007, 5; "Private Profits and Socialized Risks," *GARP Risk Review*, July 2008, 24–25.

Page 139: Less than four months before the firm's. 10-Q, May 31, 2008, 10-Q February 29, 2008; 10-Q May 31, 2007.

Page 140: And the gaps between actual trading losses. 6-K, February 14, 2008, 22–25.

Page 141: Largely as a result of such change. 6-K, May 6, 2008, 10–12.

Page 141: In Q2 2008, too, the number of exceptions. 6-K, August 12, 2008, 26–28.

Page 141: As of mid-August 2008, a month before. Tom Petruno, "Banks' credit-crisis write-downs top the half-trillion mark," *Los*

Angeles Times Blogs, August 12, 2008, http://latimesblogs.latimes
.com/money_co/2008/08/now-500-billion.html.

Page 141: Short-term borrowings ($316 billion) and. 10-K, February 25, 2008, 19.

Page 142: VaR and other risk measures significantly underestimated. 10-Q, September 28th 2007 pages 100–101.

Page 142: After posting a devastating $9.8 billion loss. Christine Harper, "Death of VaR Evoked."

Page 142: Given the market experiences of U.S. subprime. 10-K, February 25, 2008, 63.

Page 143: Had the toxic stuff been kept in place. Ibid.

Page 143: Merrill's VaR continued on its southbound quest. 10-Q, May 8, 2008, 119.

Page 143: Average daily VaR was CHF193 million. 6-K, July 24, 2008, 68.

Page 143: Morgan Stanley made $2.5 billion. 10-Q, June 30, 2008, 3.

Page 144: Such a state of affairs may be harmless. "Observations on Risk Management Practices During the Recent Market Turbulence," Senior Supervisors Group, March 6, 2008, 15

Page 145: The calculation of VaR requires numerous assumptions. 10-Q, September 28, 2007, 100.

Page 146: What will be the consequences? I think. Stan Jonas, "The Limits of VaR," derivativesstrategy.com, February 1998.

Page 146: VAR has made us replace about 2,500 years. "The World According to Nassim Taleb," derivativesstrategy.com, 1996.

Page 147: That's completely wrong. It's not better. Ibid.

Page 147: VaR players are all dynamic hedgers. Ibid.

Page 148: My first premise is that after a given. Jonas, "The Limits of VaR."

Page 149: The essence of civilization is measurement. Ibid.

Page 149: Frank Knight of the University of Chicago defined. Ibid.

Page 150: It all comes back to one problem. Ibid.

Page 150: Being scientific does not necessarily mean. Ibid.

Page 151: There was no regulation that required the portfolio. "In Defense of VaR," derivativesstrategy.com, 1996.

Page 152: Nor am I swayed by the usual argument. "Against VaR," derivativesstrategy.com, 1996.

Page 155: For example, Morgan Stanley's 95 percent trading VaR. 10-Q, June 30, 2008, 95.

Page 156: In a summer 2008 revision to this. "Proposed Revisions to the Basel II Market Risk Framework," consultative document, Bank for International Settlements, July 2008, 8–10.

Page 156: As one astute commentator proposed, this would. Gillian Tett, "Volatility Wrecks Value at Risk Models," *Financial Times*, October 12, 2007.

Page 157: Fire sales that should have halved VaR. Ibid.

Page 157: For instance, Merrill Lynch. 10-Q, September 28, 2007, 101.

Page 157: The "Incremental Risk Charge" amendment. "Basel II signals the end for regulatory arbitrage," eFinancialNews, August 18, 2008, www.efinancialnews.com/homepage/content/2451551218.

Page 158: In fact, the first thing that catches one's eye. Bank for International Settlements, "Proposed Revisions to the Basel II Market Risk Framework," consultative document, July 2008, 14.

Page 158: VaR is a tool for normal markets. "A VaR, VaR Better Thing?" *Risk*, February 2008.

Page 159: That is, not only can VaR help cause. Jon Danielsson, Paul Embrechts, et al., "An Academic Response to Basel II," London School of Economics, FMG Special Paper Series, May 2001.

Chapter 6   Blue Is Not Green

Page 171: Better and more thoughtful modeling...The subprime crisis. *Cornell Engineering Magazine*, Spring 2008, 17–19.

Page 174: Modern finance is a high-tech industry. http://mitsloan.mit.edu/academic/mfin.

Chapter 7   The Black-Scholes–Merton Conundrum

Page 180: Since the appearance a couple of years ago. "Why We Have Never Used the Black-Scholes–Merton Option Formula," Espen Haug and Nassim Taleb.

Page 180: In January 1965, Fischer Black (a recently minted. Merhling, *Fischer Black*, 47.

Page 181: He began to mingle with leading academics. Ibid., 64.

Page 181: The future father of modern option theory. Ibid., 97.

Page 181: Shortly after arriving at the Massachusetts. Ibid., 99.

Page 181: So eager was Black to embark. Ibid., 100–101.

Page 181: Whatever the initial inspiration, by June 1969. Ibid., 127.

Page 182: It was thus with more than a passing interest. MacKenzie, *An Engine, Not a Camera*, 130.

Page 182: Scholes was familiar with arbritrage–enforced pricing. Ibid., 131.

Page 182: Scholes' arbitrage arguments thus provided confirmation. Merhling, *Fischer Black,* 130.

Page 183: Since the formula satisfied the differential equation. Ibid., 131.

Page 183: His attention was certainly piqued when. MacKenzie, *An Engine, Not a Camera*, 135.

Page 186: Here the only unobservable involving human. Ibid., 133.

Page 186: In their 1967 book *Beat the Market*. Espen Haug, *Derivatives: Models on Models* (John Wiley & Sons, 2007), 41.

Page 186: He didn't think that enormous errors would. Ibid., 127.

Page 186: The methods, technical details, and probabilistic summary. Ibid., 42.

Page 192: In November 2007, I published an article. Pablo Triana, "Smiling at Black-Scholes," *GARP Risk Review*, November/ December 2006.

Page 202: Figure 7.1 plots the relationship between. *My Life as a Quant* by Emanuel Derman, John Wiley & Sons, 2004, page 227. Reprinted with permission of John Wiley & Sons, Inc.

Page 203: Figure 7.2 (also from Derman. Ibid., 228 and 230.

Page 205: This time, the piece was run on June. Pablo Triana, "The Day When Black-Scholes Made Black-Scholes," *Futures and Options World*, June.

Page 212: The weakening of the American markets. MacKenzie, *An Engine, Not a Camera*, 205–206.

Page 213: Futures on the S&P 500 (the contract. Ibid., 2.

Page 213: At 7:17 a.m., the wire transfer was. Ibid., 3.

Page 214: At 11:45 a.m., the Chicago Board Options Exchange. Ibid., 188.

Page 214: A cascade of reassuringly good news. Ibid., 189.

Page 222: In a potentially revolutionary paper released. Espen Gaarder Haug and Nassim Nicholas Taleb, "Why We Have Never Used the Black-Scholes-Merton Option Formula," January 2008. Working Paper.

Page 227: options on commodities were banned in the United States. Nicholas Dunbar, *Inventing Money: The Story of Long-Term Capital Management and the Legends Behind It* (John Wiley & Sons, 1999), 31.

Page 227: activity levels were in the doldrums. Ibid., 41.

Page 228: These efforts were fruitful and in May 1972. MacKenzie, *An Engine, Not a Camera*, 145–150.

Page 229: "Black-Scholes was really what enabled. Ibid., 158.

Page 232: In an idealized fantasy world, dynamic. Haug, *Derivatives: Models on Models*, 32–33.

Page 233: "If competitive intermediaries can hedge perfectly. Lasse Heje Pedersen et al., "Demand-Led Option Prices," June 2007, 2. Working Paper.

Page 234: Taleb cites the example of a three-month. Nassim Taleb and Emanuel Derman, "The Illusions of Dynamic Replication," *Quantitative Finance,* Vol. 5, No. 4, August 2005, 323–326.

Chapter 8   Black Swan Deceit?

Page 253: The fund became so eager to do so. Dunbar, *Inventing Money,* 178.

Page 254: Precisely because of its newfound role. Ibid., 181.

Page 254: It has been estimated that for every. Ibid., 212.

Page 254: In all, LTCM's equity index volatility. Ibid., 224.

Page 255: Armed with a computer presentation, core LTCM. Ibid., 235.

Page 257: At least one. Michael Lewis, "The Memoir of a Wall Street Winner and Squash Champion," *New York Times,* March 23. 1997.

Page 259: As recently as a year ago. Kate Kelly, "How Goldman Won Big on Mortgage Meltdown," *Wall Street Journal*, December 14, 2007.

Page 260: If the normality tale seemed fitting. Ibid.

Page 260: With the subprime market experiencing a. Ibid.

Page 263: Leading risk manager and famed quant Ricardo. Ricardo Rebonato, *The Plight of the Fortune Tellers* (Princeton University Press, 2007).

Chapter 9   An Unhealthy Yearning for Precision

Page 271: Finance theory can thus present us. Nassim Taleb, "The Fourth Quadrant: A Map of the Limits of Statistics (September 15, 2008), www.edge.org/3rd_culture/taleb08/taleb08_index.html.

Page 272: It doesn't matter that formal insurance policies. Bruce Jacobs, *Capital Ideas and Market Realities* (Wiley-Blackwell, 1999), 45.

Page 273: by the end of 1995, a dollar. Dunbar, *Inventing Money*, 149.

Page 273: almost $1 billion, not too far from. Ibid., 180.

Page 274: And their VaR was telling them. Ibid., 188.

Page 275: That is, VaR-guided risk-reduction is. Ibid., 202–205.

Page 281:Science continues to be represented by some. Ian Hughes, "We Are Only Human," *New Scientist*, March 23, 1996, www.newscientist.com/article/mg14920227.100-forum–we-are-only-human–biian-hughesbi-ponders-the-limit-of-what-we-can-know.html.

Page 281: This dangerous idea threatens to knock away. Ibid.

Page 284: While the assumption of normality, in a sinister. MacKenzie, *An Engine, Not a Camera*, 208–210.

Page 285: An unabashed VaR critic, inconsolably wondering. Richard Hoppe, "It's Time We Buried Value-at-Risk," *Risk Professional*, July/August 1999, 14.

Chapter 10   We Need FAT Tony

Page 297: And he is a fictional character. Nassim Nicholas Taleb, *The Black Swan: The Impact of the Highly Improbable* (Random House, 2007), 122–125.

Finale: Should the Nobel Prize in Economics Be Eliminated?

Page 310: whose brother Ludwig was Peter's great-grandfather. Jonathan Thompson, "Take the Nobel Name off Economics Prize, Say Relatives," *Independent* (London), December 2, 2001.

Page 311: The Prize Award ceremony takes place. http://nobel prize.org/.

Page 313: The stated main reason for the choice. http://nobel prize.org/nobel_prizes/economics/laureates/1997/press.html.

Page 314: Black, Merton and Scholes made a vital. http://nobel prize.org/nobel_prizes/economics/laureates/1997/press.html.

Page 314: The real significance of the formula to the. Haug, *Derivatives: Models on Models,* 40.

■ *Acknowledgments* ■

This book would have never happened without the support of two extraordinary persons who, for whatever reason, chose to believe in my abilities. Nassim Taleb first proposed that I consider doing such a book, and the legendary Pamela van Giessen at Wiley concurred that it would not be an outrageously insane idea. They both appreciated the relevance of the topic (which, serendipitously if sadly, was made exponentially more urgent by the neverending, ever-escalating unfolding of the credit crisis) and they believed that a plain-English treatment could be in good order. I, certainly, couldn't agree more.

I didn't contact (bother?) too many third parties when penning this work. It was, in the most explicit sense of the term, a solo effort. Of course, implicitly speaking, it was far from so. While the fountain may have been made of electronic and hardbound documents rather than telephone or restaurant conversations, I indeed drank enormously from many different sources. It should be excitingly obvious that without the prior contributions of such individuals, this text would have evolved at a much less dignified pace. Many are the thinkers and doers (most of the times thinkers-doers) who have influenced, even if from afar, the ideas and contents of this book. I thank them all for their invaluable intellectual gifts.

I am indebted to Emilie Herman at Wiley, who patiently re-re-re-read the draft chapters and provided insurmountably beneficial suggestions. And to Kate Wood and Stacey Fischkelta also at Wiley, of course.

Finally, let me go back to Taleb. My gratitude to the famed iconoclast extends beyond his endorsement of my persona as author of this text, or his generous willingness to share his ideas and time both online and onsite. I want to thank him too for having shown the courage, clarity, and determination to launch a battle well worth fighting (and from which many have, sadly, shied away). The world needed to hear how deleterious flawed theoretical and quantitative finance concoctions can be, how our blindness to academic credentials and equations-laden dictums can send us to the poorhouse. Those were not comfortable messages to send. Resistance was expected to be (and amply proved to be) exceedingly stiff and brutal. Yet Taleb persisted, for more than a decade. These days his views, to the abundant displeasure of his most vicious opponents, have become unredeemably widespread and accepted within plenty of intellectual and professional circles and, most importantly, the general populace. I strongly believe that we are the better off for it. If going forward newly-minted B-school graduates, journalists, regulators, and pros become indisputably accustomed to seriously (and healthily) doubt the validity of financial modelling we will owe such beneficial development to the groundbreaking valiant musings of a maverick free-thinker who inspired us by relentlessly marching along in the presence of unremitting enemy fire.

■ *About the Author* ■

Pablo Triana has a Master of Science from New York University's Stern School of Business and a Master of Arts from American University's Economics Department.

He boasts varied professional experience, and is most proud of having proven his value in widely different fields all around the world. Mr. Triana has succeeded in many low-probability endeavors. He has authored books and articles for internationally leading imprints, *and* helped lift off into preeminence a globally recognized e-commerce start-up, *and* taught at a charts-topping business school, *and* peddled derivatives from a bulge-bracket investment bank.

For the past few years, Mr. Triana has been based in Spain but travelling abroad extensively, enjoying a quality of life characterized by long spells on the beach, daily visits to the country club, and a decent amount of jogging sessions in New York's Central Park (all fittingly combined with challenging and interesting work). And it was during such time that he began to type thoughts into Microsoft Word.

During the period January 2007 through March 2008, Mr. Triana was the most published business school staff member worldwide in the *Financial Times* (tied with a Harvard professor). His previous book was *Corporate Derivatives* (Risk, 2006).

▪ *Index* ▪